More Praise for *Leadership Lessons from West Point*

Many of our graduates will tell you that over their four-year careers at West Point, the lesson they have learned to value most can be expressed in two words: "Leadership matters." Some of the best leaders in the world have contributed to *Leadership Lessons from West Point*. They articulately and earnestly explain the key points of leadership strategy, values, development, styles, and situations. Readers of all backgrounds will learn from the experts' personal anecdotes, accessible prose, and sage advice.

> —Lieutenant General Franklin L. Hagenbeck, 57th Superintendent of the
> U.S. Military Academy at West Point and 1971 West Point graduate

This is a wonderful primer for the student of leadership whether young or old, regardless of profession. Doug Crandall has expertly crafted some of the latest commentary on leadership, from both a practical and theoretical perspective, into an easy and extremely relevant work. *Leadership Lessons from West Point* is a must for your professional collection and a great tool to help you develop your followers into future leaders.

> —John W. Rosa, Lieutenant General, U.S. Air Force (Ret.), president of The Citadel,
> The Military College of South Carolina, and 1973 Citadel graduate

The U.S. Military Academy has proven without a doubt that leadership skills can be developed and strengthened. The same leadership skills required to prepare troops, to plan logistics, to formulate military strategies, to execute tactics on the battlefield, and to motivate soldiers in combat can be applied to business.

> —Henry Cisneros, chairman, CityView

Can a book on leadership from a military academy help leaders who don't march to breakfast? If your organization has a mission and people, then stop what you're doing and read this book. After that take your team for a tour of any military installation and learn about its mission. Then . . . hold on . . . watch what happens!

> —Brigadier General Randal D. Fullhart, U.S. Air Force, Commandant, Air Command and Staff College

The U.S. Military Academy is a national treasure. It lives, breathes, and inculcates leadership skills into those bright young men and women who enter the gates and go through the forty-seven-month immersion process. The front of these skills is the Department of Behavioral Science and Leadership, so ably led by Colonel Tom Kolditz. This book captures the essence of what we collectively teach the future leaders of our Army and our Nation.

> —Seth F. Hudgins Jr., Colonel, U.S. Army (Ret.) and president, Association of Graduates

The essays in *Leadership Lessons from West Point* offer insights from authors with many years of experience in the field. Topics such as learning from failure, gaining confidence as a leader, developing leadership qualities in others, and the various aspects of leadership discussed can be applied to all walks of life. Whether you are involved in the military, business, or civil service, if you want to be an effective leader, the lessons in this book will be relevant to you.

> —Richard W. Schneider, Rear Admiral, U.S. Coast Guard (Ret.) and president, Norwich University

The first thing you will notice about this book is that the authors are mostly Captains and Majors—people on the front lines of leadership issues. It is a hands-on work for leaders in every walk of life. Great stuff!

> —Dennis M. McCarthy, Lieutenant General, U.S. Marine Corps (Ret.)
> and executive director, Reserve Officers Association

Other Publications from the Leader to Leader Institute

JB JOSSEY-BASS

LEADERSHIP LESSONS FROM WEST POINT

Major Doug Crandall
Editor

John Wiley & Sons, Inc.

Published by Jossey-Bass
A Wiley Imprint
989 Market Street, San Francisco, CA 94103-1741   www.josseybass.com

Jossey-Bass books and products are available through most bookstores. To contact Jossey-Bass directly call our Customer Care Department within the U.S. at 800-956-7739, outside the U.S. at 317-572-3986, or fax 317-572-4002.

Jossey-Bass also publishes its books in a variety of electronic formats. Some content that appears in print may not be available in electronic books.

Library of Congress Cataloging-in-Publication Data

Leadership lessons from West Point/Doug Crandall, editor.
    p. cm.
  Includes index.
  ISBN-13: 978-0-7879-8773-2 (cloth)
  ISBN-10: 0-7879-8773-5 (cloth)
  1. Leadership. I. Crandall, Doug, date.
  HD57.7.L4342 2006
  658.4'092—dc22   2006025136

Printed in the United States of America
FIRST EDITION
HB Printing   10 9 8 7 6 5 4

leader to leader
INSTITUTE

Established in 1990 as the Peter F. Drucker Foundation for Nonprofit Management, the Leader to Leader Institute furthers its mission—to strengthen the leadership of the social sector—by providing social sector leaders with the wisdom, inspiration, and resources essential for leading for innovation and for building vibrant social sector organizations. It is the social sector, in collaboration with its partners in the private and public sectors, that is key in changing lives and building a society of healthy children, strong families, decent housing, good schools, and work that dignifies a diverse, inclusive, cohesive community that cares about all of its members.

The Leader to Leader Institute provides innovative and relevant training materials and resources that enable leaders of the future to address emerging opportunities and challenges. With the goal of leading social sector organizations toward excellence in performance, the Institute has brought together more than four hundred thought leaders to publish over twenty books available in twenty-eight languages and the award-winning quarterly journal, *Leader to Leader.*

The Leader to Leader Institute engages social sector leaders in partnerships across the sectors that provide new and significant opportunities for learning and growth. It coordinates unique, high-level summits for leaders from all three sectors and collaborates with local sponsors on workshops and conferences for social sector leaders on strategic planning, leadership, and cross-sector partnerships.

Building on a legacy of innovation, the Leader to Leader Institute explores new approaches to strengthen the leadership of the social sector. With sources of talent and inspiration that range from the local community development corporation to the U.S. Army to the corporate boardroom, the Institute helps social sector organizations identify new leaders and new ways of operating that embrace change and abandon the practices of yesterday that no longer achieve results today.

Leader to Leader Institute
(formerly the Drucker Foundation)
320 Park Avenue, 3rd Floor
New York, NY 10022 USA
Tel: +1 212-224-1174
Fax: +1 212-224-2508
E-mail: info@leadertoleader.org
Web: www.leadertoleader.org

CONTENTS

PART TWO: LEADERSHIP STYLES AND SITUATIONS

PART THREE: LEADING ORGANIZATIONS

A NOTE FROM THE
LEADER TO LEADER INSTITUTE

It is a great honor to write the opening words to this book; the chapters were written by a group of highly qualified educators who are teaching or have taught at the U.S. Military Academy at West Point, Army officers and civilians who live "Duty, Honor, Country." This is one of the most important leadership books the Leader to Leader Institute (formerly the Peter F. Drucker Foundation) has published in our sixteen years. Providing leadership resources for leaders in all three sectors, twenty-one of our books are now traveling the world in twenty-eight languages, and *Leadership Lessons from West Point* will now join this group in providing leadership wisdom and practices as relevant to a corporate executive as they are to a leader of a social sector organization, university students and faculty, and government leaders at every level. This is a book for our tenuous times, a book "just in time."

At the Leader to Leader Institute, we believe this book will become an indispensable guide for leaders of the future, leading the organizations of the future. This book brings together remarkably gifted Army officers, educators, and leadership developers to look at every aspect of leadership. The chapters are based not just on academic theory but on the on-the-ground experience of these leaders, their own impressive educational backgrounds, and their research as faculty members. Although the authors make references to war, life-and-death decisions, and heroic action, their focus is on leadership, mission, values, teamwork, organizational learning and culture, leading change, and other topics that cut across all organizations, across public, private, and social sectors. This is a book for leaders searching for authenticity and relevance, and for philosophies to make their own. Each chapter is a gift to leaders who are challenged to redefine the future—some would say "called" to help redefine the future.

Leader to Leader's twentieth book, *Be, Know, Do,* adapted from the U.S. Army Leadership Manual, was our first collaboration with the U.S. Army. Now we bring you another amazing leadership resource from expert military leaders. These authors and faculty are part of a moving, inspiring adventure in learning that prepares our young men and women, cadets at West Point, for a future that no one can adequately describe, yet a future in which these young officers must lead well, playing their part in sustaining democracy.

These leadership lessons will resonate across the sectors and around the world. *Leadership Lessons from West Point* is a book to keep close at hand as an indispensable leadership handbook, even as we share it widely with fellow travelers on their own leadership journeys.

August 2006   Frances Hesselbein
                                                                          New York

FOREWORD

Jim Collins

In 2005, I had the privilege of visiting West Point for a gathering of leaders from business, social sectors, and the military. One of my hosts, a captain in the U.S. Army, had obtained an M.B.A. after graduating from West Point. "What most surprised you about business school after your West Point experience?" I asked.

"The misperceptions my M.B.A. classmates had about Army training and its relevance for leadership outside the military," he responded. He then described a debate that had erupted in one of his classes, and how one of his classmates had challenged, "In the Army, you don't really need to lead because soldiers are so well trained to follow orders."

If leadership exists only if people follow when they have the freedom not to follow, I thought perhaps his classmate had a point. After all, civilian life does not have the same clear chain of command as the U.S. Army. When I pushed on this point, the captain responded that, yes, the Army has a clear chain of command, but Army leaders face one giant reality that business leaders rarely face: "In business, if you make bad decisions, people lose money and perhaps jobs," he said. "In the military, if you make bad decisions, nations can fall and people can die."

The phrase stuck in my mind: *people can die.* In the Army, it matters to your very existence if your leaders are competent. It matters if your leaders are trustworthy. It matters if your leaders care more about themselves than they do about their people or the mission. Your life may well depend on it. Combine this truth with the larger mission of protecting national interest and advancing the cause of freedom, and you get a context for leadership rarely faced in the normal course of business.

This wonderful book gives us a glimpse into the lessons of leadership that can best be grasped in the face of high stakes and large consequences. Upon receiving the manuscript, I began my standard reading process of flipping through the chapter title pages to get a sense of the overall work before delving into a page-by-page read. But along the way, I found myself drawn in, stopping to read entire chapters before completing my initial scan, increasingly excited by the project. These writers blend their very real experiences with thoughtful frameworks, bringing them to life with vivid stories.

Disciplined people who engage in disciplined thought and take disciplined action: this framework captures much of what separates greatness from mediocrity. The Army has long embraced this concept with its own framework of leadership: Be, Know, Do. This framework runs through these chapters, like a thread of DNA. The beauty of this book lies in the dualities of leadership—knowing when to follow and when to not follow, the responsibility to question and the responsibility to execute, dedication to mission first and dedication to your comrades above all. These dualities highlight the point that disciplined action does not mean rote action. Disciplined action means that you begin with a framework of core values (be), you meld those values with knowledge and insight (know), and finally you make situation-specific decisions to act (do). Leadership, the chapters in this book teach, begins not with what you *do* but who you *are*.

Encoded into the West Point approach are two eternal truths. First, the medium- and long-term future cannot be predicted, and second, the best "strategy" in a volatile environment lies in having the right people who embody your organization's core values and can adapt to unanticipated challenges. West Point exists not to train soldiers for a specific war but to develop leaders who can adapt to whatever war might be thrust on our nation—no matter what continent, no matter what conditions, no matter what form of warfare, no matter what enemy.

West Point answers the question "Can leadership be learned?" with the idea that whether you like it or not, you *are* a leader. The real question is whether you will be an *effective* leader. In reading this book, I realized that West Point also addresses a question that I've been wrestling with: Can Level 5 Leadership be developed? In our research into why some companies become great while others do not, my colleagues and I observed that leadership capabilities follow a five-level hierarchy, with Level 5 at the top. At Level 1, you are a highly capable individual. At Level 2, you become a contributing team member. At Level 3, you become a competent manager. At Level 4, you become an effective leader. Stepping up to Level 5 requires a special blend of personal humility and professional will—the capacity to channel your personal ambitions and capabilities into a larger cause or mission. Level 5 leaders differ from Level 4 in that they are ambitious first and foremost for the cause, the organization, the mission, the nation, the work—*not themselves*—and they have the will to do whatever it takes (within the bounds of the organization's core values) to make good on that ambition. These chapters show that West Point is in the business of developing not just leaders, but *Level 5* leaders; the ideals of service, dedication to cause, loyalty to comrades, sacrifice, courage, and honor shine through these pages.

Toward the end of my visit to West Point, I had the privilege of conducting a small seminar for soon-to-graduate cadets, invited by a few members of the faculty who penned some of these chapters. One senior cadet, who would almost certainly graduate to dangerous duty in the Middle East, said to me that he felt more fortunate than his friends who had gone to places like Harvard and Stanford. "No matter how the rest of my life unfolds," he explained, "I know that I have served a larger cause than myself." Earlier that day, a senior general officer commented that this current generation of West Point graduates stands as one of the most inspired—and inspiring—since the graduating class of 1945.

I came away from those sessions struck by the contrast between these young men and women and my graduating class from college in 1980. For two decades, we lived in a world of artificial stability, made possible by America's triumph in the Cold War, combined with an era of perverted prosperity culminating in the stock market bubble of the late 1990s. My generation had no larger cause, no overriding ethos of service, no great object that extracted our sacrifice. And we are poorer for it. The West Point leaders who introduced me to these inspired cadets, and who write so passionately in this book about the principles of courage, sacrifice, and commitment, helped me to see that this younger generation of idealistic men and women deserves not to be just students of their elders but—equally—our teachers.

September 2006
Boulder, Colorado

ACKNOWLEDGMENTS

We in the Department of Behavioral Sciences and Leadership (BS&L) at the U.S. Military Academy are tremendously grateful to all those who have helped us share our ideas with readers beyond the gates of West Point. Larry Olson of John Wiley and Sons is the true hero. This book stems from his creative energy and his tremendous efforts. *Leadership Lessons from West Point* (and our special edition of the *Leader to Leader Journal*) never would have happened without his belief in our mission, our talents, and our ideas. Similarly, we thank Frances Hesselbein and Brigadier General (Retired) Robert Gaylord for the Leader to Leader Institute's continued support of BS&L and West Point. Their contributions have certainly helped strengthen our department. We hope that the nineteen chapters in this book help to strengthen the leadership of the social sector.

We thank Ruth Mills, Allison Brunner, Elizabeth Forsaith, and Beverly Harrison Miller for their tremendous contributions to this book. Their constant guidance throughout the editing and publishing process transformed our raw ideas into what we hope are valuable lessons for others.

Most important, we thank the soldiers, colleagues, and cadets who have inspired us, helped us, and kept us on track during our own leadership journeys and teaching endeavors. Without you, we would have nothing to share.

ABOUT THE CONTRIBUTORS

Major Jeff Bergmann is an assistant professor of psychology in the Department of Behavioral Sciences and Leadership at the U.S. Military Academy (USMA). He currently serves as the course director for Educational Psychology and Foundations of Counseling and teaches General Psychology for Leaders. Bergmann has served in a variety of leadership positions, including aide-de-camp to a commanding general and commander of a military police company. He deployed in 2001 to the border of Afghanistan in support of the Global War on Terrorism. His current research focuses on the psychological impact of combat on service members and their families. He has a B.S. from the USMA and an M.A. from New York University.

Captain Dena Braeger is an instructor in the Department of Behavioral Sciences and Leadership at the U.S. Military Academy (USMA), where she teaches Leading Organizations Through Change and Military Leadership. She has led in a variety of assignments as both a medical services officer and logistician. In 2003, she deployed to Iraq in support of the Global War on Terrorism. She has a B.S. from the USMA and an M.A. in organizational psychology from Columbia University's Teachers College.

Major Doug Crandall is the executive officer to the Dean of the Academic Board at the U.S. Military Academy (USMA). He was previously an assistant professor in the Department of Behavioral Sciences and Leadership where he served as course director for Leading Organizations Through Change and Advanced Military Leadership and received the Excellence in Teaching Award. Prior to his assignment at West Point, Crandall served in an array of leadership capacities as an armor officer. He has a B.S. from the USMA and an M.B.A. from the Stanford Graduate School of Business.

Major Chip Daniels served as an assistant professor in the Department of Behavioral Sciences and Leadership at the U.S. Military Academy from 2003 to 2005, where he taught military leadership and served as an assistant course director. Previously he served as a platoon leader, executive officer, staff officer, and company commander at various posts across the Army. He has a B.S. in management from Virginia Tech and an M.B.A. from the Fuqua School of Business at Duke University, where he received the Spaulding Award for Leadership. Daniels is currently deployed to Iraq with the First Cavalry Division.

Dr. Morten G. Ender is the sociology program director and associate professor of sociology in the Department of Behavioral Sciences and Leadership at the U.S. Military Academy. He is an award-winning teacher at both the University of Maryland and at West Point. His research has appeared in scholarly journals, and he has written two books: *Military Brats and Other Global Nomads: Growing Up in Organization Families* (2002) and *Inequalities: Readings in Diversity and Social Life* (2004). His current research compares military and civilian university undergraduates and their attitudes toward contemporary social issues, such as women in combat and the role of the United States in the Global War on Terrorism. He has an M.A. and Ph.D. in sociology from the University of Maryland.

Major Remi Hajjar served as an assistant professor in the Department of Behavioral Sciences and Leadership at the U.S. Military Academy (USMA) from 2002 to 2005, where he taught military leadership, introductory sociology, and sociological theory; he also served as the deputy director of the sociology program. His leadership experience includes a broad array of assignments in the Army's military intelligence community. His current academic interests include the topics of culture and diversity in the armed forces, particularly how the military can bolster its ability to process cultural diversity effectively to enhance performance. He has a B.S. in leadership studies from the USMA and an M.A. in sociology from Northwestern University.

Lieutenant Colonel Sean T. Hannah is the director of leadership and management studies for the Department of Behavioral Sciences and Leadership at the U.S. Military Academy. He has twenty years of experience leading infantry units in both peace and combat and at strategic levels at the Pentagon. He has an M.B.A. and M.P.A. from Syracuse University, an M.A. in military science from the Marine Corps University, and a Ph.D. in leadership from the University of Nebraska.

Second Lieutenant Greg Hastings graduated from the U.S. Military Academy in May 2006, where he majored in the Department of Behavioral Sciences and Leadership's Psychology Program and conducted award-winning academic research on performance enhancement for combat soldiers. Upon graduation, he received a commission as an officer in the infantry and will serve as a platoon leader with the 82nd Airborne Division. His interests while at West Point included mountaineering, foreign languages, combatives, and skydiving, where he earned a National Championship for the West Point Parachute Team.

Lieutenant Colonel Todd Henshaw is a U.S. Military Academy professor and director of the core course in military leadership. Previously, Henshaw directed the Eisenhower Leader Development Program, a graduate program in leadership and leader development affiliated with Teachers College, Columbia University. He has served in a variety of leadership and staff positions in the Army, from platoon through division. He earned his M.B.A. from the University of Texas at Austin and Ph.D. in business at the University of Kansas.

Jack Jefferies is an adjunct instructor in the Department of Behavioral Sciences and Leadership at the U.S. Military Academy, where he speaks to the cadets about group dynamics and high-performing teams. He currently works with Oneteam, an organizational and leadership development firm that helps diverse client partners define and achieve their goals by focusing on the interplay of individual, team, and organizational systems. Jefferies has won multiple world championships and national titles as captain of the U.S. Skydiving Team. He holds an M.S. in organizational development from American University and National Training Laboratories.

Lieutenant Colonel Eric G. Kail is a doctoral candidate in industrial/organizational psychology at North Carolina State University en route to teach in the Department of Behavioral Sciences and Leadership at the U.S. Military Academy. He has served in numerous command and staff positions in U.S. Army conventional and special operations units and as a company tactical officer at the U.S. Military Academy. He holds a B.A. from Radford University and an M.S. in psychology and leader development from Long Island University and in national security and strategic studies from the U.S. Naval War College.

Colonel Thomas A. Kolditz is professor and head of the Department of Behavioral Sciences and Leadership at the U.S. Military Academy. He holds a B.A. from Vanderbilt University, three master's degrees, and Ph.D. in social psychology from the University of Missouri. He teams with his faculty to think, study, research, write, and teach leadership. His background includes command of a multinational military organization on the demilitarized zone in Korea, leadership consultant roles in the Pentagon, and coaching as an air-to-air videographer for the Academy's national champion parachute team.

Robert Morris served as a company tactical officer and instructor at the U.S. Military Academy (USMA) from 2002 to 2006. He taught the core leadership course and served as the executive officer for the Eisenhower Leader Development Program in the Department of Behavioral Sciences and Leadership. Morris has served in various leadership and staff positions from the platoon to the division level. He has a B.S. in leadership from the USMA and an M.S. in counseling and leader development from Long Island University. He is currently pursuing a Ph.D. in social psychology at Columbia University.

Lieutenant Colonel James Ness is an associate professor in the Department of Behavioral Sciences and Leadership at the U.S. Military Academy, where he serves as the director of the Leader Development Research Center. He is course director for Sensation, Perception and Psychophysics; teaches biopsychology; and directs senior theses in the psychology honors program. Ness has commanded a medical research unit, directed key research assets, and served as a principal investigator researching the bioeffects of nonionizing directed energy. He has a B.S. from Florida Institute of Technology and an M.S. and Ph.D. from Virginia Tech.

Major Dennis P. O'Neil is an assistant professor in the Department of Behavioral Sciences and Leadership at the U.S. Military Academy (USMA), where he teaches Military Leadership and Psychology for Leaders. In spring 2006, he deployed overseas to assist in the development of leadership curriculum at the National Military Academy of Afghanistan. Prior to joining the faculty at West Point, O'Neil held a number of leadership positions in armor and cavalry units at Fort Carson, Colorado, and Fort Hood, Texas. He has a B.S. in management from the USMA and an M.A. in psychology from Duke University.

Major Everett S. P. Spain served as an assistant professor in the Department of Behavioral Sciences and Leadership at the U.S. Military Academy (USMA), where he was the course director for Leading Organizations Through Change.

He has served in the 82nd Airborne Division, was part of the Kosovo Stabilization Force, and deployed to Operation Iraqi Freedom. He earned a B.S. from the USMA and an M.B.A. from Duke University's Fuqua School of Business, where he received the Spaulding Award for Leadership. He is currently the aide-de-camp to Lieutenant General David Petraeus, commander of the U.S. Army Combined Arms Center.

Colonel Patrick J. Sweeney is an academy professor and the deputy head of the Department of Behavioral Sciences and Leadership at the U.S. Military Academy (USMA). He holds a doctorate in social psychology from the University of North Carolina at Chapel Hill. He currently directs the Eisenhower Leader Development Program. His background includes command and leadership positions at multiple levels in the Army, service as the executive officer and researcher for the USMA's Center for Leadership and Organization Research, and service as a leadership mentor for the Army Football Team.

Major Brian Tribus served as an assistant professor of management in the Department of Behavioral Sciences and Leadership at the U.S. Military Academy (USMA) from 2002 to 2006. Prior to his teaching assignment, he served in a variety of leadership positions as an armored cavalry officer. He holds a B.S. in economics from the USMA and an M.B.A. from Harvard Business School. He currently serves at the Army's Strategic Outreach Directorate at Fort Knox, Kentucky.

Major James Tuite is an assistant professor in the Department of Behavioral Sciences and Leadership at the U.S. Military Academy (USMA). He currently is the course director for Advanced Military Leadership and the coordinator for the department's Outreach program. He has led at multiple levels in the Army's elite airborne and ranger units. He has a B.S. from the USMA and an M.B.A. from the College of William and Mary.

Major Eric J. Weis is a former psychology and leadership instructor in the Department of Behavioral Sciences and Leadership at the U.S. Military Academy and now serves at Fort Stewart, Georgia. His previous military background is in light, airborne ranger, and mountain infantry units—all of which helped him bring real-world and frontline combat leadership applications into the classes he taught and the continuing small unit leader adaptability research he conducts. He has a B.S. in psychology from James Madison University and an M.S. in social psychology from Pennsylvania State University.

Major Todd Woodruff served as an assistant professor in the Department of Behavioral Sciences and Leadership at the U.S. Military Academy from 2003 to 2005, where he taught military leadership and a sociology course, Armed Forces and Society. He has led almost a dozen Army units in locations around the globe as both an officer and noncommissioned officer. He holds an M.B.A. and an M.A. in sociology, and his research on leadership, identity, and families has appeared in scholarly journals and books.

INTRODUCTION

Doug Crandall

Strong leadership may be the most important factor in an organization's success, because what happens at the top (of the company, group, team, or squad) has an impact on everything else. If the leader's attitude is poor, the team's attitude will follow. Be it a Fortune 500 company, a small business, a nonprofit, an infantry platoon, a school, a community, a family, or any other group that has a common purpose, leadership matters. As James Tuite, the author of Chapter Sixteen, wrote, leadership is "not just about crafting sound policies and incentive programs; rather, it's much more about inspiring the people who implement the policies to care enough about the organization and each other so that they will act as good stewards . . . even when no one is watching."

Leadership Lessons from West Point came about because of the enormous interest in a special supplement to the *Leader to Leader Journal,* a quarterly publication from the Leader to Leader Institute and Wiley Subscription Services. That supplement presented articles from active-duty Army leaders who were teaching in the Department of Behavioral Sciences and Leadership at the U.S. Military Academy (USMA) at West Point, New York. The articles offered insight into what leadership meant to them—in both war and peacetime—and described their views on quiet leadership, mission, values, taking care of people, organizational learning, and leading change, among other topics. This book develops those ideas much further than the special supplement could, with nineteen chapters from a range of contributors at all levels of the Army, from cadet to colonel. It captures the essence of what we do: synthesize experience, scholarship, and teaching in an effort to educate, train, and inspire our Army's future officers. This synthesis of leading, studying leadership, and teaching leadership is a unique aspect of our academic and developmental experience. In our classrooms, as in this book, we bring forth concepts and theory, relate stories from our own leadership endeavors, and help cadets make sense of their own experiences as they look toward the future. Throughout this book, we open a window into this world of leadership development that is the Department of Behavioral Sciences and Leadership at West Point and share some of our candid reflections, compelling stories, best practices, and frontline ideas.

We begin the book with our passion and our reason for being. In the opening chapter, "Becoming a Leader Developer," in Part One, on the topic of leadership and values development, Eric Kail turns what is sometimes seen as an organizational responsibility into a personal mandate. Developing leadership skills is not the ultimate goal of great leadership, argues Kail. Great leaders seek to develop other leaders because those leaders will affect hundreds, if not thousands, of other people. Kail identifies three phases of leader development: learning from the best leaders, leading, and reflecting on why you lead.

In Chapter Two, "Learning from Failure," I share lessons from my own leadership experiences and my time in the classroom at West Point. Reflection on failure is often championed as a recipe for leader growth. But reflection on true failure can be distasteful, humbling, and difficult. I wade through three distinct levels of leadership failure: failures in what we do, failures of who we are, and failures of who we want to be, using the three examples that have taught me the excruciating pain but immense value of honest reflection: two from my days as a young lieutenant and one as a parent. The lessons I have learned can apply to any leader in any organization: that failure requires us—that is, those who desire to do better—to solicit candid input from others, take a hard look at our actions, and diagnose our own needs for improvement.

Chapter Three provides a real-time picture of leadership development from someone just embarking on his leadership journey. Recent West Point graduate Greg Hastings, in "You Must Lead Yourself First," reflects on a few lessons he has learned during his time as a cadet: to take responsibility for his own actions, that great leaders need to be great followers, and that even just one person can make a difference and lead successfully. He not only reminds us of some leadership basics but also demonstrates the reality of what we do at West Point: turn high school students and young enlisted soldiers into men and women ready for immense leadership challenges on the front lines.

Chapter Four demonstrates how important it is for an organization to ensure as it develops and supports leaders that those individuals internalize the established core values. In "Influencing Your Organization's Moral Philosophy," Brian Tribus describes a wide variety of situations in which people need to embody their organization's values in order to make the right decisions: from corporate America, with examples from Beech-Nut and Johnson & Johnson, to wartime, in Somalia in 1993 and in Iraq today. And he offers many recommendations for how to live up to your organization's "honor code," as the students at West Point are taught the meaning of theirs—that "a cadet will not lie, cheat, steal, or tolerate those who do."

Chip Daniels follows up on Tribus's theme with a reminder that values are the bedrock for our decisions and organizations must inculcate those values from the outset. Chapter Five, "Developing Organizational Values in Others," describes the Army's systematic approach for developing values, which is useful for leaders in all walks of life. This approach uses five steps or methods: attracting people who already share the organization's values; socializing new members; establishing role models; telling stories, myths, and legends about positive or negative actions that reinforce those values; and using feedback mechanisms and performance evaluations to embed the organization's values.

Internalization of values is a crucial aspect of organizational success because values cannot be faked. As Sean Hannah articulates, the very best leaders are those who exhibit authenticity. In Chapter Six, "The Authentic High-Impact Leader," he makes a case for leadership development that produces a strong commitment to a core self-concept. In times of great social pressure, role conflict, or other dilemmas that pull us away from who we are, leaders who know themselves and act in accordance with their values, beliefs, and self-understanding will ultimately prove most effective.

Chapter Seven concludes Part One on leadership and values development with advice for all organizations. In "Leader Development and Self-Awareness in the U.S. Army Bench Project," Dennis O'Neil, Patrick Sweeney, James Ness, and Thomas Kolditz collaborate on a description of how the Army develops great leaders: just as successful baseball teams can look down the bench and call prepared players into the game, the Army is developing a future generation of leaders who are prepared to assume command at the highest levels. O'Neil and colleagues describe a 360-degree rating system for three levels of leaders: executives, midlevel managers, and direct leaders (in Army terms, senior leaders, junior leaders, and noncommissioned officers). At each level, "the bench" has identified the top behaviors that set apart exceptional leaders—for example, senior leaders should keep cool under pressure and be able to handle bad news well, junior leaders need to have guts and be trustworthy and dependable, and frontline supervisors need to be good role models and build and motivate their teams—in all organizations.

The chapters in Part Two take up the topic of leadership styles and situations. The authors in this part look at specific aspects of leadership that translate into lessons for all. Chapter Eight opens this part with "Teaming High-Potential Talent." Jack Jefferies writes about the difficulty of managing groups of people who all want to be leaders, drawing on his own experiences as a member of a championship skydiving team, as well as situations in corporate America (at Aetna and Lotus Development Corporation during the creation of Lotus 1–2–3), and in sports teams—from West Point's Sprint Football Team to the National Football League and the Philadelphia Eagles. Jefferies offers five strategies to leaders who want to lead teams of elite performers who are also often brash and reluctant team players.

In Chapter Nine, "Leading as if Your Life Depended on It," Thomas Kolditz shares his ideas on leading in dangerous and high-risk situations. He calls these *in extremis situations,* where leaders must give purpose, motivation, and direction to people when there is imminent physical danger and where followers believe that leader behavior will influence their physical well-being or survival. He draws on experiences with military troops and SWAT teams, as well as skydiving teams and mountain-climbing guides. He identifies seven characteristics of such leaders and offers lessons on how to develop such leaders and how to lead in dangerous and high-risk situations. Moreover, these lessons help develop great leaders in all situations, in any organization; in extremis leadership is authentic leadership.

In Chapter Ten, "Creating Urgency and Inspiring Your Team," Robert Morris shares lessons for leaders who struggle (or have ever struggled) to move their people beyond mediocrity. He describes how important leader motivation is: leaders need to provide focus and direction to the people they are leading. They also need to build strong relationships, one on one, because it is not possible to build a relationship with a group. Simultaneously, to achieve their goals, leaders need to set priorities and never lose sight of the overall mission or goal.

"Quiet Leadership," by Eric Weis, wades into the nuances of leadership style. In Chapter Eleven, he paints a picture of leaders who communicate intent, inspire, listen, care, and drive optimal performance, all without fanfare or cheerleader personas. Weis brings a new perspective to the challenge of leadership, for successful leadership is not high-energy volume but, as he writes, a "hidden reserve of formidable strength."

Chapter Twelve shows the importance not only of what leaders say but how they say it. In "Leading Without Words," Jeff Bergmann describes how communication affects leadership and provides a primer on how people can more effectively read and use body language; physical space; facial expressions, body movements, and touch; voice level, pitch, speed, and volume; and the perception of time (for example, a leader who keeps someone waiting is sending a message). Some people use these signals deliberately to reinforce or even contradict what they are saying verbally; others have no idea of the message they are sending with these nonverbal signals. Good leaders need to be aware of these nonverbal communications so that they do not undermine themselves unwittingly.

Chapter Thirteen looks at one of the pitfalls of strong leadership: charisma. In "Developing Charisma with Caution," Dena Braeger describes how charismatic leaders can draw in their followers and wield profound influence, and although that may be appealing, charisma—even in well-meaning leaders—may limit an organization's ability to develop and grow. She explores some of the dangers of charisma that she has witnessed firsthand and offers some suggestions on how to avoid these dangers.

In Chapter Fourteen, "Trust: The Key to Combat Leadership," Patrick Sweeney addresses trust, which he says is the key to combat leadership. In May 2003, Sweeney fought with the 101st Airborne Division during Operation Iraqi Freedom, and he interviewed seventy-two members of that division to explore the relationship between trust and influence in combat. They identified ten attributes of a leader who can be trusted in combat: competence, loyalty, honesty/good integrity, leadership by example, self-control (especially in terms of stress management), confidence, courage (physical and moral), sharing of information, a personal connection with subordinates, and a strong sense of duty. Sweeney's insights regarding trust in combat are applicable to all organizational settings and leaders everywhere.

The final part of this book delves into leading organizations. Todd Henshaw begins this part with a look at the socialization of new leaders. In Chapter Fifteen, "Socialized Leadership," he draws on research he assembled while studying the cadet basic training regimen at West Point. The goals of those organizational members who are actually executing a socialization program do not always mirror senior leadership's intent. Because of this, senior leaders must take an active role in shaping newcomer programs and communicating a clear, consistent message. Socialization of new leaders has long-term cultural implications: it is where organizational success begins—or ends.

In Chapter Sixteen, "Leading at the Business End of Policy," James Tuite follows Henshaw's theme, pointing out that many leaders do not understand how to motivate so that people in their organization will behave in a way that embodies organizational values and purpose. He emphasizes that it is not the leaders themselves who communicate an organization's values; instead, it is all the other workers who are executing their duties as agents of that organization. And he describes how leaders cannot enforce every policy and must not micromanage; instead, they need to inspire others.

Remi Hajjar and Morten Ender have done extensive research on diversity, the subject of Chapter Seventeen: "Harnessing the Power of Culture and Diversity for Organizational Performance." They begin by offering statistics on the core values of Americans in general and the Army in particular. They then describe "the (un)lucky seven" factors that differentiate people—race and ethnicity, religion, social class, sex and gender, age, physical ability or disability, and sexual orientation—with some supporting statistics on the demographics of religion, race, and ethnicity in the United States, as well as statistics on all seven factors in the U.S. Army. Knowing and accepting these statistics sets the stage for the authors' recommendations for how to lead a diverse group.

Todd Woodruff wrote Chapter Eighteen, "Developing Organizational Commitment by Putting People First," to show how the U.S. Army continues to retain highly committed, skilled professionals without the benefit of large salaries—even in the face of the sacrifices Army personnel need to make in terms of not only wartime demands (including the risk of loss of life or extreme injury, as well as the time away from family) but even the routine demands of Army life (such as unpredictable and frequent moves and the decreased access to and support from families and friends). To foster commitment to the organization under those circumstances, leaders need to develop multiple supportive commitments that reinforce members' identification with the ideals of their organization. Leaders must also foster a climate of caring about their people and their families and make available personal development, training, ongoing education, and opportunities for advancement.

We conclude the book with a look at organizational improvement. In Chapter Nineteen, "Managing Expectations When Leading Change," Everett Spain describes how important it is to identify who will be affected by change. Successful leaders will clarify their own character and intentions, describe the benefits of the long-term change process, define what constitutes short-term success, and spell out their stakeholders' specific responsibilities that are required to achieve the short- and long-term outcomes. Spain offers a detailed case study of how various leaders recently working in Iraq have successfully led change by following those precepts, and he wraps up with eleven lessons he learned about managing expectations, from the importance of promising less than you think you can achieve and then delivering more to meeting and communicating regularly and often— and how best to handle those meetings.

Editor's Note: The views expressed in this book are those of the respective authors and do not reflect the official policy or position of the U.S. Military Academy, the Department of the Army, the Department of Defense, or the U.S. government. Furthermore, the inclusion of authors and contributors from outside the Department of the Army does not imply endorsement of those individuals or their organizations by the U.S. Military Academy, the Department of the Army, the Department of Defense, or the U.S. government.

LEADERSHIP
LESSONS FROM
WEST POINT

PART ONE

LEADERSHIP AND VALUES DEVELOPMENT

CHAPTER ONE

BECOMING A LEADER DEVELOPER

Eric G. Kail

It's what you learn after you know it all that counts.

—JOHN WOODEN, HALL OF FAME BASKETBALL COACH

I was one month away from promotion to major in 1998 when my father, a career Army officer of thirty-two years, passed away. In our final conversation, I asked him how I would know if I was a successful leader. His answer provided me a definition of success that changed the way I see myself as leader, whether leading as a soldier, husband, father, or community member. He told me not to look at my rank or, for that matter, any of the medals or badges on my uniform: these are just things created to make ourselves feel important, and they are really the results of the efforts of others. He told me not to read my efficiency reports or performance reviews: these were merely overinflated pieces of paper designed to get me promoted. He also told me not to ask my boss: the boss might tell me only what I wanted to hear or whatever it took to get me out of his office so he could get back to work.

My father told me that for a leader, the true measure of success is found in the eyes of your direct reports, the embrace of your spouse, and the hearts of your children. I believe him. The embrace of your spouse and the hearts of your children are subjects for another venue. But when was the last time you looked into the eyes of those who work for you in order to measure yourself as a leader?

When you look into the eyes of your soldiers, or employees, or direct reports, you cannot escape your real worth as a leader. Every time I have turned the leadership of my soldiers over to another officer, I gathered them around me for one last face-to-face good-bye, one last chance to thank them for their service to me, each other, and our nation. What my boss had written in my performance reviews about my leadership performance faded from my mind as I looked each soldier in the eye for the last time. Their eyes told me they would be better leaders not because of who *I* was but because of the time and effort I had invested in the deliberate development of them as men and women. No medal can trump that feeling.

One of the most important things you can do as a leader is to develop other leaders. Those leaders will affect hundreds, if not thousands, of other people.

Leader Development: The True Measure of a Leader's Success

Are you successful as a leader? Before you answer, consider this scenario. I am looking for a master carpenter to produce a handcrafted wooden desk for you as a token of appreciation for all you have done for the organization. This is not just any desk, but a great desk that reflects the strength and integrity of both giver and recipient. I have selected a master carpenter based on the quality of the products of his labor. By selecting this carpenter to build your desk, I passed up other carpenters with more impressive woodworking power tools and state-of-the-art showrooms. I also ignored some carpenters who have created thousands of production-line desks in their manufacturing plants. These others are very efficient, but to them, your desk was just another dollar figure in their profit margins. The bottom line is that I judged each carpenter by evaluating the wood on which they labored, not the carpenters themselves or their tools.

That brings me back to my original question. Are you a successful leader developer? Along with managing resources and setting direction for your group or unit, you have a responsibility to develop your subordinate leaders. As leaders, we often place heavy emphasis on the bottom line and our personal accomplishments. But think ahead to your retirement dinner or ceremony: Would you prefer a slide show and handouts detailing all the deals you made, complete with statistics and charts demonstrating your prowess at leading within the organization, or do you want to share one last evening with those whose lives your leadership changed? These are the people who will carry on in your place primarily because of your investment in their lives. One of the most important things you can do as a leader is to develop other leaders. Those leaders will affect hundreds, if not thousands, of other people.

Leader Development Is a Deliberate Process

Being a leader is harder today than ever before because information processing and decision-making requirements are temporally compressing every year (in other words, you need to assess situations and make decisions faster than ever before), and risks that were once easy to recover from may in fact be fatal in today's environment. One critical decision you must make is whether to let your subordinate leaders develop themselves in a do-it-yourself style or deliberately exert your energy and resources to develop them. And keep in mind that making no decision on this matter is the same as deciding to let your subordinate leaders develop themselves. Leader development must be done deliberately for three reasons.

One critical decision you must make is whether to let your subordinate leaders develop themselves in a do-it-yourself style or deliberately exert your energy and resources to develop them.

First, it is bad reasoning to believe that you were a total self-starter and others wanting to be leaders should be self-starters too. There are psychologically valid theories to support this, but suffice it to say that our memory tricks us into believing that we owe our successes to our own efforts, but our failures are the result of other people or factors beyond our control. If you really believe that you developed yourself into a great leader and somehow dodged the efforts of fate and others to drag you down, you are not only wrong but most likely lonely too.

Second, a good leader would never leave to chance factors that he or she could directly affect; that would be negligence. We exert tremendous energy in setting the conditions for the success of our organizations, whether on the battlefield or in the commercial market. Investing energy and resources to develop subordinate leaders—people who will execute your organization's business at hand and eventually fill your shoes—is a great form of condition setting.

Third, if you do not get personally involved in leader development, you will miss out on the significantly rewarding experience of watching leaders grow personally and professionally. If you have experienced firsthand the satisfaction of watching a subordinate leader grow in confidence and competence, you know what I mean. But if you have not or if this reward sounds pointless, you really should change your title from "leader" to simply "gatekeeper."

Three Phases of Leader Development

There are several ways to develop leaders, and what works for one leader may not work so well for another. My experiences as a leader developer, as a developed leader, and as a formal student of leadership research have convinced me that leader development takes time, focused energy, and even risk. (This risk, by the way, is the reason leaders get the big bucks. Reading one book or article or attending a seminar is not enough.)

Three phases of leader development require understanding: learning, leading, and reflecting. These three seasons of reflective leader development form a perpetual cycle, and as a leader matures, the phases occur concurrently as well as sequentially. As a leader developer, you have a role in each phase.

Does your organization value the learner, the teacher, and the learning process itself? By "value," I mean respecting and providing resources for all three, not merely tolerating the process of formal leadership education as something to complete prior to starting a "real" job.

Phase One: Learning from the Best Leaders

Not all leaders are given the opportunity of a formal leadership education process prior to leading, but it most certainly helps those who get it. The average Army officer spends most of his or her first year in uniform in a formal leadership education system, and the benefits are apparent for these leaders and the soldiers they lead.

If your organization includes formal leadership training and education, take a close look at it. Does your organization value the learner, the teacher, and the learning process itself? By "value," I mean respecting and providing resources for all three, not merely tolerating the process of formal leadership education as something to complete prior to starting a "real" job. The military, and many other organizations as well, has improved dramatically in this area since the war on terror began.

For example, the BP Group, a petroleum merger of British Petroleum, Amaco, and ARCO, has developed a model program for formally educating and developing its first-line leaders. Its leader development program was not mapped out at a one-weekend leadership summit or decided on by a single leader. Instead, the senior leadership of BP Group met repeatedly to determine why their junior leaders were not performing well, and they devised and carried out experiments to back up their perceptions. The key to its junior leader development program is the energy and focus the senior leadership of the organization placed on it. This was not just another initiative the company was undertaking; it was a priority. Today, graduates from BP Group's first-line leader training program are running petroleum operations on every continent, and their performance ratings are significantly better than those of nongraduates.

There are specific things you can look at within your organization to assess how valued your leader education and training systems are. Who trains and educates emerging leaders? If your organization truly values the process of leadership development, some of the very best and most experienced leaders will be directly involved as instructors and trainers. Is this the case with your organization? Or is your leader development cadre made up of those who have outlived their usefulness in the organization's operational endeavors?

Not so long ago, there was a time in the Army when being assigned as an instructor or trainer was tantamount to being put out to pasture. That sends a message to everyone in an organization that leader education is unworthy of precious personnel resources, and therefore that it belongs at or near the bottom of the list in terms of priority.

The good news is that the Army has gotten smarter about who trains and educates its leaders. The cadre of leaders in any officer basic course or captain's career course are the Army's best warriors and leaders, most of whom have led troops in combat within the past six months. Assigning the best and brightest as leader trainers benefits the Army significantly. Its leader development systems gain credibility, as does what is taught in the leadership curricula.

Let us say that you are a brand-new second lieutenant attending your officer basic course and your instructor has just returned from commanding a company of 120 soldiers in combat in Iraq or Afghanistan. What he or she teaches becomes more real and relevant by how that instructor teaches it. The experiences of these instructors will directly relate to what their students will experience on graduation.

For example, suppose it is a typical Monday morning at Fort Benning, Georgia, and Second Lieutenant John Doe is seated in a classroom ready to learn how to provide leadership while reacting to enemy sniper fire. In strides Captain Jim Smith, walking with a slight limp: the bullet wound in his left thigh still aches from where he was shot by an enemy sniper in Mosul, Iraq, just three months ago. His unit was two weeks away from returning home when he and several others in the company were on their last combat patrol. Smith does not have to make up a scenario; he is going to be teaching today's class using his own unit's reaction to an enemy sniper.

The class begins with, "There I was . . ." and ends with the honest recounting of how Smith's actions as the company commander that day saved the lives of several of his soldiers and how his mistakes could have cost others their lives. His students ask questions like, "What did *you* do? and "What were *you* thinking?"

What the students learn now becomes personally and professionally inspirational and gripping. Captain Smith remembers when he was Lieutenant Smith just four years ago, sitting through the same class and staring at the clock waiting for the class to end; he cannot even remember which fictional vignette his instructor used that day. Today his students stay late to hear more of his story and how much he misses leading soldiers. The story continues tomorrow for the class as Smith reminds them that not every soldier was as fortunate as he was that day in Mosul. The subject for tomorrow is casualty evacuation, and Smith's primary training aid for the class is the dirty, blood-stained scrap of paper he used to record the battle roster numbers and nature of wounds for his unit's casualties that day.

You do not have to have a limp to be an inspirational and gripping leader developer in your organization. You just have to be willing to talk about your scars to those who will be in similar situations in the near future. Find the Captain Smiths in your organization, and show the organization that you care enough about developing leaders—and those they will lead—by valuing their development enough to give them instructors fresh from your battlefields.

Do you ever look at your subordinate leaders, especially those holding jobs that you once performed so well, and wonder why they are not as good as you were? It is unfair to expect your subordinate leaders to know what they have not yet learned or experienced.

Phase Two: Leading

Think back to what it was like to lead for the first time professionally, that is, when it was your job to do so. You may have been a leader on a high school or college sports team or a leader in a Girl or Boy Scout troop or some other civic group. All those experiences are good preparation, but leading in your chosen line of work and getting paid to do so is different from them. This first professional leadership opportunity becomes the cornerstone of your life as a formal leader. It can be many things: a realization of a calling to lead, a test of perseverance, or even a sense that leadership is not for you.

There is one universal truth, though, to every leadership opportunity: it is your chance to lead and take ultimate responsibility for whatever your group or unit does or fails to do. This is a critical fact for all leaders to embrace, but if there is one group of leaders that needs to be reminded of this, it is the leaders who lead other leaders.

Here is an example of what I mean. As a young lieutenant, I was a platoon leader. I led thirty-three men in training and in combat, and I loved every minute of it, especially the cold and rainy days when we were accomplishing difficult missions together. To be certain, I am not the best platoon leader in the history of the U.S. Army, but I was good.

Three years later, I was a captain commanding a howitzer battery roughly triple the size of my old platoon. I got a lot of advice the day I took command, but the phrase I heard more than any other was, "Remember, you're not a platoon leader any more, so make the ones you have do their job. Don't do it for them."

That was great advice but hard to follow at first. In order to move from being a good platoon leader to become a developer of good platoon leaders, I had to understand two things. An opportunity hit me square between the eyes only one month into command.

First, I did not know then what I do now. Do you ever look at your subordinate leaders, especially those holding jobs that you once performed so well, and wonder why they are not as good as you were? If you do, do not feel guilty; it is only natural to do so. We remember all our triumphs and maybe those bad times that turn into funny stories over time, but all the times we were mediocre at best are usually flushed from our memories. It is also natural to look back on our past through the lenses of the competence we hold today. It is hard to remember what it was like when we did not know what we know now, but it is unfair to expect your subordinate leaders to know what they have not yet learned or experienced. Keep in mind that the leaders you develop do not need to relive your experiences; they need their own.

The other thing I had to come to grips with was the fact that my platoon leader days were over. It was someone else's turn now. If I was busy being a platoon leader again, who would be commanding my battery? So there I was, one month into commanding a light-howitzer battery in the 101st Airborne Division (Air Assault). It was a cold, clear night at our local training area on the Tennessee-Kentucky border, and my unit was about to conduct what is called an artillery raid. Our mission was to insert six howitzers using helicopters behind enemy lines, fire forty-eight rounds of artillery on an enemy target, and extract by helicopter back to a secure area, all within thirty minutes.

I was excited but also overwhelmed. Doing anything at night using only night-vision goggles and no flashlights was hard enough. But we were going to be sling-loading howitzers beneath the helicopters we were flying. The safety considerations were enormous enough without all the pressure of accomplishing a mission that we might have to do in combat some day.

Time, which I thought was my enemy, really turned out to be on my side after all: I simply did not have the time available as we prepared for this mission to do everything myself. My senior noncommissioned officer, my first sergeant, was with me when our battalion commander gave us the mission. First Sergeant Scott asked me, "This is your first artillery raid. Are you nervous?" As I told him how this mission reminded me of a similar mission I took part in as a young lieutenant in Iraq during the First Gulf War, his eyes lit up. "You know, Sir," he said, "your lieutenants will have memories just like yours after tonight." His words carried instant wisdom for me: every leader needs to grow from his or her own experiences in order to reflect later. That was just the beginning of many things I would learn from my first sergeant over the next two years.

Take stock of your subordinate leaders. Write down what they need the most work on and those tasks they accomplish to standard. Then write down those things that they do better than you did when you held their job. If you are truly objective, those things they do better than you did are undoubtedly directly traceable to qualities they already had when they came to your organization. The chances are good that your subordinate leaders are better than you were in ways that you have yet to influence.

My first platoon sergeant, Vern Croley (now a command sergeant major), made this point clear to me when I was his new platoon leader. One of my most important jobs as an artillery platoon leader was to oversee the occupation of a firing point so that my platoon could fire when called on. Croley took me out to the field and had me watch our platoon occupy a firing position without the two of us running things. It was a miserably cold autumn day in Germany, and it was pouring rain. We watched together from a few hundred yards away as our platoon did their job in knee-deep mud and met every time standard in achieving firing capability.

I was incredibly proud and grinning from ear to ear, but Croley was not. "Don't miss the point, Lieutenant," he said. "They are very good at doing this. Now you and I need to find out what they're not good at and make them better." Eight months later, Croley and I led that platoon into combat. Next to my father and my father-in-law, both Army officers, Croley taught me more about what my duties as an officer and leader were than any other person I have met.

All organizations have men and women just like Vern Croley. You will not meet them at the watercooler or at social functions: they are out getting things done. If you ask them for their advice, be prepared to listen without getting your feelings hurt or your executive ego bruised.

Now go back to the lists of things your subordinate leaders need to improve on or sustain: these are the areas of their leadership performance you can have an impact on. They are also the areas of their performance for which they will remember you as their leader—a leader who cared enough about them and their soldiers or subordinates to make a difference, when others may have just written them off or let them try to figure it out on their own.

In addition to developing leaders, you have a job to do and missions to accomplish. How should we as leaders balance the need to develop leaders and lead winning organizations? For example, as an Army officer, my job is to fight and win the nation's wars. I can develop a good leader stable, but if we cannot get the job done, there are severe and lasting consequences. This is true no matter what line of work you are in. The challenge is to create opportunities for subordinate leaders to learn, and that means letting them fail miserably without dire consequences.

The best way to do that is through training. In the Army, we send units to well-resourced training centers in the California desert, the swampy forests of Louisiana, and the hills of Germany. The goal of the cadre at these training centers is to challenge each unit with a real enemy (we fire blanks against other Army units trying to defeat us) and other stressors of combat. Leaders are given more to do than they or their units have time to accomplish. Little or no sleep is the price for poor time management. The cadre also causes things to go wrong at the worst possible time. The challenges are so extreme that some leaders return from combat to say that getting through a training center rotation was much more difficult than actual combat. What is not the same are the consequences of failure: in combat, people die and lives are changed by wounds and loss, whereas back at the training centers, consequences are felt by the embarrassment of losing a battle to the enemy, only to have your soldiers brought back to life to fight again.

Following each battle at a training center, a unit conducts a lengthy after-action review. These reviews can take hours to complete, and we film them so that the unit can take them home and study them repeatedly. Every soldier, from private to colonel, is required to publicly explain his or her intent and actions during the battle. We are hard on each other and ourselves during this process because we are committed to being as good as we can be when the bullets are real. Without our training centers to challenge us and allow us to fail miserably, only to pick ourselves up and do it again over and over, we would enter combat with nothing more than our imaginations and hope.

Not every organization has the time or resources the Army has to build and run training centers. But our training centers started with a vision that our leaders needed to be challenged and to learn from individual and collective mistakes, and a realization that in order to do this, senior leaders had to create the opportunities for such challenges. You can exercise that same vision within your organization. It takes determination to place leader development over the excuse that "you and your organization are just too busy to do anything about it." In fact, you should be arguing that you cannot afford not to do any leader training.

The best leaders loved leading, which meant they placed the welfare of the organization and each of their soldiers ahead of their own self-interests.

Phase Three: Reflecting on Why You Lead

The final lesson for young leaders of practicing leadership is the understanding of why they lead, and perhaps an objective assessment of whether they should continue to lead. This is where the leader development component of reflecting begins. Some of the most dynamic and competent leaders I have worked for in the Army all had a few things in common.

First and foremost, they loved leading, and for each of them, that meant placing the welfare of the organization and of each of their soldiers ahead of their own self-interests. They also led in a manner demonstrating that exercising authority meant exercising good stewardship. For the steward leader, this means believing that leadership exists for the good of the organization and the follower, not for the ego or reputation of the leader.

Colonel Ken Keen is an outstanding example of this. In spite of all his accomplishments, he is amazingly humble. I was serving in the 75th Ranger Regiment in 2000 when the Army chief of staff, General Eric Shinseki, decided that the Army would begin wearing the black beret as standard-issue headgear. This decision generated much discussion, especially because since 1951, the black beret had been worn only by rangers serving in the 75th Ranger Regiment or in the Ranger Training Brigade. The black beret was part of our persona as rangers; it immediately made all rangers distinctive within the Army. Army Rangers conduct highly specialized combat operations as the U.S. Army's most elite airborne infantry regiment. The 75th Ranger Regiment is the only operational ranger unit, and it is made up of roughly twelve hundred rangers. Just to be considered for service in the Rangers, a soldier must complete months of specialized training, the successful completion rate of which is less than 50 percent.

The commander of the 75th Ranger Regiment at this time was Colonel Keen, now a brigadier general. Keen was the epitome of what all special operations soldiers should be: a quiet professional. He was not meek by any means, and he led by example from the front, where everyone could see him. When it became public knowledge that the entire Army would soon wear the black beret, Keen received a lot of encouragement from many directions to dig his heels in and resist giving up the black beret as something only for rangers.

As he met with the rangers he commanded, they all asked him about what he thought about the rest of the Army getting the coveted black beret. He never dodged the question once, and he never said anything negative about General Shinseki or his decision. Instead, he left every ranger knowing that he cared about them, the ranger regiment, and the Army more than he did about his own ego or personal pride. And in June 2001, every soldier in the Army donned the black beret, and Colonel Keen's rangers donned their new tan berets. Mountains did not crumble, and neither did the ranger regiment. This leader with a long-term vision was able to place the welfare of his organization over his or her own ego and legacy.

Self-effacing leadership makes sense for the Army. But what about organizations where profit is most important? If this is the case in your organization, I suggest you make two decisions. First, you need to decide whether profit really is the most important thing in your organization. Then you need to decide how well you can achieve profit with poor subordinate leadership or by allowing your leaders to develop in a do-it-yourself manner.

If you are fortunate enough to survive with the leader development philosophy of letting the best naturally rise to the top, I caution you on the outcomes of doing so. Those who naturally rise to the top will probably do so by pleasing you or whomever they work for within the organization. They will probably be the best-looking people in your organization, and they will most likely be upwardly focused and very good at taking care of their boss or bosses while depriving their subordinates of real leadership.

There are simple ways to check to see if this is the case:

- Ask their followers about what kind of leadership they are getting, and really listen to what they say.
- If their answers are vague and generic, ask tough questions that get to the heart of assessing good and poor leadership.
- Listen to how your junior leaders talk to you about their subordinates. Are they all too willing to point the finger of blame at a subordinate rather than taking responsibility?
- When your junior leaders ask you for resources, consider whether they are concerned more with pleasing you as the boss or with getting their followers what they need and deserve.

If your assessment leads you to the conclusion that your subordinate leaders have forgotten (or perhaps never learned) that their authority is not a perk but a responsibility, then set the example for them by communicating clearly that you bear the blame for allowing them to practice sycophancy instead of leadership.

When you begin assessing what type of development your subordinate leaders need, remember that any shortcomings are more your responsibility than theirs. Unfortunately, some young leaders will never see beyond themselves to the responsibilities they have for their followers and to the organization. Others will be wonderful with people but incompetent in critical skills. Do your absolute best to develop such leaders, but if they do not or will not improve, then it is probably time to remove them from a position of leadership, and perhaps even from the organization. As leaders determine why they lead, they need to always remember that leadership is a privilege, not a right.

Imagine yourself as a head football coach and your team is down by six points with two minutes left in the final quarter. Then your team gets the ball deep in your own territory. Who do you want taking the snaps as quarterback: some hot-shot rookie or a seasoned veteran who has been in this position dozens of times? My guess is that even if the seasoned veteran led the team to wins in this position only half of the time, you would still want him leading your team. What makes his experience so valuable is not merely the fact that he has been in this situation before, but that he has had years to reflect on those experiences of leading under pressure. Reflection is the ideal synthesis of what we have learned and what we have done, and there are things to be learned by reflecting on both our successes and failures as leaders.

While reflecting on what we learn about leadership and what we do while practicing leadership, the goal is not to be too impressed with our successes or too disheartened about our failures. Part of leader development is requiring leaders to become better because of their leadership experiences but not to live in their past, bad or good. Reflection makes a leader greater than the sum of just his or her experiences and things he or she has learned. It is the cognitive process that allows us to be exponentially better leaders following each evolution of our own leader development and prior to taking on increasing leadership responsibilities.

Some people are naturally reflective through introspection and constantly seek ways to improve as a leader. Others need a little coaching to start the reflective process in motion.

It would be nice if leaders could reflect on what they have learned and their leadership experiences without distraction, and some leaders may get this opportunity. But reflection can occur even while driving to and from the office. I have always done some of my most effective reflecting when I run. If you and your subordinate leaders do not have a regular routine when reflection comes into play, set aside some time each day for reflection.

Final Thoughts

Successful leader development comes down to your deciding what your legacy as a leader will be. Remember that desk I am having made for you, the one I described at the beginning of this chapter? I am glad I did not hire the carpenter with the impressive power tools and the state-of-the-art showroom: he thought too much of himself. I am also glad I did not choose the one who produces thousands of great desks; he was interested only in getting done with your desk, like countless other desks, so he could get paid. Instead, the carpenter I selected understands that he is judged as a carpenter by the quality of the wood on which he labors, not his tools or the number of desks he makes.

Being a good leader developer begins with the realization that the judgment of your leadership that will mean the most to you will be based on the wood on which you labor. The development of your subordinate leaders is much more important to your organization than any of your other credentials.

I am willing to bet that on the day you finally leave your current leadership position, knowing that you have developed your subordinate leaders will be more personally and professionally satisfying than any watch or plaque you might receive.

CHAPTER TWO

LEARNING FROM FAILURE

Doug Crandall

I n the fall of 1996, I came a split-second from launching a 120-millimeter tank
round that had it flown its course might have killed a number of American infantrymen participating in a live-fire exercise at the Army's Joint Readiness Training Center. Just a few months later, in the dead of winter at Yakima Training
Center, about a hundred miles from Seattle, I retreated to the warmth of a small
restaurant called the Oasis and bit into a tasty cheeseburger while seventy of my
soldiers suffered outside in the cold. Fast-forward nearly a decade, to just a few
months ago, and you would have found me embarrassing my own nine-year-old
son through the public correction of his mistake on a soccer field.

That first paragraph is painful for me to read because it is embarrassing and
stomach stirring, and my conduct was inexcusable. It is a window into three
episodes of my own personal leadership history that might leave one to wonder
who exactly the Army has chosen to develop its future leaders. Yet I am sharing
these accounts—rife with lapses of principle, flaws of personality, and moments
of incompetence—because they represent an essential element of learning leadership: the ability to reckon with one's own failures, make meaning of those experiences, and resolve to lead more effectively in the future.

This is not new: from the pages of *Harvard Business Review* to the Center for
Creative Leadership's *Handbook of Leadership Development* to countless volumes of
wisdom from luminary authors, a student of leadership will read again and again

about the importance of diagnosing personal failure in any drive toward leadership excellence. Unfortunately, the advice consistently seems sterile. As often as I have read about how hard it is to stare failure in the face and learn from it, I have come away unconvinced that the authors cut to the heart of the true difficulty of these personal explorations. I am not writing about the difficulties of reckoning with failure because I moonlight as a part-time psychologist; rather, I write about it because as a leader, I am a part-time failure. I write about it because as a teacher, I have observed how difficult it can be for leaders to face themselves.

Leaders from boardrooms to the front lines lack the ability to take a hard look at themselves and thus bear the fruit of improvement that comes from such personal pruning.

Teach Yourself to Lead by Reflecting on Your Strengths and Weaknesses

Our core leadership course at West Point puts reflection on challenging experiences at the center of leader growth. Our job in the leadership program is not so much (or even not at all) to teach cadets how to lead but to help them learn how to teach themselves to lead. If successful, we facilitate their ability to relate new knowledge to their experiences—past, present, and, most important, future—in a lifelong journey of leadership development.

As a first step, we have them write a reflective essay. Their task is to detail a key experience from their recent leadership travails and then diagnose their own strengths and weaknesses from that experience. During my first semester teaching this course, I received a submission that highlighted the challenges of facing one's own failures or shortcomings. One cadet, whose strength could be categorized as self-confidence, surmised that his principal weakness was as follows: "I will be such a great leader, that I will need to take measures to ensure that I don't set my successor up for failure. Because my soldiers will be so disappointed when I depart, it is possible that their loyalty to me will make it very difficult for whoever takes my place."

This is not exactly the type of candid self-examination that leads to personal growth. Nevertheless, it served as an early reminder as to the challenge of inspiring honest reflection—the type of reflection and mirror-gazing scrutiny that leads to true self-development.

There are three distinct categories of leadership failure: failures in what we do, failures of who we are, and failures of who we want to be.

I found the cadet's essay, although wayward, refreshing in the genuine nature of its bold observations. That college junior may have lacked self-awareness, but he is hardly alone. Leaders from boardrooms to the front lines lack the ability to take a hard look at themselves and thus bear the fruit of improvement that comes from such personal pruning.

When I handed the reflection essays back that semester, I took some time to talk with this cadet about his paper and his "weakness." I asked him how he thought his peers would respond if all of them had the chance to read his essay. He shuddered at the thought that his classmates might be afforded a glimpse into his arrogant thoughts.

"Maybe your peers already know," I suggested. "If your arrogance is this unabashed on paper, it is likely your actions and behaviors communicate the same. Will your soldiers truly love and admire such a self-important leader?" It became clear to this cadet that his true weakness was a lack of humility and an inability to be self-critical. He left a bit shaken but, I hope, a more skilled learner and self-developer.

As a teacher, I decided that there is no better way to inspire honest self-assessment than to demonstrate it. Painful as it can be, I spend each semester tactically uncovering some of my own difficult experiences and the lessons of each. In doing so, I have come to the conclusion that there are three distinct categories of leadership failure:

- Level One: Failures in what we do
- Level Two: Failures of who we are
- Level Three: Failures of who we want to be

To reckon with each type involves varying degrees of personal pain. The consequences of failures in what we do may be great, but these shortcomings are usually the easiest to come to grips with and learn from because they strike only at the surface of our leadership self. And because they are on the surface, the learning relates primarily to the improvement of knowledge and skills.

In the middle are failures of who we are: when our temper flares and we damage a relationship, when we fail to foster innovative ideas because we are threatened by the talents of direct reports, or when a presentation we make is poor because our public speaking abilities are lacking. These Level Two failures force us to take a critical look at our own abilities, emotions, and personality; they strike at the heart of who we are and are therefore more painful to face.

At the far end of the spectrum are failures that violate who we want to be: departures from our own value systems or deeply held principles. Examinations of these failures are the most difficult and rare, but they are powerfully developmental.

Level One: Failures in What We Do

I never actually made the mistake of launching the tank round into the formation of fellow soldiers. Consummation of that disaster would have required me to command, "Fire." But just before I uttered that word, the sergeant in charge of observing and controlling our live-fire exercise came across my radio and warned, "Don't fire at that one."

My tank was leading a column of five vehicles, including three other tanks from my platoon and a truck full of combat engineers. The engineers had just breached an obstacle, blowing a hole in a span of barbed wire with their torpedo. Our tanks moved through the breach and turned a corner on a wooded Louisiana trail. Appearing to our left as we came around the corner was an enemy vehicle (for training purposes, the shell of an old armored personnel carrier). I issued the appropriate fire commands to my gunner. He traversed our turret toward the enemy vehicle and responded, "Identified," indicating he had eyes on the target. We were both ready to fire our first round of the day (and were an instant from doing so) when the sergeant trailing in a Humvee behind us issued his warning. My stomach turned as I realized what we had almost done.

During the safety briefing (a somewhat artificial addendum to what was otherwise a very realistic exercise), the range controllers had instructed me not to fire at the first vehicle we encountered. To remain consistent with the live-fire scenario, they had told me that the infantry company to our left flank would have already destroyed that vehicle, and thus we could bypass it. But the real impetus for the restriction was the presence of an actual infantry unit. Directly in line with the enemy vehicle, just several hundred yards to our left front, were a hundred or so soldiers from Charlie Company—our own soldiers. Had we launched into and through that personnel carrier, the tank round almost certainly would have continued on into the heart of Charlie, possibly killing someone's father, son, husband, or friend.

I tell cadets that at best, leaders above me would have stopped the live-fire exercise and relieved me of my duties, and my career would have been quickly over. I certainly would not be enjoying the privilege of teaching leadership at West Point. At worst, I could have been sent to jail and lived my life knowing I had been responsible for the death of one of my fellow soldiers.

Leaders make decisions—sometimes hundreds each day—and many of them will be wrong. With almost all of these actions and decisions comes feedback telling us whether we have done well or fared poorly. Failures of what we do should not be hard to face up to and learn from.

We never fired that round. Instead, we turned our turret to the front, collected our thoughts, and continued the mission. Upon completion, the team assessing our performance told us we were the best platoon they had seen in two years. Of course, they had no idea what we had almost done. Even the sergeant who warned us not to fire had no real knowledge of our intentions. He had simply seen our gun tube zero in on the target and had reminded us (just in case) not to fire. He could not hear our internal communications, and his timing, just an instant before I had given the order, was merely happenstance.

Description of this near failure conjures substantial emotion to this day. It is the penultimate example of a failure involving what I do. That said, it is not one that I find extremely difficult to share. Breaking the failure down is quite simple. There would have been extreme consequences, but the act of firing that round says very little about who I am as a leader.

I have repeatedly revisited the moment in which I almost gave the order to fire. We had received the safety briefing nearly twenty-four hours earlier. It was my first live-fire exercise. Everything at the Joint Readiness Training Center (JRTC) was designed to approximate a real combat situation. As the major who was second in command of our battalion told us before we departed, "The only thing that doesn't seem real at the JRTC is the blood that flows when you are shot." Given the realism, the adrenaline associated with a desire to perform, and the somewhat artificial nature of this particular safety constraint, our near-firing of that round is almost understandable.

Nonetheless, it would have been a failure of enormous proportions, and it would have been my mistake. But it would have been a failure of what I do, and those are failures that we can usually reckon with.

Leaders execute and sometimes fail to execute. Leaders make decisions— sometimes hundreds each day—and many of them will be wrong. Go left or right. Acquire or develop new business. Change or stay the course. Run or pass. Fund the venture using debt or equity. Focus on discipline or development. Retain or release the star performer who also happens to disrupt the team. Go to market with that new product or set it aside.

With almost all of these actions and decisions comes feedback telling us whether we have done well or fared poorly. We chalk up successes and failures. Failures of what we do, unless we make the same ones repeatedly, should not be hard to face up to and learn from. Examination of these first-level failures contributes to the development of our knowledge and skills. The lessons learned build our competence in a specific area, and we can draw on them as we endeavor in the future. They make us wise.

The pain of Level One failure often depends on the consequences, which is deceptive because the lessons entwined in Level One failure are not consequence based. A decision may cost shareholders millions, or it may double earnings; the choice to reflect on our decisions should not necessarily proceed from the outcome. Fortuitous decisions may be fundamentally flawed. Ill-fated decisions may be clothed in deep and solid analysis. Even a mistake of enormous proportions, if it is a mistake of what we do, has only limited capacity to teach. If we are examining our actions at this level alone, there is much more to be learned.

The live-fire episode gives me perspective. It humbles me when I start to believe others' praise (for example, "You are the best platoon we have seen in two years"). It paints the picture of the fine line between success and failure. It reinforces an Army officer's need for vigilant attention to detail, especially in the area of safety. But it does not even compare to the learning potential of temperamental criticism that I issued my son on a cold soccer field in southern New York (my Level Two failure) or the immense leadership lessons that proceed from the bite I took out of that cheeseburger at Yakima Training Center's Oasis (my Level Three failure).

I tell the tank round story on the first day of class to establish an environment of honest reflection. If I can share with leadership students that I nearly committed fratricide, then I expect that they do more than come up with a faux strength clothed as a weakness. What I am hoping for is much deeper than failures of what we do: I am hoping for the deep learning that comes from the discovery and exploration of Level Two and Level Three failures.

Level Two failures are ignorable. Because they rarely come with feedback, we must decide to reckon with them, to hunt for and find them. These failures require us to solicit candid input from others, take a hard look at our own actions, and diagnose our own needs for improvement.

Level Two: Failures of Who We Are

Level Two failures get a little more difficult, because who we are is a collection of our own history, our genetic makeup, and our intelligence—analytical and emotional. Failure is now more about us and less about our actions. Failures of who we are may come wrapped in the packaging of what we do, but the actions and decisions are more calculated or more connected to our personal traits, abilities, and emotions.

In every Level One failure, we must look for Level Two. Did we choose investing in equity because we are risk averse? Did we stay the course because we are afraid of change? Did we almost fire the tank round because we are careless by nature? We will often stop at Level One, even when there are Level Two failures to be learned from. We will rationalize, run, and hide because failures of what we do are more bearable than failures of who we are.

The learning of leadership comes from a variety of contexts. With my leadership development antennas up for the last several years, I have garnered important lessons from parenting, volunteering, movies, books, and myriad other sources. Youth sports is another arena ripe with development for us all, not just the players.

This past fall, a friend and I coached our sons' soccer team to a 0–9 record. The West Point Rockets scored three goals, whereas the opposition scored well over twenty. As each week passed, we attempted to keep the junior athletes' spirits up, focusing on what they were learning and helping them make sense of an increasingly tough experience. Of course, children play soccer in the third and fourth grade for fun, but fun becomes a little more elusive with each loss, even at nine years old.

During week eight, my son asked if he could play goalie. There were all sorts of reasons I should have said no. Reason 1 is the overly competitive nature John inherited from his father. This upcoming game was likely to be a tough one, and I knew my son would not respond well to the peppering of shots on goal that were likely to season our end of the field.

Reason 2, connected to reason 1, was the successful hiatus John had taken from goalkeeping duties. The year prior, he had spent a portion of every game minding the net. In the season's last game against the league's best team, we were clinging to a one-goal lead, when John experienced a Level One failure of his own. A very large nine-year-old launched a shot from midfield. As the ball sailed into the air, my coaching colleague and I quickly calculated the trajectory and began to bark instructions to John. The ball was dropping out of the sky toward a spot at the top of the penalty box from a height of probably thirty feet. John was rushing toward that spot, but he was not going to make it before the ball hit. Time seemed to stand still.

I knew my son's disposition, and I knew this was an impending disaster. As the ball approached impact, I could hardly bear to watch. John was still en route as the ball hit the ground and then leaped over his head toward the net. He turned around just in time to watch it trickle into the goal. Magnifying his disappointment was the loud roar from the opposing sideline as the parents of the other team celebrated the score. John took his gloves off, threw them down, and stormed off the field, understandably unable at nine years old to handle the seeming enormity of the moment: his failure, the tying goal, the crowd's response. And although he learned a Level One lesson from that goal—to play the bounce on shots launched into the air—we decided together that John would take a break from goalkeeping duties during the following season.

But in week eight of this season, our regular goalie was away with her family, and John asked if he could fill in. He made several good saves to start the game, but the volume of shots proved to be overwhelming. The opposition scored, and then it scored again. The third time they scored, I yelled across the field to John that he needed to get in front of the ball and use his hands. The tone of frustration in my voice communicated my dissatisfaction with my son's performance and the progress of our game. John heard me. The other players heard me. Even the parents heard me. In fact, the yell still echoes in my head. My nine-year-old son, putting behind him a very tough bounce from the year before, volunteers for goalie duty once again—and I embarrass him.

There are several different reasons that I shouted the instructions: because he was my son; because I was frustrated; because we were headed toward another loss; because I had told him before to use his hands; because I still have a lot to learn about myself, coaching, and leadership.

John came out of the game. I did not think about my failure until a week or so later. A colonel whom I work with, also a youth sports enthusiast, passed me a book about coaching. It is failure, not success, that pushes us toward learning. Headed toward an undefeated season, I probably would have set the book aside. But winless and feeling that I was letting the kids down, I was anxious to soak up some help.

I read the book (Jim Thompson's *Double-Goal Coach*) in two days. Tucked among a number of compelling lessons was one that took me back to John. Thompson reminds coaches (in fact, leaders) that the moment after a mistake is usually the worst time to make a correction. Wait, he says, until the pain of that moment has passed, and then lead when the time is right. Combine that with the most basic of leadership precepts—that one should praise in public and correct in private—and it occurred to me that I had failed.

This was more than a Level One failure. I did not simply learn how to become a better in-game coach. Correcting John in public at that moment was a failure of who I am. The specific things I have learned from that failure are personal, important, and tough lessons that I am forced to face if I want to become a better leader, parent, and coach. They go far beyond how I address young soccer players and delve into why I say what I say and why I do what I do. They are about me. And that makes this particular failure tough to reckon with (tougher even than the near launching of that tank round in 1996).

John and I sat down for lunch not long after that fateful game. The first thing I did was to ask his forgiveness for the embarrassment I had caused him. I learned from my own father that even simple apologies from Dad can endure as lifelong lessons in humility. John and I talked about how I could improve as a coach (not about how he could improve as a goalie). And before we got up to leave, we resolved to go out and just have fun.

As I shared lunch with our team's part-time goalie, I resolved to build his confidence rather than damage it with the hammer of my pride. No matter how many times you tell yourself you will not be *that* parent, sometimes you still are. Sometimes you still shout instructions because who John is as he flounders a bit on the field is also a little bit of who you are. Parents, coaches, leaders, humans: we all suffer from differing levels of pride, insecurity, and a lack of self-awareness. The choice is whether we suffer long from those maladies, or learn day by day how to overcome them by looking through the lens of our own failures.

I am sure I am a better coach and a better leader because of those wayward soccer instructions, the book I read in the aftermath, and the lunch with John. In the months that followed, we spent a lot of time tossing the football at Michie Stadium, the home of the Army Black Knights. John struggled to catch pass after pass the first few times we threw to each other. His confidence waned. There was part of me that wanted to show frustration once again. "I could catch those balls when I was nine," I thought. "Why can't he?" But I did not. I just kept throwing and encouraging as John got better and better. Last week, we went back up to Michie and played a fun, interfamily game with some of our best friends. John caught everything in sight. After the game, he beamed; he felt like a hero. My failure on that soccer field—and more important, my decision to face up to and learn from it—led to John's success on that football field. Leadership matters.

Level Two failures are avoidable and ignorable. Because they rarely come with feedback, we must decide to reckon with them. In a way, we almost have to hunt for and find them. These failures require us to solicit candid input from others, take a hard look at our own actions, and diagnose our own needs for improvement. When we lose our temper at a critical time, feel the discomfort of inadequacy, or fail to build the team, it is rarely readily apparent; these failures are not the same as wasting the advertising budget on a failed campaign or calling the wrong play at the wrong time. They are more subtle, more personal, and more important. Learning from Level Two failures requires the admission of imperfection and the ambition to become a better leader. Without that ambition, we may glide through leadership in ignorant but blissful mediocrity, learning from the Level One mishaps that circumstances force us to face but never learning more.

At the outset of this chapter, I shared words from a cadet who seemed unwilling to address his own weaknesses—who instead dressed his own self-perceived greatness in the clothing of a shortcoming. But I have seen the opposite. I have spoken to and counseled cadets who were just beginning the lifelong journey of learning leadership.

One cadet in particular (I will call him Mark) has taken some huge first steps. He has plunged deep into his own Level Two failures and pulled out valuable lessons. Read Mark's own words as he reflects on his role as a cadet basic training platoon sergeant: "Throughout the summer, I felt like the smartest dumb kid in the entire regiment. I couldn't seem to do what others made look easy. For example, I struggled in dealing with poorly performing subordinates and had difficulty unifying the platoon. The leadership situations seemed straightforward; however, I always seemed to struggle to define what needed to be done and how to get it done within the platoon. All too often, I was indecisive and unsure of myself."

Mark goes on to diagnose some of his weaknesses, pointing out that he fostered a climate of indiscipline because of a lack of force in his directives; often he failed to correct his direct reports and peers because of the all-too-familiar fear of not being liked. Embedded in Mark's self-diagnosis is a tapestry of recently acquired leadership theory, masterfully applied to both explain his failings and outline self-prescribed remedies.

Such candid and poignant self-examination is not only rare for a college student; it is rare, period. Leaders at every level and in every walk of life hesitate to make decisions, worry about what others think of them, and fail to manage relationships. Only the very best leaders look in the mirror, admit these Level Two failings, and improve. Mark is one of those leaders.

Serve others. Put others first. Wash their feet. However this core value was supposed to manifest itself in my actions, I doubt it involved staying warm and fed while my soldiers suffered outside in the cold.

Level Three: Failures of Who We Want to Be

In a class I teach on leading organizations through change, we spend one lesson juxtaposing the organizational with the individual. Each student reads the description of vision in a classic *Harvard Business Review* article authored by Jim Collins and Jerry Porras. The cadets then take the key concepts from that article and craft their own personal vision statement.[1]

The objectives are twofold: to provide cadets a vehicle for further understanding of the concept of vision and provide them a vehicle for further understanding of themselves. Embedded within Collins and Porras's discussion of vision are core values (three to five fundamental and deeply held principles) and core purpose (an organizational or individual reason for being).

Failures of who we want to be violate our core leadership values or our core purpose, or both. They impinge on our fundamental beliefs about leadership or our reason for leading. We must not make them often if we hope to lead effectively. But we will make them, and when we do, we must have the courage to reflect, learn, and become a better leader.

Serve others. These are two words that help define who I want to be as a leader, two words that I would place on my short list of core values. Many ascribe to the concept of servant leadership, and to different leaders it probably means different things. My desire to be a leader who serves others comes from my love and respect for my father and mother, who provided examples of leaders who served. My desire to be a leader who serves others comes from my faith—from Jesus's example of washing the feet of those who followed him. My desire to be a leader who serves others is inextricably linked to where I come from and who I want to be. So when the telephone rang in the warm confines of that Yakima Training Center hangout as my greasy burger stared me in the face, I realized that I was not who I wanted to be—not yet.

Almost every soldier who has lived and served at Fort Lewis, Washington, has crossed the Cascade Mountain range destined for "The Yak." Yakima, home to some of the world's best-tasting apples, is also home to a desert-like expanse of land fit for tanks, infantry-fighting vehicles, self-propelled artillery pieces, and thousands of soldiers. It is blistering hot in the summer and brutally cold in the winter, with winds that whip upward of fifty miles per hour. Yakima Training Center has few redeeming qualities, notwithstanding its excellence as a proving ground for Army units.

When redeeming qualities are lacking, your imagination and desperation create them. For the soldiers who have spent months on end at Yakima, the imagined redemption comes in the form of a tiny short-order restaurant that affords an occasional departure from Pop-Tarts and the Army's meals-ready-to-eat. The Oasis sits in Yakima's cantonment area, wedged between the makeshift barracks and a rarely used parade ground.

Yakima was nobody's idea of a vacation. When the wind blew, it was all you could do to keep your lips from freezing together. I remember waking up in the mornings and being afraid to unzip my sleeping bag because the impending blast of cold seemed so unbearable.

It was on one of those unbearably cold Yakima days that my commander summoned a few of us back to the cantonment area, about a thirty-minute ride from the training areas. Seventy of my soldiers were doing their jobs—manning machine gun positions, repairing vehicles, improving camouflaged concealment net—as our driver, a fellow officer, and I headed back to our meeting. I honestly do not remember the sequence of what happened next: whether we met with our commander and then went to the Oasis, or whether we went to the Oasis while waiting for the meeting. But to the Oasis we went.

Because leadership is about who we are, reckoning with leadership failures is extremely difficult. When we admit failure as a leader, we are looking in the mirror and admitting that we have violated the very essence of what we do, who we are, and who we want to be.

There were only a few other people inside; the rest of our five-thousand-soldier brigade was out in the cold training. The Oasis was warm. A big-screen television played in the corner. We were in no hurry to move on. I ordered a cheeseburger, a soft drink probably, and some fries. We talked a little—about what, I have no idea. And then the telephone rang. The cook, with his tall white hat and grease-stained apron, called out a name, my name. And then I heard it again.

"Is there a Lieutenant Crandall here?"

"Yeah, I'm Lieutenant Crandall."

"Phone," he said, as he held it out toward me.

I walked the twenty feet to the counter, wondering who would be calling me. And as I put the phone to my ear, my stomach turned and my heart sank. I have no recollection of what was said or why he was calling me, but it was my platoon sergeant: my second-in-charge. He asked me a simple question. I answered it. And then I went and ate the most distasteful cheeseburger I have ever had.

Serve others. Put others first. Wash their feet. However this core value was supposed to manifest itself in my actions, I doubt it involved staying warm and fed while my soldiers suffered outside in the cold. I doubt it involved serving myself.

I am not overstating the enormity of this moment in my personal path toward being a leader who serves others. Maybe I had been hypocritical before. Probably so. Maybe I had left my team in the lurch many times as I comforted my own needs. But when that telephone rang and I was caught with my hand in the cookie jar by my platoon sergeant, my personal failure came into full view. There was no running from it.

I have told this story to students in class several times, and many of them do not recognize the failure—or at least the magnitude of the failure. Some of them reason that if I had some extra time, why not have a cheeseburger? Possibly Yakima, the cheeseburger, and the telephone call fail to resonate with you even as you read this. But that is the essence of Level Three failure: you know it when you feel it. Unlike Level One, there may be no feedback; unlike Level Two, you need not solicit input. At Level Three, your gut wrenches, your actions clash with your values, and you realize quickly that you have failed to be who you want to be. Maybe getting caught eating a cheeseburger would not be your call for reckoning. But something else has been, and something else will be.

I truly believe in serving others. I want to wash others' feet. I want to be a leader who puts the interests of the people on my team well above my own, who works beside them and suffers with them. That cheeseburger and telephone call became a mental symbol, stored away for recall when I am tempted to turn my back on my own core leadership value of servanthood.

Remembering Our Own Personal Leadership Failures

Over the last few years, the National Aeronautics and Space Administration (NASA) has gone through a public struggle to understand and learn from its mistakes. Its culture has been one that suggested failure is not an option. In diagnosing what the space agency might do to alter this culture and learn as an organization, one of my students suggested that NASA place a huge picture of the *Challenger* explosion at the entrance to its headquarters. Each day, the student said, this would remind those working on the space program of the consequences of their mistakes. It would provide a daily shot of vigilance. Next to that picture, another student suggested, NASA could place a separate photo of the moon landing. These would convey both messages: "We are great" (moon landing), but "we can always learn from our mistakes and get better" (*Challenger* explosion).

Yakima is one of my personal reminders about my own leadership failures. I have captured that moment in my mind so that I might constantly pursue service to others—understanding the personal consequences of failure in this area.

It is important for teachers and developers to jump into the chilly pool first. For others—those simply desiring to become better leaders on a personal level—it is entirely appropriate to wear the wet suit of private reflection. But do not allow your private reflection to be full of excuses; be as hard on yourself as necessary to extract learning from your endeavors.

If you have never felt sick to your stomach while reflecting on the implications of one of your own failures, either an isolated event or an ongoing struggle, then you have probably never delved deeply into an examination of a failure involving who you want to be. Mine make me sick and disappointed, but resolved to live up to my own core values in the future—to fulfill my own personal leadership vision.

"Our Life Is Our Message"

A former instructor from our department, whom I know only through his stellar reputation, used to remind fellow faculty that "our life is our message." Leadership is about who we are; when we teach leadership, we are our own first lesson. Because leadership is about who we are, reckoning with leadership failures is extremely difficult. When we admit failure as a leader, we are looking in the mirror and admitting that we have violated the very essence of what we do, who we are, and who we want to be.

Two things have enabled me to take a hard look at my own failures. First, it is my job to teach others how to teach themselves—how to develop themselves as leaders. Because of my unyielding belief that reckoning with one's own failure, especially at Level Two and Level Three, is such an important part of the leadership development process, I have to lead the way. I cannot ask cadets to candidly reflect on their own experiences and then step aside. I must show them that I am willing to candidly reflect on my own and that I have benefited greatly from doing so.

A few summers ago, two colleagues and I conducted a leadership seminar with a group of students from Columbia University's Executive M.B.A. Program. During that session, we equated facing up to one's own failures with jumping into a chilly swimming pool. Everyone stands around the pool, and no one wants to jump in. But once someone takes the first leap, others almost always follow. If your job entails developing others as leaders, you must be the one to take that first leap into the chilly pool of learning. It will give those you lead the courage to follow, and your organization will improve as a result.

The second key thing I keep in mind when facing up to my own failures is that everyone has made mistakes. This is simple but powerful. I truly believe that I am flawed and need to improve. But I also truly believe that everyone else is flawed and needs to improve—that everyone has failed at Levels One, Two, and Three. This belief has cost me as a teacher: on a few occasions, I have received feedback from cadets that I lost a bit of credibility as a leadership instructor by sharing such tremendous failures as the near-fatal launching of that tank round.

Because my goal is to espouse the merits of candid reflection, I am less than concerned about their individual perceptions of me as a leader. But I am concerned with their perception of failure and its link to credibility. I want them to believe what I believe: that we have all failed and that reckoning with our failures contributes greatly to our development as leaders. I want them all to be like Mark.

To mitigate against the idea that failure directly results in a lack of credibility, I turned to Colin Powell, in my mind, one of the few greatest leaders of our time, and if nothing else, an undoubted success as an Army officer. In his best-selling autobiography, *My American Journey*, General Powell details two compelling Level One failures. As a second lieutenant, he lost his pistol and had to inform his commander, Captain Miller, of the error. Miller later put a scare in him by telling Powell that the weapon had been found by some children in a local German village. "Luckily," Miller said, "they only got off one round before we heard the shot and came and took the gun away from them." Powell was later told that he had left the pistol in his tent. Powell goes on to say that just a few months later, he lost his entire platoon's train tickets, stranding him and his men in Frankfurt.

If General Powell can admit his failures (albeit at Level One), so too should we be able to face up to our own.

Ultimately the primary goal is admission to self. I believe it is important for teachers and developers to jump into the chilly pool first. For others—those simply desiring to become better leaders on a personal level—it is entirely appropriate to wear the wet suit of private reflection. But do not allow your private reflection to be full of excuses. To reflect in private is to be as hard on yourself as necessary to extract learning from your endeavors: about knowledge and skills at Level One, about who you are at Level Two, and about what you need to do to become who you want to be at Level Three.

Make no mistake, whether into the mirror or into a loudspeaker, the admission of failure at all levels is often discomforting, painful, and gut wrenching. And as we put more leadership experience under our belt, it becomes more and more painful. Lieutenants are supposed to make mistakes. Recent college graduates have a built-in excuse of inexperience. An apprentice is there to learn; failure is part of the job description. But by the time we are the CEO, or the senior partner, or a colonel, failure becomes less and less tasteful. It is much easier to admit that five years ago, we committed a failure of who we were than it is to admit that five days ago, we committed a failure of who we are.

When I picked up that book on coaching and my failure struck me in the gut, I felt foolish. I teach leadership at West Point; I have been coaching soccer for years. I love kids. Could I still be making this type of leadership mistake? Yes, and it would do me no good to hide in the comfort of Level One or ignore the shortcoming altogether. The quicker we face up to our failures, the quicker we will learn. And when we lead by example and jump into the chilly pool first, we will inspire others to follow suit and learn as well.

If our life is our message, then imperfection is a given. And one thing is clear: the comfortable illusion of infallibility is the biggest failure of all.

Note

1. J. C. Collins and J. I. Porras, "Building Your Company's Vision," *Harvard Business Review,* Sept.–Oct. 1996, pp. 65–77.

CHAPTER THREE

YOU MUST LEAD YOURSELF FIRST

Greg Hastings

E ach of the three stories here that span my recent leadership journey, from my freshman to senior years at West Point, takes place at a different level of responsibility, and each has helped me become a more effective leader as I head out into the Army. These stories, the ones I have grown from, are typical and serve as a window into the world of leadership development that is the U.S. Military Academy.

Take Responsibility for Your Own Actions

I learned my first lesson about leadership while still a freshman at the Academy, happy and proud of where I was but also miserable most of the time—by design. West Point first-year students are called *plebes*, from the Latin word *plebeian*, referring to the lowest class. So I was at the bottom of the rank structure, performing extra duties like delivering newspapers, cleaning the common areas, and setting the mess hall tables before each meal. But I knew and expected all of this before I showed up, and I soon was able to perform all these duties with my focus on the future, when I would be an upperclassman and, eventually, a graduate of West Point and an Army officer.

A common release for plebes was spirit mission. We were able to do things in the name of "spirit" that would never be allowed otherwise—for example, carrying cadet commanders away from formations on our shoulders, temporarily taking necessary uniform items (like a hat) from exchange cadets from other academies, and attacking the mascots of other cadet companies. The height of this spirit came during Army-Navy Week, when classes were deliberately light, Army pride was high, and artifacts of spirit were everywhere. The dozen or so Navy midshipmen attending West Point for the semester were victims of constant, good-natured harassment, but they were also the perpetrators of their own Navy spirit missions.

In the days leading up to the famous Army-Navy college football game (December of my plebe year), the signs of a stirring rivalry were everywhere. Posters dotted the campus, and the uniform for the week, typically a gray class uniform, included a "Beat Navy" spirit shirt and our camouflage battle dress uniform. On Thursday night, the corps of cadets ate dinner in the mess hall and watched spirit videos—short, creative clips, many of them parodies of popular commercials—about the upcoming victory. After dinner, all four thousand cadets marched over to the athletic fields to enjoy a bonfire, the centerpiece of which was a boat symbolizing Navy.

When we learned that the plan was to trash the room of a Navy midshipman, we plebes were hesitant. "Don't worry," we were told, "as long as there's an upperclassman involved, you guys won't get in trouble."

When some upperclassmen approached a few other plebes and me about a spirit mission, we were excited. But when we learned that the plan was to trash the room of a midshipman, we plebes were hesitant. "Don't worry," we were told, "as long as there's an upperclassman involved, you guys won't get in trouble." That night, well after our required curfew of 11:30 P.M., a third-year cadet, Sergeant White, assembled the team.

In the morning hours, we gathered the tools for the mission and went over the plan. We looked over the buckets of Gatorade, old cartons of milk, and cans of foam shaving cream, and we rehearsed the teams' sneaking into a barracks room. Quietly we scrambled up the stairs to the room of our target: a Navy midshipman on a semester exchange. A few floors up, the teams got into position, supplies were passed out, and we swung the door open.

As planned, I moved in with a sophomore, each of us carrying a bucket of cold Gatorade. When we were both standing over the midshipman's bed, we flashed a look to the others waiting in the hallway. They were in position, so the sophomore counted to three, emphatically but silently, and we dumped almost five gallons of sports drink on the sleeping "Squid" (the cadets' perjorative term for those from the Naval Academy). Immediately we leaped out of the room. As I cleared the door, a plebe on either side pierced two cans of shaving cream and tossed both in the room. Foam shaving cream sprays out in all directions when a new can is pierced, and these two shaving cream bombs worked perfectly. The final cadets on the spirit mission tossed spoiled milk cartons in the room, and we were off. Our security, guarding the hallway in both directions, collapsed in, and we all ran downstairs, splitting up and taking circuitous routes to our rooms just in case the midshipman jumped up and followed us.

Back in my room, I laid down in my bed and tried to calm down. After all, there was one more day of classes to get through, then a full weekend in New Jersey at the game. I was thinking about the free weekend that we were about to enjoy away from West Point when I heard a knock on my door. No one is supposed to be up at 3:00 A.M., so I knew something was up. I opened the door to see Sergeant White, who had led the spirit mission. "We have to go see the CO [the commander, a senior cadet in charge of the company]. Right now."

We were soon standing at attention while the CO yelled. Apparently the victim of our spirit mission and his roommate woke up furious and called the central guard room to let them know what happened. A series of telephone calls ended with our CO, who knew some of his cadets were planning a spirit mission, although he did not know the details. He went to the room of Sergeant White and asked him if we had trashed the room in question.

This cadet had no choice but to answer truthfully. At other schools or in other organizations, an individual might be tempted not to admit to an offense so quickly, but under the cadet Honor Code, which states that "a cadet will not lie, cheat, steal, or tolerate those who do," denial was not an option. Had we all chosen to deny our involvement, I am sure we would have gotten away with it, but no one even considered lying to avoid the potential trouble that followed.

I was surprised to be standing at attention in the lineup that morning because I was, after all, only a plebe. My earlier concerns were relieved when the upperclassmen told us they were responsible for the mission, and we had nothing to worry about. "If anyone gets in trouble, it will be me," I recalled Sergeant White telling us. And now that he was in trouble, he did try to spare us. But the CO was furious, and he was not letting anyone off the hook.

The problem was our choice of spirit mission. The missions are supposed to be approved by the CO or higher to ensure that they are appropriate and harmless. Our spirit mission, in hindsight, was neither. The combination of Gatorade, shaving cream, and milk is not harmless when it splashes on a desk full of electronic equipment and a suitcase full of uniforms and civilian clothes. We realized the damage we caused as we spent most of the remaining time before breakfast formation cleaning the room that took so little time to destroy. With the room cleaned and clothes in the laundry, we were back on the CO's wall.

Again Sergeant White argued, "The plebes were just following my orders. Let them go." The CO did not see it that way, nor did the tactical officer (TAC), a commissioned officer who oversees and is legally responsible for our company (the cadets at West Point are divided into 32 equal companies, each with about 125 cadets). Despite thinking we were protected from any punishment by plebeian ignorance, we were now facing the same consequences as the upperclassmen who had convinced us to participate.

That morning, we had to face the TAC in a formal meeting, and she took away our weekend privileges. So instead of enjoying a weekend away from West Point celebrating the Army-Navy Game, we would spend most of it in our rooms on call for various duties. Sergeant White knew he could get in trouble for this mission, but he was furious that the plebes were also punished. Spending that weekend with White and the other participants in the spirit mission, I also grew upset. After all, I was just a plebe; I had not known any better when I participated in this mission.

I was sure to mention how innocent I was and how I had been wrongly punished just for being a follower. My coach listened intently but unsympathetically. When I finished explaining what took place, the coach asked me one question: "Did you do anything wrong?"

The final punishment consisted of marching for several hours each weekend, the standard West Point punishment. This meant that I could not participate in athletics on the weekends (I was on the mountaineering team). At the end of a team meeting shortly after the incident, I spoke to the coach. I was sure to mention how innocent I was and how I had been wrongly punished just for being a follower. He listened intently but unsympathetically. I knew there was a chance he could cut me from the team because my trouble represented the team poorly. As he listened and occasionally asked questions, getting cut seemed to become more of a possibility. When I finished, the coach sat back and asked me one question: "Did you do anything wrong?"

At first I was upset. The coach was clearly taking the side of the officers, who did not understand what it was like for plebes (or so I thought) who were accustomed to following orders all the time. I thought about his question and tried to answer in a way that would convince him to go easy on me. I explained how we had not thought through the spirit mission and how badly we all felt when we saw

> *"You may not have been in charge of the mission, but you were in charge of yourself. It doesn't matter how high or low you are in the chain of command. You are always a leader because, if no one else, you are a leader of one: yourself."*

the damage as we cleaned the room. But I also explained that when I expressed initial doubt about participating, the upperclassmen urged us on. As plebes, we figured that was just the way things happened—that during Army-Navy Week, you get the Navy midshipmen however you can. We just did what we were told, I explained, trying to make the case. It was not as if we had thought it up and led the spirit mission.

This last statement seemed to bother the coach. He looked at me, thinking about what I had just said. Under his gaze, I questioned whether I really was innocent in this whole mess. After a long pause, he told me one of the more important things I have learned in my development as a leader: "You may not have been in charge of the spirit mission, but you were in charge of yourself. It doesn't matter how high or low you are in the chain of command. You are always a leader because, if no one else, you are a leader of one: yourself."

My initial reaction to the coach's words was anger and defiance, but I had a lot of time during the following weekends to think about what I had done and what he had told me. As I marched back and forth, I considered the coach's words. I realized that I was not responsible for that spirit mission, but I was responsible for my own actions. For my part, I deserved the punishment I was serving. I was grateful to the coach for passing that lesson on to me. I was also sorry for my classmates, whose perspectives on the issue did not change as mine did. They continued to feel victimized and bitter about their punishment. Although it was a difficult way to learn it, I learned a fundamental skill as leader: leading yourself.

Great Leaders Also Need to Be Great Followers

I learned another important leadership lesson almost two years later, when I was spending my summer at West Point leading thirty-eight new cadets through cadet basic training. New cadets are incoming first-year students who are undergoing basic training over the summer; only after they complete cadet basic training are they accepted into the corps and earn the title "cadet." I was in charge of a platoon of these new cadets: four squads of about ten each. Each squad had a squad leader (also juniors).

There were forty-two people under me, and throughout the basic training, I worked alongside and in front of them eighteen or more hours a day. There were several levels of cadets above me, but the cadet I worked closest with was the first sergeant, who was one level above me in the chain of command. I knew First Sergeant Miller before that summer, and we were classmates and roommates for the training. Although we had not been good friends, we worked together well.

I understood that cadets in leadership positions are learning and therefore will make mistakes, but it was still frustrating to see mistakes made, especially because the new cadets were often the ones to suffer.

Cadet basic training is different from regular Army basic training in several ways. First, new cadets are taught a lot about West Point, in addition to learning basic soldier skills such as marksmanship and working as a team. Second, it is run entirely by cadets, with oversight from regular Army personnel. This is a big responsibility and a great opportunity for the upperclass cadets in charge of the new cadets, but inevitably things do not always run smoothly. Having spent two years at the Academy, I understood that cadets in leadership positions are learning and therefore will make mistakes, but it was still frustrating to see mistakes made, especially because the new cadets were often the ones to suffer. They were often small things, like time lines or incorrect packing lists.

But there was one mistake that bothered me the most. One day we had to get to one of the training sites that required a long, hard march. This march was nothing extraordinary for the cadre or even some of the older or stronger new cadets, but some of the new cadets struggled to climb the West Point hills with a full rucksack on their backs. It took a lot of effort from everyone in the platoon just to get to that training site.

We arrived a few minutes late and with one sprained ankle, so by the time we marched in, the soldiers at the site were upset. They took me aside and explained the importance of arriving on time, and they asked why we were carrying rucksacks. I had been told we needed them, but I was informed that no one else brought rucksacks to that site and someone must have been wrong. The march up to that training site benefited my platoon because it challenged them, but it also cost them training time because we were late and one new cadet spent some time on crutches after twisting his ankle under the weight of the apparently unnecessary rucksack. I was sure to let my superiors know about my dissatisfaction.

A few days later, we were preparing to ride the trucks out to another training site. Most mornings built in a few minutes after physical training for everyone to change, shower, and clean their rooms before coming back outside for breakfast formation. This particular morning had a tighter schedule because after physical training, everyone had to prepare their training gear and arrive back downstairs to meet the trucks. We would ride the trucks out and eat breakfast at the training site. I released my platoon with specific instructions, and I gave them fifteen minutes to be back in formation, showered and with the proper gear. I hurried upstairs after them to shower myself and beat them back to the formation area. On my way, the first sergeant informed me of a change.

"Everyone is going to have to wear camo [camouflage face paint]."

"Are you serious?" I replied angrily. "We're leaving in five minutes. My guys are already on their way downstairs. No one told them anything about camo, and it takes them ten minutes to do it right."

"Well, we have five minutes, and everyone has to camo up," the first sergeant explained patiently.

"Look, we can't do it. There's no way every new cadet can accomplish that and still make it to the trucks on time." I was bordering on insubordination, but I thought I had to be honest. Besides, he was a classmate of mine I knew well, so I had some latitude with him.

"Hey," he was angry now. "I've got three other platoons who are working on it right now. You're the only platoon sergeant wasting time arguing with me. It's not my decision; if it was, I'd change it. But it has to get done, so get it done."

I knew it was not his decision, and I knew that arguing with him would not change the decision. I gave up and told my four squad leaders about the change. They were just as angry with me as I was with the first sergeant, but we were able to get all the new cadets down to formation on time, with some type of camouflage paint on their faces, necks, and hands. The first sergeant gave us a few extra minutes to finish the camo before departing on the trucks, as the other three platoons were struggling as well. By the time we arrived at the site and finished breakfast, everyone's frustration from the camo paint issue had melted away, and we got on with the training.

As basic training continued, there were more miscommunications and mistakes. I met each one with as much opposition as was appropriate, but I was often dismissed in the same way as I had been during the argument over camo paint. I thought I was protecting my subordinates by sticking up for them. I did not want them to have to suffer unnecessarily for someone else's mistakes.

First Sergeant Miller and I were sitting in the room one night, and we started talking about all these changes that come down the chain of command. I explained that for the person making the change, it is just a decision: he tells his two or three subordinates, who pass it down to their subordinates. For most of the chain of command, that decision requires them only to follow the change themselves and pass the message along. But at the lowest level, platoon sergeants and squad leaders have to ensure that every new cadet understands and follows the new guidance. This can be time consuming, because new cadets have not been around long enough to know how to react to the change. For example, when one of the cadet leaders decided we would wear camouflage, they just told their subordinates and then put on some camo. But the squad leaders had to apply their own camo, then instruct and inspect the camo application of eight to ten new cadets, all at the last minute.

"But you argue with me as if I make these changes. I don't. They are made several levels above you and me. And you can't go argue with the leader several levels up the way you argue with me."

"Well, somebody up there doesn't understand the effect of these last-minute changes," I complained.

With all my arguing and complaining, I was not the honest
but effective subordinate I wanted to be; I was just a pain.
My platoon was the best in the company, there was no doubt.
I had been an effective leader—but a terrible follower.

"You're missing the point. Whether they do or not, you still have to follow orders. You still have to follow *my* orders. It doesn't matter where those orders originated."

I saw his point but did not want to concede.

"Look," he continued, "I have four platoon sergeants, and you're one of them. The other three will take orders, and if they're bad, they might sigh or moan, but they turn around and get it done. You will stay there and argue with me. I'm almost afraid to give you bad news because of the reaction you will have."

Now the first sergeant's point was sinking in. With all that arguing and complaining, I was not the honest but effective subordinate I wanted to be; I was just a pain. My platoon was the best in the company, there was no doubt. I had been an effective leader—but a terrible follower.

My first sergeant helped me realize that focusing on the welfare of my subordinates limited my effectiveness in the chain of command. I finally fully understood the role of followership, a role that I was currently teaching the new cadets. I also gained an understanding of the duality of leaders as followers.

One Person Can Make a Difference and Lead Successfully

I learned a third leadership lesson during my senior year at West Point. All cadets fit into the military hierarchy and fulfill jobs through all four years at West Point. As a senior, I held a staff job as the physical development officer: I was responsible for all of the physical requirements of the cadets in my company. Because my company (one of thirty-two in the corps of cadets) had the highest average score on the physical fitness tests for the past three semesters, I saw it as my job to maintain that preeminence.

Early in the fall semester, I began preparing for the Army physical fitness test, a test that everyone takes a few months into the semester. I held voluntary—and even some mandatory—workouts in the mornings, evenings, and on weekends. I even held a practice fitness test to get a good idea of our average and to identify what each individual needed to work on. The BrewDawgs (my company's nickname) had been at the top physically for most of my time there. But as cadets graduate and new ones come in, a company's identity can change, and I worried that the BrewDawgs were losing their emphasis on physical training.

I set goals for the company that the company leadership agreed with, but I do not think all the cadets shared the same goals. And if they did not share those goals, they would not be motivated to achieve them.

As classes started, attendance at workouts dropped off drastically. The scores from the practice test were pretty low, and I rarely saw people working out on their own. The worst part was that no one else seemed to care that we were about to lose our title as the top physical company. I talked to the whole company almost every day when we were all together at lunch formation. I went door to door in the evenings to get people to join us for push-ups and sit-ups in the hallway (the whole company, roughly thirty cadets from each of the four classes, lives in the same dormitory-style hallway). These techniques would work, but the effects were individual and temporary. As the fitness test neared, I worried about the outcome for my company.

I saw the problem as one of motivation. I did not know what the reason was, but the company as a whole did not seem to have the same level of motivation as in previous years to pass the fitness test—let alone to score the maximum points of three hundred out of three hundred. I set goals for the company that the chain of command agreed with, but I do not think all the cadets shared the same goals.

And if they did not share those goals, then they would not be motivated to achieve them. So I tried to find a way to align all of the BrewDawgs' physical goals with those I had already set.

I thought back to an instructor of mine who had told me how he had set goals for his platoon when he was a junior officer. (A clear advantage of taking academic classes with military officers as instructors is the way they can relate material to our future jobs in the Army.) The instructor I was thinking about got sidetracked one day into a discussion of platoon goals. He told us that he put up posters around the platoon area. At first the soldiers laughed at and even mocked the posters, but eventually they grew so accustomed to seeing them that they accepted the goals.

Months later, the posters were still up, and this officer asked his men what some of their goals were. To his surprise and delight, many responded with the goals on the posters. He even witnessed a soldier from a different platoon come through their area, read the posters, and start mocking them in the same way his soldiers had only months before. This time, though, his soldiers defended the goals as their own.

Those results sounded dramatic, but I needed something to elicit change in the next six weeks. Time to prepare for the fitness test was running short, but if the BrewDawgs started working, they could still bring their scores up significantly. I went through my own books and notes and searched the Internet for motivation. After an evening of searching, I had several quotes and sayings that I organized on several fliers:

> "To give anything less than your best is to sacrifice the gift." (the motto of Steve Prefontaine, former American record holder and distance-running cult hero)
>
> "The more you sweat in peacetime, the less you bleed in war." (a Chinese proverb)
>
> "Someone who wants to kill you worked out today." (my favorite, because it is such an ominous reminder)

In all, I created sixteen different fliers, each one containing the words "WORK-OUT! BREWDAWGS." Many also contained the company goal, the workout schedule for the voluntary workouts I held, and the date of the fitness test.

I printed out two or three copies of each flier and posted them on the walls around our company area. By the time I was done, there was one flier about every ten feet and several in each of the bathrooms: no one in the company could miss them. Some people saw them that first night, but most did not see the fliers until the next morning. I did not know what to expect, but I was pleased that I got everyone's attention. The BrewDawgs were at least reading them, and they were reminded several times a day of the goal for the company average.

For the most part, people were amused by the sayings, especially one story about a gazelle outrunning a lion and a lion outrunning a gazelle, resulting in a moral that "no matter who you are, you better be running." People outside my company heard about them and were repeating some of the sayings that were less well known. Just as in my instructor's story, the BrewDawgs were having fun with the signs, but I did not know if that would turn out to be good or bad.

A week went by, and talk about the fliers died down. There were not any more people at the workouts or signs of an increased emphasis on physical training (PT). With another week for preparation gone, I decided to get more aggressive. I put up new posters, each one with the goal for the company average and a few extra words—for example:

"Don't let the team down."

"BrewDawgs—Building a PT dynasty."

I put out fewer posters for this week, but people still walked around to make sure they read all of them.

When I started posting the goals and motivational quotes around the company area, I saw an immediate effect. Many cadets credited the fliers, especially some of the harsher ones, like, "Don't let the team down," with motivating them to prepare.

I noticed some new faces at the workouts that week, and I encouraged those BrewDawgs to bring more people out. When I went door to door, cadets were already making their way to the hallway for the evening workout. In the afternoons, more people were leaving with towels to go to the gym or coming back from a run. And those who were working out encouraged others to do so. For the first time, it felt as if I was not the only one in the company urging physical training. And when I asked people what they were going to score on the fitness test, it was no longer an uneasy "I don't know" but a more confident, "Definitely over 270, maybe 300" (out of 300).

The increase in physical training could, of course, be credited to several different factors. Maybe some cadets had planned to wait until the test approached, or maybe I was just seeing what I wanted to see. I asked around to be sure. Many cadets credited the fliers, especially some of the harsher ones, like, "Don't let the team down," with motivating them to prepare for the fitness test.

And when the test finally came, the BrewDawgs were ready. Although we did not maintain our previous rating as the top physical company, we were close behind the highest average, and we scored significantly higher than in the practice test at the start of the semester.

I had been struggling to find a way to motivate my company and maintain physical fitness as a top priority. When other methods failed, posting these messages around the company area worked. A side conversation with an instructor years ago had sparked an experiment that helped me achieve important goals for my company. Before this experience, I would have doubted the potential impact that one individual can have on an organization.

Three Great Leadership Lessons

West Point allows the maximum opportunity for cadets to learn about leadership at any time, anywhere. My first leadership lesson taught me that I had made a mistake as a plebe, and I almost missed that lesson. But a coach provided me with a piece of advice that taught me leadership at the lowest level.

As I continued to grow as a leader, I had an opportunity to lead a platoon of about forty. And although I looked out for their best interests, I neglected the other part of my responsibilities in my chain of command, and a conversation with a classmate—a peer—led me to a lesson about the dual roles of leaders.

And finally, near the end of my time as a cadet, I was able to influence a 120-person company, helping to align the company goals to those identified by the leaders. Through the change I witnessed and the ensuing performance of the company, I learned the impact one person can have on an organization. These were significant lessons in my cadet career and ones that I learned in ways unique to West Point.

It is important for leaders to focus on growing and developing. While attending the military Academy, my job was to prepare to lead soldiers in the U.S. Army. But all leaders, young or old, experienced or not, share the task of bettering themselves. The privilege to lead must be continually earned; this field is one where perfection is never achieved but always sought. The overall West Point leadership lesson is for leaders to continue to learn.

CHAPTER FOUR

INFLUENCING YOUR ORGANIZATION'S MORAL PHILOSOPHY

Brian Tribus

During the summer of 2005, I had the opportunity to travel to China to interact with students enrolled in the Beijing International M.B.A. Program. I led discussions about leader development and shared some insights from my experiences at West Point and in the Army. Following a presentation about the West Point Honor Code, one of the students asked me a tough question: "I agree that it is admirable to live by the spirit of the Honor Code and values of the Army. However, we live in the real world. Sometimes we have to compromise our ideal values in order to get the job done and keep our business alive, for example, by giving a client a gift to build a relationship (that is, a bribe). Should we sacrifice our livelihood in order to uphold our values?"

It took me some time to respond because I had so inadequately assessed my audience and their context. However, I eventually responded that it would be okay to give a bribe provided that the leadership of the organization was aware that this type of behavior was occurring and was prepared to accept the short- and long-term consequences of their employees' behavior. This question helped spark the idea for this chapter. I do not intend to preach about values and honorable living. I simply hope to raise some questions about the status of your organization's moral philosophy and offer some ideas about how you can shape it.

Being Preyed on Taught Me a Hard Lesson

My first day of negotiations class at Harvard Business School was different from the other classes I had taken: here, I wanted to be called on by my professors, whereas in other classes, I had dreaded it. I was confident because my first negotiation exercise had gone extremely well. I had met with my counterpart, Kendra, and we had immediately established a comfortable, productive rapport. We had shared information and explored possibilities, just as negotiations theory prescribed, until we reached an agreement that appeared to be beneficial to both Kendra's organization (Easterly, a bed and breakfast) and mine (Brims, an incoming coffee shop looking to purchase space from Easterly). I was eager to share the details of our success with the rest of our classmates. Who says that negotiations have to be win-lose? And so when I was called on, I smiled and happily explained how Kendra and I had cracked the code. Then the professor put up a PowerPoint slide with the results of the value created or captured in the negotiation: "Kendra, $2.4 million; Brian, $15,000."

"How would you explain these results, Brian?" the professor asked.

My heart sank, my face turned red, and I could feel myself starting to sweat. There were whispers and even some giggles throughout the room. I could not help myself: "You lied to me!" I shouted at Kendra from across the room. Kendra's face turned red, and the chatter in the classroom reached a roar. I had openly shared my organization's information with Kendra, trusting her to do the same. Instead, she used the information to her advantage and led me to believe that we had reached a mutually beneficial outcome.

Despite getting crushed by Kendra in our first negotiation exercise, the Academy allowed me to teach negotiations theory to cadets. I used this story to illustrate what happens in a distributive (win-lose) negotiation when one party (me) uses symbiotic tactics and the other party (Kendra) uses predatory tactics.

Recently I told this story in a management class about control systems. More specifically, I described how officers can influence their organization's moral philosophy—the principles, values, and rules that people use in deciding what is right or wrong. Kendra had lied to me during our negotiation; she misrepresented her organization's information and took advantage of my honest (albeit naive) disclosures. Was she wrong? I wonder what would have happened to Kendra if the negotiation had been real. Perhaps her results would merit a bonus and a promotion.

My students pointed out that she might get in trouble for damaging the relationship with her client or tarnishing our organization's reputation. Surely she would not fare so well in future negotiations now that her tactics were revealed

In the absence of proactive measures, members of an organization may be left to make critical, strategic decisions on their own. Good intentions aside, they may make decisions that the organization will later regret.

(indeed, she did not do nearly as well in subsequent negotiation exercises in class). I was quick to remind them how great I had felt before our professor revealed that Kendra had raked me over the coals. Kendra's actions could have led to negative consequences for her organization *if* her tactics were uncovered.

The point of my class was not to put Kendra on trial. The point is that Kendra should have been acting in accordance with her organization's moral philosophy. It is the responsibility of the leaders in Kendra's organization to set the boundaries for her to operate within. What is important is that the organization is comfortable with the way that she handled the negotiation and is prepared to deal with the associated consequences. In the absence of proactive measures, members of an organization may be left to make critical, strategic decisions on their own. Good intentions aside, they may make decisions that the organization will later regret.

The Army's Case for Shaping Moral Philosophy

The U.S. Military Academy's mission is "to educate, train, and inspire the Corps of Cadets so that each graduate is a commissioned leader of character committed to the values of Duty, Honor, Country; and prepared for a career of professional excellence and service to the Nation as an officer in the United States Army."

The service that Academy graduates sign up for will not be easy. The U.S. Army is engaged in the Global War on Terrorism in the villages of Iraq and Afghanistan and elsewhere around the world. The situations that junior leaders will find themselves in are volatile and complex, and they must make decisions rapidly—decisions that sometimes have the potential to affect national objectives.

For example, imagine being asked to win the hearts and minds of the Iraqi people while simultaneously having the task of identifying and capturing or killing insurgents, while enemies engage in tactics that are devoid of ethical standards. There are many things that could go wrong in those situations, so the Army has a lot at risk.

Therefore, it is imperative that officers have the ability to shape the moral philosophy of their organization: they are instrumental in establishing the principles, rules, and values that their subordinates use in deciding what is right or wrong. My assumption is that the business environment that other organizations operate in is also volatile and complex and that sales reps, customer service agents, project managers, and others are called on to make decisions that could have strategic implications.

The business environment that other organizations operate in is volatile and complex, and sales reps, customer service agents, project managers, and others are called on to make decisions that could have strategic implications.

Recruiting and Selecting People Who Match Organizational Values

It is easier to establish an organization's moral philosophy by selecting people who generally subscribe to its values already. The U.S. Military Academy trains a team of Army officers to identify potential cadets who have "the right stuff." In addition to looking at the academic and physical performance of candidates, recruiters look for examples of leadership and service.

For example, Mike Barger, the chief learning officer for JetBlue, spoke to some cadets and described JetBlue's process of conducting peer interviews, where flight attendants interview potential attendants to determine if they will fit into the customer-service-centered culture at JetBlue. Of course, it is critical to make sure that the flight attendants who are doing the interviews live by the values of JetBlue.

When selecting people for your organization, what processes do you have in place to look for soft attributes? We tend to look at hard figures because they are more readily quantified and reported on performance evaluations and résumés. We need to be more creative when looking for soft attributes. For example, one of the values we try to live by in our academic department is being "cadet-centric"— in other words, taking a genuine, personal, and professional interest in our cadets. How can we tell if a prospective faculty member possesses an inclination to connect with cadets? If this person is at West Point for an interview, we take notice if he or she seizes opportunities to interact with nearby cadets.

Socializing Recruits to Embrace Organizational Values

Despite best efforts at recruiting the right people, chances are that incoming employees will not automatically believe in and live by an organization's values. Leaders have to initiate and manage a socialization process designed to help new employees understand the right way to do things and help them become productive members of the team. For example, David Barger, chief operating officer of JetBlue Airways, had mentioned the importance of his company's orientation program in Orlando, Florida. New employees receive briefings about the company's history and values. They all are issued a JetBlue values card and learn what those values mean and why they are important. Barger said that he could count on one hand the number of times that he or chief executive officer David Neeleman was not at the orientations, which take place several times a year.

That being said, I offer the following story about my first day as a cavalry troop commander and the consequences of not having a solid socialization program.

My first day in command of an armored cavalry troop, called Charlie Troop, at Fort Hood, Texas, had gone well. The ceremony and reception went smoothly, and I had a few productive meetings with the senior leaders of our troop.

My first evening, however, was a disaster. At approximately 2:00 A.M., I received a telephone call from my first sergeant (the senior noncommissioned officer in our troop and my right arm) informing me that Private Morris had been arrested. "Who is Private Morris?" I asked. I had memorized the names of all of the members of our 140-man organization, and this name was not one of them. "He arrived at the troop last night," the first sergeant responded. It turned out that Private Morris had been arrested for driving under the influence of alcohol, and he was under age, did not have a driver's license, had no insurance, and his car was not registered.

After retrieving Private Morris from the police station, I called in the senior leaders of my troop for a 3:00 A.M. meeting on Saturday morning in order to get some answers and prevent this from ever happening again. Private Morris had arrived at our unit at 5:30 P.M., after I had released everyone for the weekend. Our supply sergeant had to come back in order to give him some bedding and assign him to a room in the barracks. After showing Private Morris to his room, the supply sergeant had told him to report in physical training gear on Monday morning at 6:30 A.M. Not knowing anyone yet, Morris had changed his clothes and headed downtown to find a place to get drunk.

That evening, my senior leaders and I had laid the groundwork for a formalized socialization process for Charlie Troop. That is, we had developed a plan to receive and integrate new members of our organization so that they would be taken care of and eventually be able to contribute to the troop and behave in a manner consistent with our standards and values. The plan included simple things like an itemized checklist to inspect each newcomer's driver's license and registration on arrival, as well as ideas to help make the new member feel socially accepted and to assess his skill level and develop a training plan.

On the day of his arrival, Private Morris would have been assigned a battle buddy—a more senior enlisted soldier whose mission would have been to make Morris feel welcome and orient him to the "Charlie Troop Way." We had been careful in selecting these battle buddies, picking soldiers who were mature and had internalized our standards and values.

In our plan, I had also required that all new soldiers would meet me on the day of their arrival. I would introduce myself and explain our standards, as well as take some time to get to know our new member and see if he had any concerns that needed to be addressed. This was an important part of our plan because in the absence of a formal socialization process, new members of an organization will be socialized anyway, and sometimes in a manner that is inconsistent with the moral philosophy we were trying to establish. Our organization failed Private Morris, but the implementation of our new socialization program undoubtedly prevented similar failures from occurring.

Establishing Clear Rules of Acceptable Conduct in the Organization

An important part of the Army's ability to be successful in the Global War on Terrorism is our soldiers' ability to understand and abide by the rules of engagement (ROE), clearly established, written rules for conduct for Army personnel to follow during operational deployments and combat missions. The ROE explicitly describe the circumstances and reasons for soldiers to apply escalating means of force when threatened or faced with uncertain hostilities and possible personal or unit danger—for example:

- When is it okay to shoot a weapon at someone with the intent to kill?
- When is it not okay?
- What other nonlethal measures are acceptable to use in trying to accomplish your mission?

Soldiers at lower levels of our Army units need to be able to answer these questions with as much accuracy as higher-level leaders. Killing an innocent noncombatant, a tragedy in itself, can also have a disastrous effect on the long-term success of our mission.

Leaders play a critical role in developing the ROE and evolving the ROE as necessary. They also have the responsibility to teach their subordinates what the ROE are and why the ROE exist. They must then have a plan to enforce the ROE.

An example of the ROE in action can be found by looking at the fighting that occurred in the streets of Mogadishu, Somalia, in October 1993. American soldiers were caught in one of the most intense firefights in recent history—a long and bloody fifteen hours of close combat. Tasked with the mission to capture Somali warlord Muhammed Farrah Aidid and his top lieutenants, the ranger and special forces soldiers unexpectedly found themselves making on-the-spot ethical decisions that would test their moral character and challenge the established ROE outlined by senior military and civilian leadership.

According to the ROE, soldiers were authorized to use deadly force when they "saw someone with a weapon in the vicinity of a target area." This is not hard to understand and abide by when someone is pointing a weapon and shooting at you. However, what if the enemy does not abide by the same moral code? Local Somali warlords and their clansmen were aware of American ROE and the constraints the rules placed on soldiers to engage with deadly force, and some began using women and children as human shields as they advanced and fired on U.S. forces. In this situation, American soldiers saw someone with a weapon in the target area, but that person was standing behind an innocent noncombatant who was likely to be killed if they shot back.

Fortunately, the soldiers had also been educated on the rules of the Geneva Conventions regarding the use of human shields, a tactic used in the past on other battlefields (like Vietnam) and anticipated by U.S. leaders. Authorized to fire, soldiers used their marksmanship skills to attempt to minimize unnecessary deaths of noncombatants. Some soldiers asked their leaders for permission prior to engaging, even though their own lives were in danger.

In Somalia, the ROE were clearly established: they were written in codified operations orders, briefed to all military members, clearly expressed by leaders at all levels throughout the chain of command, and provided in classroom settings, as well as on individual laminated cards for soldiers to carry and memorize.

The humanitarian focus of the overall mission in Somalia, coupled with American ideals for clearly distinguishing between combatants and noncombatants, was understood at all levels and prevented American soldiers from indiscriminately taking the lives of innocent Somalis and using deadly force without clear rationale to do so. The ROE reflected Army values and adherence to the rules of land warfare and the Geneva Conventions, establishing a moral code and ethic for operations in the less-than-hospitable environment of the streets of Mogadishu.

Situations like these became the topic of intense discussion in the Army following the events in Somalia. How do we balance the need to protect soldiers and accomplish our mission with the desire to live by our Army values and defend the dignity of noncombatants? ROE training has become heightened at military national training centers and a critical training task for leaders in units called on to deploy.

While developing their own organizational rules of engagement, leaders should ask:

- What could go disastrously wrong in the organization?
- What rules are in place to prevent disaster from striking?
- How well do employees understand the rules?
- What pressures might tempt them to break the rules?

Clarifying Boundaries by Punishing Those Who Step Outside Them

No one can always select employees whose values are directly aligned with the organization, and socialization is a process that may take several months depending on the employee and the effectiveness of the process. Therefore, it is okay to start by seeking compliance—having employees understand the rules and live by them by virtue of knowing the consequences of not doing so. At West Point, plebes (the first-year students) are taught the meaning of the Honor Code: "A cadet will not lie, cheat, steal, or tolerate those who do."

They are taught the Army's values of loyalty, duty, respect, selfless service, honor, integrity, and personal courage (LDRSHIP) by senior cadets and Army officers through historical and personal stories that illustrate what the values mean and why they are important. The plebes are also informed of the consequences of not living by the values, which range from being counseled to being separated from the Academy. Leaders in any organization need to develop necessary rules, clearly articulate and live by the rules, and have a system to enforce the rules. Those who step outside the boundary lines drawn should be dealt with in a manner consistent with their violation, which helps send a message to the rest of the organization that reinforces its prescribed values.

One of the values we lived by when I commanded Charlie Troop was teamwork. Our troop consisted of scouts (hunters), tankers (killers), mortarmen (indirect fire support), mechanics, and administrative personnel, all with a key role to play in order for our troop to succeed. Perhaps the hardest-working yet least-celebrated team members in our troop were the mechanics, so I made an extra effort to point out their contributions and reward them for outstanding performance.

One day it came to my attention that one of our mechanics, Private First Class Hunter, had failed out of lifeguard school on Monday (organizations were occasionally tasked to supply a lifeguard to the installation pool). Because the school was scheduled to last until Friday, Hunter figured he would let his chain of command know about his failure on Thursday, after spending a couple of days in his air-conditioned room playing Nintendo while his fellow mechanics worked on tanks in the 110-degree motor pool.

Ben Franklin once said, "Anger is never without a reason, but seldom a good one." In my opinion, this was one of the few times that anger had good reason. I was furious. How could Hunter do this to his teammates? I held his punishment hearing in my office at 4:30 P.M., just as the rest of the organization was gathered outside for an end-of-day formation. Hunter admitted to what he had done but told me that he felt his punishment should be "light," given that this was his first time being in trouble and that what he did "wasn't that bad."

I was later told by the other leaders in our troop that they were taken aback by the veins bulging from my neck, the redness of my face, and the general ferocity with which I launched into Hunter. How could he have done anything worse? He had let his teammates down. I brought Hunter to tears, and the rest of the troop knew that a sure way to cross the commander was to not be a team player.

Pushing Beyond Compliance: Toward Internalization

We cannot stop at compliance. Too much time and energy would be wasted trying to supervise subordinates and enforce the rules. In addition, many of our subordinates will be in positions to act in the absence of supervision. We need junior leaders to internalize our values and in turn be role models and help instill values in their subordinates.

A quick (and often overlooked) way to step closer toward internalization is to explain the purpose behind your own values and regulations. Given our busy schedules as leaders, we have a tendency to adopt a "do-it-because-I-said-so" mentality. I remember being told this as a child, and I did what I was told only out of fear of

We cannot stop at compliance. Too much time and energy would be wasted trying to supervise subordinates and enforce the rules. In addition, many of our subordinates will be in positions to act in the absence of supervision. We need junior leaders to internalize our values and in turn be role models and help instill values in their subordinates.

punishment. Granted, there are times when subordinates need to simply comply with orders, as when in the Army the enemy is shooting at you or in a business setting when you are approaching a production deadline and action needs to be taken. However, there are plenty of times when a quick explanation would help a subordinate see the value in complying and take that step toward internalization.

Another way to push toward internalization is to avoid putting employees in situations that may require them to compromise organizational values in order to get the job done. Leaders must understand the implications of their orders. For example, when I was a support platoon leader, one of my missions was to provide fuel for our squadron's vehicles when and where it was needed. Our squadron deployed to the national training center in Fort Irwin, California, to be evaluated by experts on our readiness to go to combat. Prior to the squadron's leaving the base camp to conduct simulated combat operations, I had to make sure that my fuel trucks were tested to ensure that the fuel was not contaminated. It was the day before moving out, and my fuel section sergeant told me that our fuel was not certified.

Apparently drawing some of the trucks from the draw yard had taken longer than anticipated, and he did not have time to circulate the fuel in some of the trucks. (Circulating the fuel means that the truck routed the fuel continuously through a series of filters in order to remove any water or other contaminants, a process that took several hours.)

"Am I going to have to tell the squadron commander that we can't go into combat because we don't have enough fuel? I need those trucks ready to go by 0500 hours tomorrow morning," I said.

My fuel section sergeant replied, "Don't worry, Sir, we'll make something happen."

Comments like "just make it happen" or "I don't care how, just do it"
can have disastrous consequences and are leadership failures.

Later that evening, he reported back to me that all the samples were certified. At first, I was elated: "Awesome job, Sergeant! Great news!" Then I began to wonder how he pulled this off. It turned out that he had taken several samples from one truck that had completed circulating the fuel and turned them in to the lab marked as samples from the other trucks. The sergeant assured me that the other trucks would complete the circulation process before moving out in the morning but that we did not have time to get the samples tested because the lab was closed for the evening.

I struggled on what to do. My fuel section sergeant had assured me that the fuel would be fine, but the regulation stated that the lab needed to certify the fuel. I knew that contaminated fuel could cause damage to an engine (tank engines can cost $500,000) and at worst could lead to an accident and injury to soldiers. Telling my commander would illustrate my incompetence and perhaps delay our squadron's deployment, which would embarrass the whole unit.

I told the commander. Fortunately, he was able to pull some strings and get the lab reopened and the samples tested (the fuel sergeant was right; they all were certified). I held a meeting with my fuel sergeant and the other leaders of my platoon and said that although I appreciated the fuel sergeant's desire to accomplish the mission, we could not behave like that. As the platoon leader, I should have anticipated this problem by knowing what it would take to get the fuel certified.

What will it take for your subordinates to do their work? Do you want to know? Comments like "just make it happen" or "I don't care how, just do it" can have disastrous consequences and are leadership failures. How can we expect employees to internalize our values when we knowingly ask them to do things that require inconsistent action? Here is another example. My wife, April, worked for a major telecommunications company for twelve years. One of her duties was to compile profit-and-loss statements from different business units. When her boss was dissatisfied with her numbers, he would say to her, "These numbers are unacceptable. Our vice president won't be pleased. Take them back and work them a bit." What does that mean? Is April supposed to learn how to change rounding rules in the spreadsheet? The only difference between her boss and certain executives at Enron is that the latter were caught.

The Next Level: Embodying Your Organization's Values

Leaders are responsible for helping to alter their employees' sense of identity. Over time, employees should start to view the organization as part of who they are. For example, if you were to ask me to tell you about myself, I would certainly include the fact that I have been an Army officer for fourteen years. My time in the Army has had an impact on who I am as a person.

In working toward this goal of having employees associate themselves with the organization, leaders must articulate why the organization exists (that is, its purpose) and the values that members of the organization live by and why they are important, and then leaders must consistently reinforce these messages through their behaviors. They should ask themselves Theodore Levitt's classic question, "What business are we in?" and their direct reports should be able to answer the question correctly.[1] People at all levels of the organization should understand the reasons behind what they are doing and how their work fits into the bigger picture.

A Values Case Study: Beech-Nut Then and Now

One of the important cases I studied at Harvard Business School was about Beech-Nut, the baby food company.[2] In 1978, executives from the company became aware of a potential problem with the purity of the apple juice concentrate bought from its sole supplier. Nevertheless, it continued to purchase the concentrate over the next few years despite increasingly accurate information that a problem existed. The reason was that the concentrate was 25 percent cheaper than prices offered by other suppliers, competition with Heinz and Gerber was intense, and the executives felt pressure from their new parent company to turn a profit.

As evidence became more compelling, the executives decided to dump the product overseas and play a shell game by moving finished product between warehouses in order to minimize product seizure and the potential loss to Beech-Nut. By this standard, they thought they had done a decent job of handling the problem.

However, the executive who was in charge of quality control and had been raising issues about the concentrate decided to write a letter to the Food and Drug Administration (FDA), and it sparked an investigation. In the end, the Beech-Nut president, Niels Hoyvald, and the plant manager, John Lavery, were sentenced to a year in jail and $100,000 in fines. If they had been asked Levitt's question of what business Beech-Nut was in, I would imagine that Hoyvald and Lavery would have replied: "We are in the business of selling baby food products at a profit." If you visit Beech-Nut's Web site today, you can get an indication that the answer to the question might be: "We are in the business of helping parents nourish their children by providing delicious food made with the highest-quality ingredients." If this had been the answer in 1978, perhaps Beech-nut would have avoided the largest fine in FDA history and a loss of consumer trust.

People at all levels of the organization should understand the reasons behind what they are doing and how their work fits into the bigger picture.

An Alternate Values System: Johnson & Johnson

In contrast with the Beech-Nut case is the way Johnson & Johnson handled the Tylenol crisis in 1982 by making a voluntary recall that resulted in a $100 million charge against earnings.[3] The actions of CEO James Burke and other executives involved were consistent with the first line of J&J's famous Credo: "We believe our first responsibility is to the doctors, nurses and patients, to mothers and fathers and all others who use our products and services. In meeting their needs, everything we do must be of high quality."

Absent leader actions that are consistent with our prescribed values, company values become nothing but meaningless signage and may even generate counterproductive cynical behavior.

Teaching Ethics

In addition to modeling the values of their organizations themselves, many leaders implement a values education system. For example, as an assistant professor at West Point, I volunteer some of my time to teach in our professional military ethic education (PME2) program. Given my participation in the program and my belief in our organization's values, I was taken aback by some comments one of my marketing students made about one of the PME2 classes he had recently attended.

"Sir, have you ever seen *The Office?*" he asked, referring to the television comedy series about office behavior.

"No, why?" I replied.

"Because the PME2 class we just had was just like the ridiculous values training they did on one of the episodes. What a joke and complete waste of time. I mean, we keep hearing the same stuff over and over like they're trying to beat the values into us."

That is not the type of feedback anyone wants to get about values training. Leaders cannot afford to have classes that feel this way. Granted, this may have been this sole cadet's opinion. But if the majority of the students felt that way, there is a problem. Not only do these classes waste resources, they have the potential to inspire cynicism. We make our classes effective by meeting a few criteria:

- *The content is relevant.* The examples we use to teach values are realistic scenarios that lieutenants have actually dealt with in the Army. It is important that your organization is in touch with situations that your employees are likely to face.
- *The teachers are credible.* Our teachers have been in situations similar to what their students will face. They have struggled with similar decisions before. Sometimes they have failed in those situations. In addition, we bring in lieutenants and captains directly from the operational Army to share their experiences. They believe in and try to live by the values they are trying to instill. Imagine my wife April's boss trying to teach her the importance of honest and accurate reporting.
- *The teachers know their audience.* Teachers have to know what their students may be thinking and how they are feeling if they want to craft their instruction in a manner that will be well received by their students.

- *The teachers do not preach.* The goal is not to beat your organization's values into your employees. Instead, the goal is to have them question who they are and what they stand for—to have them see how the organization's values might apply to realistic situations.
- *Leaders supervise.* How can we say that values education is important if we never spend time observing classes or reviewing the curriculum? Leaders also need to continue their education. By sitting in on a class, we can learn a lot about how our junior leaders are framing and dealing with issues at their level.

Policing Their Own Ranks

Organizational rules may be established and clearly understood, but they need to be enforced until all employees internalize them. It would be a lot easier to enforce the rules if junior members of the organization helped senior leaders police the ranks.

My first deployment exercise in the Army in 1993, a year after graduating from West Point, provides an example. My cavalry troop went to Arizona for six weeks to conduct a counternarcotics mission along the Mexican border. A few days into the mission, I noticed that our commanding officer, Captain Smith, was using the government credit card to purchase snacks and drinks for himself and his driver. Prior to deploying, we had all received instruction on how to use the card, and I clearly remembered that the card was supposed to be used primarily for fuel and oil purchases and, if necessary, "mission-essential items that cannot be procured through other channels." Smith was stealing from the government.

I was apprehensive about approaching him to discuss his behavior. I was a very junior officer with little experience, and he was my boss. Before going to him, I talked to one of my fellow lieutenants who had been on a deployment before in order to get some support and make sure I was on track. His response was, "Yeah. It's no big deal. I've seen Captain Smith doing it before. The finance folks don't really check your charges when you get back."

I was stunned. I was looking for validation of my feelings and instead felt even more unsure of myself. Should I let the issue slide? After all, it was only a few dollars. Smith was the boss and would be the one to settle the accounts when we got back. But I could not let it go. How could we complain about not having enough money for training and equipment while we were using resources to buy chips and soda?

While we were back at the base camp for a day of rest, I went to talk to Smith in his room. "What's your problem, Lieutenant?" he asked before I could get anything out. I suppose he sensed that something was wrong.

"I'd like to talk to you about the government credit card, Sir. I don't think you're supposed to use it for personal items."

"What the hell do you know, Lieutenant?" he responded. He was clearly agitated that I had disturbed him in the first place, and now he was angry. "I've been on more deployments than you have months as a platoon leader. I know how to use the card, and I'm the one who settles the accounts. Perhaps you should mind your own business. Now get out of my room, Sherlock, so I can get some rest."

Leaders need to be aware of the reasons
that their employees might tolerate unacceptable
behavior and empower them to police their own ranks.

Now what? I am not sure what I had hoped to achieve before I went to see him. However, it was clear that his behavior would continue, and it did. Should I go to Smith's boss with the issue? That would have been the right thing to do. The American people had paid a lot of money to send me to West Point, and now I was expected to live by the Army values. Smith's unethical behavior permeated his whole organization. It was not just chips and soda; I would come to find that corners were cut with regard to equipment accountability, costing the government hundreds (perhaps thousands) of dollars. I had had a chance to put a stop to it. I had a responsibility to put a stop to it. But I failed. After I left his room that day, I kept my mouth shut.

People tolerate unethical behavior for a variety of reasons. Reflecting on my experience with Smith, the biggest reason was that I was weak: I lacked the moral courage to do what was right. I was worried about straining my relationship with my boss. I feared what might happen if I went over his head and brought the issue to our squadron commander. I was also concerned about being socially outcast. Smith was well liked by most of the men in our troop. Getting him in trouble would not win me any popularity points. In addition, I wondered if this was really my problem. After all, Smith was the boss, and the finance department back at Fort Stewart was responsible for reviewing purchases made with the card. And finally, was I making too big a deal of this? After all, it was only a few dollars.

There are lots of reasons that I tolerated his behavior, but there are no excuses. Leaders need to be aware of the reasons that their employees might tolerate unacceptable behavior and empower them to police their own ranks.

The Problem of Tolerating Unacceptable Behavior

Addressing toleration of unacceptable behavior is no easy matter. Yet toleration is one of the biggest obstacles that must be overcome if leaders want to succeed at having their moral philosophy take roots and guide employee behavior. Again, the West Point Honor Code reads, "A cadet will not lie, cheat, steal, or tolerate those who do."

The tenet that we struggle with the most in terms of influencing cadet internalization is the toleration clause. Perhaps the biggest reason is that cadets, like most other college students, are trying to fit in. They want to be accepted. Certainly informing the chain of command that a fellow cadet committed a violation is not the preferred method of making friends. In many cases, loyalty lies with friends, teammates, and classmates rather than with the organization. Given these conditions, consider a story that one of my colleagues (I'll call him Jason) told me about his experience with the toleration clause as a cadet.

In the spring of his yearling (sophomore) year, Jason became an honor representative for his company; he was one of seventy-two who helped conduct investigations of possible Honor Code violations, sat on honor hearings, and helped teach classes about the code and West Point's values. Soon after his appointment, Jason faced one of the biggest challenges of his life: turning in his roommate, Bill, for violating the code.

Jason and a few of his classmates found out that Bill had stolen another cadet's economics assignment and submitted it as his own work. The cadets aware of the situation turned to Jason, who had volunteered to be an honor representative, to do what needed to be done. Despite being Bill's roommate and friend, Jason turned Bill in after Bill's refusal to self-report. Faced with an honor investigation and possible separation, Bill decided to resign from the Academy.

I asked Jason what went through his mind when he turned Bill in, and he said that although it was extremely difficult, there was no doubt that it was the right thing to do. Jason had grown up as the son of a West Point graduate and had heard his dad tell stories about the Honor Code, why it was so important, and how it made West Point a special place. Jason believed in West Point's values and had volunteered to be a guardian of the code.

Jason paid heavily over the months following turning Bill in. Some cadets labeled him a snitch. He found the words "Honor Nazi" written under his nametag in the hallway, and his nickname became "Honor Boy." Even Jason's mother paid, because Bill's mother (formerly a friend as well) could not understand how Jason could turn on her son.

As a faculty member looking back on Jason's story, I find it troubling to think about what he had to endure as a result of doing the right thing, doing what the organization expected. Jason told me that a senior member of the faculty never counseled him about his situation. Without question, Jason's tactical officer (a captain or major assigned to the company as a trainer, mentor, and coach) knew about the incident. This officer should have been aware of what Jason was going through and given him mental support, even a simple statement from an Army officer to the effect of, "I know it's tough, but you did the right thing and I'm proud of you. Believe it or not, several of your classmates respect what you did; they just lack the courage to say so." A five-minute pep talk would have gone a long way. Positive feedback from a fellow cadet would also have nurtured Jason's soul.

Jason and I laughed at the idea of the tactical officer gathering all of the cadets in a room and preaching about the merits of Jason's actions. What the officer could have done, however, is single out a senior cadet who was well respected by other cadets and believed that Jason had done the right thing. Not only could this cadet have talked to Jason, but he or she could have stood up for Jason in certain situations and put an end to some of the demeaning behavior. Without support, Jason could have convinced himself eventually that doing the right thing was not worth it.

During his junior year, Jason faced another difficult situation. He was getting ready to head to Boston on weekend leave with his friend John and John's friend Tim. The three of them were approached at West Point prior to their departure by a group of sophomores looking for beer. Although John and Jason refused to help them, Tim said he would purchase the beer for them, using the fake ID card he had. Jason and John convinced Tim that they needed to get going and that the sophomores would have to find another supplier. The mention of a fake ID troubled Jason because using one would constitute a violation of the Honor Code, and he hoped the issue would just go away.

But the problem would not go away: they were headed to Boston, and John and Jason were both twenty-one years old. Jason watched Tim use his ID card to gain access to a club. Now what? Should he turn in another cadet? Deal with more abuse for doing the right thing? This time, Jason decided to let it go.

Several weeks passed, and Jason found himself at a leadership conference with students from other colleges. He was explaining the value of the toleration clause when it hit him that he had tolerated Tim's behavior. He was a fake. He was talking about values that he did not live by. Jason could not bear the guilt and decided to turn himself in for violating the toleration clause. This action carried significant potential consequences: Jason could have been separated from the Academy, Tim would likely be charged with a violation and could be separated, and Jason would certainly reinforce his "Honor Nazi" reputation and endure more harassment.

In reflecting on his story, Jason commented that he wished he had just told Tim not to use the fake ID when the sophomores were asking for beer. This would have been difficult, placing a damper on the weekend trip to Boston and being made to feel like a "tool" (a cadet term for cadets who enforce the rules—in other words, an "agent of the man"). But that would have been a lot easier than what he went through as a result of addressing the issue after the fact.

Perhaps we as leaders can remind our subordinates of this point and encourage them to display the personal courage to address issues at their level before they happen. We must also be able to identify with the pressures our subordinates face when confronted with the decision to turn in a fellow employee and provide support so that the spirit of an employee like Jason is not quelled. Leaders who possess the personal courage that Jason exhibited as a cadet are essential in the Army today. Without them, the potential for more atrocities like Abu Ghraib increases.

Who are the Jasons in your organization? What issues are they dealing with? Will you empower them to help you shape your organization's moral philosophy? By the time Sherron Watkins blew the whistle on improper accounting practices at Enron, it was too late: billions of dollars in shareholder value had been destroyed. Were there others who knew something was wrong but had not said anything?

Conclusion

Regardless of whether we work for a civilian or military organization, the global environment in which we operate is increasingly volatile and complex. Subordinate leaders make decisions quickly with incomplete information, decisions that sometimes have an impact on our organization's short- and long-term success. Organizational officers get paid to make sure they set the conditions for their subordinate leaders to make the right decisions, to establish their organization's moral philosophy. Incidents like Abu Ghraib and Enron provide examples of the consequences associated with failing to accomplish this critical leadership function.

Notes

1. T. Levitt, "Marketing Myopia," *Harvard Business Review,* July–Aug. 1960, pp. 45–65.
2. L. S. Paine, *Beech-Nut Nutrition Corp.* (Boston: Harvard Business School Publishing, 1992).
3. F. J. Aguilar and A. Bhambri, *Johnson & Johnson (A)* (Boston: Harvard Business School Publishing, 1983).

CHAPTER FIVE

DEVELOPING ORGANIZATIONAL VALUES IN OTHERS

Chip Daniels

Many organizations have crafted a set of core values that express to their employees, customers, and stakeholders what the company is all about and how it operates. Values statements are posted on company Web sites and office walls. Some companies ask employees to carry a list of the core values with them. They seem to be ubiquitous.

Yet all too often, people in an organization do not share or even know the organizational values. A lack of alignment between personal and organizational values causes stress for the company and for the person. The employee is unhappy and usually unproductive. Moreover, a person in this situation is much more likely to violate the organizational values.

We see violations of organizational values in all sectors: social, business, and government. In some cases, the perpetrator is a person who has been with the organization for many years. How can this be possible? How is it that after years in the organization, a person cannot know or, even worse, knowingly violate the organization's core values?

Violations of core values can be costly in any company. In the Army, these violations can be catastrophic. Men and women in the Army not only need to know the values but must truly inculcate them and share them. The work being done by young soldiers, and the high-stakes arena in which they operate, demand it. Consider the following story and the impact of organizational values.

All too often, people in an organization do not share or even know the organizational values. People in this situation are much more likely to violate their organization's values.

On December 10, 2003, Staff Sergeant Tracey Stremming and his squad were conducting a patrol in the northern Iraqi city of Mosul. He was about to find out how much he and his soldiers had internalized the Army values, which are listed in Exhibit 5.1. Here is his account:

> We were just returning from a patrol in the northern Iraqi city of Mosul when a bomb detonated alongside the roadway, seriously damaging one of the Humvees in my column. Simultaneously, we were ambushed by a group of Iraqis hiding in and around the buildings about fifty meters away. I quickly jumped out of my vehicle, dropped to one knee, and began to return fire, as did the other guys in the patrol.
>
> The firefight did not last long. Most of the attackers were killed quickly, and the others ran away. I got back to the truck and saw that the gunner was wounded in both legs. They were later amputated. Our medics pulled him out, applied a tourniquet, and I am sure they saved his life.
>
> At first, I thought the truck commander, also my roommate and friend, was just knocked out. He was sitting straight up in the passenger seat, like he was asleep. The passenger door was buckled in from the blast, so I had to pull him out of the top of the truck.

EXHIBIT 5.1. THE ARMY VALUES

Loyalty—Bear true faith and allegiance to the U.S. Constitution, the Army, your unit and other Soldiers.

Duty—Fulfill your obligations.

Respect—Treat people as they should be treated.

Selfless Service—Put the welfare of the Nation, the Army and your subordinates before your own.

Honor—Live up to Army values.

Integrity—Do what's right, legally and morally.

Personal Courage—Face fear, danger or adversity (physical or moral).

When Tracey started to pull him, he saw the grievous wounds to his friend's lower back. He had died instantly when the blast rocked the vehicle. Tracey experienced grief, tremendous anger, and frustration all at the same time. On the day of his friend's memorial service, his squad—the same squad that had just said good-bye to one of its own—was given the mission to conduct new searches for improvised explosive devices (IEDs). This would surely test the values of everyone involved. Here is Tracey's description of how his squad handled this mission:

> We stayed focused on the mission by talking to each other about it and staying in the streets. We were always hard on our soldiers to make sure they were always doing the right thing; we demanded it, and sometimes the soldiers thought we were too hard on them. They understood more why they needed to stay in the fight and stay focused, and they pushed each other to do the right thing because we did not want to experience anything like [the ambush] again.

Tracey knew that each soldier ultimately would have to decide how he or she was going to react when the squad went back out on patrol. To focus them, he reminded them of their values as American soldiers as well as their overall mission. When asked what values he considered, Tracey said:

> I would have to say that a few of the Army values were always in play. Personal courage, selfless service, and duty stand out. I felt that after the ambush, honor and integrity became more obvious due to the fact that it could have been easy to distrust and take revenge for the casualties we took on December 10. Knowing that all Iraqi people were not responsible for what happened to us, we very well could not harass and fight every civilian we crossed.
>
> Even in our last days in Iraq, we were given a mission to raid a house one night. Along with us, we had the battalion commander and a reporter from the *Army Times*. Some of the soldiers wondered why we had so much company. The truth was that we were going after the man who was said to be responsible for planning the ambush that happened to us.
>
> With the knowledge of who the target was, we still did the right thing by taking him down without firing any shots or punches when we apprehended him. As easy as it could have been to say that he resisted, we did the right thing. We valued discipline. We train our soldiers to be disciplined and do what is right. Anyway, we risked damaging the relationships we had built with our Iraqi allies. Our mission was to protect them and help them build a new nation.

Even under extreme duress, Tracey and his soldiers stayed true to their values. If those soldiers had decided to take the law into their own hands, it would

"In Iraq, a few of the Army values were always in play. Personal courage, selfless service, and duty stand out. After the ambush, honor and integrity became more obvious due to the fact that it could have been easy to distrust and take revenge for the casualties we took."

have been an international incident, potentially damaging the strategic position of the U.S.-led coalition. Their ability to stay focused on the mission and make decisions based on shared values prevented that from happening.

The Enduring Nature of Army Values

Soldiers and officers pay much more than lip-service to these values. These values create a common framework within which all soldiers operate. We know what to expect from each other, and we hold each other accountable to those expectations: two soldiers, whether they know each other or not, can always expect the other to hold true to these values. Because soldiers and officers internalize these values so deeply, they affect our lives long after our military careers are over. They truly change how we view the world and our place in it.

My neighbor, Major Andy Hilmes, and I were recently discussing how Army values have affected our lives and how the concept of loyalty carries over from one organization to the next. Many organizations see loyalty as a one-way street: supervisors expect employees to be loyal to the company but fail to understand why or how the company should reciprocate that loyalty.

Andy told me a story about his father, Jerry Hilmes, who had spent thirty-three years in the Army after graduating from West Point in 1959. When he retired from the Army, Jerry was hired by a Fortune 500 company. It was not long before he was serving as a division president, responsible for five thousand people. One day the company CEO contacted Jerry and informed him that because the company had lost a contract in another division, it would be making job cuts of about 140 people in the Raleigh-Durham area in North Carolina. He basically said that these people would be "on their own."

Jerry protested, telling the CEO that these people had worked loyally for the company for several years. They therefore should be told in person about the layoff and taken care of as much as possible. The CEO claimed that he understood the problem. He said, "I know that you are a former Army officer and you feel you must be loyal to your men and take care of them, but this is different.

This happens all the time in the business world. People expect to be laid off. It happens."

Jerry volunteered to visit these people himself and try to relocate them to his division or elsewhere in the company if they were amenable to that course of action. He did that and recruited fourteen men to transfer. He was still working on the details the week before he and his wife were scheduled to spend a weekend with Andy, who was serving at Fort Hood, Texas. They had been looking forward to this visit for months.

Andy told me he barely got the chance to talk to his dad the entire weekend because his father seemed highly agitated and was constantly on his cell phone. Andy asked his mother what was going on, and she told him about the layoffs. Jerry was calling all of his contacts in the company and trying to get new job interviews for all fourteen people. (The others decided to stay in the area, but they were highly impressed that a division president would care enough to visit with them about the layoffs.)

It cost Jerry his weekend with his son, but he managed to get all fourteen people placed within the company. That is loyalty.

Why Values Are So Important

A set of core and shared values allows people in an organization to operate independently while still working toward the same goals. Shared values are not restrictive; rather, they provide freedom of action for subordinates when it is not possible for higher authorities to provide constant guidance. This freedom of action allows leaders to act when they are faced with a crisis or an ambiguous situation, or when they need to make a decision and do not have time to collect all pertinent information.

Shared values are not restrictive; rather, they provide freedom of action for subordinates when it is not possible for higher authorities to provide constant guidance.

Initiative such as this is essential when operating in the environment in which Tracey and his soldiers found themselves. Young leaders must recognize opportunities and seize the initiative in order to make decisions in a manner timely enough to have a positive impact on the situation.

Where do these values come from? When people join any organization, they bring with them their own deeply held set of values, shaped from their backgrounds and previous experiences. The Army culture, though, fosters the development of shared organizational values. As shown in Exhibit 5.1, the U.S. Army's espoused values are loyalty, duty, respect, selfless service, honor, integrity, and personal courage. Notice that if you take the first letter of each value, it spells LDRSHIP. Positive, effective leadership has become one of the Army's core competencies over the years. For example, Army leaders recently have led combat operations in Iraq and Afghanistan; disaster relief operations after the Asian tsunami, Hurricane Katrina, and the Pakistan earthquake; and peace support operations in other parts of the world. Leaders in the Army need to be able to adapt to a host of circumstances and lead capably, no matter what the mission. Reliance on shared values allows leaders to be flexible.

How Leaders Get Others to Internalize Organizational Values

It is important to note some of the key differences between the military and social or business sector organizations before describing how the Army develops values in its soldiers and officers. Only after understanding these differences can a person make an informed judgment about whether this process of developing values is relevant to his or her organization.

First, the Army (and the rest of the military, to a large extent) is nearly a total institution: all aspects of the lives of the individuals in the institution are controlled and influenced by the authorities of the organization. The Army does not quite meet this definition, but it comes much closer than most business and social sector organizations. A person does not "have a job with the Army." Instead, that person is "in" the Army. We all dress alike by wearing the same uniform; even the language is very different from that of corporate America.

For example, on business school campuses across the country, when the time comes for job interviews, one can overhear M.B.A. candidates saying, "I hope to land a *job* with [company name]." People in the military do not speak this way. They are *in* the Army, Air Force, Navy, or Marines. In fact, ask people who served in the Marine Corps about being an ex-Marine. They usually answer first by saying, "Once a Marine, always a Marine." There is no such thing as an ex-Marine because it is a lifestyle, not just a vocation. Being a member of the military service is part of their self-identity.

The impact of this difference in self-identity is strongly influenced by the infrastructure of the military. For example, Army posts are designed to provide all essential services to sustain the typical Army family:

- A soldier may be provided a house on post, with the cost of most utilities covered by the installation.
- That soldier and his or her family members can purchase food from the post commissary and clothing and other household consumer goods from the post exchange.
- The family can do its banking with the post credit union.
- The family has access to on-post medical facilities to meet all health care needs.
- The children can attend on-post schools during the day and then participate in the youth services and athletics programs after hours.
- The family can enjoy a movie at the post movie theater or golf at the post golf course.

In short, facilities on post can meet almost every need. It is not uncommon to talk to Army families who have not driven out of the gates of the post in several days or even weeks, depending on the location of the post.

Obviously this creates a tightly knit community. Neighbors not only live beside each other, they also work together. Dinner parties and other social gatherings are common and often impromptu. A soldier can arrive home from work, and the spouse will inform him or her that they will be dining with the Smiths and the Joneses that evening. This social construct adds greatly to the Army culture. The culture, which is developed at the workplace but continually reinforced in formal and informal social settings, strongly influences the development of values in the soldier and family members.

The Army is almost a total institution. The Army culture, which is developed at the workplace but continually reinforced in both formal and informal social settings, strongly influences the development of values in the soldier and family members.

Although this "it's a lifestyle, not a job" attitude and self-identity provide fertile ground for the inculcation of values, the Army does have a systematic approach for developing these values that may be informative to social and business sector leaders. Some of the steps of this process may be more applicable than others, depending on the organization and its environment. Exhibit 5.2 lists these methods.

Following is an overview of the methods the Army uses to internalize its values; the rest of this chapter discusses each step in more detail:

Step One: Self-identification and selection. Generally the Army works to attract people who already share the Army values to some extent. The hope is that

EXHIBIT 5.2. FIVE STEPS TO
ACHIEVING INTERNALIZATION OF ARMY VALUES

1. Self-identification and selection

2. An early socialization process

3. Role models

4. Sharing of stories and examples

5. Feedback and performance evaluations

a potential recruit will already value what the Army values and self-select into the Army.

Step Two: Early socialization process. The Army has a structured early socialization process during which new members are formally introduced to the Army values, with the goal of developing a psychological contract between the person and the Army as an organization.

Step Three: Role models. During this early socialization period and throughout a person's life while in uniform, there are plenty of role models who exemplify the Army values. The presence of these role models is hugely influential, especially with younger soldiers and officers. Not all role models are organizational superiors; many are peers and even subordinates, and this creates a sense of accountability that is very effective at inculcating values.

Step Four: Sharing of stories and examples. Occasionally a role model fails to uphold the Army values, and this leads to a story or example that is shared informally. The stories can also be tales of positive role models and actions. In both cases, positive and negative, they greatly shape a person's understanding of organizational and personal values.

Step Five: Feedback and performance evaluations. The Army values are closely integrated with the Army's formal performance evaluation and feedback mechanisms. If used properly, these mechanisms provide an excellent tool to embed and reinforce organizational values.

Step One: Self-Identification and Selection

Although the Army's strong culture heavily influences the internalization of the Army values in members once they are in the organization, the process truly starts long before any person takes the oath of enlistment or oath of office.

One need only watch an Army recruiting commercial to see an illustration of Army values at work. These commercials show young people performing a multitude of missions in hostile and complex environments. The message is, "If you like a challenge and have a sense of adventure, and if you are willing to serve a cause larger than yourself, the Army is for you." Moreover, the seven Army values are prominently displayed on the Web sites www.GoArmy.com and http://www.Army.mil/. The online ads clearly spell out the values, along with numerous videos that show these values in action. The television and online ads appeal to people who already subscribe to similar values and will readily subscribe to these values after they join the Army.

Contrast this with the old Army recruiting ads from the "Be All You Can Be" campaign. Those ads conveyed the message, "Join the Army for a few years, and we will give you money for college so you can get on with your life." This approach enticed many to join the Army using the Montgomery GI Bill, but it also contradicted the Army's retention efforts down the line. The Army was using college money to attract new soldiers but then asking them to reenlist and not use the very GI Bill benefits they had accumulated. The Army still offers money for college as an enlistment benefit, but it is no longer the centerpiece of the recruiting campaign. The "Be All You Can Be" campaign appealed to young people who valued self-improvement. Self-improvement is a noble thing to value, but it often comes into conflict with the concept of service to a cause other than yourself.

The current war against extremists in Iraq and Afghanistan serves as an excellent backdrop against which prospective recruits can measure their values. The war has made it clear to everyone that those who do not have a concept of duty or value service to the nation should look into another line of work. Values are changing in American society, and many people believe that today's young people are more concerned about their own self-interests. The Army's recent recruiting struggles are perhaps a reflection of this.

Interestingly, though, the same conflicts in Iraq and Afghanistan are perhaps part of the reason that many soldiers are electing to reenlist and stay in the Army. Those who value service, duty, loyalty, and courage see in the war an excellent opportunity to exemplify those values. Researchers believe this phenomenon partly explains why the military's retention rates remain high.

The bottom line is that the Army and its recruiting campaign now target people who are already predisposed to adopt the organizational values that the Army espouses. Moreover, the campaign dissuades people who believe they will not be a good fit with the Army values and culture. A young person who chooses the Army as a vocation today knows exactly what he or she is getting into and can make the transition from civilian to soldier much more smoothly than the person who joined the Army for other reasons.

How Businesses and Other Organizations Can Use Self-Identification and Selection

The implication of this self-identification and selection process for business and social sector organizations is clear: companies that have a strong set of core values that are truly shared by employees should leverage these values when recruiting. Make it clear what your organization is about and how it operates. This transparency will serve to cull out people who do not, or will not, share these values from the recruiting pool. Look for evidence that indicates whether potential employees do or do not already share your organization's values.

Companies that have a strong set of core values that are truly shared by employees should leverage these values when recruiting. Make it clear what your organization is about and how it operates.

One such piece of evidence that carries weight with West Point and Reserve Officer Training Corps (ROTC) admissions boards is whether a candidate has served in some other service-based organization, particularly the Boy Scouts or Girl Scouts. In fact, data show a strong correlation between service in the Scouts as a youth and the likelihood of continued service in the Army as an adult. Social sector organizations are usually able to align personal and organizational values more easily than for-profit ones because of the nature of this work. A person usually joins a social sector organization because he or she is intrinsically motivated to perform the work. Values are more or less already aligned, and people who join such organizations view their work as a calling instead of simply a way of making a living.

Although business organizations face more of a challenge, they can also employ this technique, and some do it exceedingly well. For example, people who work for General Electric are usually very clear on what their company's values are. They know them and live them and are held accountable to them formally. This is another effective way to inculcate organizational values.

Step Two: Early Socialization Process

Most Americans are familiar with the military's basic training concept. The Army and other services bring new recruits to basic training posts across the country to train them to be soldiers, airmen, sailors, and marines. They learn specific techniques and skills such as marching, rifle marksmanship, and physical training.

Values education also takes place during this early socialization process. For both new enlisted soldiers and new officers, this process plays a critical role in ensuring that personal values and the Army values align. If the values are not already aligned, then the internalization of the Army values is an express goal of early socialization.

Socialization is truly a never-ending process and is simply part of maturing as a person, but entry-level training for new soldiers and cadets is particularly critical. The process is very similar for enlisted soldiers and officers and differs mostly in its duration. For enlisted Army soldiers, basic training and the follow-on advanced specialty training are usually four to six months long, depending on the soldier's specialty, and then the soldier is placed in a unit. The socialization process for aspiring officers is usually much longer. ROTC cadets and West Point cadets are in college for four years, and perhaps more. On graduation, these new officers attend branch-specific officer courses for up to an additional six months.

For both soldiers and officers, the Army uses a formal and collective approach that is designed to result in a person who knows and lives the Army values. Ultimately the process leads to the development of a strong psychological contract between the person and the organization. Both parties are committed to each other and strive for a mutually beneficial relationship. For some, this may require that their personal values be stripped away and replaced with new values. This is increasingly the case as societal values and norms change.

Some effective techniques to ensure that the specific Army values are internalized is to use both a formal and collective approach if possible. Recruits and cadets are separated from other members of the Army until they successfully complete the early socialization process. This allows the Army to design a specific set of experiences particularly for them.

The recruits are introduced to the Army values in classes. In addition, in the case of West Point cadets, the values are used as a benchmark to track the progress of the cadet toward graduation.

Due to the number of recruits and cadets entering basic training or an officer commissioning source such as West Point, the Army can leverage the benefits of a collective socialization process. The ability to train people together ensures a set of somewhat common experiences. This leads directly to group cohesion, which is crucial in the military. The collective approach results in a person with more homogeneous views than if he or she were socialized individually.

The ability to train people together ensures a set of somewhat common experiences. This leads directly to group cohesion, which is crucial.

This collective approach can stifle innovation and creativity somewhat. Although this may not be desirable for many organizations, it is beneficial in the military, where a mistake could cost lives. Early in a person's military career, conformity is necessary, and the collective approach fosters this. As soldiers mature, initiative and innovation become necessary and are expected.

An Early Socialization Case Study: How I Learned About My Duty to Others

I underwent a formal and collective approach when I was a new cadet at Virginia Tech in 1989. Virginia Tech and Texas A&M are the only two schools in the United States that have a corps of cadets within a larger student body. All new cadets, called "rats," had to report to Tech in the summer before the civilian first-year students arrived. During this time, new cadets were socialized and trained in a manner similar to West Point and Army basic training. We were subjected to mental and physical stress, and many people decided that the military lifestyle was not for them.

I had an advantage, though, or so I thought. My older brother had graduated from Virginia Tech a few years earlier, and he had told me what I could expect as a "rat." I was mentally prepared for the high-pressure environment, and it was not long before I had mastered the individual tasks required of me.

One of the ways that the upperclassmen would induce stress was to run what we called "fashion shows." During a "fashion show," the upperclassmen would order us to go into our rooms and change into various uniforms. Then we would have to report back out into the hallway so that they could inspect our appearance and bearing. They would give us about two minutes to change from a daily class uniform into our formal dress uniform. There could be no loose threads or stains, all the brass accessories had to shine, and our shoes had to be polished to a mirror-like finish.

At first, no one ever made it, and we would get harassed and dropped for push-ups because we had failed. Eventually I learned to put my uniform on correctly in almost no time. We would then rush out into the hallway before our two minutes were up and the upperclassmen would descend on us.

I felt confident until one senior, Cadet First Lieutenant Katie O'Brien, stopped in front of me and remarked that my uniform looked great. She then asked me why one of my fellow rat's uniforms looked terrible. I replied that I had no idea why his uniform looked bad. In my mind, that was his problem, not mine. I think she read my mind. She proceeded to verbally rip me apart because I had come out of that room knowing that my classmate's uniform appearance was unacceptable. I could not believe that I was getting punished because someone else had made mistakes. She told me I had mastered my uniform appearance, but that I had failed in my duty to ensure that others were prepared correctly. I now had a responsibility to help my classmates, and if I were to be viewed as a leader, I needed to start fulfilling my duty. I have never forgotten that message. I learned what duty meant that day.

Early Socialization of Families

Because of the Army's similarities to a total institution, it is important to also socialize families along with individual soldiers. This is important because if a person adopts the organizational values but his or her spouse does not, this creates a great deal of stress on the family. The spouse may not understand why the soldier must work long hours or deploy frequently. The spouse may not understand the soldier's need to bond with fellow soldiers and take part in the unit's social activities. Ultimately this can lead to either a divorce or the soldier leaving the Army.

Effective leaders work to mitigate this values conflict by introducing the family to the Army culture as early as possible. Newly arriving families are assigned a sponsor, whose job is to help the family get settled and answer the many questions they will inevitably have about the post, unit, and other soldiers and families. In addition, leaders meet with the new family and describe the Army values and the unit culture. Leaders ensure that the family has access to all the agencies on post that assist with the transition from civilian to soldier. Perhaps most important, the unit leaders share the training schedule that depicts all deployments and other periods of extended separation with which the family will have to cope. By welcoming the family into the unit and the Army at large, leaders can have a positive impact on the family's perception of military life. This results in greater satisfaction and commitment and can even directly improve soldier retention and productivity.

How Businesses and Other Organizations Can Use the Early Socialization Process

Whether social sector and business organizations can learn from this socialization process largely depends on the mission and role of the organization. A company may want to consider this process if the following circumstances apply:

- The mission of the company requires common shared values.
- The cost of mistakes is very high.
- The company has the ability and resources to formally and collectively socialize new members.

If the company requires immediate creativity and innovation on the part of its employees, this approach is certainly not optimal.

The socialization process never really ends in any organization. Although it starts as a formal and collective approach in the Army, it becomes an individual and informal process after the early socialization process. Consequently, as soldiers become more experienced, the Army is able to foster more innovation and creativity.

Step Three: Use of Role Models

The next time you talk to people who were enlisted in the Army at some point, ask them if they recall the name of their drill sergeant. They almost certainly will, because a drill sergeant has such a profound impact on a new soldier that the lessons learned last a lifetime. Positive or negative, the drill sergeant is a powerful role model.

Role models surround cadets during the early socialization process as well. West Point's faculty is largely made up of midcareer officers who hold a master's degree instead of a doctorate. These officers are in their early to mid-thirties and recently served in assignments where they led lieutenants, exactly what the cadets are striving to become. The administration at West Point could build a faculty of entirely civilian Ph.D.s and probably save the Army a great deal of money in the long run. After all, once selected to serve on the Academy faculty, the Army must send these midcareer officers to graduate school so they can receive a master's degree in the discipline they will teach at West Point. Service at West Point keeps them out of the deployable Army, but it does put them right in front of cadets, exactly what the Army wants to do.

West Point elects to bring in these relatively young officers so they can serve as instructors, coaches, and other role models. The intent is that they show the future officers of the Army "what right looks like." ROTC programs and especially senior military colleges like the Citadel, Texas A&M, and Virginia Tech, place officers in similar positions as role models.

Role Models Who Sponsor Cadets

West Point has a program where faculty members and similar role models can sponsor cadets. Usually the faculty member sponsors a cadet starting in his or her plebe year, the first year at the Academy. Occasionally sponsors provide plebes with an opportunity to escape the rigors of barracks life by inviting them over to their homes on weekends. The cadets can relax, eat dinner with the family, and perhaps watch television (a privilege not afforded to cadets during their first semester at West Point). This also provides the sponsors with numerous opportunities to introduce cadets to the Army culture and lifestyle.

Sponsor-cadet relationships frequently develop into lifelong relationships. Cadets often ask their sponsors to deliver to them the oath of office and commission them. Sponsors are also frequently invited to attend cadet weddings. These relationships and the presence of other role models continue to influence officers long after graduation from college.

Just as officers sponsor plebes at West Point, a more senior soldier or noncommissioned officer commonly sponsors soldiers new to their units. These sponsors introduce the new soldier and family to the Army and the unit. They are usually influential, so leaders should take great care in selecting sponsors to prevent the wrong people from inadvertently becoming role models.

Senior Leaders as Role Models

Role models are abundant at nearly every point in a person's career in the military. From their first assignment, soldiers are surrounded by senior leaders who strongly influence soldiers' personal and professional lives. Squad leaders, platoon sergeants, and commanders demonstrate proper behavior and norms on a daily basis. They also illustrate "what right looks like."

Nevertheless, from time to time, they model the wrong behavior. Still, good leaders can use poor role models to help others internalize values by telling stories about how the improper behavior or values choices had a negative impact on the organization. The influence of role models is magnified by the fact that the Army approaches being a total institution. Young soldiers look to their squad leaders for professional advice and skill training, but they also closely watch how that squad leader conducts himself or herself when off duty as well.

Role models are found not only among supervisors in the Army, but, particularly with young officers, are also frequently found among peers and even their subordinates. Young officers and their families spend so much time together that peers strongly influence the inculcation of values. This results in the creation of a culture of accountability where peers set the example for each other. People discuss with their peers why they made the decisions they did and the thought process behind those decisions. These conversations usually take place off duty and in informal settings, and the peers implicitly or explicitly offer approbation or condemnation for the decisions made by their counterparts.

This implicit peer pressure is a strong influence, but in the Army, subordinates also heavily influence the internalization of values. A young officer's platoon sergeant, or noncommissioned officer (NCO), serves as that lieutenant's foreman, so to speak. Although this sergeant technically works for the officer, he or she has a tremendous amount of influence over the lieutenant. A platoon sergeant usually has fourteen to seventeen years of experience, compared to the lieutenant's one year of experience. Consequently, it is common for the NCO to serve as a role model for the younger officer. NCOs teach officers how to operate on a day-to-day basis. Ultimately the platoon sergeant will follow the orders of the lieutenant, but usually a great deal of coaching occurs first.

It is a somewhat complex relationship, but the U.S. Army strongly believes in the value of it, so much so that commanders at every level have an NCO counterpart, all the way up to the chief of staff of the Army. This professional NCO corps, and its ability to serve as role models and coaches to the officer corps, is one of the factors that contributes to the Army's being such a dominant fighting force.

A Role Model Case Study: How I Learned About Honor, Integrity, and Moral Courage

One of the most influential role models in my career worked for me when I served as a company commander at Fort Hood, Texas, from 1999 to 2001. A company commander's right-hand man, so to speak, is the company first sergeant. The first sergeant is the senior enlisted NCO in the company and effectively runs the day-to-day operations of the unit. I was privileged to have one of the best first sergeants around.

When Carlos Fuentes-Lopez enlisted in the U.S. Army at age twenty-four, he could not speak a word of English. He told me he joined because the prospects for a stable life were not very good in the neighborhood in San Juan, Puerto Rico, where he lived. Most of his childhood friends had already suffered violent deaths or were imprisoned. Carlos and his young wife were expecting their first child, and he knew he had to do something to provide a better life for his family. He told me, "I hoped that I would be allowed to serve a full twenty-year career and retire as a staff sergeant, with enough money saved to buy my own home." I was surprised to hear him say "*allowed* to serve." I had never heard anyone refer to his or her career quite that way. He viewed the opportunity to serve as a privilege.

Carlos taught himself to speak English through on-the-job training in the Army. He told me that early in his career, his sergeants had to assign him to work for other Spanish-speaking soldiers so he could function. That did not last long. Soon his leaders recognized that he was extremely committed to the organization and exceptionally talented. He worked harder than anyone else in the unit and began to get promoted ahead of his peers. Eventually he was promoted to first sergeant, two ranks higher than the staff sergeant grade he had hoped to achieve.

First Sergeant Fuentes could motivate soldiers and NCOs like the best drill sergeants you see on television and in the movies. He would yell at a soldier and tell him to jump, and the soldier would ask, "How high?" with a smile on his face because he knew that yelling was just the first sergeant's way. The soldiers loved him because of his wisdom, his competitive spirit, and the fact that he always took care of them. They respected him and he respected them, even though he yelled at them from time to time.

Once we redeployed from a training mission, and I failed to ensure that certain standards were met with our equipment maintenance on the part of my unit. My boss, the battalion commander, called First Sergeant Fuentes and me into his office that night and informed us that he had discovered the infractions. He said he did not expect infractions from our unit and thought we were better than that. I began to speak, but Fuentes snapped to the position of attention and told the battalion commander that it was his fault and that it would never happen again. He felt he had failed in his duty, and he had too much honor for that. To this day, I think the fault was clearly mine, but he took part of the blame. He never allowed our unit to make a similar mistake again. I learned a great deal about honor, integrity, and moral courage that night.

Fuentes retired in May 2001 after twenty-four years of service to the United States. He bought a house in Louisiana with the money he and his wife had saved over the years. I consider it a singular honor to have been his last company commander. I stay in touch with him to this day.

Role models reinforce proper values and try to help their protégés make sense of what is happening in their lives. This mentoring relationship and investment in protégés is crucial to long-term satisfaction.

Lasting Relationships

It is not uncommon for mentoring relationships to develop between a young soldier or officer and his or her role model. Senior NCOs invest time and energy into turning privates into junior NCOs. As these junior NCOs grow up in the Army, they often maintain relationships with senior NCOs even after their tour of duty together. Mentoring relationships are perhaps more common in the officer corps. Many officers have several mentors whom they seek out for both personal and professional advice. They ask questions like, "How do I achieve a proper work-life balance in the face of so many deployments?" "What unit or job would be best for my professional future and best serve the Army?" These conversations almost always come down to a discussion concerning values.

The role models reinforce proper values and try to help the protégé make sense of what is happening in his or her life. This mentoring relationship and investment in the protégé are crucial to long-term satisfaction. Junior officers often elect to stay in the Army because of the relationship they have with their first battalion commander, a leader two levels up in the hierarchy. If the lieutenant views the battalion commander as a positive role model who has successfully aligned personal and organizational values, that lieutenant is much more likely to continue his or her service as an officer in the Army.

The Army recognizes the value of role models and is developing ways to facilitate even more mentoring relationships. Role models have a huge influence on the internalization of values for their protégés, and any organization can benefit from this process. It is part of human nature to seek out those who live the kind of life we want to live.

How Businesses and Other Organizations Can Use Role Models

Social and business sector organizations are filled with potential role models. Research indicates time and again that people are more satisfied with their jobs if they perceive that their supervisors and the company they work for are willing to invest in their development and growth. People are asking to be developed; this is the perfect opportunity to work on the development of proper organizational values.

Research indicates time and again that people are more satisfied with their jobs if they perceive that their supervisors and the company they work for are willing to invest in their development and growth.

Step Four: Sharing of Stories and Examples

Supervisors, peers, and even direct reports can serve as powerful role models that heavily influence others in the organization. Because the Army is almost a total institution, this effect is greatly magnified. Constant interaction, on and off duty, provides countless informal opportunities to discuss organizational values and their effect on decision making. During the early socialization process, leaders can state the organizational values and may require new entrants to memorize them. These values are brought to life through stories and examples. People may read the statement of organizational values every day and may carry their values cards in the wallet at all times. But what they remember are the stories and examples of how those values were put into action. A person need only read a few Medal of Honor citations before he or she can visualize what it means to value selfless service, loyalty, duty, and courage.

For example, dinner conversations among Army families are often about which officer, sergeant, or soldier made the right choices or wrong choices. Soldiers and spouses alike take part in these discussions, which serve to reinforce values on many levels. During informal counseling sessions, supervisors frequently tell soldiers or officers stories about how one person made a values-based decision that saved the reputation of the unit or even the life of another soldier. Good leaders can leverage the value of these organizational legends by developing a culture of accountability.

Inculcating Values Through Negative Stories

Company stories are not always positive. In the Army, it is not uncommon to share stories about leaders who made poor decisions that had a severe impact on the ability of the unit to execute its mission. For example, because of the tightly knit community in the Army, an act of marital infidelity can have severe repercussions for morale and unit discipline and will not remain hidden for long. This is why the Uniform Code of Military Justice (the set of rules that governs the behavior of Army officers and soldiers) expressly prohibits it. When one person is unfaithful with another person's spouse, obviously problems between those two individuals will arise.

The implications of infidelity in the Army can go way beyond the people directly involved. Normally everyone in the unit will hear about the incident, and the reputation and credibility of the alleged adulterer is destroyed. In an environment where trust is absolutely critical to mission accomplishment, this can be devastating for the entire unit. It drastically reduces cohesion, and cohesion is what keeps people motivated to perform when faced with adversity.

By telling stories of how destructive such violations of organizational values can be, leaders can reinforce why the values are important in the first place. For example, the leaders of Enron and Tyco today should openly and freely discuss with employees how unethical accounting practices were allowed to take place and how the executives in those companies either failed in their supervisory responsibilities or committed outright fraud. The lessons learned from such mistakes must never be forgotten.

*By telling stories of how destructive violations of
organizational values can be, leaders can reinforce why
the values are important in the first place. Formal values
statements are important, but people remember stories.*

That is why the Department of Behavioral Sciences and Leadership's Psychology for Leaders course regularly invited Hugh Thompson and Larry Colburn to speak to first-year cadets about a decision they made on a fateful day during the Vietnam War. Thompson, Colburn, and Glen Andreotta were three American helicopter crewmen who stopped the My Lai massacre on March 16, 1968. From their position in the air circling the My Lai area, these men witnessed what was happening on the ground as American soldiers rounded up and killed Vietnamese civilians, mostly women, children, and elderly men.

Thompson decided to land his helicopter in the line of fire between the soldiers and the fleeing civilians. His crew even pointed their weapons at the other American soldiers. He was threatened by some of the soldiers, but he decided to try to save some of the Vietnamese civilians anyway. It is believed that Thompson, along with Colburn and Andreotta, saved at least ten Vietnamese people by flying them out of the area in his helicopter.

Until his death in January 2006, Thompson spoke to cadets about the importance of values and what can happen if those values are so grossly violated. When asked, he would also discuss the tremendous moral courage it took for him to report the massacre and testify during a time when many in this country were sympathetic to the perpetrators. Glen Andreotta died in combat shortly after My Lai, and Thompson and Colburn were forgotten by the American public until recently. In fact, it took nearly thirty years for the U.S. military to officially honor them. The My Lai massacre continues to be used as a case study during values training sessions across the Army.

Leaders in all organizations should identify stories and examples that illustrate proper behavior and depict their organizational values. These stories can provide a clear picture of how employees can put values into action when making decisions. Although formal values statements are important, people remember stories. People will also share stories with each other, and this can serve to create a culture of accountability by depicting the proper or improper use of values. Through this process, people express their approbation or condemnation of the actions of others and therefore ensure that personal and organizational values are properly aligned. This sense of accountability helps to create a healthy culture where people can hold certain expectations of each other. This type of culture fosters trust, a key component to successful leadership.

Leaders in all organizations should identify stories and legends
that illustrate proper behavior and depict their organizational values.
These stories can provide a clear picture of how employees
can put values into action when making decisions.

How Businesses Can Use Their Own Stories and Examples to Inculcate Values

Nearly all companies have stories that clearly illustrate how someone successfully put the organizational values into practice. These legendary examples show others "what right looks like." This is the idea behind the awarding of medals in the military.

The successful retail company Nordstrom has always valued customer service above all else. The company values customer service so much that new employees are told the story of how a Nordstrom employee helped a customer change a blown tire on her car as she was trying to leave the parking lot. Similarly, people at Johnson & Johnson (J&J) still talk about former Chairman James Burke's masterful handling of the Tylenol cyanide tamperings. In 1982, several people in the Chicago area died under unusual circumstances. Eventually authorities were able to determine that in each case, the individuals had recently taken Tylenol, and they found that it had been laced with cyanide. This caused panic among consumers and could have been a public relations nightmare for J&J.

Instead, J&J immediately recalled all Tylenol capsules and offered to replace them with tablets. The company began a large-scale media campaign to educate the public about the issue. J&J also worked closely with the Chicago police, FBI, and other authorities to solve the crimes, and it offered a $100,000 reward for anyone with information leading to the conviction of the culprit.

Although no one was ever convicted, Burke and J&J assured the public that the company would take measures to prevent this from ever happening again. This was the advent of tamperproof seals on most consumer products. Johnson & Johnson has a statement of values, the Credo, that all employees know and respect. Company leaders referred to this statement of values when making their decisions during this crisis. Although the Tylenol crisis cost the company millions of dollars, Burke and the other executives were able to preserve the reputation of the company by following their Credo. Because of the Burke legend, current employees at J&J know how to use the Credo to guide their decisions.

At West Point too, officers use many stories, often personal ones, to help cadets understand why values are important. One day a friend from graduate school told me about a young West Point graduate with whom he had worked prior to beginning business school. This man joined my friend's firm when he left the Army after fulfilling his service obligation. My friend and he were chatting in the break room and buying some soft drinks from a vending machine. Two cans of soda dropped out of the machine, even though the young man had put in enough money only for one.

As they were leaving, the Academy graduate put the extra can on top of the machine and my friend asked him what he was doing. He replied, "I didn't pay for that. It's not mine." After witnessing that, my friend knew that he could give his complete trust to his new colleague. He even went on to say that it forced him to evaluate his own concept of integrity. It is not hard to see how such a story affects the young cadets who hear it.

Step Five: Feedback and Performance Evaluations

Few organizations incorporate their organizational values into the feedback and evaluation process. Yet this is one of the most powerful tools that leaders can use to achieve internalization of values. There is a common saying in the Army that captures the spirit of the message that this sends: "A person [or unit] does well that which the commander checks."

Few organizations incorporate their organizational values into the feedback and evaluation process. Yet this is one of the most powerful tools that leaders can use to achieve internalization of values.

Although this might sound draconian initially, there is a strong psychological reason for it. Employees from many companies are not able even to recall what their company's values are, let alone discuss how the company puts these values into action. A few companies, however, like General Electric and Johnson & Johnson, are successful at linking values to performance.

Feedback Through Counseling

In the Army, soldiers and officers receive feedback through regular one-on-one counseling sessions with the person's direct supervisor. For enlisted soldiers, this is usually the first NCO in the chain of command. For officers, it is normally the first commander in the chain of command. Counseling can come in many forms. Initial counseling takes place when the soldier arrives at the unit. Here, the supervisor lays out the expectations for the soldier, including organizational values and priorities. The soldier is told, in general terms, "what right looks like." Goals and objectives are developed jointly and documented.

Performance counseling happens throughout the evaluation period, usually one year in length. Many Army leaders use this time as an opportunity to reinforce the values by reviewing not only performance and potential but also how the person's specific actions over the evaluation period have supported or violated Army values. First, the soldier is reminded of what the values are. Second, the message that the values are important is communicated clearly. Finally, the soldier knows that how he or she chooses to put the values into action will bear on the performance evaluation.

Disciplining Mistakes of Omission versus Mistakes of Commission

Occasionally a direct report may need disciplinary counseling (called negative counseling in the Army). This is required when the soldier has done something wrong, usually related to a violation of Army values. If a soldier makes an honest mistake that leads to poor results because of the complexity or ambiguity of the situation, that is a mistake of omission, and most Army leaders will tolerate those, especially when the soldier or officer is young and inexperienced. Leaders should quickly correct such a mistake but focus on the lessons learned and the initiative demonstrated rather than the results of the actual decision.

Senior leaders can model the acceptance of mistakes of omission by being transparent and honest about their own failures. The best time for senior leaders to pass on these lessons to junior leaders is during formal and informal counseling sessions that are constructive, not disciplinary, in nature. Also, external reviews or after-action reports provide important opportunities for senior leaders to model how they tolerate mistakes and accept criticism.

A violation of Army values is a mistake of commission, which is a different matter entirely. It is a mistake of commission because the soldier knew the organizational values and knowingly committed the violation anyway. A person who makes mistakes of commission either does not share the organizational values or may be acting in his or her own self-interests. These mistakes are much more serious and often affect the organization on a strategic level.

That is not to say that these mistakes cannot be corrected and the behavior of the offender changed. Inexperienced soldiers and officers who make mistakes of commission are frequently placed into a remediation program. This is quite common at West Point and other military schools. The West Point Honor Code is "A cadet will not lie, cheat, steal, or tolerate those who do."

If a first-year cadet commits an honor violation by lying to another cadet or instructor, then the cadet's case is investigated and heard by the cadet honor board. If the cadet is found to be guilty of lying, the board will review how long the cadet has been "under the code." This means that the other cadets will determine whether they believe that the offender has been subject to the Honor Code long enough to have internalized it.

If it is determined that the cadet has not internalized the values espoused by the Honor Code, the board will frequently recommend that the cadet be placed in an honor remediation program. This program requires that the cadet be counseled by a commissioned officer at the Academy. During these counseling sessions, the officer and cadet discuss the nature of the offense and why the cadet chose to commit it. The intent is to rehabilitate the cadet and help him or her come to the realization that what he or she did was wrong and especially to understand why it was wrong. Once the chain of command is convinced that the cadet has internalized proper values, the cadet is removed from the program.

When a more experienced cadet or soldier violates organizational values, the case is handled quite differently. It is expected that a more senior person would have already internalized the values, so a violation can be only a mistake of commission. Usually this person must be removed from any leadership position he or she holds and is frequently separated from the organization.

Formal Performance Evaluations

Whereas counseling and disciplinary action reinforce values, formal performance evaluations take it one step further. The Army uses the noncommissioned officer evaluation report (NCOER) to evaluate NCOs and the Officer Evaluation Report (OER) to evaluate officers. The Army values are listed on the front page of both the NCOER and OER. Beside each listed value, the supervisor must fill out a block that tells the reader whether the rated NCO or officer upholds that value. A negative rating requires justification because it is extremely damaging to the rated person's career. It will almost certainly delay promotion for junior NCOs. For an officer or senior NCO, a violation of the Army values effectively ends that person's career.

Army leaders are evaluated not only on their own values. Part of their performance evaluation comes from how well their units seem to have internalized values. Army leaders are held accountable for the actions and behavior of their soldiers. This is not to say that if one soldier is convicted of driving under the influence that the leader will be held personally responsible. However, if there is a consistent pattern of driving under the influence, drug use, or other problems, the leader will be held accountable. It is not uncommon to find companies in the same battalion that have very different rates of alcohol and drug violations. In most cases, this can be traced back to the failure of company leaders to model proper behavior or deal swiftly with unacceptable behavior. This creates a dysfunctional organizational culture that leads to more problems.

Regular formal and informal feedback counseling and formal performance evaluations are powerful tools to help leaders reinforce organizational values. These feedback sessions must include frequent discussion of organizational values and how these values are put into action. A productive way to do this is by telling some of the stories and legends associated with correct and incorrect values choices. This perpetuates and reinforces the culture. It also helps managers and leaders to "manage out" people who do not share organizational values by making it clear to them that their personal values do not align with the organizational values.

Many companies have successfully linked performance evaluations with how employees put values into action. To make any impact, companies must first put their values in writing. Employees must be briefed on these values and introduced to them formally. Subsequently, supervisors should refer to these values during feedback sessions and discuss how an employee is upholding the values or failing to do so. Serious violations of values should be documented, and the supervisor, along with the employee, should develop a remediation program. The supervisor and the employee then can refer to this plan to gauge development and progress.

A written evaluation of how the employee upholds organizational values also should be included in the employee's annual or regular formal performance evaluation. This sends a strong signal to the organization that values are equally or perhaps more important than performance metrics.

Conclusion

Values are so ingrained in each of us that we usually do not consciously think of them when making decisions. Yet these values affect nearly every decision we make, from how to spend company resources to how to raise our children. Because values are so deeply rooted in the subconscious, it is imperative that organizations are able to find people who already share organizational values or are able to internalize these values over time.

Organizations must have a clear set of core values that aligns with the overall purpose of the organization. Employees who have internalized organizational values offer many benefits to the organization. Research shows that the alignment of personal and organizational values increases personal satisfaction and fulfillment. In these circumstances, people feel that they have worth and are contributing to the larger mission or purpose of the company. Consequently, productivity and commitment increase. A person who has achieved values alignment is much less likely to make a catastrophic decision that could have strategic consequences for the organization. Supervisors can trust them and therefore allow them to operate with some autonomy and independence. This tends to be reciprocated on the part of the employee and creates a virtuous cycle.

Developing organizational values in employees is not a difficult process. It does, however, require commitment on the part of the organization's leaders. Leaders must clearly express and exemplify organizational values at all times. This is especially critical when recruiting new members. By making the core values transparent from the beginning, the organization gives potential recruits the opportunity to self-identify and select whether they want to work in that organization. This saves leaders a great deal of time, effort, and pain in the long run.

A formal and collective early socialization process can establish a psychological contract between the employee and the company that results in increased commitment and internalization. It also results in higher levels of cohesion, which in the military is crucial to mission success and dramatically increases a person's chance of surviving combat.

The presence of positive role models is particularly important during this early socialization process, but it remains important throughout a person's career. Role models show "what right looks like." They model proper behavior and values. In many cases, role models can become mentors, and these relationships often last a lifetime. A personal relationship with a trusted mentor significantly raises the chance of internalizing organizational values.

An effective way to communicate the real meaning of values is by telling stories or employing examples. People remember stories, which bring to life how others have put values into action, and examples show "what right looks like."

Finally, by using values during the feedback and evaluation process, leaders can strongly reinforce organizational values and how they are to be put into action.

Organizations made up of people who have internalized proper values are more productive and healthier places to work than those where employees are constantly stressed because personal and organizational values are at odds. Employees who have internalized organizational values are more loyal and committed. The power of internalization is that it is transformational, not transactional. Transactions are temporary. A transformation lasts forever. In such circumstances, human beings are capable of achieving wonderful things.

CHAPTER SIX

THE AUTHENTIC HIGH-IMPACT LEADER

Sean T. Hannah

There is but one cause of human failure. And that is man's lack of faith in his true self.

—WILLIAM JAMES

Why will some followers afford great influence and referent power to their leader while merely complying or even attempting to sabotage the efforts of another leader? During times of crisis, why are followers drawn to certain leaders while others are marginalized? What is at the core of trust, emulation, idealization, and other positive factors that speak to high-impact leader-follower relations? These questions get at the heart of true leadership: authentic leadership, which is not based on reward, coercive, or other powers based on the leader's position, but occurs when followers idealize their leader and internalize the leader's vision and ideals.

Through the hands-on leadership opportunities and challenges I have experienced in two decades of Army leadership and reinforced through research as a leadership scholar, one primary tenet has consistently emerged: at its core, true leadership stems from the leader's authenticity. What is authenticity, and how does one become an authentic leader? When faced with challenging circumstances, what are the characteristics that allow an authentic leader to consistently create high-impact leader-follower relations? Examining the components of authenticity reinforces that over time, a leader who behaves authentically and promotes similar behavior in their followers will create a culture of authenticity that can prove valuable and beneficial to the organization and perhaps a source of proprietary competitive advantage.

Through the hands-on leadership opportunities and challenges I have experienced in two decades of Army leadership and reinforced through research as a leadership scholar, one primary tenet has consistently emerged: at its core, true leadership stems from the leader's authenticity.

Challenges to Authenticity

A leader's authenticity is constantly challenged as his environment and the expectations of others pull at him to betray his true self to meet social and situational demands. A corporate CEO has to balance the demands of her board, shareholders, investment bankers, employees, regulatory agencies, and others. The shop foreman must balance his leadership between making his plant manager's production quotas and the health and welfare of his line workers. Senior Army leaders have to balance the demands of Congress, White House, and Department of Defense political appointees, their soldiers, and the American people. The platoon leader in Iraq struggles between the tactical focus her soldiers require on the ground and the operational and strategic focus required to win the support of the local population, all while the CNN camera beams her every move back to millions of viewers. Leaders are always tempted to arbitrage between competing interests and find the best-calculated solution, one that will meet the demands of the most important factions in their environment. These struggles can cause leaders to show different faces to different audiences and to act sometimes in conflict with their core values and beliefs—in essence, to be inauthentic.

A leader's authenticity is constantly challenged as his environment and the expectations of others pull at him to betray his true self to meet social and situational demands.

Inauthenticity has consequences; although attempts to manage the impressions of others may be productive in the short term, the long-term impacts to the leader's power and influence are disastrous. Followers want guidance and leadership, and they need leaders they can trust—who say what they mean and walk their talk. Inauthentic leaders will eventually be discovered, as their multiple faces will in time be noted and come back to haunt them. In the U.S. Army Ranger

School, these leaders are called "spotlight rangers"; they are the students who try to impress the instructor cadre when they are around but otherwise fail to meet standards or support their team members. These spotlight rangers are eventually discovered and quite often do not make it through the course, often due to poor peer evaluations.

People similar to spotlight rangers can be found in any organization, making it important to distinguish the genuine authentic leader from the pseudo-authentic leader, who may be adept at presenting himself or herself as authentic but does so only to manage the impressions of others. Depending on their level of impression management skills, some leaders may appear authentic for an extended period, but over time—particularly when faced with stress, crises, or other diagnostic moments—followers will eventually uncover their inauthenticity, lose respect for the leader, and negate the leader's ability to have further influence over them. This backlash is amplified because the followers feel duped by the leader and then see that leader as lacking morals and virtue. (See Chapter Two, this volume.)

In stark contrast to this pseudo-authentic leader stands the leader who is proven authentic: the leader who holds to principles under times of great challenge and is highly trusted and idealized by her followers, allowing her great power and influence in her leadership.

Bruce Avolio, a top leadership scholar and one of the primary architects of transformational leadership theory, along with Fred Luthans and other colleagues at the Gallup Leadership Institute, recently advanced the study of how authenticity can be developed in leaders.[1] Powerful models of leadership, such as transformational or charismatic, have shown that certain leader behaviors lead to positive outcomes, but they have not fully addressed how who the leader is promotes certain positive leadership behaviors. Authentic leadership theory addresses this void to propose that a leader who is highly developed will be more likely to use positive leadership behaviors, genuine behaviors such as individualized consideration or idealized influence (as proposed in transformational leadership theory), and in turn will have greater impact on followers because they are trusted and exemplified. This highly developed authentic leader will have a multiplication effect on followers, in that regardless of what leadership style he or she may use, the effects of his or her influence attempts will be greatly increased.

Components of Authentic Leadership

Along with Avolio and colleagues, I believe an authentic leader must exhibit both the ability and the motivation for self-awareness and self-regulation. These are the two major facets of leadership authenticity: (1) the level of self-awareness one has of one's true self, gained through one's personal search and life journey, and (2) the level of self-regulation one displays—the ability and motivation to present one's true self to others across differing situations. High levels of self-awareness afford the leader a deeper level of understanding and increased level of clarity over her true self and how she relates as a leader to her social environment. The leader's ability to self-regulate comes from cognitive processes, while the motivation facet comes from personal virtue (the leader must have a high level of commitment to self).

An authentic leader must exhibit both the ability and the motivation for self-awareness and self-regulation. These are the two major facets of leadership authenticity.

Because leadership is a bidirectional influence process between the leader and his or her followers, two additional interpersonal criteria of authenticity emerge: (3) the leader must be transparent so that his or her observed behavior leads to accurate perceptions of authenticity by their followers, and (4) as the leader acts authentically and receives positive verbal and nonverbal feedback cues from followers such as increased trust, morale, and engagement, the leader's own authenticity is reinforced and thus sustained.

Self-Awareness

Authenticity is a state of being, a level of coherence with one's self. It is a matter not of feeling authentic but of being authentic and being aware of one's true self. We all know people who have a severe lack of self-awareness, even a distorted view of their true self, and yet still feel that they are being true to that (false) self. In contrast, an authentic leader has heightened ability and motivation to achieve self-awareness.

Through life experiences, leaders form a self-concept reflecting the beliefs, values, goals, roles, attitudes, attributes, emotions, and other factors that define who they are and how they relate to their social environment. The term *self-awareness* denotes the level of clarity one holds over one's self-concept—in essence, how well you know who you really are. Self-awareness is heightened through developmental experiences and is driven, among other things, by the leader's cognitive abilities and level of commitment to self.

Highly effective cognitive abilities give increased capacity to monitor and control the leader's self-concept while leading. Psychologists call this *meta-cognitive ability,* broadly referred to as thinking about one's thinking. This is the difference between deciding how to best lead in a given situation (thinking) versus determining whether you are processing that decision in the best way (thinking about thinking). In the latter, a leader may ask herself questions such as, "How are my values represented in this decision?" or "How are my personality and emotions affecting the way I am leading?"

It is very difficult, given the demands of leadership, to take time from tasks for self-reflection, but this meaning-making step is perhaps the most critical in development as an authentic leader.

This cognitive ability helps leaders to better assess and make meaning of their self while leading and to monitor and adjust their behaviors accordingly to stay true to themselves. This cognitive oversight is critical in achieving authenticity, as research has shown that although we may seek accuracy, people are cognitive misers and normally stop processing information once their preconceptions (which may in fact be misconceptions) are confirmed. We thus have a sufficiency threshold, and to go beyond that threshold—to truly assess our self and self as leader in a controlled manner—requires dedicated effort. It is very difficult, given the demands of leadership, to take time from tasks for self-reflection, but this meaning-making step is perhaps the most critical in development as an authentic leader.

Self-Regulation

To achieve authenticity, heightened self-awareness is necessary, but it is not the only necessary trait. I knew a fellow officer who was extremely introspective, always reading self-help books, who thought he knew himself very well. This leader, however, was a social chameleon, always acting to impress his audience; he lacked the ability or motivation to self-regulate. The authentic leader must practice behaviors that are true to the self. The ability to translate self-awareness into action—to present one's true self—requires heightened cognitive abilities, as well as the ability to make an accurate assessment when under stress. Leaders must think about thinking and ponder various possible courses of action that may be available at any given time in a leadership situation, then assess the adequacy of each of these actions not only to the situation but also as to compatibility with their own self-concept. Leaders must reflect on and make meaning of how their actions may positively affect their followers and organization while maintaining consistency with their values, attitudes, and other facets of the self. We all know, however, that choosing the right solution does not equal action. Leaders must be virtuous and resolutely committed to be themselves and to overcome situational demands and carry their assessment through to action.

Commitment to Self

Being authentic is not easy and often means choosing the hard right over the easy wrong. It is usually easier to meet the demands or desires of others and of one's situation than to buck convention and stick to internal principles and values. To overcome this external pressure, authentic leaders must hold a value-laden commitment to self that they manifest while leading. This commitment is a core belief of the leader, a form of internal virtue whereby the leader values self-consistent behavior and sees such behavior as a moral imperative. This commitment is self-reinforcing; as the leader achieves positive outcomes by being authentic with followers, positive feedback sponsors further commitment to self. Leaders who succeed in being authentic will build confidence in their own ability to act authentically, propelling them to overcome future social resistance or expectations.

Being authentic is not easy and often means choosing the hard right over the easy wrong. It is usually easier to meet the demands or desires of others and of one's situation than to buck convention and stick to internal principles and values.

Follower Perceptions and Attributions

Leadership is bidirectional; ultimately the follower must perceive the leader as being authentic, which gives the leader much greater influence and power. A leader who is transparent and shows his or her true self in interactions with followers will continuously reinforce the follower's perceptions that he or she is open and genuine—that is, truly stable and authentic.

Authentic leadership is therefore both an intrapersonal and interpersonal process. In essence, authentic leadership is a reciprocal process between the leader and the follower in which an authentic relationship is formed. Over time, as a leader behaves authentically and promotes similar behavior in followers, a climate and ultimately a culture of authenticity may arise that can be a source of proprietary advantage for an organization and prevent some of the moral lapses that have recently plagued major corporations.

The Essence of Authenticity

The key components of authenticity therefore include a virtuous commitment to be oneself, as well as a heightened ability for self-awareness and self-regulation that manifests in transparent behaviors. Over time, as consistent authentic leader behaviors reinforce their perceptions, followers attribute authenticity to the leader and afford that leader greater trust, influence, and power. Having outlined these components, we can better explore how being an authentic leader has high levels of positive impact on followers and organizations.

High-Impact Leadership: The Multiplying Effects of Authentic Leadership

Authentic leaders have a positive impact on leader-follower relations, as evidenced by greater levels of trust, respect, predictability, and idealization in the relationship. As outlined in Figure 6.1, these more immediate outcomes increase the effects of any chosen leadership style used by that leader and increase the effects of those efforts on follower outcomes, such as performance, engagement, and productivity, which I call a leadership multiplication effect. My experience is that this leadership multiplication effect is increased in times of crisis where followers demand greater levels of virtuousness and trustworthiness in their leaders.

FIGURE 6.1. IMPACTS OF AUTHENTIC LEADERSHIP ON FOLLOWERS

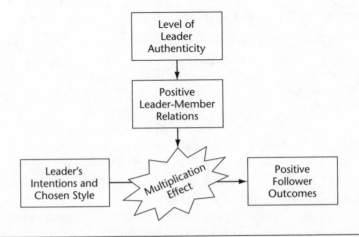

Leadership Multiplier Effects

A leader achieves the multiplier effect because her behaviors engender trust, respect, liking, and similar positive effects and allow followers to easily and confidently infer authenticity from her actions. An authentic leader is transparent and consistent, and as she acts out her values, followers attribute morals and virtues to her. The leader's observed behavior, or values-in-use, support her espoused values. When authentic leaders set a standard, they practice it themselves. When they say something is important, they put their focus and resources there. These behaviors help followers make accurate inferences about a leader and achieve a level of stability, predictability, and psychological safety in their relationship. They know what to expect and what is expected of them.

We can view this multiplying effect using transformational leadership theory as an example of a leadership style. Consider a case where a leader uses the transformational leadership behavior of individual consideration in a counseling session that was called to address a follower's drop in performance. If a leader is perceived as genuine and has been consistently considerate and built strong trust with the follower, his or her attempt to discuss the performance issue will be positively received. The follower will be more likely to be open and disclose relevant personal and professional information to that leader, allowing the two to work through the problem and increase the success of that session. An inauthentic leader, conversely, may be seen as patronizing or manipulative, leading to the follower's resistance to disclose pertinent facts, not knowing whether he or she can trust the leader with that information. The follower may rightly ask, "Why does he care *now*?" Most leaders tell their followers to bring them both the good and bad news but rarely see the latter. Authentic leaders may ask people to bring them problems and actually see it happen.

Trust has been shown to be sponsored by a willingness in the parties to be vulnerable to one another. The transparency and routine self-disclosure shown by an authentic leader will likely be interpreted as a willingness to be vulnerable and will therefore create higher levels of trust in their followers. Leaders' consistent behavior will also increase the likelihood that they will be seen as possessing integrity, which is foundational for trust building. In essence, the leader is seen as moral and virtuous and thus deserving of trust and respect.

Beyond positive effects such as increased trust, respect, and liking, authenticity provides healthy stability to the relationship. Consistency and transparency makes the leader-follower relationship more manageable. There is a level of predictability where both the leader and the follower spend less focus trying to figure each other out or anticipate what each other's next actions will be. These pairs will also be more likely to achieve a base of mutual understanding or shared mental models that will guide their future interactions and create the basis for, or psychological contract regarding, their future behaviors and performance expectations. This stability is a further sponsor of psychological safety, where members feel secure and positive in their organizational roles, leading to increased performance.

Referent Power and Idiosyncrasy Credits

A leader's powers of coercion are not limitless. I have seen soldiers in combat refuse orders of a leader they do not respect, fully willing to take any punishment that may be given. Followers must agree to be led, and by doing so they afford the leader their power. Leaders who have proven themselves worthy in an organization build what Edwin Hollander calls *idiosyncrasy credits* from their followers, credits that they can then "spend" to exercise their influence.[2] These credits must be replaced and continuously earned from their followers as they are used. My experience is that while expert power credits may be earned through demonstrating technical expertise or prowess at their job, referent power is earned through a leader displaying authenticity and in being moral and transparent. Referent power is, I believe, the most influential source of power a leader can have, yet it is the most difficult to earn and the easiest to lose. Referent power is the most likely power source to lead to a follower's idealization of the leader and subsequent desire to emulate that leader's actions. Beyond the personal attraction of the leader, emulation sets the stage for internalization of the leader's ideals, values, and vision, which can facilitate achieving the organizational goals and objectives that the leader envisions.

Leader Latitude

In building various forms of credits, leaders have much greater latitude with their followers and can thus be more flexible and have a higher impact across various situations. Consider an authentic leader who has built strong referent power with his followers, and place him in a crisis situation. This leader can "spend" some credits and be demanding or directing in this circumstance. His followers are more likely to think this is out of character for him and trust that the circumstance requires the leader to be directive, but that they can ultimately trust the leader to make the right decisions on their behalf. A more transactional leader who has based his power on his position by being instrumental and doling out rewards and punishments to gain compliance will be marginalized in such a situation and perhaps disobeyed; his followers will feel they cannot trust him to care for and look after them in difficult situations or to make moral decisions. Having lost his referent power, this leader will be relegated mainly to his reward, coercive, and other position powers that will likely lead to compliance from followers at best and resistance at worst.

Pseudo-Authenticity and the Boomerang Effect

Referent power, as the easiest form of power to lose, can come crashing down should a leader lapse or be uncovered as pseudo-authentic. The uncovering of an unfortunate succession of corporate, political, and other scandals attests to the fact that pseudo-authenticity and impression management cannot be maintained indefinitely. Because organizations have become less hierarchical, flatter, and more transparent, with a wider variety of information and data available to all, followers are more likely to eventually uncover a lack of true authenticity.

This discovery of a leader's inauthenticity leads to what Edward Jones calls a *boomerang effect* and can devastate a leader-follower relationship to a point where recovery may not be an option.[3] In essence, followers tend to punish a leader whom they wrongly thought was authentic more for a moral or other lapse in their authenticity than they do a leader who conducts a similar transgression but whom they had previously perceived as less authentic.

The uncovering of an unfortunate succession of corporate, political, and other scandals attests to the fact that pseudo-authenticity and impression management cannot be maintained indefinitely.

Authentic leaders are idealized and motivate their followers to emulate their exemplary behavior. This exemplification elicits underlying feelings of guilt from followers, as they feel inadequate in comparison, causing them to attempt to emulate and live up to the example set by the leader. If followers later discover that they have been duped by the leader, their guilt can easily turn into anger as they feel manipulated, and they will then attempt to discredit or damage the leader. Retribution would be less likely among followers with lower expectations of their leaders (and hence lower levels of experienced guilt) in the beginning.

Forms of referent power, exemplification, and idealization can also boomerang on a leader as the sources of this power are very one-dimensional: followers tend to look at things like morality in an all-or-nothing fashion. For example, leaders may show some technical shortcomings and still maintain most of their expert power as long as they show expertise in most areas of their position. Any moral lapse, however, will likely be looked at one-dimensionally and the leader labeled as immoral, a label from which the leader will be challenged to recover.

I am not naively proposing that authentic leaders do not have moments of error or transgression. However, I do propose that due to their high levels of moral development, self-awareness, and self-regulatory abilities, the frequency of these transgressions will be fewer than those of an inauthentic or pseudo-authentic leader. In addition, having built a base of trust and strong interpersonal relationships with their followers—an authentic relationship—the parties will be more likely to disclose, openly discuss, and work through the issue than to allow it to fester. In turn, followers are more likely to see the lapse as an anomaly, a one-time error versus indicative of the leader's character, and the leader will maintain referent power. In summary, idealization and referent power must be built and sustained on the leader's authenticity.

Authentic Leadership in Operation

Being authentic does not mean being rigid to an inflexible true self. Great authentic leaders are not robots driven by some central processor that determines their behavior. Authentic leadership extends beyond the (intrapersonal) authentic person. Authentic leaders are true not just to themselves but also to their role as a leader. They are highly aware of social cues and followers' needs, expectations, and desires. This awareness allows them to react to their environments and make certain aspects of their true self more salient than others at any time. What is critical here is that they bring to any situation part of their true self but not a false self. This nimbleness results in what psychologists term a working self-concept that is adaptive and responsive to situational cues and is situation specific, yet is a subset of their true self.

To clarify this idea of a working self-concept, we must venture into the complex field of cognitive psychology. Our knowledge about our self is the largest and most complex of the types of knowledge we hold about anything else. It is critical to understand that this memory store is too vast for any leader to access all of the self-information held in long-term memory at any given moment or situation. A simple exercise to clarify this is to ask yourself, "Who am I right now?" and then write down your answer. Most people find this a difficult question to fully answer and struggle to articulate all the emotional, cognitive, and behavioral aspects of the self, particularly aspects that are not necessarily relevant or activated at that time. They would likely give a different response to that question if asked now as they read this chapter and are intellectually stimulated than if I asked them at a sporting event or while watching TV. This human cognitive limitation necessitates that only a portion or working part of the self-concept is available to us at any time.

This working self-concept is also tied to your role as a leader. For example, the working self-concept that is activated when you deal with your followers at work most likely differs from your working self activated as a parent when you return home in the evening. The working self therefore is cognitively primed from cues in the environment that activate select parts of the self while suppressing others. I can assure you that the parts of my self that were activated by the environment and drove my thoughts and behaviors when leading an infantry unit in combat differed from those when I mow my grass now—although in both situations, I try for authentic representations of parts of my self.

What is paramount is that all the working selves of an authentic leader include or overlap the core—one's values and beliefs.

Authentic leaders can therefore remain true to themselves and still display an adaptable range of behaviors to meet situational demands and lead effectively across situations. What is critical within this range of behaviors, when looking to differentiate authenticity from pseudo-authenticity or inauthenticity, is that the leader does not betray that part of the self that is activated at any given time— the self that this person brings to the table in a situation. As an example, if a follower fails in a particular situation, one leader may activate empathy and also a level of personal responsibility for his or her failure to train or develop the follower—and yet this leader may betray that self and punish the follower in order to eschew personal responsibility for the failure and look like a forceful leader in the eyes of his or her own boss. An authentic leader, conversely, may take personal responsibility for a follower's failure with his or her own superior and then take a developmental approach toward that follower, choosing to coach and mentor, which will lead to great trust, respect, and ultimately future power for the leader with that follower. What is paramount is that all the working selves of an authentic leader include or overlap the core—one's values and beliefs.

A leader's level of authenticity varies on a continuum. Leaders are not entirely authentic or inauthentic, but are more or less authentic in particular situations. Beyond this person's level of ability and motivation for self-awareness and self-regulation, his or her level of authenticity varies as a function of his or her current role. This highlights the need for organizations to understand their people and use that information in determinations of personnel assignment, training and development, and person-role fit. I have too often observed cases where an authentic person is assigned to a role that renders him or her inauthentic as a leader when strong role demands prevent that leader from acting true to self. Ultimately a leader's self-concept must be compatible with his or her position. Leaders must see themselves as having the attributes and dispositions needed in a particular leadership role in order for them to act authentically as a leader in that role. A mismatch will create role conflict, which requires the leader to leave the position or act inauthentic in it, which is dysfunctional to both the leader and the organization.

An army leader, for example, may have developed a role-based true self that is replete with the attributes and identity of a combat leader. This self-defined warrior may rise through the ranks by being an authentic leader and have great success and positive impacts on followers at tactical levels of the organization. In my five years in the Pentagon, I too often saw these great warriors assigned to a strategic-level post at a senior rank for the first time in their career. Despite their prior successes at tactical and operational levels of the organization, some of these leaders experienced role conflict because they were not developed for such a strategic post and not prepared for the business and political aspects of their position. In some cases, they chose not to fully immerse themselves in their new role. These warriors often saw the role of "riding a desk" as incompatible with their self-concept or as a necessary evil in their further advancement versus playing a major role in the organization's strategic success. The misfit of such a leader to a high-visibility post creates strong pressures for the leader to be inauthentic and use impression management to meet the expectations of the new role. This same phenomenon is found in corporations when people are pulled from the field to work at senior corporate headquarters positions for which they have not been developed.

This discussion of person-role fit is not to say that leaders cannot be developed for certain types of positions. In fact, true leadership development is all about creating lasting positive changes in the leader and therefore changing who they are—their true self—thus enabling them to take on greater roles and responsibilities and be themselves in those roles. However, such development must precede assignment to those positions so that role conflict does not have a negative effect on the well-being of the leader, their followers, or organizational effectiveness.

Authentic Leadership Development

Becoming an authentic leader is a developmental and lifelong journey. Authentic leadership development is about positively changing the leader—who this person is—not teaching some new styles or techniques of how to behave, like those that are often seen in leadership workshops and symposiums. In positively changing the leader's self, positive behaviors come naturally. A huge sum of money is spent every year on corporate leadership development programs, where consultants push their one-size-fits-all programs. I often cringe as both a practitioner and scientist of leadership when I see this approach, and I challenge you to ask your consultants or in-house trainers to back up their training proposals with empirical, causal evidence of the results of those programs in raising leader or organizational effectiveness over time. Many can give anecdotal evidence, but few can offer evidence that their programs possess acceptable levels of scientific rigor.

Becoming an authentic leader is a developmental and lifelong journey. Authentic leadership development is about positively changing the leader—who this person is—not teaching some new styles or techniques of how to behave, like those that are often seen in leadership workshops and symposiums.

True development takes time, and thus for the most part it needs to be an integral part of the organization and its daily operations, not something that the organization takes time out for once in a while. Purposeful, integrated leadership development programs can accelerate development, such as those embedded along preplanned points in an Army officer's career. Such development should be targeted at raising the ability and motivation for self-awareness and self-regulation, and through moral development. I turn now to explore some of these developmental processes to determine how authentic leaders are matured.

Developing the Self-Concept

Leadership researchers such as Robert Lord and Douglas Brown propose that there is a temporal dimension to the self-concept in that we hold not only a current self-concept (who I am now) but also a more distant possible self-concept (who I can become).[4] In essence, we can conduct "mental time travel" which allows us to articulate both the end state and path of our development. I argue that to set the framework for development, it is critical that senior leaders assist junior leaders in reflecting on and discovering these two selves, conducting a gap analysis between the two and guiding them in dedicated thought of the paths, ways, and means that will move them toward their possible self. Senior leaders must make this possible self tangible and provide support, resources, and opportunities to enable their junior leaders to have robust experiences, or what Bruce Avolio and Fred Luthans call developmental trigger events, and then plan reflection periods to make meaning of and internalize the lessons from those events into their developing self-concept.[5] We often turn from one task to the next, never properly reflecting on the previous one. Much like organizations must stop, reflect, and codify knowledge gained from their operations to become a learning organization, so must individuals, or that knowledge is lost and developmental opportunities squandered.

Psychologists have shown that people who have more complex and better organized self-concepts are then able to make better sense of new information about the self and thus acquire new self-knowledge. These more developed people also tend to spend more time deliberately reflecting on new, self-relevant information. Therefore, heightening the robustness of one's current self-concept accelerates future development in an ever-accelerating cycle or loop. In this manner, the self-concept is constantly evolving, and as long as that process is managed and oriented toward authentic leadership development, it can be accelerated to achieve great growth and, ultimately, effectiveness as a leader.

Our self-concepts are mental representations stored in what are called schemas held in long-term memory. At its simplest function, the self-concept can be made more robust and complex through increasing one's memories of oneself—through exposure to developmental trigger events—and then reflecting on those events to ensure they are encoded into long-term memory and linked with one's existing self-concept. The process of metacognition enhances self-awareness and self-regulation of this robust information. Fortunately, another cyclical process that accelerates leader development is a by-product of this experience-reflection cycle; the act of processing and making meaning of self-related information both exercises and increases the effectiveness of one's cognitive abilities. In essence, the more you use it, the better it gets.

There is a strong goal-setting component inherent in this model of leadership development. The envisioning of a possible self is in itself a goal-setting process—in this case, the desired end state. Senior leaders should help their followers not only in this envisioning process but also in establishing incremental goals to strive for as milestones, coupled with specific forms of performance feedback along that path to the possible self. These incremental goals should include specific trigger events that will expose the leader to key growth experiences.

These trigger events should be what I call major self-diagnostic moments where the leader is tested beyond her normal bounds or comfort zone, and thus provides her opportunities—in fact, forces her—to diagnose her true self. Such a major milestone may be a platoon leader giving his first vision statement to his new platoon, or a young executive giving her first presentation to the corporate board, or a leader dealing with a failed product launch she was responsible for. After these events, it is vital that guided reflection interpret not only how well the leader did at the task at hand, but, more important, what this person learned about her self, and her self as it related to her social environment and as a leader in that situation. Unfortunately, most after-action reviews focus on performance outcomes and not the harder questions that address the interpersonal leader-follower interactions that contributed to success or failure. I have found great success asking probing questions such as the following:

- How do you think you made your followers feel in that situation?
- What did you learn about your own beliefs of yourself as a leader?
- How did your values guide you in making that decision?
- Do you think that your decisions inspired your followers?

In summary, as leaders experience numerous growth-oriented trigger events over time and reflect on those events, they will build a more complex and robust self-concept that will further enable their cycle of development. Through continuous self-reflection, they will also heighten self-diagnostic skills and habits that will increase their self-awareness and self-regulation when leading in the future. Research suggests that through habitual reflection on the self and self-regulation, a highly developed leader may reach the point where these can become automatic cognitive processes. Just as when riding a bicycle, controlled cognitive effort is expended on watching one's direction of travel and traffic, but the pedaling and balancing eventually become mostly automatic processes. If leaders consciously emphasize and practice self-awareness and self-regulatory processes while leading, they eventually focus more on where they are going—on leading their people and the organization—while being more authentic becomes at least partially automated. Maintaining a leader reflective journal is one tool that may help reinforce and make habitual this process.

"Can't I be an authentic jerk if that is who I really am?" A leader, short of one with psychological pathologies, could hardly have reached authentic self-actualization by clearly envisioning a possible "self-as-jerk."

Moral Development and Virtue

A strong commitment to self is required to resist the social pressures of leadership. My own research has proposed that authenticity and moral development are mutually reinforcing and cannot be entirely separated. I often get questions such as, "Can't I be an authentic jerk if that is who I really am?" A leader, short of one with psychological pathologies, could hardly have reached authentic self-actualization by clearly envisioning a possible "self-as-jerk." I argue that a leader cannot be authentic and also immoral or antisocial, as the processes that lead to moral development and authentic development cannot be separated. I believe such questions are more a product of the adage that "we don't know what we don't know"; thus, a person may feel that she is being herself but truly does not possess sufficient ability or clarity over her true self to know that is the case. If you need evidence, ask a teenager. He will tell you he is not only confident that he has his self all figured out but you figured out too!

To achieve true authenticity, high levels of awareness must cause one's developmental path to be one of great self-exploration. Through that journey, the leader's perspective of his self as it relates to his social environment are simultaneously developed. This development sponsors a more prosocial, or what Lawrence Kohlberg calls a *postconventionalist,* level of moral reasoning and perspective. The leader at this level also becomes more internally driven and acts based on his or her held values. In essence, the person becomes more value driven and able to exercise what Robert Kegan terms *self-authorship* over his or her own life.[6]

To achieve true authenticity, high levels of awareness must cause one's developmental path to be one of great self-exploration.

Being authentic itself is a moral imperative and is associated with the leader's internal virtues. To betray one's beliefs, values, or other aspects of the self by using impression management is perceived as a lack of virtue by the authentic leader. Authentic leaders hold behaving in accordance with their true self as a key value that is central to their self-concept. This value is manifested in their strong commitment to self, which gives these leaders both the motivation to take the effort and time to self-reflect and to overcome resistance and social demands and regulate their behaviors consistent with their beliefs. Authenticity therefore is predicated on the individual's having a sound core on which to build and develop authenticity.

Being authentic itself is a moral imperative and is associated with the leader's internal virtues. To betray one's beliefs, values, or other aspects of the self by using impression management is perceived as a lack of virtue by the authentic leader.

By changing the leader's core, positive forms of leadership behavior come naturally. Virtuous and ethical leaders care about their people, are empathetic, and are individually considerate. They want their followers to succeed and truly believe in leadership that is associate building in its orientation. These transparent leaders build relationships where their followers perceive these positive behaviors as authentic, and the result is high-impact leadership and its development in followers.

Taking Authenticity to the Collective Level: A Culture of Authenticity

I propose that authenticity can be raised to the collective level. If leaders shape each individual they come in contact with and those individuals in turn shape others, then their organization's culture and the shared values and assumptions on which it is built will create a culture of authenticity. I have argued that authenticity is itself a value held by the leader; thus, inasmuch as leaders can get their followers to emulate them and internalize those same values, they can then diffuse shared values of authenticity in the culture. In addition, if the leader manages the authentic development process of followers through dedicated goal setting, trigger experiences, and periods of reflection, over time they can raise the average level of authenticity across organizational members.

Leaders must create a sustainable, growth-oriented learning organization and ensure that followers feel psychologically safe and enabled to be creative, self-expressive, and open to self-development. They must have room to learn, explore, and, at times, fail within reason. Leaders must also establish that members are expected to be authentic and align reward systems to sponsor transparent, moral behaviors, and positive interpersonal interactions. Role models who exemplify authenticity and serve as catalysts of social learning must be embedded throughout all levels of the organization.

Authenticity Revisited

Leadership authenticity is a state of being that acts as a leadership multiplier, increasing the positive effects of a leader on followers to achieve organizational effectiveness. Authentic leaders build advanced levels of referent power with and are emulated by their followers. They are transparent and build trust, respect, and positive relations. Reaching authenticity is a lifelong developmental journey during which, through cycles of experiences and reflection, leaders increase their ability and motivation for self-awareness and self-regulation as they interact with their followers. This virtuous developmental cycle corresponds with moral development and continuously moves leaders toward their possible self.

It is often difficult to be authentic under social pressures or when in role conflict, requiring leaders to hold the value of commitment to self as core to their self-concept. Authentic leaders are, and are known to be, prosocial and thus more likely to use positive and inspiring forms of leadership that their followers interpret as genuine. Ultimately authenticity is at the heart of high-impact leadership.

Notes

1. B. J. Avolio and F. Luthans, *The High Impact Leader* (New York: McGraw-Hill, 2006); B. J. Avolio and others, "Unlocking the Mask: A Look at the Process by Which Authentic Leaders Impact Follower Attitudes and Behaviors," *Leadership Quarterly*, 2004, *15*, 801–823; A. Chan, S. T. Hannah, and W. L. Gardner, "Veritable Authentic Leadership: Emergence, Functioning and Impacts," in W. B. Gardner and B. J. Avolio (eds.), *Authentic Leadership Theory and Practice: Origins, Effects, and Development* (New York: Elsevier, 2005); S. T. Hannah, P. B. Lester, and G. R. Vogelgesang, "Moral Leadership: Explicating the Moral Component of Authentic Leadership," in Gardner and Avolio, *Authentic Leadership Theory and Practice.*
2. E. P. Hollander, "Leadership, Followership, Self, and Others," *Leadership Quarterly*, 1992, *3*(1), 43–54.
3. E. E. Jones and T. S. Pittman, "Toward a Theory of Strategic Self-Presentation," in J. Suls (ed.), *Psychological Perspectives on the Self* (Mahwah, N.J.: Erlbaum, 1982).
4. R. G. Lord and D. J. Brown, *Leadership Processes and Follower Self-Identity* (Mahwah, N.J.: Erlbaum, 2004).
5. Avolio and Luthans, *The High Impact Leader.*
6. L. Kohlberg, *The Philosophy of Moral Development* (New York: HarperCollins, 1981); R. Kegan, *In Over Our Heads: The Mental Demands of Modern Life* (Cambridge, Mass.: Harvard University Press, 1994).

CHAPTER SEVEN

LEADER DEVELOPMENT AND SELF-AWARENESS IN THE U.S. ARMY BENCH PROJECT

Dennis P. O'Neil
Patrick J. Sweeney
James Ness
Thomas A. Kolditz

The U.S. Army is charged with developing the future generation of leaders—a generation prepared to assume command at the highest levels. To this end, the Army has rolled out a new program, coined "The Bench." The term *bench* was derived from a baseball analogy, where successful teams have the ability to look left and right down "the bench" and call prepared players into the game. To develop its bench, the Army has created several tools designed to assist leaders in increasing self-awareness through reflection, including an easy-to-use 360-degree feedback instrument specifically tailored to leaders at various levels. Through the lens of multirater feedback, the characteristics of an ideal leader come more clearly into focus. These instruments provide a reflection to increase self-awareness and allow for personal growth by providing feedback on one's own behavioral tendencies from various perspectives. In order to develop a bench for an organization, effective leaders must be strategic and creative thinkers, builders of teams, competent and professional, effective managers, and diplomats. Self-awareness lays the bedrock essential to developing these multiple skills of effective leaders.

Goals of the Bench

The Army is on the cusp of a cultural change in the self-awareness possessed by its future officers at all levels—a change to a climate where leaders of varying levels are encouraged to systematically seek feedback from superiors, peers, and subordinates to stimulate discussions on improving leadership abilities. The Bench, as a key part of this change, creates an environment where individuals seek open, candid, leadership proficiency feedback, not just from superiors but from peers and subordinates as well. To support this climate, leaders and subordinates need to understand that the assessments are only for personal development, are secure, and are seen only by the rated individual. Through self-reflection or mentor coaching, or both, leaders gain insights into their strengths and weaknesses and develop strategies on how to improve. Integration of feedback provided in the 360-degree assessment with senior officers and noncommissioned officers (NCOs) as coaches for junior officers is critical for improving self-awareness. To understand the importance of systematically seeking feedback, we review the theory of self-awareness in relation to leader development.

The Role of Self-Awareness in Development

Awareness of the self is the essence of reflective learning. Self-awareness is having an accurate perception of how others perceive you. When our self-awareness is high, a comparison is activated between how we think of ourselves versus how other people see us. Highly self-aware individuals have a more accurate perception of how others perceive them.

When highly self-aware people recognize a discrepancy between how they see themselves and how others see them, the potential for inner personal conflict exists. For example, if I think I am a great athlete and I learn that others whose opinions I value think I am uncoordinated, then there is a discrepancy between how I perceive myself and how others perceive me. In this case, I have two choices: I can dismiss their criticism as being incorrect or can change my view about how I see myself. Either way, I am motivated to reduce the inconsistency between how I see myself and how others see me. People tend to actively engage in comparative processes. When we discover we are not as good in one area as we thought we were, then we generally are motivated to improve ourselves in this area. Accurate self-awareness becomes a mirror that gives us a reflection of our true selves. If we are not satisfied with the picture in the mirror, then we are motivated to improve.

> *Awareness of the self is the essence of reflective learning. Critical to increasing self-awareness is feedback from multiple perspectives over time.*

Traditionally the Army has given individuals feedback through only one lens. The traditional lens has been a built-in system of top-down feedback through formal periodic counseling and annual evaluations. This traditional feedback has painted only part of the picture. But given what we know about the motivational aspects of self-awareness for improvement, the Army has a rich opportunity to enhance leader development by providing tools to give us a more accurate and arguably more honest reflection of our strengths and our weaknesses.

The continuous variety and scope of self-awareness research suggest not only the importance of the work, but strong practical implications as well. Based on the motivational component, the Army has sought to design assessments and feedback tools that will increase self-awareness in leaders and thus build the bench of future leaders. However, there has been little empirical research documenting the link between leader self-awareness and the position or rank of the leader. If leaders are motivated to reflect based on a comparison of self to a standard, then the question becomes, What is the comparison against?

In other words, what are the standards to which the ideal leader should be held? More important, do the comparisons differ across various levels of leaders? What is the ideal leader at each level? That is, do leaders of various ranks need different mirrors to give them an accurate reflection of their true strengths and weaknesses? Three studies are discussed in this chapter in an attempt to answer these pressing questions.

Developing Leader Adaptability and Self-Awareness

The Bench initiative seeks to spur a professional developmental discussion between a leader and a trusted adviser. To accomplish this goal, the Bench has three 360-degree feedback assessments: a senior leader assessment, a junior leader assessment, and a senior NCO assessment. The intent of the assessments is to compare feedback from others against one's own self-assessment. This comparison allows us to focus on our discrepancies and provides great potential for growth in self-awareness. The three instruments are designed to stretch leaders to develop self-awareness centered on concepts determined as important to leadership at higher levels.

The Army, like many other organizations, has initiated 360-degree assessment previously, with marginal results. Most of these attempts have failed because they were too complex and required substantial amounts of interpretation on the part of a behavioral scientist. Also, they were extremely time-consuming and expensive because the assessments were usually tied to formal coaching.

In contrast, the assessments in the Bench are unique for several reasons. First, the assessments are simple and easy to use and interpret. In designing the assessments, a primary goal was simplicity. To get leaders to participate, the time required to initiate and complete an assessment needed to be short. Therefore, each assessment had a target of twelve questions that would require less than five minutes to complete. In addition, the Bench needed a favorable low-cost-to-high-benefit ratio. In other words, the cost in time to an individual would be very small, while the benefit of unbiased input from subordinates, peers, and superiors would have potential for high impact on leader reflection. To ensure ease of use, the assessments are Web based, to allow worldwide access at any time.

Critical to increasing self-awareness is feedback from multiple perspectives over time. In all cases, the feedback is only developmental, nonjudgmental, and never evaluative. The self-aware truth can help a leader develop by activating the drive to reduce the discrepancy between how we see ourselves and how others see us. The feedback facilitates an honest evaluation of leadership and is intended to spur candid discussions with a trusted adviser on our strengths and limitations as a leader.

To create the assessments for use in this leadership development program, three separate studies were conducted to tailor the assessments to three levels of leadership in the Army. An overview of how each of the three assessments was created and the leadership insights gained from each follows.

Leaders must possess mental adaptability, which includes being technically and tactically proficient, understanding the capabilities and limitations of their organizations and the enemy's, and maintaining an optimistic warrior attitude.

Assessment One: Senior Leaders

The Bench's field grade assessment is targeted for the Army's field-grade officers—majors, lieutenant colonels, and colonels—who are the business equivalent of middle- to senior-level managers and junior executives. This assessment was designed using attributes, skills, and behaviors that distinguished highly successful general officers (senior executives in other organizations) from their peers.

The intent behind the assessment is to have the field-grade officers become aware of and develop these important skills, traits, and behaviors through 360-degree feedback and coaching. The development of this set of distinguishing attributes and skills should increase each field-grade officer's likelihood of developing into a future general officer, thus helping the Army maintain its bench of future senior leaders.

Mentorship and coaching are the key to the field-grade officer's development with this assessment. Mentors will help officers process and understand the feedback and work to develop strategies to overcome deficiencies noted in critical skills, attributes, or behaviors. When a mentor is not available, officers can use the Bench's Web site to conduct self-development.

The field-grade assessment was formulated using the results from a U.S. Army War College study that investigated leadership at the division command level.[1] An Army division is an organization that has between twelve thousand and seventeen thousand personnel and is commanded by a major general (two-star). The purpose of the study was to capture insights regarding leadership at the division level gained from more than twelve months of combat in Iraq. Seventy-seven officers from four divisions were interviewed in an effort to determine the senior leader behaviors that were important in establishing an effective command climate that motivated subordinates and behaviors that differentiated good senior leaders from poor ones. The top twelve leader behaviors that distinguish exceptional senior leaders are listed in Exhibit 7.1.

EXHIBIT 7.1. THE TOP LEADER BEHAVIORS THAT SET APART EXCEPTIONAL SENIOR LEADERS

1. Keeps cool under pressure
2. Clearly explains missions, standards, and priorities
3. Can make tough, sound decisions on time
4. Sees the big picture; provides context and perspectives
5. Adapts quickly to new situations and requirements
6. Can handle bad news
7. Gets out of the headquarters and visits the troops
8. Knows how to delegate and does not micromanage
9. Sets a high ethical tone and demands honest reporting
10. Builds and supports teamwork within staff and among subordinate units
11. Is positive, encouraging, and realistically optimistic
12. Sets high standards without a "zero defects" mentality

Source: W. Ulmer Jr. and others, *Leadership Lessons at Division Command Level—2004* (Carlisle Barracks, Pa.: Army War College, 2004), p. 4.

From the list of distinguishing leader behaviors provided in Exhibit 7.1, one can discern the underlying attributes and skills that set good senior leaders apart from their peers. Insights gained from an evaluation of these attributes and skills should help promote the development of the Army's future senior leaders. The lessons learned from the U.S. Army War College's study exploring leadership at the senior levels should be equally applicable and relevant to leaders of any type of organization. The following sections examine the leader attributes and skills that appear to be necessary for effective leadership at the senior leader level in the Army.

Mental Adaptability

Effective senior military leaders need the mental flexibility to anticipate, assess, and decisively act to exploit opportunities and meet ever-changing requirements on a dynamic battlefield. To do this, leaders must:

• *Be technically and tactically proficient.* This provides the foundation for mental adaptability or flexibility because it allows leaders to quickly identify opportunities to be seized.

• *Understand the capabilities and limitations of their organizations and the enemy's.* This enables leaders to quickly leverage their units' strengths against the enemy's weaknesses while at the same time protecting or hiding their unit's vulnerabilities.

• *Maintain an optimistic warrior attitude.* This provides senior leaders with the strength of will to win and the confidence to make bold decisions to seize opportunities.

• *Effectively manage sleep.* In combat, an effective sleep plan helps ensure that senior leaders' primary weapon system, their mind, is operating at peak efficiency. Research exploring the effects of sleep deprivation on military units who were training at the National Training Center has found that leaders who went twenty-four hours without sleep operated at about 70 percent of their initial effectiveness, and those who went forty-eight hours without sleep operated below 60 percent of their initial effectiveness.[2] As sleep deprivation increases, leaders lose the ability to concentrate and encode information, comprehension and reasoning slow, memory becomes impaired, and communication skills become degraded.[3] Thus, sleep deprivation will seriously erode senior commanders' abilities to exercise mental adaptability.

Keeping a Broad Perspective

Maintaining a broad mental perspective appears to help senior leaders to best position their organizations, use resources most efficiently to accomplish the mission, and effectively manage perceptions in the media or local populace. Leaders can develop this broad perspective by having a thorough understanding of:

- How their organization contributes to the parent organization
- The mission and intent of the parent organization two levels up
- How the missions of peer organizations contribute to and affect the parent organization
- The cultural context they are operating in
- The local populace's perceptions and level of support
- The enemy's mission and intent

Thorough understandings of the above factors provide leaders with a higher-level perspective. This broad perspective provides them with the capability to:

- Identify opportunities
- Make sound, decisive decisions to exploit them
- Set clear priorities that significantly contribute to the accomplishment of the mission
- Anticipate the enemy's actions and take measures to counter them
- Focus organizational attention and resources on tasks that significantly contribute to their unit's success and their parent organization's success
- Maintain local populace support, which greatly facilitates operations

Furthermore, delegating and trusting subordinate leaders to handle their assigned responsibilities allows senior leaders to keep focused on the big picture. Maintaining a broad perspective provides the senior leadership the opportunity to set the conditions today to negate central enemy strengths and exploit enemy weaknesses in the future.

Leaders who try to handle subordinate leaders' responsibilities or micromanage direct reports will get lost "in the weeds" and lose perspective on their higher-level responsibilities. When senior leaders place their primary focus on subordinate leaders' responsibilities, they lose their ability to command effectively. Senior leaders who are focused downward and inside their own organizations are not able to see the battlefield at their level of responsibility, and they lose temporal focus. This loss of appropriate focus prevents them from identifying and exploiting opportunities, looking deep into the enemy's formation to set conditions for future success. Thus, they forfeit the initiative to the enemy. Once "in the

---

Leaders who try to handle subordinate leaders' responsibilities or micromanage direct reports will get lost "in the weeds" and lose perspective on their higher-level responsibilities.

---

weeds" or in subordinate leaders' business, senior leaders are more likely to set priorities and expend resources on objectives that do not efficiently contribute to the accomplishment of their own and the parent organization's missions.

In addition, when senior leaders trust subordinate leaders to handle responsibilities, that communicates trust and respect in the subordinates' competence and professionalism, which serves to bolster subordinates' motivation to perform and serve. The extension of trust also prompts subordinate leaders to reciprocate in kind, thus facilitating the development of mutual trust. Therefore, the delegation of responsibility to subordinate leaders and not engaging in micromanagement helps in all of the following ways:

- Plays a significant role in helping senior leaders maintain a broad perspective
- Keeps them focused on their level of responsibilities
- Facilitates synchronization of effort within the organization
- Enhances subordinate motivation
- Fosters the development of trust

When senior leaders trust subordinate leaders to handle responsibilities, that communicates trust and respect in the subordinates' competence and professionalism, which serves to bolster subordinates' motivation to perform and serve.

Stress Management

Maintaining composure in stressful situations or when being given bad news was another critical skill that set exceptional senior leaders apart from their peers. Possessing the skills to manage stress provides leaders with the ability to keep their composure or prevent them from being overwhelmed by emotions in stressful situations. This ability to remain cool in stressful situations facilitates leaders' making sound and decisive decisions in situations when their organizations have the greatest need and dependence on them.

Confidence plays a critical role in the management of stress. Leaders have to believe that they have the capabilities and skills to meet any demands that arise from a dynamic battlefield or business marketplace. The foundation of leader confidence is technical and tactical proficiency. This provides leaders with the knowledge base to creatively solve problems and make sound decisions. Furthermore, leaders' level of physical fitness plays a significant role in combating stress. Good physical conditioning tends to bolster leaders' confidence by helping them ward off the reduction in cognitive efficiency associated with long-term exposure to stress.

Social support from peers or trusted key subordinates is another technique leaders can use to manage stress. Having the opportunity to talk out problems, issues, or concerns with a trusted confidant can provide leaders insights into solving problems or helping to deal with doubts and fears.

Confidence plays a critical role in the management of stress. Leaders have to believe they have the capabilities and skills to meet any demands that arise from a dynamic battlefield or business marketplace.

Relaxation techniques such as deep breathing can help leaders clear their minds in stressful situations in order to provide focus for dealing with the situation at hand.[4] Leaders must also ensure that in stressful situations, they are eating and sleeping on a regular schedule and getting a minimum of six hours of sleep a night.

Finally, maintaining an optimistic warrior attitude helps reduce stress because leaders will view tough situations as opportunities, focus on the positive aspects of situations, and have a higher perception of their capabilities to meet the demands of the situations, which serves to reduce stress.

To summarize, tactical and technical competence, an optimistic warrior attitude, and the practice of stress management techniques will help maintain leaders' confidence in their abilities to handle any stressful situation that arises, with the composure necessary to make bold, sound decisions.

Subsequently, leaders' ability to maintain composure when negative information is provided to them has an impact on communication within the organization. Leaders who lose control when they receive disturbing information and lash out at the source isolate themselves. Followers will therefore hesitate to bring important negative information to these leaders; instead, they will try to hide or distort it, which results in leaders' getting untimely or inaccurate information. Thus, the isolation caused by leaders' inability to handle bad news has a detrimental impact on their opportunities to handle problems in a timely manner.

Communication Skills

At the division command level, leaders exercise their greatest influence through the communication of the commander's intent and mission statements. First, the commander's intent must:

- Clearly state the purpose of the operation
- Outline key tasks to accomplish

- Articulate what the end state will look like in terms of friendly and enemy capabilities and positioning of forces on the terrain (in nonmilitary environments, in the marketplace)

By having a thorough understanding of the purpose of the operation, key tasks to accomplish, and the end state the senior commander wants to achieve, subordinate leaders are now empowered to exercise initiative to take advantage of opportunities or make changes to achieve the senior commander's intent.

Furthermore, a clear mission statement provides subordinate commanders with specific guidance on:

- What tasks they must accomplish.
- When and where they must be accomplished.
- Most important, why the task must be accomplished. This portion of the mission statement helps subordinate commanders understand their organization's role in helping peers and the parent organization accomplish their missions and provides them latitude to exercise initiative to exploit opportunities on a dynamic battlefield.

Both the intent and mission statements are critical for synchronizing purposes and priorities of effort throughout all subordinate organizations. Therefore, senior-level commanders who can formulate and communicate succinctly help synchronize the efforts of subordinate organizations and provide subordinate commanders with the opportunity to exercise the initiative needed to be successful on the battlefield or in the marketplace.

Moving Around the Front

Getting out of headquarters or the office to visit subordinates is vital for senior leaders for a number of reasons:

- *Keeping abreast of the current situation as seen from the eyes of the subordinates.* Moving around the front and visiting subordinates provides senior leaders an invaluable view of the organization's posture that they will not get from their headquarters.
- *Understanding the organization's strengths and weaknesses.* By piecing together each one of their subordinate's views, senior leaders will have a richer and more insightful perspective on the organization's capabilities and limitations and the next likely course of action by the enemy or a competitor.
- *Monitoring morale and the will to fight.* Most important, senior commanders get a sense of the morale and the determination of each of the subordinate units.

- *Streamlining communication with subordinate leaders.* These visits also streamline communication among leaders because they provide the opportunity to discuss, synchronize, and immediately implement changes to a plan to take advantage of opportunities that arise. Thus, senior commanders can influence an operation without going through the more time-consuming staff procedures. The visits also allow senior commanders to assess how well peer organizations are working together, gain insights into resource needs that the senior staff can provide, and determine if priorities need updating.
- *Demonstrating to subordinates the courage to share the danger and risks with them.* Finally, moving around the front to visit units demonstrates that the senior leaders have the courage to share the dangers with their soldiers, which fosters the development of trust.

Therefore, effective senior leaders exercise leadership on a dynamic battlefield by moving around the front and visiting units.

The Ability to Develop Subordinates and Build Teams

Senior leaders who take the time to coach and provide subordinate leaders with developmental feedback demonstrate loyalty and promote a positive, developmental command climate. In a developmental climate, subordinate commanders will grow and feel comfortable exercising initiative, which is critical for success on a dynamic battlefield. This is not to say that senior leaders should not set and demand high standards; they must realize that their subordinate commanders are human and in the process of mastering the leadership challenges of their current position. Investing the time and having a realistic developmental perspective provides senior leaders with the ability to improve their organization, create the conditions that foster the development of teamwork between subordinate commanders and the staff, and develop the Army's future general officers.

---

*Senior leaders who take the time to coach and provide
subordinate leaders with developmental feedback demonstrate
loyalty and promote a positive, developmental command climate.*

Senior commanders who expect perfection and do not look at mistakes or shortfalls as developmental opportunities will soon create a zero-defects command climate that will stifle initiative and creativity, fragment teamwork within the organization, and stunt the development of subordinates, which all serves to hinder organizational effectiveness.

To build subordinate organizations and the staff into a cohesive team, senior commanders should:

- Work to establish a positive relationship with all subordinate commanders
- Give each subordinate commander the opportunity to provide feedback on upcoming operations
- Ensure that they all are in the communication loop to receive important information

Senior commanders should endeavor to make all subordinate commanders feel that they are valuable and contributing members to the organization.

Commanders who are optimistic, positive, and encouraging bolster group members' motivation to perform and, most important, their will to win.

Integrity

Senior commanders' integrity sets the ethical tone for their organizations. These commanders must live by moral integrity, be honest in word and deed, and demand that others in the organization do the same. They must ensure that operations are planned and executed in accordance with legal standards and ethical principles.

By setting a high ethical tone for the unit, senior commanders firmly establish the ethical boundaries for subordinate units to operate within. These boundaries are important for keeping the distinction between socially sanctioned and morally justified application of lethal violence and unlawful murder. Therefore, ethical boundaries serve two purposes: they protect the country's moral justification for fighting and protect soldiers from unlawful application of violence, which all serve to protect the soldiers' will to fight and their psychological health.

A Positive and Optimistic Outlook

Units will take on the outlook of their senior commanders. Commanders who are optimistic, positive, and encouraging bolster group members' motivation to perform and, most important, their will to win. When faced with a tough situation, followers will look to their senior leaders to confirm their assessment of the impact and seriousness of the situation. Therefore, commanders have to:

- View challenging situations or crises as an opportunity and then focus on the positive aspects of the situation
- Communicate optimism in their organization's ability to accomplish a tough mission
- Be out front encouraging subordinates to give their all

A senior commander's positive and optimistic outlook can provide followers with hope and the motivation to continue to fight even in the bleakest of situations.

In addition, a positive, encouraging, and optimistic outlook helps senior commanders effectively exhibit all of the behaviors mentioned thus far, allowing them to:

- Adapt to new situations
- Make bold and decisive decisions
- Manage stress
- Maintain a broad perspective
- Promote trust in subordinates
- Build teams
- Promote the development of subordinates

As retired General Colin Powell has proposed, a commander's optimism is a force multiplier regarding an organization's ability and motivation to accomplish a mission, especially in tough circumstances.[5]

Assessment Two: Junior Leaders

The Bench's 360-degree assessment at this level is designed to assist in the leader development of company-grade officers—second lieutenants, first lieutenants, and captains—the business equivalent of entry-level to midlevel managers. This assessment was designed to emphasize behavioral tendencies of successful company commanders. For company-grade officers, the company commander is the premier position with a great degree of autonomy and responsibility. The questions used in this assessment were designed to allow for a developmental trend in leader self-awareness. Specifically, the company-grade assessment is designed to stretch the lieutenants to consider key attributes and behaviors required for successful leadership up to two levels senior to their current level of responsibility.

The company-grade assessment was obtained from a study designed to investigate the leadership attributes, skills, and behaviors needed for successful company command. This study interviewed former company commanders in order

EXHIBIT 7.2. THE TOP LEADER BEHAVIORS
THAT SET APART EXCEPTIONAL JUNIOR LEADERS

1. Listens with genuine interest

2. Is trustworthy and dependable

3. Is the type of person you would go to for advice

4. Enforces the standards fairly and consistently

5. Knows his or her job

6. Manages resources effectively

7. Has priorities straight

8. Makes the right decisions at the right time

9. Provides useful feedback

10. Solicits and incorporates others points of view into decisions (when possible)

11. Performs well under pressure

12. Has guts

Source: Original research by Thomas A. Kolditz.

to answer the question, "What twelve things do company commanders need to know about themselves in order to be successful?" The insights from this study formed the basis for the company-grade assessment. The top twelve leader behaviors that distinguish exceptional junior leaders are listed in Exhibit 7.2.

The distinguishing attributes and behaviors listed in Exhibit 7.2 offer insights into what makes successful midlevel leaders. Developing these traits and skills through self-awareness will help entry-level managers successfully move into positions of increasing responsibility. These behaviors are not unique to the Army, but rather reflect a variety of dimensions that can be seen in developing leaders in most organizations. The following sections describe several of the traits that appear to influence effective leadership for entry to midlevel managers.

Competence

The single strongest trend found in the top leader behaviors of exceptional junior leaders is competency—specifically, whether the person knows his or her job.

Another component of competency at the junior leader level is the ability to manage resources effectively. For most leaders, the midlevel management equivalent of company command is probably the first time they have allocated resources to accomplish missions. One of the most valuable resources held by company commanders is time. Effective commanders are able to use time to maximize training and increase the proficiency level of the organization daily.

The end state productivity for a company is the ability of each individual soldier to know his or her job. In business terms, the Army produces soldiers. The measure of success is how well each individual soldier in a unit is able to master warrior tasks successfully. Competent leaders who are technically and tactically proficient and properly allocate resources are able to maximize the training productivity of individual soldiers and increase the competency level of the entire organization.

> *Competent leaders who are technically and tactically proficient and properly allocate resources are able to maximize the training productivity of individual soldiers and increase the competency level of the entire organization.*

Character

Exceptional junior leaders possess great integrity, which is defined as doing what is right, both legally and morally. To paraphrase General J. Lawton Collins, a former Army Chief of Staff, Americans expect their military leaders to be simultaneously technically proficient in their profession while possessing great integrity.

Specifically, leaders are expected to be both trustworthy and dependable. They should be trustworthy for leaders in both word and deed. That is, leaders set the example by what they say and what they do. Trust among subordinates is built when a leader consistently acts according to his or her values and beliefs. Building trust enables leaders to seek extraordinary feats from their subordinates. Leaders who possess high levels of integrity are more likely to behave morally and ethically under pressure because they make values-based decisions.

> *Leaders are expected to be both trustworthy and dependable. Leaders should possess moral courage and set the example by what they say and what they do.*

In addition, leaders are expected to have guts, that is, moral and physical courage. By combining this with trustworthiness, leaders demonstrate their integrity. Overall, leaders who possess character are the individuals anyone would turn to for advice.

Development of Subordinates

Exceptional captains constantly develop their subordinates at the small-unit level. Company commanders serve as role models, mentors, coaches, and teachers to lieutenants.

Part of developing subordinates includes providing useful feedback. Exceptional leaders are able to develop their people by offering an accurate picture of strengths and weaknesses. Feedback is given both formally and informally by the leader. Junior leaders take every opportunity to develop the next generation of commanders.

Communication Skills

The final behavior possessed by exceptional junior leaders is the ability to communicate. This includes an ability to listen with genuine interest. Furthermore, these leaders are able to solicit and incorporate others' points of view into their decisions whenever possible.

The ability to communicate includes a cognitive component. Exceptional junior leaders are able to interpret guidance from higher organizations and translate that guidance into specific action plans that subordinates can understand and use. The abilities to receive a mission, listen to the advice of others, and make timely decisions are critical components of effective communications for junior leaders.

Assessment Three: Senior Noncommissioned Officers

The Bench's senior NCO assessment is targeted to develop the Army's sergeants first class (SFCs) and master sergeants (MSGs). NCOs in the Army are equivalent to frontline supervisors in business organizations. Here is how the hierarchy works:

- The highest senior NCO rank in the Army is sergeant major, who is responsible for developing and supervising groups of MSGs.
- MSGs are responsible for supervising and developing groups of SFCs and junior NCOs.
- SFCs are responsible for supervising and developing a group of junior NCOs or frontline supervisors.
- Junior NCOs are responsible for developing and supervising soldiers or first-line employees.

The NCO Corps is the backbone of the Army and is responsible for ensuring the execution of missions. Senior NCOs are part of the command team at all levels of the Army and serve as advisers, leader developers, and confidants to the commanders.

Similar to the Bench's senior and junior leader assessments, this senior NCO assessment was designed using attributes, skills, and behaviors that place sergeants

EXHIBIT 7.3. THE TOP LEADER BEHAVIORS THAT SET APART EXCEPTIONAL FRONTLINE SUPERVISORS

1. Is an effective leader
2. Clearly communicates missions, standards, expectations, and priorities
3. Coaches and gives useful feedback to develop others
4. Takes care of subordinates
5. Is honest in word and deed
6. Thinks globally; sees the big picture
7. Leads by example; is a role model for others
8. Possesses integrity and values
9. Builds a cohesive team
10. Thinks ahead; anticipates organizational needs
11. Makes sound and decisive decisions
12. Is fair, consistent, and impartial
13. Motivates subordinates to excel
14. Is competent

major apart from other senior NCO leaders. The intent behind the assessment is to have SFCs and MSGs become aware of and develop these important skills, attributes, and behaviors through 360-degree feedback and coaching from mentors, which should increase each senior NCO's likelihood of developing into a future sergeant major. The key to this development hinges on a mentor's helping the individual process and understand the 360-degree feedback and helping the individual create strategies to enhance critical attributes, skills, or behaviors. When mentors are unavailable, NCOs can use the Bench's Web site to conduct self-development.

The senior NCO assessment was developed using feedback from sergeants major serving at the U.S. Military Academy and the U.S. Sergeants Major Academy. They were asked to list the ten most important qualities they needed to know about themselves as leaders. The responses were analyzed to determine frequency counts for various skills, attributes, and behaviors mentioned, and those receiving the most mentions were used to develop the assessment. This distinct set of skills, attributes, and behaviors seemed to be critical for effective leadership at the highest level of the NCO Corps. Therefore, having more junior NCOs reflect on and develop these skills, attributes, and behaviors should prepare them for the leadership challenges at the senior NCO ranks. The top fourteen leader behaviors that distinguish exceptional frontline supervisors are found in Exhibit 7.3.

Analyzing the attributes, skills, and behaviors the sergeants major selected as the most important to them provides insights into leadership at the senior supervisor levels. Increasing proficiency in the skills and developing the traits portrayed in the senior NCO assessment should help the Army develop its future sergeants major. The following sections describe some of the general observations pertaining to leading at this level.

Sees the Big Picture

Similar to senior officer counterparts, successful senior NCO leaders are able to develop a broad organizational view. Seeing the big picture allows senior NCOs to understand how their organization contributes to the success of the parent organization and the Army, which helps them to do all of the following:

- Recognize opportunities to exploit.
- Assist commanders in establishing priorities that will yield a significant return regarding organizational effectiveness.
- Most important, provide them with a long-term developmental perspective pertaining to personnel and resources.

This broad developmental perspective enables senior NCOs to make decisions to forgo short-term benefits to realize long-term gains not only for the unit, but for the Army as well.

For instance, if the organization is about to take part in a major training event and an opportunity arises for some key personnel to attend an important career school, senior NCOs with this broad perspective would send the personnel to the schooling even though the organization's training event performance could suffer. These NCOs know that the benefits in the long term will be greater for the personnel, the unit, and the Army. Thus, having a global organizational perspective allows senior NCO leaders to make decisions and establish priorities that will have a significant, long-term, positive impact both inside and outside their organization.

Successful senior NCO leaders are able to develop a broad organizational view, which enables them to make decisions to forgo short-term benefits to realize long-term gains not only for the unit but for the Army as well.

Moreover, this broad organizational perspective enables senior NCO leaders to recognize and exploit opportunities to help their own and the parent organizations achieve their respective missions. This broad understanding of purpose enables senior NCOs to help maintain priorities on what truly matters to the organization. Meaningful priorities help ensure that organizations are moving in the right direction to achieve their missions, while at the same time taking care of and developing their personnel.

Forward Thinking

Senior NCO leaders must develop the ability to think ahead in order to anticipate the unit's future needs. This forward-thinking ability rests on their technical and tactical competence and their broad organizational perspective. Having a full understanding of the organization's mission, commander's intent, the probable enemy's intent, and how each subordinate unit contributes to mission success provides senior NCOs with the information needed to anticipate future needs. This anticipation allows the organization to prepare fully for future challenges and thus maintain the initiative in combat.

Communication Skills

Similar to senior leaders, sergeants major must have the ability to clearly communicate intent, missions, standards, priorities, and expectations. They influence and ensure the unity of effort of subordinate NCOs by clearly articulating their intent, missions, and priorities. They must do all of the following:

- Communicate purpose of tasks.
- Outline key tasks to accomplish.
- Clearly outline the conditions that constitute success of a given mission.

To facilitate the clear communication of missions to subordinate NCOs, sergeants major should communicate missions in the form of task, purpose, and end state and provide each subordinate with the missions the others are working on. After issuing intent and missions, sergeants major should ask each subordinate to provide them with a briefing to ensure that intent and mission were clearly understood.

Following these communication techniques enables sergeants major to communicate the direction the organization needs to move toward and helps ensure unity of effort throughout the organization. Finally, an important aspect of communication is the ability to listen to subordinates' feedback. Senior NCOs should take steps to develop systems for routinely getting feedback from subordinates and truly listening to it. Reflective listening techniques can be used to help ensure that subordinates' feedback is listened to and processed. It has the following benefits:

- Demonstrates respect
- Helps senior NCOs make good decisions
- Increases subordinates' motivation because they feel that their input is valued
- Opens lines of communications with subordinates
- Facilitates the establishment of cooperative interdependence, which leads to the development of trust
- Provides senior NCOs with feedback for improvement

Developing Others and Building Teams

Successful senior NCOs coach and mentor their subordinate NCOs as well as officers in their organization. They focus on ensuring that their subordinate NCO leaders can accomplish responsibilities of their current jobs and prepare them for future responsibilities. To accomplish this, senior NCOs make leader development a top priority and dedicate the time necessary to coach the development of subordinates. An important need all soldiers have is the drive to realize their full potential. NCOs who help soldiers develop both professionally and personally will greatly increase soldiers' motivation to serve and also earn unflagging loyalty in return. This is why developing others is an important senior NCO leader skill.

NCOs who help soldiers develop both professionally and personally will greatly increase soldiers' motivation to serve and also earn unflagging loyalty in return.

Similarly, senior NCOs' wisdom and experience are an invaluable resource for the development of officers, especially junior ones. For instance, although SFC platoon sergeants are junior in rank to their lieutenants, they usually have more years of experience and play a critical role in the development of lieutenants, the Army's most junior officers or managers. Platoon sergeants share their wisdom and coach and mentor lieutenants as they develop into confident, experienced officers. Investing in the development of officers helps NCOs protect and take care of the welfare of their units, builds the command team, and earns the respect and confidence of the officer corps.

Senior NCOs are the team builders and continuity within an organization. They bond members of the unit together in the following ways:

- Fostering unity of purpose
- Ensuring all personnel are trained to handle their respective duties
- Enforcing standards
- Supporting the chain of command
- Taking care of personnel
- Infusing soldiers with the will to win regardless of the situation
- Getting the mission accomplished

They understand that mutual trust, developed from competence and loyalty, is the cohesion that welds team members together and provides them with the motivation to face the grave dangers for the good of the team and fellow members. This is why NCOs demand that all soldiers be trained to Army standard, and they make leader development a top priority.

Soldiers will not trust or follow leaders who do not have integrity. Therefore, to lead soldiers and serve as role models, senior NCOs must be honest and live by the Army values.

Integrity

Integrity is achieved when leaders act in accordance with their own and the organization's values. A key aspect of integrity is being honest in both word and deed. Integrity is a central character trait and greatly influences perceptions of a leader's credibility. Leader integrity reassures soldiers in the following ways:

- That the information a leader provides is truthful
- That their welfare will be looked after
- That the mission will be accomplished in an ethical and moral manner

This reassurance leads to the development of trust, which increases soldiers' willingness to accept leader influence. Soldiers will not trust or follow leaders who do not have integrity. Therefore, to lead soldiers and serve as role models, senior NCOs must be honest and live by the Army values.

Leadership by Example

Leaders who live by their espoused values and lead from the front bolster subordinates' perceptions of their integrity and credibility. NCOs know that the only way to truly lead soldiers, especially in combat, is by example. Thus, all NCOs must be competent warriors. The first two sentences of the NCO Corps' creed capture the importance of leadership by example to the NCO Corps: "No one is more professional than I. I am a Noncommissioned Officer, a leader of soldiers."[6]

The NCOs are the frontline supervisors who lead soldiers into combat to ensure that the mission is accomplished. Soldiers will follow the example set by their NCOs, and NCOs will follow the example set by their senior NCO leaders. Thus, as they have done throughout their careers, senior NCOs must continue to lead by example for the soldiers, subordinate NCOs, and officers in their organization.

Loyalty to Soldiers

A sacred duty for all NCOs is to look out for, support, and protect the welfare of their soldiers while accomplishing the mission. NCOs ensure that soldiers' welfare is considered when plans are developed to ensure the least possible risk to life. NCOs place the welfare of their soldiers above their own. They will ensure the basic needs of their soldiers are met before taking care of themselves. This loyalty to their soldiers fosters the development of trust, which leads to a greater ability to influence or lead. Senior NCO leaders must use systems to ensure that the organization is constantly considering and promoting the needs and welfare of their most precious resource, the soldiers.

Conclusion

The results of these studies provide support for a customized multirater survey specific to leaders in a variety of capacities. The results further suggest the following:

- Meta-competencies exist on what successful leaders want to know about their leadership behaviors and traits.
- These competencies are unique to leaders across specific domains in that they deviate from competencies sought at different levels of leadership responsibility and focus.
- The competencies found that set apart exceptional leaders can be used to generate assessments to promote self-awareness and thereby support the development of leadership skills among leaders at all levels.

In addition to the behaviors specific to each of the leadership levels used in this research, the competencies set out in the exhibits in this chapter organize into two general clusters—organizational leadership and individual leadership:

- Organizational leadership focuses on systems. This level of leadership competencies helps create purpose and direction for the organization by aligning the goals of the organization with systems to support subordinates. Often organizational leaders exert influence through others by establishing organizational structures, building teams, setting high standards and setting the example, and promoting an ethical and developmental climate. These traits are seen in successful senior leaders.
- Individual leadership focuses on people. It is sometimes called "muddy boots" leadership because of the direct nature of the influence. This level of leadership concerns competencies that demonstrate a desire to achieve personal goals—your own and those of others—within a moral and ethical environment.

In answering the question, "What is the ideal leader at each level?" we have found that some of the competencies are similar across all assessments, whereas others are unique to a single level of leaders.

Communication skills are one competency that spans all levels of leadership. However, senior officers and NCOs seek feedback on how well they communicate vision and organizational goals. In contrast, junior officers seek feedback on whether or not they listen well to others. All three levels of leadership examined recognize the importance of communications; however, how they define effective communications differs greatly depending on the direct versus indirect nature of leadership.

A second trend across all levels of leadership is the ability to operate under pressure. Operating in a stressful environment taxes one's coping and decision making ability. As a result, individuals fall back on their experiences and their character. When leaders are seen as making sound and timely decisions, in high-pressure situations, subordinates learn to trust the decision making of their superiors resulting in higher overall performance under all conditions.

Another commonality between the levels of leaders examined is the desire to seek feedback on values. Values include morality components of integrity, character, and leadership by example. Values-based leadership is integral to building and sustaining trust between subordinates and leaders. Morality, values, and integrity are the foundation upon which we are able to be successful leaders.

The strength of this research lies in its generalizability. Although all of the participants were selected from the Army, the behaviors that characterize top-performing leaders are likely to exist across many domains. In addition, this research suggests that competencies associated with outstanding leadership can be adopted to create straightforward, easy-to-use, simple multirater assessments tailored to specific leadership levels. These assessments can increase self-awareness and prepare future generations of senior leaders, or develop the bench, in a variety of organizations.

Notes

1. W. Ulmer Jr. and others, *Leadership Lessons at Division Command Level—2004* (Carlisle Barracks, Pa.: Army War College, 2004).
2. H. Thompson, "Sleep Loss and Its Effects in Combat," *Military Review,* 1983, *63,* 20.
3. Thompson, "Sleep Loss and Its Effects in Combat," p. 18.
4. W. Weiten, *General Psychology for Leaders,* 3rd ed. (Mason, Ohio: Wadsworth-Thomson Learning, 2005).
5. O. Harari, *The Leadership Secrets of Colin Powell* (New York: McGraw-Hill, 2002).
6. Department of the Army, "The Non-Commissioned Office Creed," http://www.army.mil/leaders/SMA/creed.htm.

PART TWO

LEADERSHIP STYLES AND SITUATIONS

CHAPTER EIGHT

TEAMING HIGH-POTENTIAL TALENT

Jack Jefferies

Standing dazed on a grassy field in Lucenec, Czechoslovakia, in 1991, I was one of the four members of the U.S. Skydiving Team who knew we had lost the world championships by the sound of French cheers coming from the crowd. The air screamed as the French national team bore down toward us at terminal velocity. Their parachutes cracked open over the field, and the crowd poured out of the viewing tent, running to greet the new champions. Bewildered and mute, our young team stood frozen as if in a dream. This wasn't, couldn't be real. We had it all: talent, ambition, everything. We were expected to win. What had gone wrong?

The 1991 U.S. Skydiving Team suffered a devastating defeat in Lucenec to a less-talented French team. That year, the U.S. team may have had the strongest individual performers, but the French most definitely had a better team. In Lucenec, the United States was represented by four elite and cocky athletes who failed to gel and as a result failed to realize their potential. As I stood in a grassy field at twenty-six years old, my arrogant youth came to an abrupt end. The dreadful experience as a member of the 1991 U.S. team changed my life forever.

The Problem with High-Potential Talent

The U.S. Army and civilian business both endeavor to produce high-performing teams from young, talented, and often brash individuals. Unfortunately, the most promising talent often proves to be the most difficult, intransigent team player. Yet

leaders are compelled to recruit only the best, and they constantly suffer the carnage left in the wake of failed teams.

The most promising talent often proves to be the
most difficult, intransigent team player. Yet leaders are
compelled to recruit only the best, and they constantly
suffer the carnage left in the wake of failed teams.

For most of their lives, high-potential individuals have been told they are better than the rest—that they are more intelligent, work harder, and have more creative ideas. This creates an unfortunate dilemma. When gifted people are brought
together, each individual readily assumes he is carrying more than his fair share
of the load. They see their own contributions as being superior to those of their
teammates. The problem is that when teammates believe they are doing more
than their fair share, they tend to reduce their commitment, hold back their effort, and sometimes act out in destructive ways.

When teammates believe they are doing more than their
fair share, they tend to reduce their commitment, hold back
their effort, and sometimes act out in destructive ways.

Consider this situation from their perspective. Becoming a member of a team
means accepting a reduction in personal autonomy. In a team environment, individuals often end up subjugating their own needs for the good of the team. For
some people, this can be worse than a reduction in pay. Losing autonomy is uncomfortable for most people raised in individualistic cultures, and particularly so
for high performers who have experienced repeated success through autonomous
action. They are loath to saddle themselves with a group's inertia and the potential for reduced performance. They fear the gravity of the lowest common de-
nominator and as a result tend to resist joining teams.

The fact remains, however, that teams produce better results than individuals. Groups of people working well together analyze situations more accurately,
generate more creative ideas, and make better decisions than do individuals working on their own. And as anyone who has recruited people for a team knows, the
best teams are made from the best raw material. So we continue to recruit for the
best and end up facing the same dilemma time and time again.

How We Became World Champions

In September 1995, four years after the Lucenec defeat, the U.S. team won the world championships in Gap, France. High over the Haute Alps region, a dynamic American team proved unstoppable. Round after competition round, we pummeled the national teams of thirty-four other countries with clean, aggressive, and consistent skydiving. There was not a team on the planet capable of matching our talent, preparation, and teamwork. The cherry on top of the win was where it took place: the 1995 world championships were held at the French National Training Center. The U.S. team won the meet in their nemesis's own back yard.

The victory in Gap was the culmination of four years of hard work and constant learning. The loss in Lucenec and other meets had quickened our resolve and forced us to reflect honestly on the reasons behind the losing performances. Simply put, there could be no place to hide inside this team if we wanted to succeed. To become world champions, we had to excel across a number of disciplines. We had to move faster, time our exits better, and synchronize the transitions more tightly. But in the end, teamwork proved to be the essential piece of the puzzle.

Talented overconfident individuals can be great team players. West Point's Sprint football team is a great example we will look at more closely in this chapter. The Sprint team consists entirely of overachievers who manage to win consistently in one of the most teamwork-dependent sports there is. In a school of overachievers, 79 percent of the Sprint team is on the Dean's List. The Sprint team, or "150s," as they are called because of weight restrictions, has a deep heritage of excellence. The culture of the team regularly produces elite performers, both on the field and in the classroom, who are able to come together and perform as a team. What makes it work? What are the specific leadership actions that enable the best and the brightest to work together collaboratively?

Strategy One: Share Responsibility Among All Team Members

In 1994, the U.S. Skydiving Team formed a completely new lineup selected from among the top competitors in the country. Dan Brodsky-Chenfeld and I formed the nucleus of the new team. Dan had captained the California-based Air Moves, my perennial nemesis and archrival within the United States. Dan, who was thirty at the time, had been winning medals at the U.S. Nationals for more than ten years but had not yet won the competition to be selected for the U.S. team. He is a charismatic, stocky man who brought a boatload of heart to our new team.

Kirk Verner, from Sparta Illinois, has been around skydiving all his life. He grew up on his father's skydiving center, learning to fly the airplane and instruct students when he was only fifteen years old. Kirk brought winning speed to the team with his fast moves and quick mind. Mark Kirkby filled the final slot. Mark was a blond-haired, strong twenty-four-year-old who had emigrated from northern England in 1990 with the sole purpose of becoming a world champion. He was determined and brought raw power to the team. My own skydiving career began the day I turned sixteen years old in Ellington, Connecticut, when my mother helped me out of the plane for my first jump. I grew up in the sport, with both parents skydiving actively and dragging my sister, Heather, and me to the airport most weekends. Not long after that first jump, I made up my mind to become a world champion, a dream that would take thirteen years to realize.

Share Leadership Power

Each team member had been playing at the top of the sport for a number of years, and three of the four had captained our own teams in the past. In January 1994, when the team gathered in Eloy, Arizona, for the first day of training, the question of leadership had not yet been addressed. Who was going to have power in this high-octane group was a question we needed to address.

The one thing we all agreed on was how difficult it would be to win the world championships. We had seen the French and Russian national teams in action and understood that to be successful, we would need to tap all of our resources. It would require everyone's ideas and each individual's full energy and passion to be applied to the challenge every training day.

One of the solutions Bob Moore helped implement in 1994
was a leadership structure that shared responsibility equally
among all team members. We delegated accountability for specific
jobs and rotated daily leadership on a schedule that forced
each person to take a turn leading and a turn following.

We knew from experience that, once established, roles and responsibilities would drive people into specific patterns of behavior. We could easily fall into patterns that would suboptimize the use of each individual's potential. Those in positions of power might begin to take on paternalistic behaviors, and everyone else would slide into a follower role and become compliant. We had all been on teams where the captain could not sleep at night over concern for the team, while the rank and file came to work each day giving the absolute minimum required. This predictable pattern would not make world champions.

Our coach, Bob Moore, brought the answer. Dr. Bob, as he is fondly known within the sport, is an insightful man with a relentless knack for unearthing hidden issues and exposing them to light. Dr. Bob and I had been working with the U.S. team since 1990 when he began by helping us prepare for the Lucenec meet. A calming, compassionate man, he brought a new awareness of and respect for the more intangible aspects of team performance.

One of the solutions he helped implement in 1994 was a leadership structure that shared responsibility equally among all team members. We delegated accountability for specific jobs and rotated daily leadership on a schedule that forced each person to take a turn leading and a turn following.

For a bunch of Type A personalities, it was the follower role that proved more difficult. For example, on a day when I was slated to take other people's lead, I would walk into the team room feeling smug. "Oh, today is going to be a cakewalk. All I need to do is keep my head down, fly my slot, and be where the captain expects me to be. How easy is that?" But it was never that easy. I had to struggle and listen hard to understand the captain's ideas. They were different and inferior to how I would have done things, or so I thought at the time. An inner dialogue would kick up in my head about how poor the plan was and how the captain should be doing things differently. Next thing I knew, my attention had drifted and I was way off plan.

For a bunch of Type A personalities, it was the follower role that proved more difficult. I had to struggle and listen hard to understand the captain's ideas. They were different and inferior to how I would have done things, or so I thought at the time. An inner dialogue would kick up in my head about how poor the plan was and how the captain should be doing things differently.

Once while in this state, I wandered around the corner after our prejump rehearsal to talk with a friend. While I was chatting, the plane pulled up and my team loaded without me. Obviously I had annoyed the day's captain with my wandering because he made no effort to corral me onto the aircraft. My first awareness was the sound of the plane rotating off the runway for its climb to altitude. The team jumped while I sat on the ground. Following other people's lead was a real eye-opener for me. It taught me some basic skills about leading from the ranks without formal authority.

The flip side had a big impact as well. Our youngest teammate, Mark, had been competing for only about three years and at first took his leadership responsibilities with a bit of trepidation. He would rather have sat back, followed a more senior member's lead, and pointed a finger when things went awry. For example, when I wandered off and missed the jump, Mark said, "Hey, you need to be with us when it's time to go." And he was right; I did. But there are two sides to this story. As the leader that day, Mark was not anticipating the next steps and failed to communicate to the team that the aircraft was approaching. As a result, with no clear direction, it was easy to lose focus and wander off.

Days in the captain position challenged the young talent beyond their comfort zone, giving them perspective and humbling their egos. In the end, taking turns being responsible for the team made everyone a better follower.

Rotating the leadership thrust Mark, our inexperienced leader, into the position of having to anticipate needs, make plans against objectives, and ultimately be responsible for the output of the training. He was accountable if we did not make our jumps on schedule or if the preparation was poor and performance suffered. When communication broke down inside the team, he had to facilitate the group through to resolution.

One Friday afternoon, the team was reviewing videos of a mock competition that had not gone well. I was getting extremely frustrated because I felt we were not addressing the issues. After hearing some soft analysis, I blew up saying, "We aren't dealing with reality here, guys. We're kidding ourselves!" Kirk, who was trying to make a point when I blew up, became offended and clammed up. It was 2:00 P.M., and we were stuck. Mark, who was captain that day, shut the situation down by calling an end to the week: "All right, that's it. We're closing out this conversation and not making any more jumps today. I want to see everyone in the bar inside the hour. Hit the shower, and let's have a drink together. We'll look at these tapes again Monday."

Situations like this challenged everyone to step it up and take on the leadership of the team. Days in the captain position challenged the young talent beyond their comfort zone, giving them perspective and humbling their egos. In the end, taking turns being responsible for the team made everyone a better follower.

Share the Burden of Leadership

The greatest gain was sharing the burden of leadership. Everyone had a piece of the monkey riding on his back. The team's performance, not just their own individual performance, became everyone's concern—and not just an esoteric, abstract thing that someone else needed to do something about, but a tangible issue we were all accountable for.

For example, exit timing is critical when we launch a CAT formation from the plane. (The CAT is a long, fragile formation where everyone is holding the legs of the person in front of them.) When the back half of the exit leaves the plane late, the CAT formation blows apart the moment it hits the eighty-knot wind. For me, in the front of the exit, the question I need to ask when this happens is, "What can I do on our end to keep this from happening again?" This is a powerful effect because it mobilizes everyone to find his piece of the solution. In contrast, as a follower on the 1991 U.S. team in Lucenec, my response would have been, "Hey, when are you guys going to get your act together back there? You're slowing me down."

Getting a team to the point where each member feels a deep sense of responsibility for the group's combined performance is about generating equality. It requires building a system that treats each person equally with regard to what they have to contribute and how they will be held accountable for results. Sharing leadership is a great method for accomplishing this.

Techniques for Sharing Leadership

Leadership sharing can be done in a number of ways and should be structured with the team's specific circumstances in mind. There are three basic options: leadership rotation, delegation, and a mix of rotation and delegation.

Leadership Rotation. The first approach to leadership sharing is a rotational structure, where the leadership role is passed from teammate to teammate on a predetermined schedule. This is best to do when the leadership responsibilities are relatively simple and straightforward so as not to overburden each new leader with undue complexity. The leadership role should be clearly described, preferably in writing, and posted in the team area. The changing of the guard, so to speak, should occur explicitly and at a predetermined time to avoid confusion over who is in charge or, worse, avoid a "nobody's in charge" situation. For example, on the skydiving team, we rotated leadership every week. Each Monday, a new person was in charge following a preset pattern.

---

*The leadership role should be clearly described,
preferably in writing, and posted in the team area.
The changing of the guard should occur explicitly and at a
predetermined time to avoid confusion over who is in charge,
or worse, to avoid a "nobody's in charge" situation.*

The rotational process offers a powerful learning opportunity for both the burgeoning leader and the senior person forced into a follower role. Each rotational period should be debriefed to maximize the learning from the experience and avoid the deep frustration that can come with repeated ineptness in either role. On the skydiving team, we met at the close of every week to give feedback to the week's captain and hand off the role to the next person in line. Each Friday afternoon (except for the time Mark sent us to the bar early), we would sit down for thirty minutes to review the past week's leadership with a quick conversation about what had worked and what needed to be improved. The team would hand off responsibility to the next week's captain by clarifying goals and addressing any questions.

Delegating to Share Leadership. Delegation, a popular leadership sharing structure, works best when there are a number of diverse aspects to the team's leadership responsibilities. This is a good option when the technical leadership role requires sustained effort to master or solid relationships are required with people external to the team.

To delegate in a way that truly shares leadership requires more than simple task delegation. It is about more than handing out to-do lists to direct reports with deadlines for completion, which will not necessarily generate an environment of accountability. True delegation is a handing out of responsibility. A set of objectives is given to an individual to accomplish, and the individual decides how to go about getting it done.

To delegate in a way that truly shares leadership requires more than simple task delegation. True delegation is a handing out of responsibility. A set of objectives is given to an individual to accomplish, and the individual decides how to go about getting it done.

For example, the skydiving team had a series of sponsors who supported our training. Most of these were equipment manufacturers based in Florida, far away from our training center in Eloy, Arizona. Kirk was responsible for maintaining the equipment to a safe standard. All of the reserve parachutes had to be inspected and repacked every 120 days. Automatic opening devices (technology designed to deploy a parachute in the event a teammate is knocked unconscious) had to be inspected and proper battery levels maintained. Kirk was responsible for all our gear. We trusted him implicitly to keep us safe in the air.

To run a shared leadership model based on delegation requires the team to delineate sets of responsibilities with objectives and clear boundaries. Individuals are assigned their roles and held accountable for results in regular review sessions. We all had specific jobs we were held accountable for, and we all took our turn in the role of captain.

A Mix of Leadership Rotation and Delegation. The third shared leadership option is a combination of rotation and delegation. This is often the most practical structure because certain, more general roles lend themselves to rotation, whereas more specialized roles lend themselves to delegation.

For example, on the skydiving team, we rotated the captain role, which was the responsibility for setting the training plan and moving the team through the day. But we delegated other jobs, such as sponsor relations, which Kirk maintained to ensure we were supporting their marketing efforts, and competition logistics, which I managed. With these roles, the responsible individuals needed to build relationships and master complex details to be successful. The point is, we all had specific jobs we were held accountable for, and we all took our turn in the captain role.

Strategy Two: Set and Maintain High Standards for the Team

Gene McIntyre, the head coach of West Point's Sprint football team, maintains high standards. "We don't lose. That's the standard," says McIntyre. And judging by their record, he has every right to hold that expectation. This is a great example of a team of high-potential overachievers. Every year, West Point ranks each student by combining his or her grade point average (GPA), athletic performance, and military leadership. For nine of the past twelve years, the Sprint team has scored the highest of all West Point teams. The average GPA on the team of sixty-five players is 3.07. These players are elite talent, and they know how to perform as a team.

The Sprint team is one of the most sought-after athletic groups at the Academy. Common knowledge is that they work hard, perform well, and win. West Point cadets want to be part of that. The promise of a challenge draws the best because the best tend to be motivated by things that are slightly more difficult than average. They endeavor to stretch beyond what is normal. Consider this: these are students who have been told their entire lives that they are too small to play football. So what do they do? They play football. Simply put, high challenge stimulates high performers. It is no coincidence that this team has as members some of the most driven and talented cadets on post.

Build a Legacy of Excellence

When West Point's Sprint football team was first formed, it was led by a group of extremely tough cadets who instilled their legacy in the team. Ever since, high standards of excellence have been the norm, and nobody will stand for less. On the Sprint football team, motivation and discipline come largely from within. Team members discipline themselves with push-ups and running when their performance falls short of standard. And Coach McIntyre did not implement that; the team did. If a player is not pulling his weight or is acting out of line, the group will castigate the low performer until he either quits or reforms his behavior. McIntyre does not need to do this because the culture does it for him.

Pat Hall, a top defensive back, is instilling his legacy in the team right now. Pat encourages his teammates by his own work ethic. He works harder than anyone else and never expects more from his teammates than he puts in himself. For example, when official practice ends, he keeps working out on his own time rather than heading back to the barracks. And most players, seeing what he is up to, join him. If a teammate does not show up for the extra work, they hear about it with comments like, "Hey, you're looking a bit weak, and we didn't see you in the weight room last night. What's up?"

Players who still refuse to fit in because their egos are just too big usually wash out because the culture inside the team will not accept them. It's analogous to an organ transplant of the wrong blood type being rejected by the body.

As with any other talented group of high-potential individuals, issues of poor attitude and self-centered behavior do crop up. For example, one great player was fast and mean, but he was not a team player. He kept acting on his own, trying to be the hero. Coach McIntyre went to a teammate close to the problem cadet and asked him to talk to the guy. The conversation happened behind the scenes, but I am sure it went something along the lines of, "You're a great player, man, but if you don't work with the rest of us, we've got no use for you here." He used peer pressure rather than top-down authority to pull the problem in line. On the Sprint team, most of the people issues can be addressed from within because the team's legacy has formed a strong culture and the cadets will not stand for a teammate's stepping outside the norms.

Players who still refuse to fit in because their egos are just too big usually wash out because the culture inside the team will not accept them. It's analogous to an organ transplant of the wrong blood type being rejected by the body. The corps closes ranks, and the odd man out knows where he stands. From there, it is a short time until the person is either cut or quits.

McIntyre intentionally promotes this strong, unified culture. For example, a few years back, a number of cadets on the team were caught sneaking off post. McIntyre disciplined the entire team for their infraction, saying, "You guys are responsible for each other." This kind of leadership action sends a strong message about unity and cohesion.

Cut Low Performers from the Team

As the head coach, McIntyre does not balk from cutting low performers. If they are not being team players or not working hard enough, he cuts them. This may sound harsh, but it sends a strong message to the team that substandard performance will not be accepted. Hard-nosed leadership can buoy the morale of high performers. They like to know their teammates are being held to as high a standard as they hold themselves.

A good business example of high standards in action is General Electric, which is famous for developing great managers.[1] GE's leadership development program (LDP) maintains high standards and as a result attracts top talent from within the company. Bob Corcoran is a committed and driven man who has put a lot of energy into creating and leading GE's LDP. He speaks passionately about the role high standards take in developing the best.

To maintain its standards, GE drops the lowest performers from the program every year. GE ranks all participants based on demonstrated performance and works closely with the bottom 10 percent. Each of these individuals is told where he or she stands and given additional support to create a set of goals and an execution plan. Anyone whose performance does not move up to the agreed-on level is cut. By relentlessly purging the program of low performers, GE drives the average level of play upward.

Hard-nosed leadership can buoy the morale of high performers. They like to know their teammates are being held to as high a standard as they hold themselves.

There can be no double standards with this approach. Everyone must be measured in the same way, and people should rarely be given slack because of special circumstances. Double standards erode the efficacy of high standards. High potentials will rarely give their all in an unjust culture.

For example, the 1991 U.S. Skydiving Team that lost in Lucenec had a leader with double standards. At the smallest mistake, he would scream at a teammate,

"What were you thinking?" Then he would turn around and explain away his own errors with comments like, "I was distracted by the pilot's flying. As the leader, I've got to pay attention to this." The rest of us knew he was covering up his mistake, and we lost respect for his leadership.

The leader needs to strike the difficult balance between justice and being humane. The team needs to maintain a basic level of compassion or risk being unjust in that regard. Coach McIntyre has this figured out: the players on the Sprint football do the heavy-handed work because they are inspired by the deep heritage and strong culture. This leaves McIntyre free to act as arbitrator, coach, and moral support for the athletes having a hard time.

Recruit Team Members Who Will Fit In

High standards begin at recruitment. Coach McIntyre reports that the Sprint football team's standards result from recruiting people who fit: "We recruit our own. Everyone on the team is on the lookout for overachieving hard workers to bring onto the team." Recruitment and selection are focused on fit as well as capability and experience. A talented individual can learn the job. The greater question is whether that person will gel with the rest of the team.

Recruiting for fit is taken very seriously on the U.S. Skydiving Team. The top concern has always been how this potential talent will act deep in the training season. When we are seven hundred training jumps into the season and three months from the world championships, how hard this person will work as an individual performer and as a teammate are the key questions.

On the U.S. team, we found that the answer to these questions lay in discovering a recruit's core motivation for becoming a member of the team. For example, if he wants to be part of a world-class team in order to meet personal ego needs, experience showed we were going to be in for a struggle. If this were the case, talented individuals would tend to act out of self-interest and try to stand out from the group in any way possible.

Recruitment and selection are focused on fit as well as capability and experience. A talented individual can learn the job. The greater question is whether that person can gel with the rest of the team.

We once had a team member who wanted to land his parachute his own way to impress and delight the spectators. The team wanted to get down quickly and all land together to save time and make more jumps. This guy would nod his head and pretend to agree with the plan and then go off and land on his own in front of the spectators.

This behavior can be destructive to the fabric of a team. People have a finite well of motivation, and the depth of a person's well dictates how hard he or she will work and how selflessly. Understanding the reason a recruit is interested in joining a team provides a clue to the depth and quality of his or her motivation.

High-potential talent is motivated in a culture defined by high standards of performance. Leadership in large part sets and maintains the team's culture and can use performance standards as a lever to gel the team. A strong culture does an incredible job of aligning an organization. The culture on the Sprint team is about high standards and work ethic: if an individual slides off the path, the rest of the team makes the correction. As the coach, McIntyre maintains the culture, and the team maintains the rest.

Strategy Three: Develop Respect Among Team Members for Each Other

Respect among team members and for the team leader is an imperative for building high-performing teams. Team leaders command respect through competence and character. Talented individuals strive to perform for leaders they look up to: leaders who display outstanding ability and unquestionable character.

In 1995, Lotus Desk Top Applications' headline product was the spreadsheet 1–2–3.[2] At the time, 1–2–3 was a major competitive player in the software industry, rivaling the up-and-coming Microsoft. But Lotus was in trouble with 1–2–3. To stay competitive, it needed to get Release 5 out the door, the product had to be good, and the company had to beat Microsoft to the market. The trouble was that Lotus had become hobbled from infighting among the various application product groups such as spreadsheets, word processing, electronic forums, and groupware. It was organizational chaos.

Around 1988, Lotus had entered the market as a small start-up company. Over the next seven years, it grew rapidly on the back of a series of successful products. As it grew, the organization adopted a traditional industrial structure that resulted in walled-off functional silos with little integration. Over the seven years of comfortable growth, the marketing and sales, finance, and separate development groups for each software product grew increasingly comfortable within their respective fiefdoms. The company had started as a collection of high-potential talented young people who by 1995 were growing older, starting to have families, and not wanting to work so hard. The infighting began as contention between silos when each tried to satisfy its customer base without regard for the rest of the organization. Lotus was attempting to be all things to all people. It had lost its focus.

Recruit the Right Team

Jeffrey Beir was the senior vice president of applications and led the desktop applications organization at Lotus. With a Harvard M.B.A., Jeffrey understood the need for high-performing teams and took great pains to recruit the best from throughout the company to produce Release 5. He scoured the company's development groups and pulled only top talent onto the Release 5 team. These architects were the best in the field and came with egos that matched their talent. They tended to be self-centered perfectionists whose drive to create original and cutting-edge products came with an unfortunate side effect: a near complete lack of empathy and patience for teammates or the rest of the organization.

For example, the architects all had their pet way of doing things, and they all wanted things to happen their way. More than once, a group of architects sat around a table and agreed to include a specific mechanism in a product. Then one of the architects, wanting a different mechanism, would go to management behind the group's back and get the decision changed. It was anarchy.

In another instance of Lotus infighting, marketing and sales came late in the game, wanting to add a mapping feature to 1–2–3. Customer research suggested mapping would help the product sell, so they came in and said, "By the way, we need this mapping feature in here too." The head of the development group responded, "We can't do that. It's not in any of the cost models, and it'll slip the date." The developers did not want it because it came late, they were already pushing the deadline, and they had already formed their image of the product. In the end, mapping got put in and ended up contributing substantially to the product's success.

These architects were the best—with egos that matched their talent. They tended to be self-centered perfectionists, which had an unfortunate side effect: a near complete lack of empathy and patience for teammates or for the rest of the organization.

Beir's right-hand man was Steve Turner, the vice president responsible for creating Release 5. Steve was the leader who would be putting together the elite team for Release 5, and he did not have a software background. He was educated in chemistry at Nottingham University, England. Nonetheless, he was accountable for bringing this group of elite developers together around the new release. He was seen as a competent professional who commanded respect from the elite Lotus developers. He had more than twenty years of experience leading large global development projects.

And although he lacked a technical background, Steve nevertheless commanded respect because of his practical experience managing technology professionals. For example, at Primavera Systems, where he had been in charge of product development, Steve had managed more than a hundred people in project management, software development, and quality assurance. He was often heard to say, "I'm not technical, but I don't need to be; that's what I'm paying you for." He was bright, knew the industry, and understood what it would take to get a product out.

Form Relationships Among the Team

Steve needed to form a fresh team. The internal competitiveness and history of conflict in the desktop applications organization had created a toxic environment. Needing to develop a team of this group of talented individuals, Steve turned for help to Bob Moore, who has considerable skills and experience in building high-performing teams. Together, Bob and Steve dismantled the structures of the old organization and re-formed the group into a single unit of about sixty-five developers.

With Bob's facilitation, the Lotus 1–2–3 development team worked diligently developing respect for each other during their first month together. Bob took them through a series of retreats that peeled away the layers of old animosity and rivalry. He was able to instill in the team a good base of interpersonal skills that allowed them to understand each other. For example, the team learned to listen to each other when individuals disagreed. After the team development work, when an architect confronted the group with an alternative mechanism for the 1–2–3 application, her teammates would understand and truly consider the alternative idea. By actively listening, they began to see the merits and efficacy of opposing points of view.

The team learned to listen to each other when individuals disagreed. By actively listening, they began to see the merits and efficacy of opposing points of view.

Ensure Leadership Competence

Leadership competence is a key underpinning to developing teams of high performers. Steve's professionalism and ability as a leader allowed him to gel this group of previously intransigent team players. For example, he was politically savvy and used this competence to manage the boundaries between the team and the rest of the company. He was able to do this with such finesse that the team enjoyed the resources and cooperation it needed to achieve its goals. The team members not only recognized Steve's competence but lived in the glow of it.

High performers want to be recognized and respected by competent bosses, and they tend to fall in line to get that recognition. We all enjoy positive feedback from our bosses, but it is a whole lot more meaningful coming from a competent professional.

For example, in my first year on the U.S. Skydiving Team, our captain, Tom Piraz, had won the world championships in 1985 and was recognized as one of the best skydivers in the world. Although he was a hard-nosed, insensitive taskmaster, he was the best. It was an honor to be in the air with him, and I worked hard to prove I belonged there. I figured, "If Tom thinks I'm good, that really means something." Wanting to live up to a competent boss's expectations has a powerful effect on everyone. But high performers who are driven to excel will work very hard to fit into such a leader's team.

Give Clear Direction

We all expect clear direction from leadership, but talented high potentials can be particularly critical if a leader does not provide it. Nothing erodes respect faster than a wishy-washy leader. Strong, well-articulated direction is crucial. Steve was an excellent communicator who galvanized the Lotus team behind a vision of quality and speed. He instilled the practice of building quality in from the beginning to save time. He set this objective and made his expectations clear. Before Release 5, prima-donna architects would use their own styles of code to create discrete pieces of the puzzle. In the end, the disparate pieces would be brought together in a messy and time-consuming triage process before going live. Steve pushed through a new revolutionary practice of having everyone put the code in the same from the beginning. He came right out and said, "From now on, this is how we're going to do it."

Talented high potentials can be particularly critical if a leader does not provide clear direction. Nothing erodes respect faster than a wishy-washy leader. Strong, well-articulated direction is crucial.

Steve established a strong culture. He laid down a new set of rules and followed them. He rewarded excellence and disciplined transgression; he was never cruel but always firm. For example, in the old culture, coming late to meetings had become normal practice. People stopped arriving on time because they expected meetings to start late. A lot of work hours were wasted, team members were being disrespected, and people were getting thoroughly annoyed. Steve changed all that. Anyone late for a meeting did not get in because the door was locked. In general, he relegated trivial distractions and focused the group on what was important.

Steve could make these changes because the team respected him. When people are competent, they are believable, and it is easy to buy into their vision and follow the direction they set.

High performers recognize strong character and will rally behind a leader's integrity, honor, and sense of duty.

Recognize That Sound Character Is Critical

"Like carbon to the diamond, character is the basic quality of the leader," says General Edward C. Meyer and former Army chief of staff.[3] The U.S. military develops exceptional leaders through the basic framework of "Be, Know, Do": the Be is about character, the Know is about skills, and the Do is about action.

Character comes first and is the essential ingredient everything else is built on. High performers recognize strong character and will rally behind a leader's integrity, honor, and sense of duty.

The developers at Lotus respected Steve's character. He was consistent and clear, and they knew where they stood with him. Steve put his career on the line building the team to develop Release 5 of Lotus 1-2-3. He believed strongly in the need to build the team and took a big risk by devoting time to the effort. The product had to get out fast, yet he spent three full days taking the team off-site because he valued teamwork and would not give it short shrift. It should be noted that what Steve was doing was not typical at Lotus. The team he built stood out from the rest of the organization. Its values were not the norm, and it required considerable courage on Steve's part to establish and maintain a team based on his beliefs.

Steve Turner built a team of elite developers who got Release 5 out ahead of schedule and with fewer bugs than any previous release. It was a quality product that generated a substantial profit, giving Lotus a new lease on life. In the end, the product was integral to helping the company gain market share on Microsoft and eventually position itself to be sold for a good price to IBM.

Strategy Four: Ensure Humility and Recognize Individual Differences

In the middle of the 2005 National Football League (NFL) season, Terrell Owens, a star wide receiver for the Philadelphia Eagles, was fired "for conduct detrimental to the team."[4] Owens, who had been playing football in the NFL for ten years since completing college at Chattanooga, Tennessee, in 1995, was fired for verbally denigrating nearly everyone on the team. The last straw was criticizing the team in the press for not publicly recognizing his hundredth career touchdown catch. He complained, "This proves the Eagles don't have any class."

The NFL is rife with talented high performers operating in a team environment. Unfortunately, they do not all manage to work successfully on a team, and when they fail, the cost to the organization can be astronomical. "TO" (as Owens is called by fans) was paid $3.5 million a year for his talent and ability to contribute to the team. Yet in spite of all his game-winning receptions, the Eagles decided he was not worth the toll he took on the team. In the end, the team canceled his contract.

Columnist Chris Shultz, who writes for TSN, Canada's leading sports media, wrote, "Why is a man with so much going for him in life so unhappy? Why does a man so bright say such stupid things?"[5] TO was unhappy with his teammates. He had been constantly criticizing his quarterback McNabb since Philadelphia lost the 2005 Super Bowl to the New England Patriots. Shultz's questions are ones many of us ask about talented people with high potential who cannot seem to integrate into a team environment. TO chipped away at the spirit of the Eagles organization like many other prima-donna players who run roughshod over their teammates. Individual talent is important, but to win, the entire team needs to be fully engaged.

Leverage the Power of Teams

In the business world, decision-making teams outperform individuals every time. As long as they are functioning well, groups analyze situations more thoroughly and make better decisions than do individuals. The primary reason is that individuals see the world from different perspectives, which, if tapped, bring an abundance of information to the process. High-functioning groups get each team member's point of view on the table before making decisions or closing out analysis.

For this to happen, individuals who come to the table with a large dose of self-confidence need to have the humility to hold their positions loosely. They need to recognize that each individual in the group, including themselves, is likely to capture only a portion of the whole story. They need to be genuinely interested in the contributions of their teammates.

But where does humility come from? Consider a business example that I have been working with over the past four years. Aetna Health's Information Services (AIS) employs more than two thousand people who develop and maintain information technology for Aetna's primary business units.

AIS operates a three-year, fast-track leadership development program that recruits high performers directly out of top schools. That may not seem fast, but imagine recent undergraduates who three years later are managing teams of experienced developers who have been at Aetna an average of fifteen years each. Program participants work their way through eight-month job rotations within AIS and the primary business units. They are given support from program management, on-the-job training from rotational managers, a third-party mentor, and external coaching. Participants move through a series of learning experiences targeted at key leadership competencies such as managerial courage, communicating vision and purpose, and self-learning.

Our experience with this program has shown a distinct pattern of arrogance developing in the participants as they progress through their rotations. This silver-spoon syndrome is the result of being chosen because they are the best, having special attention paid to them, and being continuously romanced for important positions. Nevertheless, we have found that sometime in the third year of the program, participants begin to acquire a healthy dose of humility.

Increase Team Members' Self-Awareness

Increasing participant self-awareness is a major focus of the LDP because it is a key underpinning to improving leadership effectiveness; it also leads to humility. Through the LDP, participants begin to see the impact their behavior has on a team and to understand their previously unconscious biases.

Increased self-awareness is a key underpinning to improving leadership effectiveness; it also leads to humility.

For example, one young man who had obviously had most things in life fall in his lap without much effort came to his first LDP workshop with a serious chip on his shoulder. Each day he slouched in the back of the room and rolled his eyes at other people's comments as if they were stupid and a "why should I have to be here?" attitude. It was disturbing behavior.

Within a few days, however, he had heard what a put-off his behavior was from enough of his teammates to make him realize the effect of this behavior. Through workshop feedback, coaching, and mentoring, LDP participants begin to understand the truth about their abilities as opposed to the inflated impressions we often have. Group dialogue and personal introspection work together to help participants see the truth about themselves, and with that comes humility.

The process of gaining humility can take quite a bit of time and requires a commitment to stay the course from both the individual and the team. It is too easy for immature talent to derail from the process by quitting or being fired before they have acquired the necessary self-awareness. And for some, like TO possibly, there may not be enough time.

Group dialogue and personal introspection work together to help participants see the truth about themselves, and with that comes humility.

Value Each Other's Differences

With humility, however gained, comes an appreciation for the talents other people bring with them. On the skydiving team, we learned to value the differences everyone brought and to leverage them to meet our goals. We paid attention to who had what skills and positioned players advantageously.

For example, my teammate Dan intuitively understands people and their needs. On that training day when I wandered off to talk to someone and missed the jump, Mark, who had the captain hat on that day, was annoyed. He purposely put the team on the plane without me to make a point, and after they landed, he tore into me. But because Dan is perceptive, he realized that my wandering off was due in part to my frustration with the leadership. And although he did not let me off the hook, he was able to see into me enough to mediate effectively and managed to save the rest of our day.

Because of his interpersonal skills, we positioned Dan as our liaison to the skydiving center's management. He was able to gain cooperation. For example, when we are training, we want to make up to twelve jumps in an eight-hour period. The pinch is that there are only twenty-two seats on each airplane, and management is motivated to fill them with high-revenue customers like first-time jumpers. There were times when management would bump us off a plane to make space, and we would hear the news over the loudspeaker. When this happened, I wanted to tell the person behind the counter to put us back on the plane, and to do it *now*. But Dan was able to negotiate a give-and-take agreement that ultimately got our needs met.

It requires humility to step down from a good bit of attitude you have worked up because someone has wronged you. In this example, I had to sit down and let Dan handle this very important relationship, or I could easily have pushed management too hard and the team might have been sitting on the ground the rest of the day. It also helps that we had assigned Dan the responsibility of dealing with management in a calmer moment in our annual planning sessions. When we got bumped off the plane, I just needed to remember my role and let Dan do his.

Difference is an asset. A team is well advised to catalogue who has what skills and aptitudes and position players wisely. Who is an expert at what? Who has experience where? And how do we see the world differently? These are all questions a team needs to explore with each other. Understanding around these questions enables the team to position people effectively.

In addition, understanding each other's differences enables the team to react with less judgment when individuals think and say seemingly strange things. Let's use my wandering off as an example again. My frustration that day was rooted in Mark's leadership, which I considered too laissez-faire. In that moment, I judged Mark as incompetent and went off from there. Once Dan got us talking after the three-person jump, I learned that Mark thought differently from how I did about leadership. He thought my way was too rigid and controlled and that we would perform better in a more relaxed atmosphere. This was an eye-opener for me. Instead of thinking my teammate was incompetent when he led the way he did, I was forced to pause and think, "So that's how he sees the world. Isn't that interesting?"

Strategy Five: Communicate Constantly

When Dan, Mark, Kirk, and I formed a team in 1994, we were setting out to do what had never been done before. Throughout the 1980s and early 1990s, the winning score at the world championships was increasing by approximately 10 percent a year. To generate the additional speed and coordination to make those scores required finding new techniques and using levels of power never applied before. To win, we would need to do something special, something never done before, and we would be the ones writing the book.

After the 1991 Lucenec failure, the team had to develop a new understanding of what it would take to win. The original model, which was to get the best talent and have everyone perform the best they could as individuals, obviously was not enough. We had to figure out how to learn fast, continuously push new edges, and still be able to live with each other through multiple years of full-time training. To do this, we would need to establish a few basic and lasting tenets.

One such tenet was what Dr. Bob called "real talk." He maintained that the only way to manage the daily conflict inherent in a high-speed learning environment was through constant rigorous communication. So with his help, we implemented a comprehensive communication strategy that proved to be the linchpin to our success. In the documentary *Airspeed*, chronicling the team's two years of training leading up to the 1999 world meet victory in Corowa, Australia, Kirk was quoted saying, "Communication is the one thing that sets this team apart. With it, we can work through anything." In the end, communication became a defining element of the team.

"Real talk" is open, honest, and timely communication. It is about expressing yourself fully and fully hearing what others are telling you. It is about taking responsibility for your teammate's development by giving feedback and being able to assimilate and act on feedback given to you. We did just that. We sat around a table in a team-building event the first year we were together and said, "If we're going to pull this off, we've got to be able to get in each other's face whenever someone is out of line. We can't let stuff slide or we'll lose." Real talk is hard. It may be a soft skill, but when it is really being practiced, it is anything but soft.

"Real talk" is open, honest, and timely communication. It is about expressing yourself fully and fully hearing what others tell you. It may be a soft skill, but when it is really being practiced, it is anything but soft.

Give Performance Feedback

Good communication acts like a spotlight. It illuminates and gives color to the performance and behavior issues every team has to handle. The skydiving team debriefed every jump, looking to identify what was working and where things could be improved. Although we used videotape, it became clear that each player had a different impression of what had happened in free fall.

For example, our zigzag-to-marquee transition failed on one of the last training jumps before the 1994 World Cup in Empuria Brava, Spain. The zigzag is built with two pairs of skydivers gripping the side of their partner's body so they are perpendicular to each other. The transition is particularly powerful, requiring each pair to rotate 360 degrees in a tight spin, coming out of the spin precisely on level and directly adjacent to one another so they can reach out and gently touch to score the point. Our transition failed because we could not shut down the momentum, which caused the two pieces to crash together and fling our bodies across the sky like bowling pins.

Kirk and I were partners in the piece that was out of control. My impression was that Kirk did not get his first move out of the center stopped. His impression was the opposite: he thought that I had not stopped my move. We were each certain about our experience, and the others were concerned that we figure out what happened so it would not come up in competition the next day.

There was quite a bit of tension in the debriefing that evening. It is rarely easy to determine reality when complexity characterizes the situation, so we debriefed to build a common sense of what was real so we could move forward intelligently, confidently, and as a team.

Debrief After Each Mission

On the skydiving team, we debriefed every jump. The debriefing was structured to give each person an opportunity to express his view of the performance. We needed to have everyone's ideas in order to analyze the performance and make decisions on how to move forward. As each person's perceived reality about the jump was put on the table, the team began to have a more robust and colorful understanding of reality. On the zigzag explosion, a number of subtle dynamics became clear by working through our communication process. Kirk reported feeling pulled away from the other piece, which caused him to add more power. I remembered getting tugged in my left hand when Kirk rotated around his center point, which accelerated my move and in a split second caused me to pull Kirk away. With all this information out, the preventive response was self-evident: Kirk would let me initiate his rotation, and I would begin stopping earlier.

Provide Behavioral Feedback

We need to shine the spotlight of communication on our personal behavior as well. Studies have shown that individuals are the least able to judge the impact that their behavior has on a group.[6] In other words, we are the last to know how we come across to our teammates. For example, on one training jump, I climbed outside the plane and started pounding on the roof from the outside while the team was lining up at the exit at 10,500 feet above the ground. The teammates still inside the plane heard a loud booming sound emanating from the entire aircraft. They understandably feared the plane was coming apart around us and started pushing to get out before the line-up was set. The jump was a fiasco. Even with all the best intentions, we can be acting in ways that are detrimental to the team's effectiveness. I was trying to pump up my teammates, but the only person I managed to impress was the pilot.

Banging on the roof of a plane is an uncommon example of a fairly common problem. We are often blind to the impact our behavior is having on the people around us. And those with high potential who have grown accustomed to being right all the time can be particularly blind to their impact. This was the case with the Aetna LDP participant who rolled his eyes when his teammates talked. He had no idea what his body language was communicating, and although hearing about it could not have been a pleasant experience, at least he has the information now and can manage himself more effectively. The only way we can get this information is through feedback.

---

*Even with all the best intentions, we can be acting
in ways that are detrimental to the team's effectiveness.
We are often blind to the impact our behavior is having on the
people around us. And those with high potential who have grown
accustomed to being right all the time can be particularly blind.*

"Pass the Rock"

To shine the light on our behavior, the U.S. Skydiving Team met once weekly to "pass the rock." The "rock" is an object we passed around the room symbolizing whose turn it was to talk. If you did not hold the rock, you did not speak. When it was your turn, you shared your reality. The meeting was designed to open communication channels specifically aimed at teammate behavior. The session was focused on teamwork and what each member needed to do behaviorally to optimize the group's performance.

It was in a pass-the-rock meeting that I heard about the impact my pounding on the roof of the plane had on my teammates. I had already heard the pilot's point of view in a less structured way. As with all other direct communication, getting feedback in this meeting could be difficult to swallow, so we had to learn how to listen well.

Require Nondefensive Listening

Nondefensive listening was another of the team's basic tenets. It meant that while receiving feedback, you were not allowed to explain or defend your position in that moment. You were to listen intently to everything said, ask questions for clarification only, and signal your understanding. Regardless of the accuracy or validity of the feedback, you were not to respond in any other way.

It sounds simple, but it is not. My teammate Dan gave me some feedback during a pass-the-rock meeting about how I had spoken during a debriefing. Dan was wrong. He had not been around the day before the debriefing and did not understand the context of the situation. He misinterpreted some things and jumped to a conclusion that was way off base. But when he delivered the feedback, all I could do was bite my lip and say, "Check," indicating I had understood but not necessarily agreed with his comments.

Skydiving requires a lot of visualization. We have to work the sequences over and over while climbing to altitude in the plane. The day after Dan's feedback, I could not hold my mind on anything for long. It would wander off to how Dan was wrong and all the things I was going to say in defense of myself. My performance that day was terrible. That night, I had an epiphany while drifting off to sleep with Dan's feedback churning in my head. A nugget of truth about my behavior and its impact on the team clarified itself in my mind. It was an extremely valuable nugget, and I would not have gotten it if I had not been churning on Dan's words. If I had indulged in defensive behavior by arguing my case to Dan that morning, I would have closed out the subject in my mind. Chances are that I would not have gained that nugget of truth.

Let's look at how Aetna's leadership development program used feedback. The LDP offers participants ample opportunity to give and receive feedback within the program. The feedback helped participants gain a realistic view of their capabilities and their impact. Each workshop had time set aside for participants to hear, directly from their teammates, about the impact their behavior was having.

It was in one of these sessions that the cocky participant described earlier received feedback about his body language. Participants heard it straight, and it was not easy. This was a critical first step to empowering these emerging leaders to own their own development. They are able to develop the necessary trust to go there with each other, even though they operate in a semi-static group, changing members every six months or so. With the help of a coach and facilitator, they expedite the trust and skills necessary to engage in this level of interpersonal dialogue.

Make Sure You Have a Good Coach

It takes time to get a group to the point where the members can have this level of dialogue on their own. A good coach facilitates the process by operating as lubricant in the cogs of a machine. On the skydiving team, Dr. Bob was there to take the rough edges off people's feelings after particularly difficult interactions. He would help us get unstuck and reflect on the feedback. He helped us see the interaction from other people's perspectives.

Once I was particularly stuck after a teammate told me he did not want to be pumped up just prior to exit. He needed to be calm and quiet instead and would appreciate it if I kept my pounding to myself. I did not understand this. I needed to pump myself up to perform well, and I was convinced everyone else did too. Apparently this was not the case, and Bob helped me see the situation from my teammate's point of view.

Teams of elite, high-performing individuals can accomplish amazing things. Yet convincing brash, high-potential talented individuals to subordinate their personal agendas for a common goal is not easy.

Real talk generates high-speed learning. Open, honest, and timely communication maximizes information flow and confronts individuals where they need attention. It is a challenging and uncomfortable practice that attracts high performers because it deals with reality and demands excellence.

Conclusion

Teams of elite, high-performing individuals can accomplish amazing things. Yet convincing brash, high-potential talented individuals to subordinate their personal agendas for a common goal is not easy. But it is possible, and it is being consistently pulled off by organizations that actively embrace the five leadership strategies described in this chapter:

- Share responsibility for the group's performance equally across the team. Each member on the world champion U.S. Skydiving Team took his turn in the leadership hot seat.
- Set high standards like West Point's Sprint football team did. Coach McIntyre built a legacy of high standards by recruiting for fit and cutting low performers.
- Establish respect in the early stages of team development like Steve Turner did. Steve was able to turn Lotus's elite software developers into a team by commanding respect through competence, direction, and strong character.
- Build in humility and an appreciation of difference by increasing self-awareness. Aetna's leadership development program is opening emergent leaders'

self-awareness through a series of challenging work experiences supported by coaching and a mentor program.

- Open up communication with real talk through feedback, debriefing processes, and interpersonal dialogue. The U.S. Skydiving Team reigned as world champions for eight consecutive years by turning communication into a core competency.

The U.S. Army, sports teams, and civilian business continue to search out the best performers and ask them to work collaboratively. They know what we all know: that successful teams of the best and the brightest will produce unprecedented results.

Keep in mind that high-performing teams built from elite talent are few and far between because talented individuals have little patience for inept team leadership. If you are going to put one of these teams together, consider carefully what you are doing, or your elite talent will eat you for lunch.

Notes

1. B. Corcoran, presentation at the Global Leadership Conference, U.S. Military Academy, West Point, N.Y., Nov. 12–14, 2003.
2. The information on Lotus 1-2-3 is from interviews with Bob Moore in December 2005.
3. Quoted in *FM 22-100: Army Leadership* (N.p.: Headquarters, Department of the Army, Aug. 1999), p. 1–2.
4. R. Maaddi, "Eagles Suspend Terrell Owens Indefinitely," *ABC News*, Nov. 5, 2005.
5. C. Shultz, "Into the Mind of Terrell Owens," n.d., www.TSN.CA.
6. Robert W. Eichinger, Michael M. Lombardo, and Dave Ulrich, *100 Things You Need to Know: Best People Practices for Managers and HR* (Minneapolis: Lominger, 2004).

CHAPTER NINE

LEADING AS IF YOUR LIFE DEPENDED ON IT

Thomas A. Kolditz

In situations where followers perceive their lives are threatened, leadership literally defines the promise of future life, and those at risk desperately seek capable leaders. Such high-risk situations are ideal settings to seek and find great leaders and to assess how they might be different from those who lead in more mundane contexts.

Colleagues and I have been studying authentic leadership under circumstances where the injury or death of followers must be actively avoided. We have found that men and women who lead other people in places and through situations that most of us would find intimidating, if not outright horrifying, will often behave in ways that may provide insights into our own leadership. We refer to such leaders and situations as *in extremis,* or "at the point of death."

This chapter describes in extremis situations and what characterizes the leaders who lead in those contexts. It is important to understand from the outset that examining leadership in these settings is not simply for trigger pullers or daredevils. Instead it is a way of recognizing one of the purest forms of leadership and using that recognition as a starting point for personal growth and development. Any leader can apply in extremis principles across many places and purposes. The life-or-death character of dangerous settings strips away the shallow veneer that all too often covers great leadership and management in our daily lives. Behind that veneer lies a rich array of insights about leadership, forged in the face of fear, and paid for with the blood of heroes.

What Is In Extremis Leadership?

We define *in extremis leadership* as giving purpose, motivation, and direction to people when there is imminent physical danger and where followers believe that leader behavior will influence their physical well-being or survival. In extremis leadership is not a leadership theory. It is an approach that views leader and follower behaviors under a specific set of circumstances—contexts where outcomes mean more than mere success or failure, pride, or embarrassment. Outcomes in in extremis settings are characterized in terms of hurt or healthy, dead or alive.

In extremis leadership differs from the popular concept of crisis leadership. In crisis leadership, the focus is on how leaders react when thrust unexpectedly into an extreme challenge, disaster, or circumstance. Crisis leadership is based largely on military history vignettes and corporate case studies that seem to support recommendations for leaders to communicate better, care more, and try to stay calm in the face of calamity. In contrast, in extremis leaders routinely and willingly place themselves in circumstances of extreme danger or threat and, more important, lead others in such circumstances as well. In short, in extremis leaders are self-selected; crisis leaders are not.

Many people live and work in dangerous settings: police officers, firefighters, soldiers, and mountain guides, to name a few. For leaders in such dangerous callings, the organizational outcomes, consequences, victories, or failures cannot be purchased, faked, or negotiated. The world of in extremis leaders is governed by forces of absolute power: physics, aerodynamics, fire, and weather occupy their physical domain. In the social domain, they face hatred, criminality, and war. Their place in the world is earned through competence, determination, and courage.

In extremis leaders are self-selected; crisis leaders are not.

It is nonetheless easy to ignore leadership in in extremis settings, which tend to be as dangerous for researchers as they are for the actors themselves. It is also easy to overlook in extremis leaders because they tend to be paid small wages, and their work tends to be either for the public good (as in police, fire, and military) or demanding, esoteric recreation (as in mountain climbing, skydiving, and other extreme sports). There are no strategic in extremis leaders with high-paying jobs and comfortable perks.

How We Learned About In Extremis Leadership

We have learned about in extremis leadership by watching, and sometimes living in, in extremis contexts. We sent participant-observers to the Special Operations Command Military Freefall School (HALO) in Yuma, Arizona, to conduct naturalistic observation of in extremis leaders who were participating in high-risk military training. We also conducted more than 120 in-depth interviews, taken across a range of leaders and followers, including the following:

- SWAT team chiefs from the New York City and San Francisco offices of the FBI
- Mountain-climbing guides from three states, including elite guides from the highly respected Exum Mountain Guides in Jackson Hole, Wyoming
- Leaders of jungle photographic expeditions, unarmed and in search of tigers
- The organizers of large formation skydiving record attempts
- Special operations soldiers
- The first armored cavalry commander to roll his tanks into the burning streets of Baghdad in 2003

We systematically studied the U.S. Military Academy's national champion parachute team, and we conducted comparative interviews with team leaders of conventional sports teams.

We also went to war: we interviewed thirty-six Iraqi prisoners of war (interviewed by translator) in field settings in Um Qasr, Iraq, during the initial hostilities there in April 2003. And we interviewed more than fifty U.S. soldiers and Marines during breaks from the fighting on the outskirts of al Hillah and Baghdad. All of the U.S. soldiers and Marines had had a peer killed in action in their unit in the thirty days prior.

We had to ensure that our mountain guides took clients on challenging climbs and were not simply climbing school staff. All of our interview participants were authentic in extremis leaders—the real thing. If we hoped to find truly unique outcomes, our investigation had to focus on a pure sample of truly unique individuals.

Characteristics of In Extremis Leadership

The goal initially has been to define in extremis leadership and to do sufficient exploration to define patterns of behavior for these leaders. In this early work, some unique patterns have emerged, which include the following characteristics of in extremis leaders:

1. Inherent motivation
2. A learning orientation
3. Shared risk
4. Common lifestyle

These characteristics clearly emerged in the findings and emerged poignantly in our interview transcripts. Other characteristics also emerged:

5. Competence
6. The ability to develop trust
7. Loyalty in an organization

Such characteristics are common among many types of good leaders, and this outcome serves to validate some enduring leader qualities. Competence, trust, and loyalty are leadership imperatives that span a variety of contexts.

As patterns emerge in the research findings and in the words of the in extremis leaders and their followers, a conclusion begins to take root: when it comes to matters of life and death, leadership assumes a recognizable form—the in extremis pattern. We look at these seven characteristics in more detail in the following sections.

Characteristics 1 and 2: Inherent Motivation and the Learning Orientation

We asked West Point athletes, mostly team captains and other leaders, to rank-order nine leadership competencies. The athletes fell into one of three categories: team sport athletes, individual sport athletes, or competition parachute team members.

The analysis compared high- and low-risk sports teams. The rank ordering of the leadership competencies was to represent the athletes' personal strengths in the context of their particular sport. We used the competencies endorsed by the Army in its current leadership doctrine, and the choices were presented in the array shown in Table 9.1.

As one might expect, for leader-athletes in both team and individual sports, the competency "motivating" was at the top of the list. After all, winning is about "farther, harder, faster." One might assume that in sports with risk to life, motivation would be even more important. Astonishingly, among the members of the national champion competition parachutists, "motivating" ranked second from the bottom. Instead, "learning" was first on the parachutists' list. Using interview

TABLE 9.1. THE ARMY'S NINE LEADERSHIP COMPETENCIES

Communicating	Displays good oral, written, and listening skills for individuals and groups
Decision making	Employs sound judgment and logical reasoning and uses resources wisely
Motivating	Inspires, motivates, and guides others toward goals and objectives
Planning	Develops detailed, executable plans that are feasible, acceptable, and suitable
Executing	Shows proficiency, meets standards, and takes care of people and resources
Assessing	Uses assessment and evaluation tools to facilitate consistent improvement
Developing	Invests adequate time and effort to develop individual followers as leaders
Building	Spends time and resources to improve teams, groups, and units and foster an ethical climate
Learning	Seeks self-improvement and organizational growth; envisions, adapts, and leads change

data to explore this counterintuitive finding, we discovered two characteristics of the in extremis pattern:

- In extremis contexts are inherently motivating. The danger of the context energizes those who are in it, making cheerleading much less necessary.
- The potential hostility of the context means that those who work there place a premium on scanning their environment and learning rapidly.

Those of us who lead in more ordinary contexts might do well to decide the relative importance of our own competencies.

Characteristic 3: Shared Risk

Another characteristic that sets in extremis leaders apart from other leaders is their willingness to share the same, or more, risk as their followers. This is partly true because they join their followers in challenging and dangerous circumstances. We found, however, such profound and consistent sharing of risk that it clearly stands out as a defining characteristic of in extremis leaders. Leaders themselves expressed powerful feelings about shared risk. For example, Special Agent James Gagliano, a SWAT team leader in the Federal Bureau of Investigation's New York City Office, said, "If you put the plan together and you're not comfortable being up there with a foot through the door, what the hell is up?"

Our research made clear that this shared risk was not merely a form of leader hubris, showboating, or simple impression management. Rather, it is part of the in extremis leader's style or technique. It profoundly affected the followers: they recognized it, knew what it represented in the hearts and character of their leader, and deeply respected their leader as a result. Conversely, soldiers who found their leaders to be unwilling to share the risk had little will and lost motivation, as in the case of this captured Iraqi soldier: "The leader was . . . a lieutenant colonel. An older man, forty-five, forty-six, forty-eight years of age. He was a simple person, but the instruction come from the command in Baghdad. Like, 'do this,' but he doesn't do that, and he ran away. . . . He told us if you see the American or the British forces, do not resist."

The common practice of providing business leaders with buyout plans, generous rollover contracts, or golden parachutes does little to inspire follower confidence. Certainly it puts business risk, compared to risk of life, in perspective. When performance means life or death, the best leaders do not wear parachutes unless their followers do too.

Characteristic 4: Elements of a Common Lifestyle

The fourth unique characteristic of the in extremis pattern emerged when we asked study participants about their remuneration and lifestyle. In an era where there are entire conferences devoted to executive compensation, it was refreshing to focus on authentic leaders who lacked materialism and instead focused on values.

For example, in the case of public sector employees like police officers and soldiers, the leader's pay and the followers' pay were unequal but uniformly modest. The leaders of the FBI SWAT teams were paid the same as other team members. We found that most in extremis leaders earn an average but sufficient wage. This made sense to us. In life-threatening contexts, pay should take a back seat to other concerns. Using the jargon of leadership scholars, transactional leadership is ineffective in in extremis settings. Instead, a values-based form of transformational leadership emerges and becomes part of the operating style of in extremis leaders.

Outside the contexts of military, police, and fire, the pattern of common lifestyle continues. People who live and work in dangerous environments learn to love life. They seem to live in a world where value is only loosely attached to material wealth. We believe that in extremis leaders accept, and even embrace, a lifestyle that is common to their followers as an expression of values and that such values become part of their presence and credibility as leaders.

Although many characteristics of in extremis leaders tend to set them apart from other organizational leaders, they also hold several characteristics that are widely exhibited by successful leaders across a range of contexts. We found that in extremis leaders, like most other leaders, are highly competent and engender loyalty and trust.

Characteristic 5: Competence

Followers demand leader competence, and nowhere is that more critical than in dangerous contexts. No amount of legitimate or legal authority is likely to command respect or obedience in settings where life is at risk, whether in a war zone or on the side of a mountain. This is the ironic contradiction of the common stereotype of the military leader—an authoritarian martinet who commands subordinates who must robotically obey. That is not how leadership in the military works, at least not the Army and the Marine Corps units we visited, and certainly not in combat. The average troop is likely to find court-martial to be a more attractive option compared to following the orders of an incompetent leader in a war zone. Only competence commands respect, and respect is the coin of the realm with in extremis settings. Consider this comment from one U.S. soldier in Baghdad in May 2003 about his leader: "He took charge every time that he needed to take charge. He was doing a hundred things while I am down there doing one thing. . . . He was overwhelmed, but he handled it very well. He did everything that he had to do. He maneuvered the troop or parts of the troop when nobody else was around to do it. He did more than you could ask of him."

No amount of legitimate or legal authority is likely to command respect or obedience in settings where life is at risk, whether in a war zone or on the side of a mountain.

Respect accrued from competence does not imply that in extremis leadership is merely technical or somehow emotionless or soft. Much to the contrary, dangerous settings often demand leadership styles that are unambiguous, pointed, and aggressive to the point of grating on followers. A Marine in Iraq in 2003 had this to say about his leader: "I don't like the guy. I don't know how to deal with him when we get off work, but as far as being a professional and being out there in the trenches, he is a great . . . squad leader. He [will do] the right thing, but sometimes it's a very unpopular thing, because he's the squad leader."

Leadership in dangerous contexts places heavy demands on leaders, who view virtually all outcomes as related to their personal competence and ability. These leaders work hard to achieve situational awareness and control. Yet the truth about in extremis settings is that awful things happen, often without warning and without leader competence casting a deciding vote. Nonetheless, the perception of control and personal efficacy is critical to the functioning of an in extremis leader. Imagine trying to accommodate feelings of inefficacy in a setting where effectiveness is the only link to life itself. In contrast to those who lead in settings that are benign enough to allow finger-pointing and denial of responsibility, these men and women tend to assume responsibility for outcomes, even when any objective observer would let them off the hook for circumstances obviously outside their control. Guy Wright, a professional skydiver and leader of Large Formation and World Record Skydiving Events, remembered his "worst day when . . . I was instructing some students, and got invited onto a larger skydive, . . . there was a [high-speed, midair] collision, a friend of mine was tumbling through the sky, and I went down and missed him, and he went in . . . that's a performance failure."

Competence is the building block for leader-follower trust relationships in in extremis settings. As one might expect, then, the competence exhibited by in extremis leaders must be, like their leadership style, authentic. Organizations run by appointed leaders without legitimate competence can muddle through mundane events, but will predictably crumble when pushed in a crisis that poses genuine threat. People in fear of their lives will not trust or follow leaders if they question their competence.

Organizations run by appointed leaders without legitimate competence can muddle through mundane events, but will predictably crumble when pushed in a crisis that poses genuine threat.

Characteristic 6: Trust

If competence is the building block of in extremis leadership, trust is the house. The leaders we interviewed often spoke of competence leading to trust relationships in dangerous contexts. In addition, it was made clear that such relationships were built quite deliberately. And, predictably, when such trust-based relationships were never built, organizational cohesion was nearly nonexistent with in extremis conditions.

A captured Iraqi soldier told this story: "The Mair Liwa [brigadier] left and went to his family. He was an authoritarian, and left everyone afraid of the other. Saddam made a situation where even a brother cannot trust his own brother. We don't trust anyone."

Characteristic 7: Loyalty

In extremis leaders sometimes have short-term relationships with their followers. Climbing guides, skydiving organizers, expedition leaders, and even astronauts can rapidly inspire trust and confidence among followers. In police, military, and fire departments, however, leaders have long-term associations with followers that can grow into deep loyalties. These loyalties are both personal and professional in nature. Such loyalty from followers is usually engendered by loyalty on the part of leaders. It has been well established in the leader development literature that loyalty is a two-way street. We found this point to be especially striking among in extremis leaders.

Only twenty-one days after he graduated from the Baghdad Military Academy in April 2003, a captured Iraqi lieutenant told this story: "I told them to go [flee from the fight]. Because there is an expression in Arabic, 'somebody is in my neck,' meaning I am totally responsible morally and especially morally for that person. These soldiers were in my neck; in other words, I was responsible for them. I am responsible for those people in front of guard, and I am not going to let them perish if I don't have to. I am not going to let them die for something that's not worthwhile." This comment by Special Agent Steve Carter, a senior team leader of the FBI SWAT in the San Francisco Office, resonated the same theme: "My personal heroes are the people I work with, many of the people I work with. . . . And they are motivated not by money and not by anything but the ultimate objective of doing something good for somebody else. And that's difficult to do, day after day."

Broadening the Exploration

As leaders, our most enduring legacy exists in the people we have led. We can build corporations, we can make loads of money, we can write books, we can name buildings after ourselves. In the end, for leaders, the only lasting effect is in the people we develop by giving them motivation, direction, and purpose. Competence, trust, and loyalty are all key in establishing the legacy of any leader, regardless of the nature of their organization or its mission.

The in extremis project is essential for exploring leadership under conditions of exceptionally grave risk. Those who lead in other circumstances may find the idea of in extremis leadership interesting or perhaps even useful. It takes some attentiveness and effort to peer into the soul of people led in times best forgotten and to understand fully what their leaders gave to them. For those of us who lead professionally, a look at in extremis leadership can be a magnifier, adding clarity and detail to what we already sense: that leaders can make anything possible, but without leadership, even basic tasks can seem insurmountable.

In Extremis Leadership Is Authentic Leadership

One of our researchers working in Afghanistan encountered an Army lieutenant colonel, a battalion commander. The officer had sensed that the soldiers in his command were shaken when two comrades were killed by an improvised explosive device on the streets of Afghanistan. He spoke with them before their next mission, but more important, he opted to accompany them on their next mission as a member of the squad, sharing risk, accepting the burden of their experience, and showing them the way while serving as a common participant—without usurping the authority of the actual squad leader.

In another example, Major General Eric Olson, commander of the elite 25th Infantry Division (Light), left the relative comfort of his headquarters in Bagram, Afghanistan, early Christmas morning and flew unannounced to one of his most remote bases. There he selected two junior soldiers who were getting ready to go out on patrol and sent them back to Bagram in his helicopter to relax, eat, and enjoy the holiday. Olson, along with his aide, took their place on patrol that day, riding exposed in the back of a Humvee with the infantrymen instead of receiving special treatment or perks as a general officer. The reaction to Olson's selfless action was immediate and positive, as one soldier remarked: "To sit in a cav[alry] truck in one of the worst seats and ride with us, to come and pull guard with us . . . makes lower enlisted soldiers like myself feel good about him as our leader." Both soldiers recently reenlisted in the Army.

Such leaders have worked their entire lives developing leadership skills in the worst environments imaginable, making them authentic. One of the most popular academic theories of leadership now emerging is called authentic leadership theory. One of its central precepts is that followers are attentive to, and able to recognize, a lack of sincerity or clumsy impression management strategies that someone trying to lead displays. Authentic leaders are confident, optimistic people, high in character, who are aware of their own thoughts, behaviors, abilities, and values. Many truisms such as "wearing their heart on their sleeve" or "what you see is what you get" are solid representations of authentic leaders.

Authentic leaders are also attentive to these same characteristics in other people. They can spot a phony or a fake or, more important, an inexperienced leader whose heart is in the right place but who needs more training. Because of this ability, authentic leaders make superb mentors. For real leaders, authentic leaders, optimism, hopefulness, and resiliency provide the key to understanding why leaders who are authentic are also effective at commanding follower loyalty, obedience, admiration, and respect.

It follows, then, that in circumstances where leader optimism, hope, and resilience are especially valued by followers, authentic leaders will assert a uniquely powerful influence. In dangerous situations where followers sense that their lives are threatened, feelings of optimism, hope, and resilience literally define the promise of future life and are therefore desperately sought by those at risk. This is the social dynamic in the life and world of in extremis leaders and followers. In extremis settings are ideal to seek and find authentic leaders, assess authenticity in leaders, and, especially, develop leaders. Researchers are beginning to study authentic leadership occurring at the point of death, or, more correctly, under circumstances where death must be actively avoided—in extremis, or, "at the point of death."

Authentic leadership theory and the notion of in extremis leadership are inextricably linked, because men and women who lead other people through life-threatening situations clearly behave in ways that are indicative of authentic leadership. To the delight of authentic leadership theory theorists, the in-depth study of these in extremis leaders is providing a research paradigm and insights for the development of authentic leadership.

Is In Extremis Leadership Values Based?

Since the term *values based* was first used to describe leaders and leadership, there has been much discussion as to which values apply. The definition of values that psychologists used in early work to measure American values was simply concepts to which people attached the most worth—for example, life, liberty, and the pursuit of happiness. In some circles, values-based leadership has come to mean conservative social values or even values concordant with religious beliefs. Interestingly, none of the in extremis leaders we interviewed in our study characterized themselves as religious (though about one-third regarded themselves as spiritual). It is apparent, however, that when they are in extreme danger, people place an enormous value on their own lives and often on the lives of others as well. Such circumstances are at the core of in extremis leadership.

> *The authentic qualities inherent in in extremis leadership place a much greater emphasis on experience as the way that values become embedded in character.*

Organizations that profess values-based leadership seek to find ways to embed such values in their leaders and followers. For example, General Electric uses a number of techniques, including a laminated values card, to ensure that GE employees understand the corporate values. The U.S. Army developed a values card in the late 1990s and paired it with a "values dog tag" that every soldier was to wear on a chain around his or her neck, along with the more familiar stamped metal identification tags.

There is, however, a fundamental flaw to these approaches: they lack authenticity. I recall watching several military formations and groups receive the "new" values. When the plastic dog tags were issued to soldiers, the event was often marked with howls of cynical laughter, and the cynicism was most apparent among soldiers with the most combat time and skill.

In the executive- or strategic-level leader development organizations captained by chief learning officers, the development of values seems to be cast as an issue of communication. The authentic qualities inherent in in extremis leadership place a much greater emphasis on experience as the way that values become embedded in character. One could argue, then, that in extremis leadership is the sine qua non of values-based leadership.

In extremis leadership has nothing to do with techniques. It is about authentic elements of the individual's character and the leader-follower relationship. Army leadership doctrine uses the "Be, Know, Do" framework to define the characteristics necessary of an Army leader. Recently Frances Hesselbein, chair of the board of governors of the Leader to Leader Institute, and former Army Chief of Staff Eric Shinseki released these ideas to the general public by capturing Army leadership doctrine in their book *Be, Know, Do: Leadership the Army Way*.[1]

In extremis leadership has nothing to do with techniques.

Originally the framework was quietly penned into the Army leadership manual by a young infantry major named Boyd M. "Mac" Harris in 1983. Harris, a former leadership instructor at West Point, wrote the "Be, Know, Do" concept to ensure that the Academy as an institution, and the Army as a whole, would recognize that in order for officers to be great leaders, they would not only have to have a set of skills and knowledge, but would also have to have genuineness of character. In other words, to be a leader is not to hold down a job; it is to develop a character inside one's self that is inextricably linked to giving purpose, motivation, and direction to others. This is authentic leadership. In dangerous settings, it takes on a unique pattern we have recognized as in extremis leadership.

In leading people, the degree of threat, risk, or danger is an important variable. The threat of death can have a powerful influence on human behavior. For example, in their study of soldiers during World War II, Samuel Stouffer and his colleagues found that when inexperienced soldiers sensed that their lives were threatened, they became desperate for almost any type of leader—in short, they wanted to see a leader as their key to survival.[2] If the individual is uncertain, aware of his or her own mortality, and the environment is hostile, the only real hope is a leader.

Among psychologists, an individual's enhanced awareness of death is termed *mortality salience*. Mortality salience has been manipulated in experimental studies by asking people to imagine in detail the circumstances of their physical death. Following the mortality salience manipulation, researchers sought to determine the characteristics that followers desire in a leader during these stressful moments. Research subjects in the studies we have reviewed clearly demonstrated a preference for charismatic, followed by task-oriented, and relationship-oriented leaders (based on ratings of leader communications). Charismatic leader messages powerfully influence people who have been recently focused on their own mortality. Mortality salience can have enormous impact when large groups of people are being led. When coupled with messages about specific events, it has been shown to directly influence political beliefs as well as voting behavior. Readers may recall a recent political tag line aimed at the search for a specific reason to invade Iraq: "Don't let the smoking gun be a mushroom cloud." Such statements are not mere attention getters; they are subtle suggestions that conditions are in extremis. Even the most subtle death threats can influence what people seek in terms of leadership.

Putting the Theory to Work: Developing In Extremis Leaders

For those of us who develop in extremis leaders, the developmental process is simple: coach junior leaders in in extremis settings, teach skills, help impart judgment, and keep people alive. Most extreme sports, and certainly police, military, and fire trainers, establish training standards and protocols to ensure that individuals develop competence and ability in a progressive, sequential fashion.

But serious leader developers in high-risk activities—particularly the pinnacle "trainers of trainers"—press beyond established doctrine to a higher level of development. Expertise tends to be high, and the experience of the individual leader developer dictates how development progresses. For example, in the formative years of sport parachuting, usually the person on the drop zone making the decisions and developing other drop-zone instructors was the person with the most jumps. Similarly, in the high-stakes merchant banking business, it used to be common for the biggest producer to be placed in charge of running the organization as well. As we learn more and more about organizational dynamics, it has become apparent that there are much better ways to develop leaders.

Sometimes a one-size-fits-all education and training approach is applied to in extremis settings. One of the primary reasons that the first studies in in extremis leadership were undertaken was the shared perception that the Army was basing many of its leader development policies and doctrines on routine, civilian education and training principles.

For example, the leadership competencies proposed in a recent draft of the Army's leadership manual were derived by contractors with only minimal military experience, and the words therefore reflect leader skills and abilities one might find in any large organization or bureaucracy. The one-size-fits-all approach is fine for the significant portion of the Army that is a bureaucracy, but such an approach holds minimal value for combat leaders. In addition, most of the combat leadership approaches were based on either historical anecdotes or expert testimonials. We thought that lieutenants headed for the battlefields of Iraq and Afghanistan deserved something more sophisticated and tailored to their needs.

If you work with people in high-risk contexts, whether in extremis settings or high-risk businesses, you should probably spend some time thinking about what that means, about how your work is unique, and how your leadership might vary as a result. Our research tells us (and we have always sensed intuitively) that in extremis settings place unique demands on leaders and followers. Leadership in these settings requires a modified approach, and the in extremis pattern represents our best and most current understanding of how to meet the unique demand.

Whether working with skydivers on the ride to altitude, challenging firefighters with a deliberately torched inferno, or taking SWAT police through a shooting house, make use of what we know about in extremis leadership by thinking through the principles uncovered in the research, as described in the following sections.

Competence

- *Remember that confidence, not just functional ability, is the goal of in extremis leader development.* Competence is the only basis for trust or loyalty. Therefore, it is not only important to the individual leader, but it is also an important perception that followers must have in order for the organization to solidify.
- *Always emphasize that trust has to be justly earned.* People who lead in in extremis settings have to be enormously humble and unassuming. Allow for plucky confidence because followers are inspired by it. Crush self-righteousness, cockiness, and arrogance because it will eventually be uncovered as false by followers and by the leader himself or herself, thereby undermining confidence. False pride has been the fatal flaw of many in extremis leaders.
- *Demand demonstrated flawless performance.* Training developers understand this fundamental approach to high-risk training, but the primary principles bear repeating. Because in extremis settings often require perfect execution the first time,

teach simple tasks to perfection, and chain them into complex tasks. Require twenty-five repetitions of physical tasks at a minimum. When possible, teach under safe conditions first, and then transfer the task to the in extremis setting.

• *Know when to pull the plug.* Development often means tolerating minor setbacks and coaching through failure. The same is true for the development of in extremis leaders, but only to a point. The person in charge of development must sense when failures are an indication of a persistent or dispositional flaw. At that point, the developmental path for that individual ends. And there should be no apologies.

The person in charge of development must sense when failures are an indication of a persistent or dispositional flaw. At that point, the developmental path for that individual ends.

Inherent Motivation

• *Manage arousal.* True in extremis settings provide ample motivation. Do not amplify anyone's excitement when risks are high. The best leaders exhibit their calmest and most level-headed demeanor when the circumstances are most dangerous. A leader with a highly aggressive motivational style can get people killed by causing initiative to be taken at the wrong time or in the wrong way.

• *Read other people.* Learn to assess when others are in touch with the degree of threat in their environment by watching their arousal, spirit, and motivation. There should be an intuitive match.

• *"Embrace the suck."* Soldiers who endured miserable environmental conditions during the second Iraq war coined a phrase to describe how to give over to the discomfort and be at peace: "Embrace the suck." When conditions are difficult or miserable but not necessarily dangerous, it is essential to motivate even the most dedicated individuals. As the person in charge, one cannot afford the luxury of self-pity in miserable circumstances. Deal with the misery (heat, rain, cold, filth, or fatigue, for example) intelligently and with some positive energy. If conditions are bad enough to be life threatening, do not hide that fact. Use the motivating qualities of mortality salience to push others beyond their perceived limits.

Learning Orientation

• *Be aware that the environment is trying to kill you.* When people are in touch with environmental threats, they focus outward. In development, foster and reward continual scanning and analysis of what is happening. Enacted sense making helps keep the leader and the led situationally aware, which contributes to survival.

- *Read other people.* Stay alert for signs in others that their attention is turning inward. For example, injuries should be completely ignored unless they are functionally debilitating. Worry or other emotionality is an indication that an individual is turning inward rather than maintaining focus outward and continuing to learn and piece together solutions to threat.

- *Share language.* Sharing a common understanding through language is key. In extremis environments are unique, and in every profession, sport, or activity involving high risk, there is a common terminology. Ensure that definitions are completely shared and commonly understood. Miscommunication kills learning, and it often kills people as well.

Shared Risk

- *Value selflessness.* Often highly competent and ambitious individuals are drawn to the challenge of high-risk activities. Recognize, reward, and foster selflessness, self-abrogation, sharing, and looking out for others. Self-absorbed loners and extroverted egomaniacs are not people who should be responsible for others in an in extremis setting.

- *Dissect risk management.* No one, leader or follower, can afford to take foolish or unnecessary risks in an in extremis environment. Risk management is a professional tool and a required organizational process. Ensure that everyone understands how risk decisions are made and the difference between a calculated risk and an ill-advised gamble. Immediately sort out and retrain individuals who make poor decisions or take uncalculated actions that threaten their lives and, especially, the lives of other people.

Common Lifestyle

- *Build a culture of passion and devotion.* We found that among in extremis leaders, working with people in high-risk settings seemed to displace more mundane concerns about material wealth or position. In extremis challenges are equalizers: fire, gravity, war, and weather place no value on social status or public image. The best in extremis leaders align their values with the challenges they face. Success is defined as excellence survival.

- *Explore motivations.* People who place themselves at risk, whether in a leader or follower role, have personal motivations for doing so. Experts learn to understand and explore these motivations with people. Is it sensation seeking? Ego enhancement? Other rewards? When you can deconstruct people's motivations, it is easier to coach them into the right frame of mind for the challenges they are accepting and the risk they are taking with their lives.

In Extremis Approximations

Leader developers should remain undaunted by the obvious challenges to leader development inherent to the concept of in extremis leadership. The most obvious challenge is that it is not practical to expose rank-and-file leaders to genuine danger in order to develop them. There is, however, some value in less-threatening activities, for example, the excitement of taking the team to a rock-climbing wall, a pistol range, or a paintball battlefield. All of these activities have been requested for corporate team building at West Point. These are enjoyable activities, to be sure, and although they are not physically threatening, the physical element helps participants sense the nature of leadership in in extremis settings.

The Outward Bound organization has expanded its developmental experiences into executive team development. Its approach is to use physically and mentally challenging experiences to teach leadership principles. Some individuals develop personal character through dangerous climbing or risky sports like parachuting from cliffs or buildings, extreme sailing adventures, or other extreme sports.

Organizationally, however, only public servants and extreme sport professionals consistently work in the settings with sufficient threat to make mortality salience a routine experience and in extremis leadership a way of life. Leadership characteristics developed in such a crucible cannot be purchased; they can only be earned through sustained effort, personal commitment, and risk to life. Difficult as the challenge of in extremis settings might be, an understanding of in extremis leadership shows leader developers the importance of authenticity and the in extremis pattern.

There is no easy road map to follow to create these same qualities in ordinary leaders.

Does Conventional Leader Development Fall Short?

Most of the popular leader development activities with which I am familiar fall far short of producing qualities in individuals that are also found among in extremis leaders. Skill-focused leader training is the most common leader development approach in use today, yet I would argue that it is only minimally compatible with the elements of in extremis leadership. In skill-focused leader training, the assumption is that a leader is the sum of his or her capability to perform tasks. In order to perform any task, an individual has to have knowledge of what needs to be done, the skills to perform the task, and the motivation to undertake the task and carry it through to completion.

For many years, training developers and human resource managers have focused on knowledge, skills, and abilities (KSAs) as a basis for employment and for constructing training programs and development programs intended to increase performance. The logic of such an approach is undeniable: KSAs can be objectively measured and tested to ensure that an individual has the capacity to perform work at a given level of performance. Assessments of KSAs can then be matched to job requirements in an airtight way of validating the capabilities of employees. Ideally, competence is increased, and the person being developed is therefore a better leader. (Recall that competence was found to be a fundamental characteristic of in extremis leaders.)

It takes time and powerful experience
to change the character of an individual.

Skill-focused training and the use of KSAs is popular in organizations. This popularity has a lot to do with the need for leader developers to demonstrate value added to organizational leaders. All leaders in a corporate environment hope for a predictable and measurable return on investment in any training or development. It is often a challenge to assess the value of leadership development in the short term. KSAs can show a connection between measurable outcomes and organizational goals. The assumption, then, is that after the leader learns the KSAs, the organization will perform better.

Interestingly, however, organizations often do not perform better after an increase in individuals' KSAs. Although there is a host of causes behind such an outcome, one simple reason is that even after skill training, an individual's fundamental character is so dominant in his or her leadership style that he or she simply reverts to his or her original ways of leading.

In other words, skill-based leader development may change what a person knows and what a person is capable of doing, but leadership is also about what one is—the "Be" component. It takes time and powerful experience to change the character of an individual. That is one of the advantages enjoyed by service academies: their character-building leader development immersion is forty-seven months long.

Another problem with the skills-focused approach is that it usually lacks any quality of inspiration. To inspire is literally to "fill the spirit." There is a spiritual quality to the moral obligation of an in extremis leader who assumes more risk than the person he or she leads. Inspiration is key to embedding qualities into an individual's character. When we are truly passionate and inspired about something, our fundamental character changes to match.

There is a spiritual quality to the moral obligation of an in extremis leader who assumes more risk than the person he or she leads.

The mission statement of the U.S. Military Academy is "to educate, train, and inspire the Corps of Cadets so that each graduate is a commissioned leader of character committed to the values of Duty, Honor, Country and prepared for a career of professional excellence and service to the Nation as an officer in the United States Army." The three verbs at the beginning of the statement—*educate, train,* and *inspire*—are commonly shared among many who seek to develop performance in individuals and by organizations. The best leader development—whether military, in extremis, or other forms of development—will achieve the best outcome if it capitalizes on all three elements of the mission. That means the ability to inspire people.

How to Develop In Extremis Leaders

Consider the following four approaches that the leadership department at West Point has used to add to the developmental preparation of budding in extremis leaders.

Develop Inspiration by Telling Stories

At West Point, if we want to develop motivation for future in extremis leaders to prepare fully for their combat roles, we could have them study graphs that depict how quickly they might experience combat, but a story is more inspirational.

For example, in 2002, West Point's cadet first captain (the top cadet in the Academy chain of command), Andy Blickhahn, graduated as a leadership major and immediately attended follow-on Army schools at Fort Benning, Georgia. He then reported for his first assignment in the famed 82nd Airborne Division at Fort Bragg, North Carolina. He was on station at Fort Bragg only seventeen days, much of his household goods still in boxes, before he boarded an aircraft destined for Iraq.

The new officer somehow found his platoon in the maze of Baghdad; it was pitch dark by the time he joined the team he was to help lead. Their mission was to conduct an attack across a bridge in the war-torn city. By midnight, Blickhahn's platoon was attacked and was experiencing offensive success against organized Iraqi forces.

Blickhahn later wrote about how strange it was when the sun came up and he saw the camouflaged faces of his platoon sergeant and his radio operator for the first time, having fought with them all night long. Until that moment, he had only their voices to personalize the relationship.

That inspirational story helps burn "be prepared" into the identities of emerging in extremis leaders. I know of no skill-focused approach that would have similar impact. If you are developing leaders, build poignant developmental exchanges into their organization's oral history, and design ways for the stories to be retold over time.

Develop Inspiration Using Technology to Link to the In Extremis

Leader developers often assemble panels of experts—highly successful CEOs, political leaders, and combat veterans—to share experience and inspirational stories. An example is the World Business Forum, a traveling assemblage of the world's most successful leaders, who speak on leadership and leader development. Such an approach has some merit, but it uses role models that show young leaders what we want them to be in ten or twenty years. People need to be inspired about what they will be this year.

Therefore, West Point instructors now arrange two-way video teleconferences between cadets and new lieutenants serving as leaders in Afghanistan, Kosovo, and Iraq. These unscripted video teleconferences provide students the ability to communicate directly with the people who are living and working in in extremis settings. The discussion has powerful meaning for the developing leaders, because the only questions asked are those the audience themselves compose. Young, ambitious people are incredibly inspired by seeing their in extremis futures, if only for an hour or so.

In most organizations, retention of personnel is a challenge, especially the retention of highly trained leaders. One of the principal reasons for turnover is that people find their expectations unmet. By using video teleconferences to transport our leaders to their future, we empower dialogue that creates realistic expectations about what service as an in extremis leader really means.

Develop Inspiration by Fusing Reality and Development

Recently the director of the Academy's principal leadership course, Colonel Donna Brazil, deployed to Afghanistan to lead real-world change. Her purpose was to assist in the establishment and development of a national military academy for Afghanistan. She returned with experience that took the class beyond the classic work by John Kotter and other scholars of organizational change, and she created a classroom drama about her struggle to assist a country in its own rebirth.[3]

In our class on leading organizations through change, the application of knowledge management principles fused with reality to form an important lesson in change. Leaders in in extremis settings must learn how to use lateral and hierarchical communication to share knowledge and learn rapidly because unshared knowledge may result in unnecessary deaths in combat. Rather than leave the principles of knowledge management untested and only loosely tied to current events, the change instructor, Major Pat Michaelis, deployed to Iraq as an agent of change. His mission was to design and implement a secure electronic knowledge management system for this twenty-thousand-person organization in an in extremis environment. But he remained the principal instructor in his class. Over several class periods, he contacted the class using satellite communications, and he helped guide the class discussion with real-time observations. In some cases, he was able to tape combat mission briefs, sanitize them for classified information, and e-mail them to the students as the combat played out in the streets of Baghdad.

Imagine the inspirational power of a trainee making a suggestion about knowledge management and having it tested by the organization in extremis, with feedback during the subsequent class. People are invariably inspired by the fusion of their developmental experience with the actual work of the organization. In the case of in extremis settings, abstract principles presented in a classroom or off-site are uninspiring by comparison.

People are invariably inspired by the fusion of their developmental experience with the actual work of the organization.

Develop Inspiration by Exceeding People's Expectations

Creative, determined leaders can help to span the gap between in extremis and more routine settings, and the effect is powerful. In the Academy's Leadership in Combat course, bringing the war to the classroom was daunting: no fieldwork had been done in this area since the oral histories of World War II and Korea. The solution was as simple as it was profound: send the instructor to the source.

In April 2003, as coalition forces fought their way into Baghdad, two instructors deployed to combat: one a professor of Arabic, the other a social psychologist—and both were leaders. They left the United States with only what they could carry in their rucksacks, and their goal was to update our knowledge of combat cohesion and leadership by interviewing captured Iraqi soldiers and U.S. soldiers and Marines. They departed Baghdad only after President Bush declared offensive operations had formally ended in May, and immediately on their return to the Academy, they coproduced a monograph for the course that captured the nature of cohesion and leadership in the two armies.

The powerful impact of this work in the class was only partly due to the new content about in extremis leadership and the dynamics of cohesion in combat. Although the content of their work had value, an important secondary impact was inspirational: the future in extremis leaders taking the class understood that their professors assumed significant personal risk to enrich learning in the classroom. Their expectations were profoundly exceeded.

In Extremis Lessons for Business and Life

When the search to understand in extremis leadership began, the assumption was that this was a unique form of leadership, suited primarily to the rigors of extreme sports, combat settings, and actions in the face of disaster. It is, after all, the conscious recognition of the threat of death, the salience of an individual's mortality, that gives rise to the changes in leader and follower behavior typified by the in extremis pattern. Business risk is about the loss of money, not the loss of life. In businesses that do involve some physical risk, the mitigation is procedural and actuarial. Therefore, there was no intention of—and even some contempt for—a business interpretation of in extremis leadership.

But isn't it interesting that most people would call a threat to their pension arrangements a threat to *life* savings rather than career earnings? For individuals, "life savings" and "saving lives" both connote grave interests (pun intended). There are compelling parallels between leadership in in extremis settings and leadership in elite business organizations that engage in high-risk enterprises with large amounts of capital.

In fact, the study of authentic leaders in in extremis settings has significant value when applied to business practice. Authentic leadership, with its emphasis on the development of hope, resilience, and optimism, gets at the heart of what is important to followers, whether their aspirations are physical, social, or material. Authentic leaders, whose behavior often reveals a heightened moral and ethical perspective, earn the trust of followers who interpret their motives in a positive way.

In business management circles, leadership is sometimes inappropriately treated as merely a skill or ability, a mechanical array of actions to increase the effectiveness of individuals and consequently improve the performance of the organization. Such an approach is inherently transactional because the primary motivation is known to be profit based, and as a result it does not work very well. In contrast, leadership in in extremis settings exemplifies how people in organizations can move beyond purely transactional relationships. By comparison, coercive leaders or policy-oriented managers are eventually rendered ineffective by the seriousness of the circumstances. Bonuses or promises of other tangible rewards are less relevant when it comes to putting one's life in the hands of a leader. Why should people tolerate lesser leadership in matters outside dangerous environments?

---

*Competence is as much the coin of the realm
in business as in in extremis settings.*

The primary focus of both the leader and the led in in extremis settings is the preservation of life and success at the task or mission. Business leaders who find it difficult to make the transition from transactional to a more authentic transformational leadership approach may gain both understanding and inspiration from in extremis leader role models. Learning how such leaders operated in in extremis environments can provide some important lessons that can be applied to some of the stressful challenges facing leaders today, even if the risks are not of a physical or life-threatening nature.

Some of the parallels are obvious. Competence is as much the coin of the realm in business as in in extremis settings. One of my favorite, most accomplished, and successful acquaintances made millions in merchant banking, but virtually all of his gains were the result of his own competence and ability in a job where there was not much in the way of guaranteed salary. He referred to his circumstances as "eat what you kill." It is an in extremis metaphor to be sure, but the point is that elite business has an unforgiving character, much as a dangerous environment does. Competence is the price of entry for anyone hoping to take a leadership role.

Elite businesspeople live in a world where trust is a precious commodity and can be an advantage worth millions of dollars in predicting business outcomes. Under conditions where deals may result in profits and losses of such magnitude that lives are changed forever, it makes sense that in extremis principles apply. The unique in extremis pattern of inherent motivation, learning orientation, shared risk, and common lifestyle may never be as universal as competence, trust, and loyalty among most organizational leaders. The unique pattern emerges from a context that most of us either do not care to inhabit or visit on only rare occasions. Yet there are lessons with broad applicability that can be learned from in extremis leaders. Following are seven important leadership lessons for leaders in all walks of life that were uncovered, or underscored, by studying in extremis leadership.

For an average leader, motivation is a way to make people work harder. For an outstanding leader, motivation is a way to help people work smarter.

Lesson 1: Motivation Is Most Powerful When Paired with an Emphasis on Learning

Remember how the parachute team leaders mentioned earlier in this chapter focused on learning rather than motivation in their inherently motivating in extremis circumstances? When leaders find themselves among followers who are highly motivated for any reason—dire threat, tremendous opportunity, earnest obligation—leaders should not rest in the comfort caused by the followers' excitement and dedication.

Instead, the leader should pay extra attention to precursors to learning, such as awareness of the environment, creativity, critical thinking, and outcome analysis. Focus the motivated crew on new solutions, impossible problems, and unresolved issues. For an average leader, motivation is a way to make people work harder. For an outstanding leader, motivation is a way to help people work smarter.

Lesson 2: Sharing Risk Enhances Credibility and Can Improve a Leader's Effectiveness in Risky Situations

In extremis leaders place more value on taking care of their clients, followers, soldiers, and citizens than they place on their own comfort, personal safety, or ability to accumulate wealth. These are the leaders people seek when the stakes are at their highest. To be the best leader you can be, especially in a high-stakes game, you will gain the most trust and loyalty by demonstrating in tangible ways that both risk and reward are distributed fairly in the organization and that much of the risk is your own.

People often make sense of their environment by comparison to the reactions of others. That includes reading both the expressions and the actions of others, especially leaders. In in extremis settings, the principle is taken to an extreme. For example, both SWAT teams and the more recreationally oriented parachute teams frown on tinted eyewear or tinted goggles. When noise or other circumstances limit oral communication, it is an advantage for team members to read the gravity of a situation by focusing on the eyes of peers, superiors, and subordinates. In the same way, the willingness to assume personal risk is an unmistakable nonverbal cue that the leader has confidence in a given course of action and is willing to put as much on the line as the people he or she is leading.

Lesson 3: Your Lifestyle Reveals to Your Followers What You Value

The common lifestyles led by in extremis leaders broadcast an important and unmistakable message to followers: "I'm not in this role for my personal gain." But the issue is not how much money the leader makes. Leader expressions of humility influence followers in much the same way. Such messages are enormously powerful because they reflect the leader's lack of ego investment and willing commitment to followers and the organization, establishing a basis for trust and loyalty.

Mediocre leaders who nonetheless seek organizational effectiveness sometimes develop a variety of impression management strategies to appear selfless, concerned, and humble. Among outstanding leaders, however, selflessness and humility are internalized, that is, part of their character; they are characteristics, not techniques. Such characteristics are not merely things a leader should do. They represent instead what a leader must be. This is one of the major vulnerabilities of leader development training that focuses solely on KSAs. Skills such as decision making, communicating, or planning may simply manifest (albeit in more effective ways) the character one already has.

Recently a principal in a well-known bank told me that the bank's leadership personally endorsed a set of values, but he could not see how they could work because virtually everyone he knew was motivated solely for personal gain. He felt that the leaders who were espousing corporate values had no idea that there was little or no loyalty in the organization. Whether in routine or dangerous settings, it is disconcerting for the rank and file to believe that their leaders are out of touch. It is important that all leaders take the time to connect with the life experiences of the people they are leading. If one's lifestyle reflects values, then a common lifestyle reflects common values, the key to resilient, high-functioning organizations.

Lesson 4: When You Develop Competence, You're Also Developing Trust and Loyalty

The seriousness of in extremis circumstances reveals the importance of competence in the establishment of trust and loyalty. Competence has always been recognized as a valued leader attribute, and trust and loyalty are obviously important leader-follower relationships.

The real lesson, however, is that the three are inextricably intertwined and sequential, with competence coming first. Leaders who find that their followers do not trust them or are not loyal usually take it very personally, almost like a social rebuff. Leaders who wish to build trust and loyalty often turn to social events like golf, off-site meetings, or other team-building activities. Leader competence is often at the root of loyalty and trust problems, and it cannot be fixed with a trip to a rock climbing school. Use care to identify the root cause of trust and loyalty issues, and never forget that competence may be the essential, if not sufficient, characteristic of a great leader.

A corollary to this principle is when you demonstrate competence, you are developing trust and loyalty. Most leaders have gotten to their station in life through their own competence, but that becomes lost on followers unless the competence is occasionally revealed by action. Take the time and effort to show followers what you are good at and why they should be confident in your ability as a leader. Use care, however, never to upstage or embarrass someone else as you demonstrate competence. In the end, leadership is about the success of your people, not about you.

Lesson 5: Extreme Threat Reveals the True Character of Leaders and Followers

Our observations about the disintegration of the Iraqi Army provide an excellent example of how the ability to lead successfully can change in an instant when the stakes go up. In the sample of Iraqi prisoners who offered us oral histories, surrender decisions were usually made at very low levels and usually in response to immediate threat—a bomb dropping, an artillery strike, or a tank appearing on the horizon, for example. Surrender plans were usually composed among small groups of soldiers and were never attributed to the capitulation of a higher headquarters. Officers permitted their organizations to surrender—sometimes by their own desertion, sometimes by benign neglect.

The ability of Iraqi small unit leadership to invoke loyalty and influence up and down the command chain was almost completely lacking and unquestionably contributed to their disintegration in the face of advancing U.S. forces. In other words, the leaders did not surrender their Army. The Army surrendered out from under their leaders.

The important lesson is that how people act when things look bad is an indication of their fundamental relationship with their organization and their leadership. Adversity unifies a strong team and destroys a weak one. Leaders must become adept at reading individuals when the stakes are high, and especially when the future appears dim.

It should come as no surprise that further conversation revealed that if Iraqi soldiers had emotional ties, they were almost always with soldiers from their tribe or region, not with their military organization. Squads and platoons had little or no cohesion. Iraq's approximately 150 major tribes comprise more than two thousand smaller clans, with a wide range of religions and ethnic groups. Soldiers spoke of units divided by tribal or regional differences.

Lesson 6: Followers Care About What You Bring to the Table Today; Your Résumé Is Irrelevant

"Other people's money" is a proxy for "other people's lives." Make use of the life-altering quality of your business or your actions as a form of inspiration for yourself and your followers. Remember that for followers, as the importance of the leadership task increases, the relevance of what you have done in the past decreases. You are not a leader unless others depend on you for purpose, motivation, and direction. That phenomenon is about the here and now—and the future.

Lesson 7: Most Leaders Are Blind to Their Dependence on Mere Positional Authority, Rather than Leadership, Until a Threat Emerges

On March 19, 2003, the day before the U.S. Army left Kuwait and headed north across the sands of Iraq toward Baghdad, the Iraqi leadership was, by its own assessment, fully in charge of its own Army. Interviews in the in extremis setting uncovered no evidence of higher-order concepts, such as nationalism or the obligation to withstand an invasion.

Instead, the near universal theme was that Iraqi regular Army soldiers were motivated by coercion. The term *Sumoud* means "withstanding" or "steadfastness" in Arabic and is a common value in Arab culture, yet this value was not demonstrated by the Iraqi soldiers we spoke to. Their behavior was driven by fear of retribution by party loyalists if they did not complete their soldier duties and punishment by the Baath Party, or *Fedayeen Saddam,* if they avoided combat. Iraqi soldiers related stories of being jailed or beaten by Baath Party representatives if they were suspected of leaving their units, and they universally deserted with their weapons in hand to fight through death squads to their rear—unmistakable evidence of coercion because the weapons also made them targets of U.S. forces, despite their willing desertion.

If you lead a business or an organization, how much of your ability to lead is based on positional authority rather than people's desire to be on your team and to accomplish common goals? If you cannot answer that question, it makes sense to assess your influence until you can. It is a rare leader who can organize people with minimal dependence on the basic tools of human resource management: remuneration, reward, working conditions, job security, benefits. But every leader's goal should be to retain a functional organization through circumstances where those advantages are threatened or nullified.

Being easygoing is not the answer. Most of the Iraqi prisoners of war enlisted soldiers described their officers as distant but usually not threatening. In truth, many officers were politically appointed and not regarded as tactically competent by their men. Iraqi soldiers reported the common practice of constantly asking (and sometimes bribing) their officers for permission to go home to their families for ten days out of every month. Such circumstances led to little mutual respect between officers and the enlisted soldiers, even though their relationship was far from intimidating and sometimes even friendly or pleasant.

Surprisingly, fear of retribution was usually not attached to leaders serving in Iraqi units. Several prisoners reported that if their officers had tried to force them to fight, they would have simply killed them and surrendered anyway.

Leaders should endeavor to make organizations work independent of the transactional, managerially imposed motivations for people to come to work. Such strategies collapse once the organization is threatened.

Conclusion: The Best Leaders Want to Be Leaders with Passion

Consider the challenge and depth of commitment assumed by people who serve as in extremis leaders, particularly those in public service. Most of us would agree, almost without thinking, that police officers, firefighters, and military leaders are worthy of respect. It takes some intellectual work, however, to probe the depths of their commitment and understand how it influences followers. No client ever wondered if his or her guide was drafted into the sport. If you play a role in choosing leaders for your organization, choose people who want to lead, not just those who wish to advance.

Notes

1. F. Hesselbein and E. Shinseki (eds.), *Be, Know, Do: Leadership the Army Way* (New York: Leader to Leader Institute, 2004).

2. S. A. Stouffer and others, *The American Soldier: Adjustment During Army Life* (Hoboken, N.J.: Wiley, 1949).

3. J. Kotter, *Leading Change* (Boston: Harvard Business School Press, 1996).

CHAPTER TEN

CREATING URGENCY AND INSPIRING YOUR TEAM

Robert Morris

On September 11, 2001, the enemy attacked us. My rifle company was engaged in a war game exercise on the island of Oahu, and our opposition had used the cover of darkness to try to penetrate our defensive position. At 3:30 A.M., the company leadership had gathered to plan our counterattack when my radio operator interrupted me. "Sir," he implored, "you are needed on the radio. I think it is important." Although I heard the radio operator, the urgency of our planning process muted his request. Our company was on the verge of accomplishing a demanding mission for which we had been preparing for the past six months. At the outset of this half-year journey, that same company could not even account for its equipment; this exercise was an important step in our growth and a vital piece of our organizational change effort.

Frustrated by the interruption but influenced by the persistence of my radio operator, I finally heeded the call. Higher headquarters ordered me to increase our security to 100 percent (every soldier at the ready), go to Force Protection Condition (FP-CON) Black, and prepare for follow-on orders. When I returned to my planning session, my first sergeant (the senior sergeant in the company) asked me what was going on. "I don't know," I replied. "They want us at 100 percent security and FP-CON Black. I guess they can't hear the weapons firing over here." No one knew what FP-CON Black entailed, so we continued planning without much thought about the radio call until my first sergeant interrupted us. "Damn!" he exclaimed, after consulting our field training guide. "FP-CON Black means that a real-world terrorist strike has occurred on U.S. soil!" Silence engulfed the group, followed by a barrage of cell phone chatter erupting from the wood line.

In the early stages following 9/11, few military commanders had trouble motivating their units. Urgency was not just a buzzword; it was a way of life as we prepared for an uncertain future. We found that functional organizations with the right systems and procedures in place prior to the attacks faced less turmoil during the preparation for deployment in the aftermath. At the time, I served as a company commander responsible for more than two hundred soldiers and more than $40 million worth of equipment. I had seven years of experience serving on and leading teams, and I had already commanded a smaller company of 130 soldiers. I had never, however, led a change effort like the one in which we were engaged at that time. Our company had been struggling for months to develop systems and organizational discipline, and we were far from perfect. But perfect or not, we had to be ready.

As the result of this change journey and the impact of that attack on our country, I learned many lessons, both good and bad, about building a motivated team.

My First Lesson in Motivation: People Need Focus and Direction

On March 31, 2001, I stood before Lieutenant Jeff Fair, a key member of my new team, with a pit in my stomach. It was 10:00 P.M., and I was scheduled to take command of a headquarters and headquarters company (HHC) in Schofield Barracks, Hawaii, at 10:00 A.M. the next morning. Jeff and I were outside the mess hall, trying to account for our equipment (a task that had been ongoing for about five weeks), but we were still missing several items. The pit in my stomach grew as I realized that we were not going to meet the deadline. There was nothing I could do in the next twelve hours to prevent us from postponing the ceremony, and it physically sickened me.

Although the legal responsibility for this event fell on the outgoing commander (who was not even around), I felt responsible. I felt like a failure; there were a lot of people invested in this event. I thought about the ceremony and the soldiers, all of whom had been released for the day by their supervisors. All that remained was to sign for the company's equipment; however, I could not sign for equipment that was missing. And I could not find missing equipment if there were no soldiers around to produce it. Where was the company? And what was the deal with their lack of concern for meeting this deadline?

*There was no real sense of urgency within the company
about finding the missing equipment. No one else in the
company seemed to care about the deficiencies. Yet the company
could not operate to standard if it did not even have the tools
and equipment necessary to perform its assigned tasks.*

A typical HHC consists of about two hundred people and several diverse operating units, each ranging in size from a three-person intelligence staff to a scout platoon with thirty soldiers. The leader for each unit is an experienced officer or noncommissioned officer (NCO), and all should have known their responsibilities for accomplishing the inventory. In fact, because the HHC supports more than five hundred soldiers, we select the best officers and NCOs from within the battalion (about five hundred people) for its leadership. That none of them was present to resolve the last-minute issues with the inventory concerned me very much.

Jeff was physically and mentally exhausted from all of the hard work he put into the inventory. Disappointed in the process, I tried to figure out the best way to inform my boss that we would have to postpone the change of command. I felt bad for Jeff, who was extremely competent and one of the hardest-working people I have ever met, because he was new to the company as well. Jeff had been sent to the team specifically to fix the company's declining administrative and logistical systems prior to this change of command. For the last month, we had worked together to locate and count every piece of equipment in the company, and we knew there were extensive accountability problems that neither of us could fix alone.

*I felt that the company's poor performance resulted from a motivation
problem rather than a competency or training issue. These same folks
performed well in other units, and I had personally observed them
accomplish tasks during training exercises. Over time, I found that many
of them were motivated and just needed focus and direction.*

Although Jeff had informed our headquarters of the property issues as they arose, everyone, including me, thought we could work it all out in time for the ceremony. Aside from Jeff's, there was no real sense of urgency within the company about finding the missing equipment. This is what bothered me even more than the lack of property accountability itself: no one else in the company seemed to care much about the deficiencies.

We postponed the change of command three times after that night because of missing equipment, and the outgoing commander was fined about four thousand dollars due to negligence. Even after we delayed the changeover, few people stepped up to fix the problems. When the change of command finally happened, one of my peers remarked: "Look at the bright side, Rob. The company has nowhere to go but up." Left with a demoralized executive officer and a disorganized staff, I had only a long four-day weekend to figure out how to lead that company.

Because the Army has a formalized training and promotion program and every leader in the company was experienced, I felt that the company's poor performance resulted from a motivation problem rather than a competency or training issue. These same folks performed well in other units, and I had personally observed them accomplish tasks during training exercises. Without this inside look at the company, I would have never guessed the magnitude of the accountability problem.

I quickly decided to focus my energy toward motivating the company leaders to meet their full potential. Captain Bruce E. Grooms, the eighty-first commandant of midshipmen at the U.S. Naval Academy (USNA), stated at the fifth annual USNA leadership conference that his thirty-year career as a submarine leader had taught him that on any team of ten people, usually two of them accomplish about 80 percent of the work, six probably account for 20 percent of the work, and two drag the team down. Grooms claimed that the leader's job is to figure out how to motivate that middle 60 percent of the team to operate at the level of those top performers, which would usually bring the bottom performers up a level and improve overall team effectiveness.

My experience in HHC was consistent with his observation, as time revealed that many of the people were motivated and just needed focus and direction. Others required quite a bit more attention, and we ultimately had to transfer some of them or separate them from the Army. As we will see, my early efforts focused on the bottom 20 percent of the company: those we ultimately transferred and separated. The tools that follow aim to help build a complete team of inspired people who will operate at their optimum potential for the organization.

If the goal is to influence subordinates to accomplish organizational goals and improve the team, then leaders must build relationships strong enough to inspire their subordinates to rise above challenging and unforeseen circumstances.

Influencing Others: Start by Building Strong Relationships

Leadership is influencing people—by providing purpose, direction, and motivation—while operating to accomplish the mission and improving the organization.

—FIELD MANUAL 22–100, *MILITARY LEADERSHIP*

There are as many definitions of leadership as there are people who write on the topic. In fact, history has shown that defining leadership is almost as difficult as exercising it. Many scholars and practitioners would agree that leadership involves some basic components: interaction with people, influence or persuasion, and goal accomplishment. The Army's definition of leadership states that leaders must influence people to not only accomplish the mission, but also to improve the organization. Therefore, I add a fourth component on which to focus this discussion: improvement, or change. It is the job of every leader, military or otherwise, to influence others to accomplish goals and develop his or her organization.

Building Relationships Is the Bedrock Competency of Leaders

We could survey fifty effective leaders and find that each possesses different personality traits and leadership styles. Regardless of style or personality, a significant factor in most modern leadership models is the idea that a leader must build relationships with his or her followers. If the goal is to influence direct reports to accomplish organizational goals and improve the team, then leaders must build relationships strong enough to inspire their subordinates to rise above challenging and unforeseen circumstances.

Although the strength of relationships between leaders and followers does not necessarily dictate mission accomplishment, it does often influence follower commitment. As a military leader, I strive for commitment so that my subordinates will perform in tough situations almost without thinking. In this case, I saw the company's lack of commitment to meeting a simple, nonthreatening change-of-command deadline as an indicator of how it would perform in more demanding situations.

Organizations may have strikingly different goals. For example, an investment firm may focus on building wealth for its clients, whereas a police station focuses on providing security for the community. Although the leaders in each of these very different organizations will encounter challenges unique to their professions, they will also deal with similar challenges. For example, the leaders in each of these organizations must motivate their subordinates toward accomplishing core organizational goals. This clearly requires the leader to engage with people, which is where relationship-building skills become critical.

Each leader must also adapt his or her organization as the environment dictates. This requires relationship skills, as we cannot expect any leader to independently read the environment and predict needs for change. The ability and courage to surround oneself with great people, even people who may be better than the head leader, often propels organizations to operate at top levels. For these reasons, I consider relationship building a critical competency for all leaders. Later in this chapter, I discuss how to develop some of those critical skills and motivate teams to accomplish organizational goals and improve the organization.

People Are the Mission

Every leader struggles with the issue of motivating people. I have told the story of my HHC change of command to friends and colleagues who invariably ask, "Why didn't you just force them to produce the equipment? You are in the Army!" If leadership were only that easy. Have you ever missed a deadline or sales objective or lost a game because someone on your team did not pull his or her weight? How did you solve the problem? The resolution strategies range from firing someone to doing nothing. Most of us probably choose some middle ground, either formal or informal counseling, unless there is obvious negligence or ethical misconduct involved. I would argue that few leaders struggle with firing negligent or criminal employees, so I am going to focus on the more nebulous issue involving poor team performance: motivating subordinates.

During my first few months as the HHC commander, I dealt with the company almost as if it was one entity with a motivation problem. If one section within the company did not meet expectations, I called in all of the leaders to discuss company improvement strategies. I spent hours with the company leadership discussing our shortfalls, and I thought my personal involvement and group tactics were building a better team. By involving everyone in the process, I was trying not to single anyone out, and we moderately improved. I failed to realize, though, that I actually hampered progress for some.

It is impossible to build meaningful relationships with a large group. Leaders must build valuable relationships with each person in that group.

One day, my most competent leader asked me to transfer him to a new unit. He was the scout platoon sergeant, and I had handpicked him for that job.

Shocked by his request, I asked him to explain why he wanted to leave. Simply put, he was unhappy with the fact that he worked diligently to improve his platoon, yet I still treated him the same as I treated other leaders within the company who failed to meet the unit goals. In effect, I had crushed his motivation with my "We're in this together" approach.

Looking back on this experience, it seems ridiculous that I could have made such a basic leadership mistake. There are two key lessons that all leaders can learn from this.

First, to build effective relationships, leaders must be self-aware. I have been told that I wear my emotions on my sleeve. As a young lieutenant, my company commander told me several times to give him "facts, not emotions." I was fired up about the company's poor performance during the change-of-command inventories and held the unit leaders collectively responsible. My anger and embarrassment from that woeful event carried over for months until that confrontation with my seasoned platoon sergeant. My emotions clouded my ability to recognize the good individual performance within the company, and there were several people doing great things every day. By knowing yourself, you can better leverage your strengths and compensate for known weaknesses.

To build meaningful relationships, know yourself and maintain a three- to five-person span of control.

The second lesson is that it is impossible to build meaningful relationships with a large group. Groups consist of two or more people, and leaders must build valuable relationships with each person in that group. Almost every leadership and managerial training program emphasizes the span of control. Clearly chief executives who run companies with thousands of people cannot cultivate meaningful relationships with each employee, but they can connect with their key leaders: the chief financial officer, the chief learning officer, and the others at the top.

The hierarchical structure of almost every organization within the Army facilitates a three- to five-person span of control. Because I felt we were in a crisis, I tried to control the situation by dealing with groups of people. I knew I had only a year to turn the company around (September 11, 2001, actually shortened that time line), and I wanted to address problems in the most efficient manner possible. I allowed the pressure of time to alter my judgment, and that confrontation with my trusted scout leader influenced me to refocus on building my team by first developing meaningful relationships with my senior leaders.

*Each individual is motivated differently, based on his or her
values, human growth needs, and personal situation. The leader
must correctly assess and identify subordinates' motivational
needs to motivate them to accomplish group goals.*

Building Your Motivated Team

Have you ever heard someone say, "This team has no sense of urgency"? Nevertheless, someone on the team has a sense of urgency, or that person would not make this statement. More likely, when you hear a statement like this, it indicates that everyone on the team is not focused in the same direction. Each individual is motivated differently, based on his or her values, human growth needs, and personal situation. Therefore, it is up to the leader to correctly assess and identify subordinates' motivational needs to motivate them to accomplish group goals.

It is not enough to just accomplish periodic goals; we want to establish a climate in which the team develops over time and adapts to the shifting environment. To change or improve organizations, our team must identify with and adopt our values and long-term organizational objectives. The ultimate goal is to have subordinates who share our passion for growth and aggressively solve problems before they get to our level. In essence, we want them to get that sick feeling in their stomach at the thought of failure, predict shortfalls in our strategy, and offer resolution strategies that put us on the right course. In the beginning, many of the leaders in the HHC lacked this drive, but the techniques I describe next helped us accomplish goals and improve the company.

Shared Leadership: Surround Yourself with Great People

During my four years as a cadet at West Point, many of my instructors and mentors often said, almost regrettably, that it is lonely at the top, referencing the legal responsibility that accompanies leadership positions at the various command levels in the Army. Commanders have a lot of power, and they can exercise it to promote and reward or, at the other extreme, confine subordinates when necessary. Unique to my profession and other select service-oriented professions is the possibility that a commander will have to order subordinates to carry out missions that may result in their deaths.

That responsibility can be a lot to bear, but I often wondered how to mitigate the feeling of loneliness that I had heard so many officers reference. I have investment banker friends who manage multibillion-dollar accounts, and a simple math mistake can cost their clients hundreds of thousands or even millions of dollars in investments. I imagine that kind of pressure and responsibility creates similar feelings of loneliness. The key to mitigating that pressure, and decreasing the possibility of making a costly decision, is surrounding yourself with great people and sharing leadership with them.

My father-in-law, a former Army officer and current corporate leader, advised me when I entered the Army to surround myself with great people. I have heard it many times since then, but I often see leaders neglect to do this for various reasons. Some are too proud to admit they do not have all the answers; others feel threatened at the potential of having smarter, younger executives around them. But the benefits of surrounding yourself with energetic, competent people far outnumber the possible disadvantages.

I have also seen leaders attempt to surround themselves with good people, only to choose poorly and actually handicap the organization. The key is to pick the right people: people who complement your leadership style and can help you make the right decisions for the team.

Immediately following the HHC change-of-command ceremony, my boss approached me and said, "Let me know what you need to turn this ship around." Within a month, I had new leaders in four of the seven key leadership jobs, and I selected each person only after carefully considering what qualities they brought. For example, I chose Lieutenant Faulkner to be my executive officer, because he was an experienced soldier who had previously served as a supply specialist for the elite Army Rangers. His knowledge and experience in dealing with logistical systems far surpassed my own, and I needed his experience to overcome our equipment and accountability problems.

My senior NCO, First Sergeant Selman, is probably the most competent leader with whom I have had the privilege to work. Not much for fanfare, he kept his office wall almost bare except for a picture of him and his squad sitting on Manuel Noriega's couch during the 1989 invasion of Panama. He was quiet and unassuming, and the soldiers in the company respected him for his experience. Although I had been in good units, I lacked the combat experience required to earn the level of respect he had from the company. The other leaders equally contributed strengths needed to improve their respective areas, but the one commonality among all of them was that I trusted each one of them implicitly.

I shared the leadership of HHC that year with my key leaders and never felt lonely in the job. I made tough decisions, and I bore the sole responsibility for those decisions, but I always consulted my team. Let me be clear here: you cannot share your assigned responsibility; you must bear that alone. Instead, sharing leadership with others means that you consult them on decisions, empower them to make decisions in your absence and take responsibility for their choices, and, most important, trust them to do what is right for your people and the team. Sometimes they act differently from how you would in the same situation. That is part of the deal. Remember that you chose them because they complemented your style, not because they mimicked you.

Surround yourself with great people—your future successors—and encourage them to challenge everyday practices in search of better methods. Respectful disagreement and constructive criticism are vitamins that stimulate healthy organizational growth.

If you select poorly, you may surround yourself with people too similar to yourself, which could lead to groupthink, or you may pick incompetent people. I have seen leaders keep poor performers around because it made them feel superior. Their logic was, "If I surround myself with mediocre people, then everyone will need me to make the decisions, and I will look smart." Although none of us would ever admit to doing this, we have probably seen someone else do it at one time in our careers. This practice will certainly damage a team, because the team will become so dependent on your leadership that it will suffer when you leave. Those leaders severely cripple the long-term health of their organizations, and they fail to accomplish that basic leadership mandate: improve the organization. Instead, surround yourself with great people—your future successors—and encourage them to challenge everyday practices in search of better methods. Disagreement is not disloyalty; in fact, respectful disagreement and constructive criticism are vitamins that stimulate healthy organizational growth.

Leaders must figure out what motivates their subordinates and create an all-inclusive team-building routine.

Your Team Should Be Your Second Family

The most basic of all groups is the family unit. Socialization occurs earliest from within our family, and we develop values, beliefs, and personalities consistent with our parents and siblings.

Like most others, my family had pretty set traditions. For example, on Christmas Eve, we spent the evening with my mother's family, opening gifts and devouring a huge meal. My uncle Ron told the same stories every year as if no one had ever heard them before, and he topped them off by serenading everyone with one of his best George Strait impersonations. We spent Christmas Day with my father's family, again opening gifts and eating a big meal. For eighteen years, those two predictable rituals shaped me and connected me with my family. The bonds we developed have withstood the test of time and space, since I have been gone for almost seventeen years now. Leaders would do well to borrow a page from the family-building book and incorporate team-building rituals into their socialization plans.

Humans are gregarious animals, and we each have a need for companionship. Certainly there are many introverted people who would prefer to be alone than huddled in the middle of a large group. Some of my family members were introverted too, but they still went to the family gathering, if only to watch Uncle Ron sing and dance. Leaders must figure out what motivates their subordinates and create an inclusive team-building routine.

In my first assignment as an officer, my company commander had the company leadership gather in his office every Friday at 3:00 P.M. to discuss current events. The topics ranged from operations within the company to current social and political issues. He always took the antagonist point of view and argued against us to challenge us to think.

Effective team-building rituals are held at regular, predictable intervals, are all-inclusive, create interdependence, and improve vertical and horizontal communication.

In another company, my commander held monthly pasta dinners at his house. Later in my career, I had a battalion commander who reserved a table in the mess hall for the staff officers and company commanders, where we gathered every morning to eat breakfast together. Similarly, I had a different battalion commander who met the company commanders every Thursday for "Surf PT" (surfing at Barbers Point Beach on the Island of Oahu, Hawaii), followed by breakfast at a local café. In each of these situations, the participants could not have varied more in their personalities. We actually had one guy who could not swim but participated in the Surf PT, which could have been disastrous if not handled correctly. I remain in contact with those leaders and my peers from those tours even today, and I attribute our close relationships to those rituals.

---

*If we truly seek to establish a climate in which teamwork is the
core value that leads to organizational success and growth, then
we must develop our subordinates to embrace ambiguity.*

Not surprisingly, those units are the best in which I have served. In every case, our teams improved the lateral and vertical communication among the key leaders. Because we spent so much time together talking about everyday challenges, personal and professional, we had better organizational awareness, and we grew close. No boss ever communicated that he intended to increase communication or interdependence, but we bonded in a way that will likely withstand the challenges of time and space, just like those of a family.

Be a Problem Solver, Not a Problem Messenger

Even if leaders had the time to solve every problem that surfaces during the course of a day, it would be destructive to do so. We need our subordinates to analyze and solve problems at the lowest level for many reasons. Two of the most compelling incentives for us to empower our subordinates are to create ownership for the long-term growth of the company and develop subordinate leaders. If we truly seek to establish a climate in which teamwork is the core value on which we achieve organizational success and growth, then we must develop our subordinates to embrace ambiguity.

In a 2001 study, the Army Training and Leader Development Panel determined that all Army officers need to be self-aware, adaptable, and committed to a pursuit of lifelong learning. Today's information technology and globalization create a fast-paced, diverse, and changing environment in which managers must lead their companies. These competencies would serve all leaders—corporate, nonprofit, teachers, and coaches—well. The challenge is to find ways to enable that leader growth.

When planning military operations, we know that our plans are good only until we begin executing them. Immediately on executing a plan, we face changing conditions and unforeseen circumstances that cause leaders to make decisions at all levels to refocus their organizations. To ensure that junior leaders make effective choices—that is, decisions in line with the overall organizational objective—we need them to see the big picture and act according to our overall purpose. One effective method of doing this is to give operations officers and direct-line supervisors more control and less guidance. Instead of guidance, tell them your intentions for a given period or project, and link your intentions to the overall team goals.

Whether you track daily, weekly, quarterly, or annual progress, you must establish an intent for the period. Perhaps you want to increase the company's profits by 2 percent for the quarter, or you want to open a new office in a different part of the country by the end of the year. By setting intermediate objectives for the team and allowing subordinate leaders to develop the team strategy, you create in them a sense of ownership for successful execution of the plan. Your key to success lies with your ability to communicate. Your intent must support the overall company goals and should remain consistent with your personality and values.

To ensure our junior leaders make effective choices, we need them to see the big picture and act according to our overall purpose. One effective method of doing this is to give your operations officers and direct-line supervisors more control and less guidance.

Over time, your people will adeptly read you and figure out where you are headed with less guidance if you remain consistent. Furthermore, by knowing the overall purpose of their assigned tasks, subordinates can either recommend better approaches or resolve issues even before they arise. Your focus should not be their method of execution; rather, it should be their success in meeting your overall intent. After assigning the task and purpose, you still have to check on progress; this is not a laissez-faire, or hands-off, approach to leading your team. As with any other goal-setting plan, you should hold people accountable for results. The difference here is that you teach them to operate with more ambiguity so they make better decisions when unpredicted problems arise.

If you want to prepare your subordinate leaders further to understand your intent and have better situational awareness, then you can incorporate leader team training (LTT) into your plan. By doctrine, Army leaders are responsible to train the next generation of leaders by focusing two levels down. LTT facilitates the learning process by teaching subordinates to learn how to think and process problems two levels higher than their present position.

When we adopted the practice, we called it nested leader training, because all of the exercises were problems nested in the organizational goals. My brigade commander (two levels higher than a company commander) gathered me and my forty-two peers in the brigade for this exercise quarterly. He planned four ninety-minute exercises that presented a group of officers with a problem that he faced as the brigade commander. Each problem was in a different area: operations, logistics, personnel, or training. After working together in a group of four or five people, we briefed the entire group on our recommended solution to the given problem.

Commanders at every level had to conduct this exercise with their units during the quarter, so I had to attend the brigade and battalion LTT sessions, and I had to plan company LTT sessions. Here are some things people learned from that process:

- A better understanding of superiors' organizational challenges
- An enhanced perspective for the variables that affect planning and operations at higher levels
- Better situational awareness
- Better communication with people outside normal organizational boundaries, which led to the sharing of best practices among peers
- Improved problem-solving skills

Another by-product of the exercise is that many leaders found their superiors' problems so complex that they stopped complaining about higher headquarters and refocused on accomplishing their own tasks. This technique may also be a useful tool to help organizations with intergroup conflict because it enhances situational awareness and opens both horizontal and vertical lines of communication.

Whatever technique you use, it is important to involve subordinates in your decision cycle. This will not only develop them to be the future leaders of your organization, but it will also help them better understand your intent and make better team decisions in your absence.

Common Pitfalls in Motivating People

These tools helped me build a motivated team, yet I would be remiss not to add cautions about some key lessons I learned about motivating people:

- It is possible to press your team too much, creating a sense of dysfunctional panic.
- Although I advocate creating positive, meaningful relationships with people, you must always keep your eye on the organization's goals.

If you treat everything as an emergency, then you will wear your people out, and eventually your team will suffer problems such as complacency, burnout, and attrition.

Don't Instill Panic; Instead, Set Priorities and the Right Pace to Accomplish Them

I learned this lesson as an upperclassman at West Point. I reported to West Point as a freshman at 8:00 A.M. on July 2, 1990, and within two hours, I was walking at the brisk pace of 120 steps per minute. The relevance of this practice, as explained by my squad leader, then a college junior, was that leaders always "move with a sense of purpose in everything they do." I had absolutely no idea what that meant, but I went with it and walked as fast as I could in the most direct route I could find to every destination on campus. For the next year, I received plenty of mentorship on moving with a sense of purpose. I learned how to eat a full meal in fifteen minutes, complete eight hours of homework in six hours, and get from boxing class to calculus in less than ten minutes.

What about those upperclassmen who provided all of that mentorship? Well, they practically sauntered around campus in slow motion compared to the freshmen. We zipped in and out of upperclassmen as if they were standing still. In fact, it almost seems as if the freshmen are in a constant state of panic at the Academy because they are under such scrutiny.

I would like to report that things were different for my class or even for classes after us, but we fell into the same cycle of complacency when we became upperclassmen. Leaders are supposed to set the example for their subordinates, so theoretically, the upperclassmen should approach their daily routines with the same urgency they demand of the freshmen. But a year of treating every duty as a priority will drain even the most energetic student, employee, and leader.

The key for leaders is to set the priorities and pace for their teams. My first sergeant always reminded me that "slow is smooth, and smooth is fast." That was his way of getting me to pace myself and have patience with others. If you treat everything as an emergency, you will wear your people out, and eventually your team will suffer problems such as complacency, burnout, and attrition. Sometimes teams need to press in order to bring on that new client, close a deal, or meet a goal. The operative word here is *sometimes*. If you never sleep and constantly press, your subordinates will likely model your example, even if you tell them that you do not expect it. Leaders with this type of personality would be wise to designate a trusted person to temper that drive before it damages the team.

Take Care of Your People, But Don't Lose Sight of the Mission

I have heard several leaders philosophize, "Mission first, people always." I often struggle to make sense out of the saying because I see the inherent conflict that often emerges between taking care of your people, while still focusing on accomplishing team goals. Sometimes we need to sacrifice in order to accomplish the mission, whether it is traveling to a distant work location, working late hours, or taking less pay or a smaller bonus. We ask subordinates to sacrifice daily for the betterment of the team, which seemingly conflicts with this philosophy.

The 1949 war classic film *12 O'Clock High* depicts a cycle in which World War II Army Air Force leaders start out with an eye toward mission accomplishment, then let their personal relationships with subordinates cloud their judgment and have a negative impact on mission accomplishment. The first leader, Colonel Davenport (played by Gary Merrill), is relieved of his command after he refuses to relieve a subordinate responsible for a failed bombing mission. Davenport acts more like a protective parent than a combat leader. His successor, Brigadier General Frank Savage (played by Gregory Peck), took a no-nonsense approach to developing the unit into a disciplined, effective team. He was focused on the mission and seemingly less concerned about the feelings and goals of his people. Yet as the story progresses, Savage morphs into the same parental figure as Davenport, and he becomes dysfunctional in his role.

In essence, both leaders in this film grew too close to their people and lost sight of the overall mission: defeating the German war-making capability through an effective daylight bombing campaign. Just as in that poignant 1949 movie, all leaders must focus on motivating subordinates while simultaneously maintaining an eye on the organization's objective.

Consider the cost of either continually pressing subordinates toward task accomplishment or sacrificing group goals for the benefit of a personal relationship, and balance your leader behaviors as best as possible.

People generally tend to be either relationship focused or task oriented, depending on their personality traits. Over time, scholars have argued and studied the merits of each style, and there are merits to both. Some may even argue that task-oriented leaders are more efficient at achieving short-term goals because it takes time to build a meaningful relationship with one person, much less three or five people at once.

The most effective leaders balance their use of task and relationship behaviors depending on the subordinate and the situation. For example, how do you react to a subordinate who wishes to leave work early to catch a child's soccer game? On a normal day, the logical response would be to support your employee and happily send him or her out the door. But what if an important client decided at 5:00 P.M. to alter a meeting schedule and you needed everyone on the team to stay late to prepare? Would you ask that employee to stay and miss the soccer game? This kind of decision can be tough, and ideally, the motivated employee who is committed to group goals will make the right decision without putting the team—and you—in a win-lose situation.

One way to maximize your effectiveness as a leader is knowing your tendency (that is, having self-awareness) and establishing a system of checks and balances to keep you on track. When facing a tough on-the-spot decision like the one described above, it would be inappropriate to reference an operations metric or job description to help you convince your employee to stay. If you have built your team effectively, you will face problems like this less frequently, and when you do, other team members will likely empathize and step up to support their teammate.

I recommend you develop a periodic review of organizational goals while keeping in mind your own leadership style and behavior. If you pressed the team particularly hard during that time, perhaps you should consciously apply more relationship-oriented behaviors in the near future—for example, let everyone take a day off, give them a bonus, or take the team out to dinner. Whatever you do, consider the cost of either continually pressing subordinates toward task accomplishment or sacrificing group goals for the benefit of a personal relationship, and balance your leader behaviors as best as possible.

Some Final Advice

In February 2002, I spent three days with the company in the field certifying them for deployment. Members of our battalion were already in Southeast Asia planning our future operations. It was a time for urgency, but it was also a time for calm, caring leadership. No one really knew what would be ahead, but everyone expected and planned for the worst.

Our deployment was delayed, and I left HHC quietly after thirteen months, happy with my team. During the turnover to the new commander, he found only one equipment accountability issue, which I attribute to my executive officer and his staff's hard work. Because I had the right people in place, I focused my efforts on building the leadership team and developing the company's future leaders. The company has since deployed to Afghanistan and fabulously performed its mission, which makes me proud.

When I first arrived in HHC, I never imagined the challenges that company would face in three years. The circumstances have been so unpredictable since September 11, 2001, that units all over the Army have had to fall back on people skills to meet the demands. This has been a test of commitment, teamwork, and adaptability, and our leaders have stepped up to the challenge. Many soldiers are serving their third or fourth tour of duty overseas, and they remain inspired to work hard and deal with the unpredictable. They are motivated by various reasons: adventure, family tradition, buddies, college money, freedom, and other reasons. The challenge for leaders is to determine what motivates each person, unite a diverse group of people into a cohesive team to accomplish organizational goals, and develop a talented pool of leaders who can continue to improve the organization well into the future. These tools and practices are only a few from which leaders of many organizations may choose to aid them in that effort.

CHAPTER ELEVEN

QUIET LEADERSHIP

Eric J. Weis

Many management principles are universal. Walk into any bookstore, and you will find numerous books written by successful leaders of industry. These giants have all capitalized on sharing their best management practices with the rest of the world. When confronted with this wide array of organizational knowledge, covering the soup to nuts of leadership, one might question whether there is anything left to be explained, for these books detail exactly what it takes to be an inspirational leader and how to run a smooth, efficient, goal-oriented organization. But what happens when you travel beyond the general practices espoused by these best-selling books? Are their carefully choreographed strategies sufficient to motivate people to continually give 110 percent of their effort—or, in the finite terms of military action, to put their lives on the line?

Although many management principles easily move across the boundaries of the business world to the military and vice versa, the armed services enjoy some distinct applications of general leadership principles due to their unique operational environment. Military management is based on the hard truth that leaders must make life-and-death decisions and inspire themselves and others to take heroic action. Although this distinctive atmosphere does not necessarily provide

This chapter was originally published in T. A. Kolditz and others (eds.), *Leader to Leader: Leadership Breakthroughs from West Point* (San Francisco: Jossey-Bass, 2005), pp. 39–47.

a revolutionary management strategy, the perspective of heroic action does allow us to take a wider view of leadership.

In my short career, I have been assigned to elite light and airborne ranger infantry units. While commanding at both the platoon and company levels, I found myself surrounded by the subordinate doers while being mentored by the superior thinkers. One of the ironic twists in this leadership puzzle is that some of the greatest lessons on influencing that I have learned and incorporated into my leadership philosophy were not from the upper echelons of my chain of command. In fact, my special operations background has exposed me to phenomenal leaders from all levels, each capable of providing concrete purpose, direction, and motivation in ways that make the organization stronger. From the lowest-ranking privates to the division commanders, they were all volunteers who fully realized that their extra work and determination would not gain them additional pay or higher rank. They merely desired to place themselves in an environment with like-minded, powerfully driven comrades. Extraordinary leaders in all ranks find it perfectly acceptable, even preferable, to work behind the spotlight and quietly move mountains.

Cheerleading from the front or back of an organization is not a necessary requirement for successful leadership, for at an early stage in a military career, you are taught never to confuse enthusiasm with capability. It was in platoon- and company-sized assignments that I discovered a truth from many successful soldiers: it is still possible to make a lot of noise as a quiet professional. The noise merely changes form. Instead of accolades and personal accomplishments, the noise manifests itself as subordinates who identify with the leader, adopt and internalize dedication, and act to make the organization stronger. These individuals, and the other officers and noncommissioned officers whom I have had the privilege to work with, displayed an unusually high amount of skill in three domains of influence that easily cross the military and civilian boundaries of leadership: they all clearly communicated intent, they all had an ability to adopt multiple perspectives, and they all had a sustainable fortitude.

Extraordinary leaders in all ranks find it perfectly acceptable, even preferable, to work behind the spotlight and quietly move mountains.

Communicating Intent

Organizations must foster initiative and creativity in individual members. Simultaneously, organizations must also restrain individual action and maintain the control necessary to minimize potentially costly financial and human mistakes. Herein lies a paradoxical relationship: How does a leader promote individual growth and aggressive initiative within the team while maintaining mandated procedural and action-oriented safeguards? Within military circles, quiet professionals attack this issue by providing a clearly communicated commander's (or other leader's) intent. This intent articulates the commander's goals and the expected end result for a designated mission.

Military concepts such as vision and mission statements have already made the successful migration from war room to boardroom. These are both excellent tools for providing initial purpose and guidance on the direction a leader expects the team to travel, without stifling initiative. Nonetheless, business and military operations are extremely fluid. In the business community, mission changes may necessitate emergency board meetings. In the military, subordinate leaders may find themselves facing immediate asymmetrical threats, uncertainty, and issues that may not have been considered during mission statement development. Even the best-laid plans are sometimes overcome by unforeseen events, requiring a radical modification of the leader's original concept of how to execute a particular operation.

Knowing this crucial intent, all team members fully understand the overall goal desired for a particular action. It becomes a standard reference point for present and future subordinate actions, and it provides the big picture by clearly defining how each member's or team's mission fits into the grand scheme of the operation. Although the overall operation may not develop or progress exactly as planned, in the absence of follow-up instructions, subordinates can continue toward their team's objective because they understand what the finished product is supposed to look like. This becomes an especially significant factor when the command element must coordinate and synchronize the actions of several interdependent teams that must work independently of each other.

Intents do not have to be lengthy manifestos. On the contrary, they are typically quantifiable and concise statements, designed to be understood at least two subordinate levels down within a hierarchical organization. The maxim of KIS (Keep It Simple) is applied to ensure that the intent can be expressed simply and thus becomes easily internalized for the entire team. When coupled with an organizational vision or mission statement, the guidelines of intent allow subordinates to make informed decisions while taking advantage of new opportunities and to react to a changed situation when the original plan no longer applies.

This framework for action also allows subordinates to have a better understanding of how their individual actions may affect the overall strategic goal within a particular organizational operation. Militarily, the intent is generally expressed by outlining the commander's purpose, method, and desired end state relative to the enemy. Depending on the size of the element and where it fits into the hierarchical structure of the organization, the intent may be relatively narrow or broad. At lower tactical or operational levels, although it may be a technical combination of military jargon and statistics, it is always concise and understandable. At the higher strategic levels, it may become a list of bullet points outlining the long-term outlook on the battlefield or in the corporate environment.

To see how changing conditions might prompt junior leaders to take action in the absence of orders while remaining consistent with the spirit of their superior's intent, take a look at one decision made by a young West Point lieutenant who found himself in the lead tank of the lead company of the lead battalion during the initial push into Baghdad. First Lieutenant Robert Ball had already successfully led his armored platoon through heavy fighting from Kuwait to the outskirts of Baghdad. As the lead element for the Second Brigade Combat Team (BCT), Ball had anticipated a unit halt and possible relief as the battle for Baghdad was about to commence.

Much to his surprise, his unit received orders to conduct an offensive operation into the heart of Baghdad the following morning, April 5, 2003, with Ball's platoon leading the charge. The BCT leadership deemed it necessary to conduct a movement to contact as soon as possible to determine the enemy's disposition, strength, and will to fight, with the subsequent goal of linking up with other friendly elements at the Baghdad International Airport. The commander's intent was that the Second BCT successfully fight its way into Baghdad; seize defensible, important, and symbolic terrain in Baghdad; open and maintain a line of communication into Baghdad; and resupply the force sufficiently to remain overnight.

Despite stiff resistance in the form of rocket-propelled grenades and machine-gun and small-arms fire, Ball spearheaded the push into Baghdad central. At one crucial point of the battle, he encountered a concrete barricade placed across the road. Although the terrain on the opposite side of the barrier had not been previously considered key by the BCT planners, Ball recognized that the obstruction could channel future follow-on units into possible enemy ambush positions. With a seven-ton mine plow on the front of his tank, Ball rammed the blockade at high speed. His platoon continued to reduce the obstacle, disrupt the remaining enemy troops, and allow the remainder of the task force to move unimpeded through the labyrinth of downtown Iraq. This battlefield decision to take a different route and possibly risk his tank against the hasty barrier in order to lessen the enemy's effectiveness was not foreseen prior to the battle's commencement. Ball used personal initiative as he veered from the original plan and was confident in his decision because it fell within the parameters of his commander's intent.

Clear and concise intents provided by the BCT leadership created an environment conducive to fostering junior leader initiative and growth while maintaining the control necessary to synchronize the myriad individual tasks participating in the

complex collective operations. The fluid nature of any business must provide opportunities for subordinates to take independent action. Within a corporate environment, this may entail a similar progression of purpose and overall goal relative
to the competition. A clearly communicated intent ensures that this initiative remains grounded within the framework of a coordinated end result. Ball remained
mission focused even when the specifics of the situation changed.

---

*Clear and concise intents created an environment conducive to
fostering junior leader initiative and growth while maintaining
the control necessary to synchronize the myriad individual
tasks participating in the complex collective operations.*

Adopting Multiple Perspectives

The second quality I have observed in successful quiet professionals has been their
ability and genuine desire to change their perspectives frequently. Leaders sometimes find themselves farther and farther away from the people in the trenches
who actually do the majority of the work. They become so used to being the transmitter of information that they lose the all-important and perishable skill of listening. In the Army, senior leaders typically establish standards for their
organizations four levels down and assume personal responsibility for teaching junior members of their teams no fewer than two levels down. The best way to accomplish this is to seek out and observe the quality of work in subordinate
environments firsthand. Revisiting the areas in which sometimes menial activities
occur can provide a great deal of rich information. The leader only observes
whether the group is meeting established standards and can also take a hands-on
approach to junior leader development. In the military, we call this "walking the
motor pool." Although rank does sometimes have its privileges, quiet professionals never forget the hard, honest work of the common soldier. That knowledge allows them to stay in tune with the organization.

---

*Leaders sometimes find themselves farther and farther away from
the people in the trenches who actually do the majority of the work.
They become so used to being the transmitter of information that
they lose the all-important and perishable skill of listening.*

The story is told of a CEO from a world-renowned hotel chain who, for two months every year, would perform every job within the hotel. He would spend time as a bellhop, front desk manager, housekeeper, room service coordinator, and so on. It was a humbling experience for him to see how much behind-the-scenes coordination and activity are required to maintain the outward surface of a smooth and efficiently run organization. These experiences also renewed his appreciation for the hard work being done by his subordinates and reinvigorated his commitment to ensuring that he was appropriately recognizing these efforts. It is important to note that this CEO was able to extend his perspective-changing experience further than what is allowable or acceptable in the military. Military constraints make it highly unlikely that generals will set aside their stars for any length of time in order to see the world from the perspective of a new recruit. Nonetheless, even military commanders must overcome the challenge imposed by these restrictions and maximize alternative means to obtain multiple perspectives.

Taking the time to "walk the walk" in their subordinates' shoes allows leaders to get their hands dirty and usually brings back memories of how good it felt to have a finger on the true pulse of the organization. Taking the time to immerse yourself in your subordinates' environment offers the threefold benefit discussed in the following sections.

Know Your People

The first benefit of walking the motor pool is that it allows you to get to know your people on a more personal basis. Find out where they are from and what their interests are away from work. Show them that you recognize and appreciate the work they have accomplished, what they are currently working on, and what kind of challenges they may face in the future. Recalling spouses' and children's names, birthdays, and personal accomplishments are just a few of the ways senior leaders can become more intimately involved in the lives of their subordinates.

I vividly remember one occasion when a brigade commander, generally responsible for more than eighteen hundred personnel and at the time four ranks my senior, bumped into me in a cafeteria hallway, called me by name, and asked how my newborn daughter was doing as he shook my hand. I typically struggle with remembering my own anniversary, yet here was a man with tremendous responsibilities who found the time to remember the names and major events in the lives of his organization. His ability to recall my family situation had an intense impact on me.

Herein lies another critical difference between the military and business environments: size and contact. Although the business rank equivalent of the commander of a military brigade of eighteen hundred soldiers may have a smaller number of subordinates, the organization might not offer the same opportunities for making direct contact with people. Initially it may not seem feasible for the president of a company to spend any significant amount of time out on the floor. I would argue that leaders from every type and size of organization need to make this kind of effort regardless.

In the military, this connection is critical. Military leaders never ask their subordinates to do things that they as leaders would not perform first. But despite this size and contact difference, the spirit of becoming more in tune with the members of your team rings true for any organization. This type of personal connection requires more work, but the impact on subordinates and the dividend reaped will far outweigh the effort.

Listen to Your People

This leads directly to the second benefit of changing leadership perspective: a face-to-face opportunity to really hear your subordinates. Ironically, this idea was supplied by my first driver when I solicited his advice on what he was looking for in a leader. He simply said, "Be a good listener and know what you don't know," an astute observation for a private first class with about one year in the Army. As a leader, it is all right if you do not know everything as long as you recognize this as a personal issue requiring hard and diligent work. All organizations expect a slight learning curve for new personnel, but the great ones also recognize their inherent responsibility to make leaders better. Subordinates may shy away from the opportunity to talk candidly about the inner workings of their organization if they believe the invitation is insincere. As you walk the motor pool and get to know people, your desire to listen sincerely becomes apparent. Ask simple questions that might produce profound answers. What do they like most? What do they like least? What would they change if they were in charge? Sometimes the top-down and bottom-up throughput of information and good ideas has the tendency to become diluted by the time it reaches its final destination. You may be surprised to discover that there might be a better way or more streamlined method of doing things, and who better is there to understand this process than the junior members of your team?

When I first took command of my 138-man infantry company, I scheduled three separate "sensing" sessions. The first and second were with my junior officers and NCOs to introduce myself and share my philosophy of command and vision for our unit. Because I would interact with these more senior leaders on a frequent basis, these first sessions were short and informal. We discussed mission-oriented training, support, and preparation for upcoming missions. The amount of experience possessed by this group of subordinates was tremendous, and the sessions focused mainly on how my vision was compatible with their ideas on how a superior company should be run.

A much more substantial, even surprising, discussion session occurred with my enlisted soldiers. I covered the same topics, but when the soldiers were given a genuine opportunity to address their concerns, I began to see the company from an entirely different point of view—concerns that never succeeded in traveling upward through the chain of command. I captured their comments and then made a point of addressing at least one of the more substantial concerns each week. One such issue was the extremely high operational tempo within our unit. The soldiers were spending an inordinate amount of time away from their families, especially during redeployment training, which was having a detrimental effect on morale at home as well as on commitment at work. After discussing options with my junior leaders, I was able to get my boss to approve a training schedule in which Monday became a preparation day and Tuesday through Thursday focused on conducting overnight field exercises, leaving Friday a full day of cleaning equipment and thus having no impact on the coveted weekend. The mere predictability of this schedule produced a tremendous rise in motivation within the ranks.

Care for Your People

A secondary advantage of this minor adjustment in training regimen was that the junior soldiers saw that I cared enough about one of their concerns to take serious action. It reinforced the idea that they too had a voice in what occurred in our company and subsequently provided the catalyst for them to assume more ownership of their piece of the corporate pie. I have discovered that potential and drive increase exponentially among subordinates once they fully realize that their leaders genuinely care for them. A famous military quotation, attributed to an anonymous noncommissioned officer, provides this same type of advice to junior leaders: "Soldiers won't care what you know until they know that you care." Substitute *subordinates* or *team members* for *soldiers,* and this maxim holds true for any organization. This type of care demonstrates that you consider the people in your organization to be important. Only by fully knowing their individual and unique talents will you be able to maximize these abilities by matching the right person with the right job. By changing your perspective, you afford yourself the opportunity to meet, understand, and capitalize on this talent for the betterment of your organization.

A Sustainable Fortitude

The final factor possessed by the quiet professionals I have had the honor to serve with has been a humble and sustainable fortitude—a hidden reserve of formidable strength and the honest ability to learn from past mistakes. Brigadier General Bernard Champoux, one of my past brigade commanders, displayed this type of fortitude. I had the opportunity to watch him ply his trade for a year while I was his brigade plans officer. Throughout this intense year, I was responsible for developing the future battle plans for a fifteen-hundred-soldier task force over six major training exercises, quite a challenge for a senior captain with only eight years of military service.

Our culmination event was a brigade deployment to the Joint Readiness Training Center (JRTC) at Fort Polk, Louisiana, in which we were about to test our skills during a fourteen-day exercise against a world-class opposing force—the veritable Super Bowl of military force-on-force training. In this rapidly changing battlefield, a fourteen-day engagement equated to developing approximately thirty battle plans. Because the (simulated) lives of soldiers in the field depended on our timely and thoughtful planning, the tempo of operations understandably left little room for any kind of normal eating or rest cycle. I recall many of us remarking how the enemy forces' ingenuity and tenacity were turning our straightforward missions into complicated and difficult-to-control operations. Although we were giving the opposing forces as much trouble as we were getting, it continued to be a constant, hard-fought struggle. Midway through the exercise, it was easy to see that the operation was beginning to take its toll on the staff.

Only the naive expect to succeed in every endeavor. For the majority of worthy pursuits, whether military missions or corporate endeavors, success rests on the foundation of several failed attempts.

Champoux recognized this immediately. In hindsight, I think he had anticipated it and was waiting for it to happen. He quickly called all of us together and said, "When faced with great challenges, don't ask that the task become easier. Instead ask that you find the inner strength to deal with the situation." Our brigade commander's quiet resolve and determination in these crucial moments became exponentially more powerful and contagious for his subordinates. His influence drove us to accomplish feats we thought unattainable, and his leadership by example sustained the strength we needed to complete our mission. His leadership also exemplified the sustaining nature of his influence—that great leaders are still present even when they are absent. Our staff found a new fortitude to accomplish our individual and collective missions beyond the training rotation and his tour of duty as our commander. To this day I draw strength when faced with difficult situations by recalling his powerful words and influence.

The second aspect of fortitude is the ability to be honest with yourself. One of the biggest mistakes awaiting young leaders who think they are invincible lies in falsely advertising what they can do. This does not mean that optimism and realism are mutually exclusive, but rather that you must be able to understand yourself well enough to recognize your strengths and weaknesses. Only the naive expect to succeed in every endeavor. For the majority of worthy pursuits, whether military missions or corporate endeavors, success rests on the foundation of several failed attempts.

Tremendous personal revelation can be gained through reflection on one's greatest failure. Where did the best-laid plan go wrong? Did you cover enough contingencies? Did you do everything within your power to mitigate the inherent risk when leading personnel through change? Only through a genuine and honest embrace of failure can we take a step back and examine the mistake with fresh eyes, capable of dissecting the issue from numerous and perhaps heretofore unconsidered perspectives. To accomplish this in the military, we use a system called the after-action review (AAR).

The AAR is simple, direct, and disciplined. It begins with a review of the original mission and plan of execution, generally supplied by the unit or project leader. Once everyone understands what was supposed to happen, an honest, and sometimes painful, review of what actually transpired follows. Personal feelings are checked at the door, and everyone in the organization is given the opportunity to express their concerns. Mistakes are highlighted, not glossed over, to ensure that similar errors are not repeated in the future. Since this process is tied to established doctrine, validated lessons that are learned become part of the unit's collective intelligence. The unit and organization become stronger from the experience.

The quiet professional who embraces this notion of self-evaluation builds the fortitude required not only to react and effect change but also to drive that change within the organization by influencing the conditions and creating new opportunities to exploit.

The abilities to accept responsibility and make a good, hard appraisal of one's status seem to be key contributors to the capacity for bouncing back from uncommon situations. Leaders, regardless of background, who continuously engage in honest personal assessment are able to identify and capitalize on strengths and challenge themselves to overcome or minimize their weaknesses. The quiet professional who embraces this notion of self-evaluation builds the fortitude required not only to react and effect change but also to drive that change within the organization by influencing the conditions and creating new opportunities to exploit.

Conclusion

Leadership does not have to be complicated just because we operate in a complex environment. Organizations tend to adopt the personality of their leaders. An organization with superior leaders at all levels, in the business world or the military, will excel. Substandard leadership, however, has a disproportionate organizational impact. In the business world, this impact may equate to less profit. In the military, the consequences may contribute to casualties on a battlefield. Therefore, it is imperative that organizations take advantage of every available gain to develop leaders capable of positively influencing their workplace environment.

The transference of leadership applications and attributes across the military-civilian boundary can provide the spark needed to maximize any leader's influence on an organization. In my experience, organizations destined for greatness have special leaders: the quiet professionals. These are the leaders who possess the ability to impart a clear intent, are willing to examine multiple perspectives, display a humble fortitude, and have a genuine desire to see their organization perform above expectations. They have the foresight to understand that lessons can be learned from personnel in both the vertical and horizontal chains of command—lessons such as junior leaders' displaying aggressive initiative in combat scenarios while operating within the spirit of a commander's intent, junior subordinates' highlighting that good listeners can gain valuable knowledge and use their position and authority to enact change within the organization, and senior mentors who can inspire us to become better leaders by being brutally honest on self-assessments and drawing on sustainable fortitude—leaders such as the Spartan hero Dienekes, who embodied these ideals most courageously as part of a three-hundred-man defense at Thermopylae against the advance of the Persian King Xerxes in 480 B.C.E.:

> His was not, I could see now, the heroism of Achilles. He was not a superman who waded invulnerably into the slaughter, single-handedly slaying the foe by myriads. He was just a man doing a job. A job whose primary attribute was self-restraint and self-composure, not for his own sake, but for those whom he led by example. A job whose objective could be boiled down to a single understatement, as he did at the Hot Gates on the morning he died, of "performing the commonplace under uncommonplace conditions."[1]

Such leadership is the hallmark of a cohesive team, a team whose members are committed to each other and to their common willingness not merely to meet established standards but to exceed them. An organization characterized by these kinds of leaders will foster people who want to succeed—not only for themselves but because they respect the quiet professionals who set the tone for the entire team.

Note

1. S. Pressfield, *Gates of Fire* (New York: Doubleday, 1998).

CHAPTER TWELVE

LEADING WITHOUT WORDS

Jeff Bergmann

I learned my first lesson on leadership and nonverbal communication when I was still a junior in high school—a naive country boy from Missouri learning about life behind the iron curtain through participation in an exchange program to Moscow that focused on learning the Russian language. My verbal communication skills failed me quickly, so I learned the utility of nonverbal communication and its effectiveness, especially when it meant my survival.

Although I did not understand the Russian they were speaking, when the man sitting in the middle threw open his jacket to reveal a machine gun, I got the message.

I should have learned this lesson during my first week in Moscow. I had been warned of criminal activities and kidnapping by rising gangs. As I walked down the sidewalk with a couple of friends I was studying with at the University of Moscow, I saw an approaching car slow down. My instincts took over when I noticed three men crouched in the back seat, looking as if they were ready to launch through the door and snatch us right off the sidewalk. Although I did not understand the Russian they were speaking, when the man sitting in the middle threw open his jacket to reveal a machine gun, I got the message.

Without thinking, I jammed my hand inside my jacket as if I were going for a weapon, and I pushed my two friends behind a dumpster we were passing. Staring hard into the eyes of the man seated in the back seat of the car with the machine gun, I nearly lost my nerve. Although my legs were planted shoulder-width apart, I felt as if my knees were knocking together as I stood there feeling naked, reaching inside my jacket for a weapon that did not exist. As I prayed silently while staring with pursed lips and firm jawbone, the gunmen muttered something to the driver, and the car sped away.

Leadership and nonverbal communication are interconnected and can lead not only to survival on the battlefield and the streets of Moscow, but also to successful communication with subordinates in any organization.

Just three weeks later, I almost made a similar mistake. How could I have been so stupid? My eagerness to get my hands on one final souvenir prevented me from reading the nonverbal cues that sent me running again. During my last week in Moscow, a friend informed me that he had been told of someone who was willing to trade my stash of Levi's jeans for a KGB uniform. I took the chance and was at least prudent enough to meet in an open park in a public area of Moscow.

The exchange was almost finished as I put the KGB uniform in my backpack, when all of a sudden, everyone took off. I stood up, zipped my backpack, and started running toward a hedge on the edge of the park. As I rounded the hedge line, I ran right into the chest of the burliest Russian I had ever seen. Before I knew it, my feet were off the ground, and a squeezing sensation in my upper arms brought me to the realization that I had just been caught.

Another man joined my captor and began speaking to me in Russian. I assumed they were undercover police and that I had to inform them that I was an American. Quickly pulling out my passport, I was careful not to disclose the contents of my backpack. Only after handing over the passport did I begin to interpret the nonverbal messages they were communicating. If they had been police, I would have been in some trouble, but my intuition told me they were probably gang members who now controlled my passport—my key to returning home to Missouri.

As they positioned their bodies to block my path, I noticed neither one made eye contact while they mumbled to each other and studied my passport. One stroked his chin, while the other covered his mouth with his hand as he spoke. Their facial expressions, body positioning, and gesturing put me into motion. Reaching down to clutch my backpack with my left hand and swinging my right hand forward, I grabbed my passport and ran.

During my juvenile adventure in Moscow at the tender age of seventeen, I learned the importance of understanding and effectively using nonverbal communication. Attending West Point and serving as a junior officer in the U.S. Army served to reinforce my respect for the power and effectiveness of nonverbal communication. Leadership and nonverbal communication are interconnected and can lead not only to survival on the battlefield and the streets of Moscow, but also to successful communication with subordinates in any organization.

As a leader, you must communicate your intent without being ambiguous. Communication involves more than what is said. In fact, the actual words spoken in any transaction are typically rated as being less important than the way in which the words are expressed.

How Communication Affects Leadership

Leadership involves communication with subordinates on organizational and individual levels. Although leaders spend a great deal of time communicating with others, they often fail to communicate as effectively as possible. Communicating properly is vital to individual and organizational effectiveness and is generally linked with leadership advancement within an organization.

Understanding nonverbal communication is a personal and professional necessity. As a leader, you must communicate your intent without being ambiguous. Communication involves more than what is said. In fact, the actual words spoken in any transaction are typically rated as being less important than the way in which the words are expressed. We are all constantly communicating, even when we are not talking. Nonverbal cues are more immediate, instinctive, and uncontrolled than verbal expressions. These subtle messages involve the way people position their bodies, use their hands, move their eyes, or alter their voices.

An awareness of nonverbal communication will allow you to become a better receiver of messages and an improved sender of signals. This awareness will also increase the degree of psychological closeness between you and others. Simply knowing whether you are connecting with someone or sending mixed messages will not only save you time and energy but also will strengthen your effectiveness as a leader. Through your use of nonverbal communication, you can lead without words.

The Leader Communication Process

Good communication involves a sender and a receiver. In the leader communication process, a leader sends a message to a receiver, who is generally a direct report. Encoding is the beginning of the leader communication process. Leaders start with a message they would like to send to a follower. As the sender, a leader converts the information into a form that can be sent to and understood by the direct report. After the message is encoded, it is ready for transmission through a communication channel to reach the desired follower.

There are many different channels by which transmission can occur, including e-mail and other written communication and organizational meetings. Nonverbal transmission often accompanies verbal channels of communication and sometimes is the primary channel for communication. Whatever channel is used, the leader's goal is always to send the encoded message accurately to the recipient.

The communication process continues when a direct report receives the transmission from the leader and then decodes the message received. Decoding is the process by which the follower converts the message received back into the leader's original ideas. This can involve comprehending words and interpreting facial expressions and hand gestures. The degree to which a leader's message is accurately decoded by the direct report determines the level of exactness of the communication.

The communication process also generally involves a feedback component, where the leader receives information back from the follower regarding the message received. Factors distorting or limiting the flow of information, known collectively as noise, may enter into the communication process at any point between the leader and direct report. Leaders who desire to communicate effectively must eliminate this nonverbal noise. Although the communication process has many channels, focusing on the nonverbal component is the primary aim of this chapter.

What Leaders Need to Know About Nonverbal Communication

Many people do not realize how much communication is accomplished without using words. Research estimates on interpersonal communication state that at least two-thirds of human communication involves nonverbal interaction. Some estimates go as high as 90 percent.

Leaders need to convey that they are listening to and hearing their team members. This acknowledgment is often accomplished nonverbally so as not to interrupt the verbal communication of the direct report. A powerful way to communicate that you are hearing what is being said is through facial expressions, gestures, voice volume, tone, appropriate silences, regulation of personal space, and eye contact—all nonverbal behaviors.

For example, my first active-duty assignment as a military police officer was serving as a platoon leader in the Southern European Task Force in Vicenza, Italy. Part of my responsibilities included providing the provost marshal (the chief law enforcement officer for a military installation, similar to a sheriff) with trained military police officers to perform law enforcement duties. One particular provost marshal consistently demonstrated her effectiveness throughout the leader communication process.

Although I was visibly nervous during our first office call, the provost marshal moved from behind her large desk and firmly shook hands while greeting me with a warm smile to welcome me to her office. Her desk displayed signs of a large project in progress, but she honored our designated appointment time and gestured for me to sit in a comfortable chair away from her desk. As she sat down nearby, I felt as if I was in a living room and not a commander's office. She communicated in a warm, welcoming tone that was professional and genuinely sincere. I immediately felt as if she had nothing more important to do at that moment than to chat with a junior officer.

She established rapport by making me feel that she understood what I was saying beyond listening to my words. Her facial expression demonstrated concern when I discussed the challenges my married soldiers were facing being stationed overseas and working various unpredictable shifts. She nodded in agreement and appeared to understand when I talked about my frustrations with having insufficient time and resources to train the soldiers in my platoon. She communicated to me that she was listening and hearing what I was saying, and she embodied the exemplary leader: she effectively employed nonverbal communication with a subordinate.

Body Language Basics

Knowing how to control your body can make your communications more effective. Learning control requires a basic understanding of the three sets of body language:

- *Natural, or innate, body language,* which is what you were born with and manifests itself automatically as when your face turns red when you are angry or embarrassed.

- *Learned body language*, which comes from social learning or from our environment and can often mean different things in various contexts and cultures. Holding your index finger in the air to communicate that your team is number 1 is an example.
- *Mixed body language*, which is a combination of natural and learned body language. Mixed body language varies from person to person, but it manifests itself with both sets of body language communicating a congruent message. Mixed body language could involve your face turning red while you slam your fist down on your desk in anger.

Through natural, learned, and mixed body language sets, you communicate without words and display your emotions. Anger, happiness, sadness: any emotion can be displayed, even if it is inconsistent with the words you use to communicate. Body language is specific from person to person, so it is helpful to look for patterns in yourself and others in order to identify disruptions in normal patterns. These disruptions in normal patterns of behavior are a form of nonverbal communication and are not normal body movements or patterns of behavior. In the next section, we explore these basic concepts in more detail.

Because body language is not always involuntary, it can be learned and therefore manipulated. If you increase your self-awareness, you can learn to control certain aspects of your body language, and you will be communicating nonverbally the same message that you are trying to communicate verbally. This congruence between your verbal and nonverbal signals increases the likelihood that others will receive the intended message.

I remember the first time I went to talk to my new commander, who, after assuming the job, held a meeting with the platoon leaders and told us, "My door is always open for you to come and discuss anything." He also instructed us to remember our duties and responsibilities and always be aware that "our soldiers were watching our actions; we should lead by example." Yet when I went to his office one afternoon, he had his feet up on the desk and was playing a game on his office computer. Although he stopped playing the game as I gave him a report on my platoon's maintenance challenges, he gazed out the window and yawned repeatedly, and his only comment after I had given him my report was, "Okay, I'll see what I can do about it." His words indicated he would address my concern, but his nonverbal communication betrayed him. I knew he did not care about our maintenance status or the perception created by his playing video games in his office during the duty day.

It is important to consider the consistency of the verbal and nonverbal message. If your words, facial expressions, and eye contact indicate interest, the sum of your nonverbal communication will be consistent with your verbal message. If you communicate boredom or disinterest with lack of eye contact or distracting gestures, you will leave your subordinate questioning your sincerity.

Dimensions of Nonverbal Communication

Nonverbal communication is generally classified in four dimensions:

- *Proxemics* refers to the social and personal use of the physical space and the interpersonal distance between the leader and the subordinate. Proxemics includes:
  Physical touch
  The use of space regarding the physical distance that separates the leader and the subordinate
  The environmental characteristics of the space within which the leader and the subordinate communicate
- *Kinesics,* or body movements, which includes the study of facial expressions, eye movement, head nods, and gestures. Although the primary focus is on changes in normal patterns of body movements, those physical characteristics that remain relatively unchanged are also part of kinesic nonverbal communication.
- *Paralanguage,* or the "how" of a message, which includes consideration of the vocal characteristics of a message as well as the fluency of speech.
- *Perception and use of time,* important elements in nonverbal communication between leaders and their subordinates. Differences in time lines or the amount of time given to different activities can raise questions about what is important to a leader. This can also lead to incorrect perceptions of power dynamics, resulting in subordinates' validating a stereotype of their leader that may be incorrect.

Proxemics: How People Define Their Relationships Through Personal Space

My first real experience with proxemics was when I became an aide-de-camp. An aide serves as a personal assistant to a general officer and accompanies the general officer wherever he or she goes during the duty day. The rules of engagement regarding interacting with a general officer can be confusing for subordinates when encountering a general officer outside his or her normal office space. As a young officer, I observed patterns of behavior when encountering subordinates en route to meetings or while visiting soldiers conducting training. If a subordinate was within arm's reach of a general officer, it meant the general was going to stop and have a conversation with the subordinate or the subordinate was going to "walk and talk" until dismissed by the general. Subordinates within earshot of a general would almost always receive a greeting from the general but if the distance remained more than an arm's reach, that was usually as far as the communication progressed. It was enlightening to me to observe how subordinates used space to facilitate interaction with the general.

I learned to detect potential intruders to the general's arm reach zone and learned to use my body language to communicate when the general did not have time to stop and have a conversation. When we were catching a flight, it seemed there was always someone trying to interrupt our departure time line. If we were walking toward the car to depart for the airport and I saw a subordinate beginning to initiate a transition from the social distance to the general's personal space, I would move into the general's personal space, placing myself between him and the approaching subordinate. Moving forward and focusing on the intruder while displaying a determined countenance, I served as a shield between the general and the subordinate. If the subordinate continued to close the distance, I would make direct eye contact and then pull my arm within six inches of my face and glance at my watch and then at the subordinate. In some instances, these nonverbal cues were ignored, and I would move out of the way and continue toward the building or vehicle. I would then open the door and stare at the subordinate as he or she spoke with the general. Every minute I would clear my throat, glance at my watch, and then stare back at the subordinate. Although I was not in a position to interrupt with words, I was effectively communicating without words to accomplish my mission.

Other subordinates assumed a defensive behavior when encountering the general. They communicated their desire to not engage in communication by moving briskly out of the area or by executing a greeting while refraining from moving closer to the general. As a leader or team member you communicate based on your use of proxemics. Being aware of your distance from others is important if you want to give off the right signals.

I knew a leader who liked to stand over her soldiers while they conducted small unit training. Many of her subordinate leaders perceived her as pushy. Another commander I knew would sit in the company operations center while his soldiers conducted training. This commander was perceived as standoffish or uncaring.

You can also determine the appropriate space between you and your subordinates by gauging their reactions to your location. For example, if you move toward someone and he or she backs away, then you have likely entered that person's comfort zone (think of the "close talker" from *Seinfeld*), and you should pull back a little. People tend to move forward when interested and away when bored or frightened. An awareness of these nonverbal responses could help you understand your subordinates' perception of your attitude toward them. If you never interact with your team members beyond the normal boundaries of social distance, you may never convince them that you are accessible, regardless of what you may have said during a welcome speech or introduction to your leadership style. Following are general guidelines regarding the four primary distances in proxemics:

- Intimate distance—skin to eighteen inches
- Personal distance—eighteen inches to four feet
- Social distance—four feet to twelve feet
- Public distance—twelve feet outward

In addition, the way we arrange our offices and public areas affects the amount, flow, and kinds of interaction that can occur in these spaces. Understanding these primary distances will increase your self-awareness as a leader and affect the factors contributing to the nonverbal messages you send to your subordinates. For example, when you talk to subordinates from behind a desk, you demonstrate dominance and even competition. Remove the desk barrier, and you demonstrate openness and concern.

The following anecdote from a deployment in support of the Global War on Terrorism in December 2001 illustrates clearly the importance of proxemics. My small tent on the Afghanistan border served as office and sleeping area for me and the military police soldiers who deployed with me. Only three weeks into our mission, one of my soldiers needed counseling regarding some family issues back home. Our interaction and communication seemed natural and genuine, and we made some progress. A short time after returning from the deployment, I was counseling the same soldier in my office. Now the communication flow seemed more difficult, and I felt we were not connecting as we had in the tent counseling session. Sensing the disconnect, I reluctantly gave up on the session. The next morning while stretching before a run, I walked over to the soldier to say, "Good morning," and decided to try talking to the soldier again. As we stood outside in the grass, the soldier began to open up and talk as if there were no barrier to communication.

---

*The way we arrange our offices and public areas affects
the amount, flow, and kinds of interaction that can occur in
these spaces. Understanding these primary distances will increase
your self-awareness as a leader and affect the factors contributing
to the nonverbal messages you send to your subordinates.*

Becoming aware of the impact that physical barriers in your office space have on the communication process can result in more effective interaction with your subordinates.

Physical Touch. Initial handshakes are key to successful nonverbal communication with subordinates. Although everyone should already know this, it is worth repeating because it is often the first impression a subordinate has of a leader.

Two of my former commanders took opposite approaches to our first handshake. One looked me in the eye, firmly shook my hand, and said, "Welcome to the unit." The other looked me in the eye, motioned toward a chair in his office, and weakly grasped my hand with his damp fingers as he said, "Welcome to the unit." My first impression was very different, although the words of both commanders were the same. Regardless of my expectations about the future relationship I would have with each commander, the firm handshake made me feel welcome to the unit, and the weak handshake left me confused. A handshake that is executed as if you mean it makes a lasting first impression, even when subordinates might not remember exactly what words were exchanged during the initial encounter. The handshake communicates whether you are meek or confident, caring or disinterested.

Environmental Characteristics of Physical Space. Seating charts and seating arrangements for meetings are often powerful forms of nonverbal communication about the status of a leader or the difference in rank of a leader and subordinates attending the same event. Higher-ranking positions of leadership are communicated by sitting at positions of authority, such as the heads of rectangular tables or at the table in front of other groups of tables. This arrangement reinforces the association of this position with power based on social observation and contributes to better functionality because the leader can maintain eye contact with subordinates.

During the Kosovo air campaign, I observed a targeting meeting where senior military leaders discussed the targets that would be bombed later that day. Although this was my first time observing a meeting of this level, it was easy to identify the senior leader: he was positioned at the conference table so that from his vantage point, he could make eye contact with each one of his subordinate leaders and their subordinates seated behind them. This location facilitated the most effective communication for the leader to conduct the decision-making process.

Kinesics: How People Use Various Body Movements to Communicate

The nonverbal dimension of kinesics deals with body position and motion. Kinesics involve a person's posture and his or her gestures. Gestures while communicating include these:

- *Illustrators,* which are movements that cannot stand alone. They accompany speech and add meaning to it, such as raising your eyebrows and pushing your head forward as you say, "No!"

- *Emblems,* which are deliberate nonverbal behaviors with precise meaning, such as nodding the head for yes or giving the "okay" sign.
- *Adaptors,* or self-touching behaviors, which are unnoticed gestures or movements that people use to calm themselves in moments of stress, such as biting one's lip, playing with one's hair, picking with fingers, scratching, or embracing oneself with a comforting hug.

Developing an awareness of the common communication gestures and their interpretations will result in more effective leader communication. Some of the common postures and gestures are described in Table 12.1.

Reflections on my last airborne mission help illustrate some of the common postures and gestures listed in Table 12.1. It was October 1, 1999, and my unit had been ordered to jump into Kosovo. It was the first jump into a hostile environment in Europe since World War II, and we were excited and ready. Soldiers waited on the tarmac for word to board the aircraft. Some sat with legs spread apart widely, hands clasped behind their heads, and some with their legs crossed in a relaxed manner. These soldiers appeared to be completely confident in their abilities and were ready to complete their mission. Others seemed to be impatient or bored, drumming their fingers as they slowly moved their bodies into more comfortable positions. Some rested with one leg crossed over the other and let their dangling foot kick lightly in the wind. This group appeared bored and would just as soon be someplace else.

I found myself in the final group I observed. I could not check my equipment enough times. I would pat my reserve parachute, check for any dangling straps, rub my hands against my pants to dry the sweat, and sometimes rest my head in my hands. I was nervous and impatient about getting into the aircraft and jumping into Kosovo. As a young officer, I was not enough aware of the nonverbal cues to understand that each leader at every level was giving off signals as to how he or she was coping with the mission at hand.

Leader awareness of basic nonverbal gestures and movements can facilitate a better understanding of unit status because verbal communication alone is inadequate. If my boss had asked me how I was doing, I would have responded, "Hooah" (meaning, "Fine") or "Airborne" (meaning, "Ready and motivated"), but this was not at all how I felt. I was worried about my ability to do the right thing. I wanted to rehearse my actions on jumping out of the aircraft. I wanted to talk with my boss about what to do in the event I could not link up with the rest of my assigned team on the drop zone. These were all signals that I was sending nonverbally but would not have put into words.

TABLE 12.1. INTERPRETATION OF
TYPICAL NONVERBAL GESTURES OR MOVEMENTS

Nonverbal Behavior	Interpretation
Brisk, erect walk	Confidence
Standing with hands on hips	Readiness; aggression
Sitting with legs crossed, foot kicking slightly	Boredom
Sitting with legs apart	Open; relaxed
Arms crossed on chest	Defensiveness
Walking with hands in pockets, shoulders hunched	Dejection
Hand to cheek	Evaluation; thinking
Touching or slightly rubbing nose	Rejection; doubt; lying
Rubbing the eye	Doubt; disbelief
Hands clasped behind back	Anger; frustration; apprehension
Locked ankles	Apprehension
Head resting in hand with downcast eyes	Boredom
Rubbing hands	Anticipation
Sitting with hands clasped behind head and legs crossed	Confidence; superiority
Open palm	Sincerity; openness; innocence
Pinching bridge of nose, eyes closed	Negative evaluation
Tapping or drumming fingers	Impatience
Steepling fingers	Authoritative
Patting, fondling hair	Lack of self-confidence; insecurity
Stroking chin	Trying to make a decision
Tilted head	Interest
Looking down, face turned away	Disbelief
Pulling or tugging at ear	Indecision
Biting nails	Insecurity; nervousness
Fidgeting	Boredom; nervousness; impatience
Hand over mouth	Disapproval; reluctance to speak openly

Leaders convey more information with their facial expressions than by words alone. An inconsistency between a leader's verbal message and facial expression is confusing, and it will cause the subordinate to reconsider what message is really being given.

Leader awareness of these typical nonverbal signals could have led to accurate decisions engendering appropriate actions. Leaders in this example could have used their nonverbal knowledge to separate the groups of waiting soldiers into those who were bored, those who were confident, and those who were nervous. By having confident soldiers interact with nervous soldiers, the likelihood of a group of soldiers gathering to talk about all the things that could go wrong would have been decreased, and procedures could have been properly reviewed. Leaders could have conducted rehearsals with the bored soldiers near the aircraft, thereby bolstering the confidence of all soldiers, decreasing nervousness in soldiers wishing they could rehearse their actions one last time, and giving the impatient, bored soldiers something productive to do.

Consider facial expressions as one example of nonverbal communication. In general, leaders convey more information with their facial expressions than by words alone. For example, I had a boss who worked hours putting together a unit social function and then failed to show up the day of the event. The following morning, I confronted him about his absence. As his face turned red, he looked away and said that he just decided not to come. It was obvious to me from his lack of eye contact and flushed face that his words were not conveying an accurate message. Many studies suggest that humans can correctly identify emotions by observing body posture or a face. Any inconsistency between a leader's verbal message and facial expression is confusing and causes the recipient to reconsider what message is really being given.

Furthermore, when people are confronted with discrepant information between verbal and nonverbal messages, most believe the nonverbal message. I had a boss who stated that it was important to get out and inspect soldiers while they were training in order to get to know the soldiers and show them that you care about what they are doing each day. Over the course of six months, I faithfully executed the guidance he gave me; however, I never saw him visit any training events, and in the few interactions that he had with my soldiers, he never knew a soldier's name unless the soldier was wearing a name tag on his or her uniform. Each time I discussed an upcoming training event, it seemed he would always stroke his chin or pinch the bridge of his nose as he tried to recall the reason he could not attend the training.

I became frustrated with this discrepancy between his nonverbal signals and actions versus his stated beliefs. Finally, I stopped inviting him to visit my soldiers. I decided to believe the nonverbal message and accept the fact that it was not important to him to know his soldiers' names and visit them in training.

Facial expressions are powerful when leaders are communicating with subordinates. The face and eyes provide strong nonverbal cues. Research has concluded that facial expressions can reflect most basic emotions. Leaders can communicate surprise, fear, anger, disgust, happiness, and sadness, all without saying a word. The power of a smile cannot be understated. It is one of the strongest tools for communicating warmth, openness, friendliness, and confidence.

The eyes are particularly powerful. Eye contact is one of the most important aspects in dealing with others. Maintaining eye contact demonstrates respect and interest in the topic at hand. Of course, there are wide cultural differences in the amount of eye contact deemed appropriate. For example, Americans typically maintain eye contact 60 to 70 percent of the time, regardless of the leader-subordinate relationship. In contrast, direct eye contact is generally avoided between subordinate and leaders in the Korean culture and can be regarded as impolite or even as a challenge. Direct staring implies intensity and aggression, whereas making scant eye contact conveys either shyness or submissiveness. Breaks in eye contact can signal something distressing or uncomfortable. Finally, when someone is talking about something that is especially interesting to him or her, the person's pupils tend to dilate. Conversely, when a person is discussing something boring or uncomfortable, pupils tend to contract.

While attending graduate school at New York University, I completed an internship at an adult rehabilitation center assisting homeless substance abusers overcome their addiction and develop a plan to reintegrate into society. I remember the difficulty I was having counseling a particular resident. Any approach I made at discussing any topic resulted in only brief responses. Using my basic counseling skills, I tried to determine what was interesting to this particular client so I could use that as a launching point to have a meaningful conversation. Unfortunately, I found I needed to do most of the talking during our mandatory counseling sessions.

At one frustrating session, I decided to talk about myself in hopes of boring him into talking. As I discussed my childhood growing up in a Christian home and attending church on a regular basis, I saw his pupils dilate. Because I did not know that was a nonverbal indicator, I confronted him, thinking he was using drugs again. That is when he started talking. Although we spent the rest of the session discussing theology instead of overcoming substance abuse, I learned an important nonverbal indicator and built a foundation from which to continue effective communication during following counseling sessions.

Paralanguage: The Way People Speak Sends a Message

Paralanguage deals with the way a message is spoken. The impact of paralanguage is strong; listeners often pay more attention to the paralanguage than to the actual content of the words spoken. Paralanguage includes the following vocal characteristics:

- Vocalizations, which are special sounds such as groans or sighs
- Vocal segregates, which are pauses, fillers, and other hesitations
- Fluency of speech, which includes elements like hesitations, errors, rates of speech, and silence
- Voice level, which refers to the volume of speech
- Pitch, which indicates intonation determined by the frequency in the verbal sound waves

For example, people tend to unconsciously increase their volume and vocal emphasis when using certain words or phrases, often concepts of particular importance to them. In addition, if a person is trying to hide fear or anger, then his or her voice will probably sound higher and louder than normal, and the rate of speech will also seem faster than usual. Sadness often produces vocal patterns that are quieter, lower pitched, and delivered at a slower rate. Speech hesitations and breaks often indicate confusion or stress. Finally, clearing one's throat often indicates that words are not coming easily for the person.

Recently my family and I were stranded at an airport. I relayed the circumstances to the attending agent and asked that we be given hotel accommodations at the airline's expense. The attending agent said that she would be happy to help me. As I explained my circumstances, the agent decided it would be best for me to speak with her supervisor. The supervisor was not available, so the agent phoned the senior supervisor at the airline's main terminal. As soon as the agent started to speak, I knew it was not good news. She spoke in a much quieter voice, with a lower pitch and slower rate. I knew that as helpful as she wanted to be, she was letting me know that she was sorry that she could not assist me further. I then asked to speak to the supervisor directly and she hurriedly replied, "Yes," in a higher-than-normal pitch that was so much louder than her previous words that I jumped back from the counter a bit.

When I met the senior supervisor, she said she would be pleased to help me. As I started to explain my situation, she sighed and stated she understood what I was saying. I could tell that she had rehearsed the exact phrases she was using to respond and was not considering anything I said. Not only was she using preplanned fillers in the conversation, but she was also clearing her throat before each statement. Her speech became louder as her speech became increasingly rapid. The structure, pace, and volume of her response belied the message she intended to communicate. I left feeling frustrated at not being heard, as she so clearly demonstrated by the inconsistencies between her verbal and nonverbal messages. (Three hours later, when I returned after the flight was finally canceled, I sighed loudly and said thanks as I received the paperwork for the hotel room the airline was now providing my family after canceling all flights to our destination for the next twenty-four hours.)

Leaders tend to communicate their position within an organization nonverbally by keeping subordinates waiting to see them. The nonverbal message sent is that the leader's time is more important than the subordinate's time.

Perception and Use of Time: Another Nonverbal Message

Leaders tend to communicate their position within an organization nonverbally by keeping subordinates waiting to see them. The nonverbal message sent is that the leader's time is more important than the subordinate's time. Although this is culturally acceptable, the actual use of the subordinate's time that the leader controls sends the most powerful message. When leaders effectively allocate time for the accomplishment of tasks without needless waiting and unfocused discussion, subordinates feel they are respected by their leaders. However, if leaders do not properly use a subordinate's time, this wasted time communicates that a subordinate's time is not valuable or worth considering when planning and executing organizational meetings.

Leaders can ensure they are sending the desired message regarding how they value their subordinates' time by limiting meetings to an established weekly event to include time, location, and duration. This structure allows subordinates to manage their time effectively and come to the meetings adequately prepared to contribute. Leaders should limit discussions to topics of importance to the organization and make opening or welcoming remarks that are brief and pertinent to everyone. They can focus the meeting time by using a preplanned agenda to prioritize the time allocated to each topic. Simple planning allows leaders to send effective nonverbal messages to their subordinates regarding the most essential aspect of organization communication: the weekly meeting.

It isn't enough to understand other people's nonverbal communication. Being able to control your own nonverbal signals can improve your image and your ultimate success in dealing with others.

Enhancing Your Nonverbal Communication

Understanding nonverbal communication is a valuable skill that can pay huge dividends in every facet of life. Knowing more about how someone feels and thinks will not only give you a personal and professional advantage, but it will also boost your confidence. Of course, it is not enough to understand other people's nonverbal communication. Being able to control your own nonverbal signals can improve your image and your ultimate success in dealing with others. Some salient points are illustrated by the following experience I had while deployed to Africa.

While traveling with a Department of Defense delegation to visit various countries in Africa, I was asleep in my hotel room in the Ivory Coast. A knock on the door startled me awake at 3:00 A.M. I was accustomed to responding at all hours of the night to new intelligence updates, itinerary changes, or other messages that required my attention in my role as the general officer's aide-de-camp. I opened the door to a tall woman wearing a long raincoat. She did not say anything, so I asked what she needed. Instead of responding, she looked around in the hallway and then walked into my room.

At first, she did not say a word, and I realized that she did not understand English. I went to the desk to get a notebook so she could write down her message and I could get it translated. It was then that she moved away from where we were standing and took off her raincoat and sat on my bed. Although it was three in the morning, I quickly realized this was not about an official message. Although I knew she did not understand English, I pointed to the door, said, "No!" and then stood with my hands on my hips, glaring into her eyes so she knew I meant for her to leave.

It is important to remain cautious in interpreting nonverbal messages. Because of the role I was fulfilling in the trip, I never thought to question the nonverbal message of a mystery knocker at my door in a foreign country at three in the morning. This proved to be the first mistake that put me in this embarrassing situation. Nonverbal cues are also important. My night caller did not have a folder, notebook, or briefcase but instead was dressed in heels, wearing makeup, and carrying a handbag. Giving proper attention to nonverbal cues and remaining cautious about interpreting nonverbal messages is essential. Following this advice, derived from a woeful performance in my unenlightened days, can increase your nonverbal communication skills.

During one of my developmental counseling sessions with a former commander, I noticed that after he asked me a question, he would feverishly write on the developmental form, which was a required product at the end of our session. He asked questions and wrote responses without visually attending to our conversation. I soon realized that he was writing down my responses to the items on the developmental form and ignoring what I had to say on related subjects that were not precisely the subject of the questions he proposed. As I reacted to his multitasking style of counseling, I started to indicate my boredom by fidgeting with my pen and jiggling my feet in impatience. It was clear that he was not paying attention to my nonverbal cues, because he did not recognize my frustration. He was simply going through the motions of developmental counseling instead of developing my responses into a basis for understanding and professional development.

As a leader, if you want to appear confident, open, and in control when communicating with your subordinates, you must be aware of the nonverbal messages you are sending. To make a developmental counseling session effective, there are some basic points to keep in mind. When communicating, look at others straight on. Meet their eyes, and then let your gaze drift elsewhere from time to time to avoid staring. Most important, do not try to multitask and communicate simultaneously with a subordinate. As a leader, you may be pressed for time. And although you may be able to rearrange your desktop, update your calendar, and scan a document while communicating with a subordinate, never do it. The nonverbal message would be that you are not listening to your subordinate, or you have better things to do than communicate effectively.

If you are communicating with a subordinate while standing, it is important to avoid postures such as hands on hips. If you are sitting, you should avoid hands clasped behind your head. Both of these nonverbal cues indicate that you are superior, ready, and aggressive—all of which may hinder your subordinate from accurately communicating with you. You should also avoid turning your body away from your subordinate when he or she is talking, and avoid keeping your arms folded across your chest. Be aware of your body movements, avoid fidgeting with your hands, and keep your gestures loose yet controlled so as to avoid excessive or frantic movements.

Leader communication should be free of jargon and fillers. Jargon can be promotional phrases or motivational cliches familiar to your culture, like, "hooah," "airborne," or "squared away." Jargon can often be as distracting to the communication process as filler words, such as "like" and "um," and "you know." Finally, ensure that your body language and your words match, or you will seem insincere. Smiling helps in confirming words of welcome and encouragement, whereas a set jaw communicates firmness or displeasure. Failing to communicate in concert verbally and nonverbally will hinder the effectiveness of the leader-subordinate communication process.

Conclusion: Gestalt Communication Facilitates More Effective Leadership

The goal of leader communication should be to develop an awareness of and to strive for gestalt communication. *Gestalt* refers to the concept that the whole is greater than the sum of the parts. In the context of communication, gestalt communication implies that a leader's combination of verbal and nonverbal aspects of transmitting a message leads to more effective communication with subordinates. A verbal message reinforced with nonverbal dimensions develops an unconscious bond of trust between the leader and the subordinate that is manifested in feedback transmitted back to the leader throughout the communication process.

Once while in command, I was faced with a leadership challenge surrounding alleged discrimination involving two of my senior subordinate leaders. I encouraged the "complainant" to come forward with the allegations through the official equal opportunity process, while at the same time asking the complainant to sit down with me and go over the issues concerning the "respondent." I asked the complainant to coordinate with an equal opportunity representative outside our unit to meet with us in an empty conference room to discuss the allegations.

It was important to me to meet in an open, neutral meeting space to reduce any barriers to communication that might have existed if we had met in my office where, sitting behind my desk, I was clearly in a position of power. In addition, I wanted to send the message that I was concerned about the communication process and about getting to the bottom of the issue, so I wanted an outside representative to serve as an advocate for my subordinate's position.

On the day of the meeting, I showed up ten minutes early so my subordinate would not be kept waiting for me. I wanted to ensure the nonverbal message was sent that I was taking this issue seriously. Throughout the communication process, I listened intently and provided nonverbal encouragers by nodding my head in understanding and muttering, "Uh-huh" and "I see," to communicate that I understood the verbal communication and was attending to the conversation. When something was said that I did not understand, I asked for clarification while demonstrating genuine interest by leaning forward and making eye contact with a facial expression that communicated a clear desire to learn more and understand the situation, instead of judging the truthfulness of the allegations. Throughout the process, I sat with an open posture, not crossing my arms or legs, and I avoided touching my face or fidgeting while my subordinate was talking. When I spoke, I used the same rate of speech, voice level, and pitch as I normally used in a counseling session. I ensured that I allowed my subordinate the time needed to discuss the allegations.

When communicating with subordinates, showing genuine interest and concern with facial expression, head nods, gestures, and body postures all reflect openness and positive reinforcement. I was able to put my subordinate at ease by appearing relaxed and breaking down barriers with friendliness. I made an effort to reduce my own defensive posture by establishing an environment that was a level playing field for my subordinate to discuss the allegations. My attention to the nonverbal aspects of the communication process resulted in clear and effective communication by eliminating all irrelevant nonverbal messages that could have distracted from the verbal message that I was open to resolving this leadership conflict between two important, senior, subordinate leaders.

With time, the communication process led to effective resolution of the complaint. The presenting issues were not as serious as originally alleged; however, the communication process brought to the light the underlying issues between these two subordinate leaders, and we achieved a successful resolution. As a leader, I was able to communicate my willingness to attend to the complainant and hear her completely. The process used both verbal and nonverbal aspects, but the consistency of the nonverbal aspects of the leader communication process led to success in this critical leadership challenge.

Leading without words is most effective when combined with consistent verbal messages that eliminate all noise in the communication process. Leader awareness of the dimensions of nonverbal communication can result in the development of communication styles consistent with the message the leader desires to send to followers. However, self-awareness is a process that must be revisited from time to time to ensure that nonverbal messages sent to subordinates are consistent with the leader's intent. You will be a more effective leader if you become aware of your nonverbal communication habits and learn to use nonverbal communication to help you bridge the communication barrier common to all human interactions—to help you lead without words.

CHAPTER THIRTEEN

DEVELOPING CHARISMA WITH CAUTION

Dena Braeger

Throughout my career in the Army, I sought out the most charismatic people to work with and for. I equated exceptional leadership with charisma and looked for charisma in my superior officers, peers, and subordinates in the Army. It felt good to be around these people. Charisma draws others in.

But history taught me lessons about the dangers of charismatic leaders who used their power to move people in immoral and hurtful ways. These were the toxic, charismatic leaders—the Hitlers, the Osama Bin Ladens, the Fidel Castros. Despite history's warning about the dark side of charisma, I still believed that charisma was a positive leadership quality. I had not thought much about the implications of charisma, even when used in moral and ethical ways, until I was commanding a company in Iraq.

In exploring the implications of charisma, I found limitations in myself and my own expectations of leadership, and I found that charisma can limit an organization's ability to develop and grow.

Everyone probably has a story about a charismatic leader. Some are our heroes and our most cherished visionaries. These are the people who occupy our memories and make up some of our most powerful schemas about what leadership looks like. Others are more everyday change makers and leaders: our parents, coaches, teachers. They inspire us to make the everyday exciting and rewarding, and they help us to move further in life than we thought we could move on our own.

Leadership Lessons Can Come Early in Life

Stu Greene, my first swim coach, was, and still is, undeniably charismatic. His imposing, athletic, over six-foot presence was matched with a warm smile that was always interested in others. He personally connected with all of his swimmers. He made everyone feel special, and it did not matter if you were the worst or the best swimmer on the team. He had a way about him that made you want to be part of his group, part of his team. He had a vision of developing a great swim team, and you knew that nothing else was possible. He was captivating, alluring, and inspiring. My Barracuda team won countless New England Championship meets under his tutelage.

I grew to be an excellent swimmer with Stu as my leader and teacher, but he also taught me more powerful lessons in leadership that I would carry into adulthood. He believed I was better than I believed I was; he may have been more dedicated to me than I was to myself. When I was not meeting his expectations (which usually meant I was goofing off at practice), he communicated his vision to me in a caring way that made me want to change and work hard. Stu set the standard for me at a young age about what a leader should be like. Therefore, ingrained in my early conceptions of leadership was the presence of charisma.

Like many of our stereotypes and biases, my own attraction to charisma was buried below the level of my own self-awareness and therefore was largely left unexamined. I liked and valued charisma in my leaders, peers, and subordinates. The presence of charisma was part of my judgment and evaluation criteria, but I lacked the self-awareness to understand why this was one of my criteria or what the implications this criterion would bring to an organization.

Charisma, with its unwavering self-confidence, is a comforting quality for a leader to have in a volatile business environment.

The Impact of Charisma on Organizations and Individuals

I have come across many charismatic leaders in the Army. In some ways, I think the organization's mission pulls for charisma. The Army is a serious life-and-death business, which is also to say that it can be a scary business. Today, the men and women in the Army volunteer to defend the policies of the U.S. government, and that can mean putting themselves and the people who work for them in harm's way. Charisma, with its unwavering self-confidence, is a comforting quality for a leader to have in a volatile business environment.

The Army is not alone in its pull for charisma. Sports teams engaged in competitive win-lose business environments pull for charisma in their players and coaches. So does entrepreneurship, with its characteristic uncertainty and volatility. In large public businesses where expectations are high and worth is highly monitored and tracked on the world stage, charisma, with its unwavering self-confidence, can be comforting. Even the field of education pulls for charisma. In a country where education is an economic dividing line, educators are asked to inspire and motivate people to learn and embody the skills that will keep this country "great" rather than just "good." Education, like the Army, may be viewed as a life-and-death business to the longevity of a great democratic nation. Many business environments are volatile, and in the face of uncertainty and fear, we find comfort in those everyday charismatic heroes in our midst.

I learned a lot about myself while commanding in combat and about people. Some of my lessons learned were clear, others more subtle. One of my more lasting lessons in leadership was the impact of charisma on an organization and an individual. My lessons and thoughts about the effects of charismatic leadership fit more under the category of subtle lessons learned. They came quietly and slowly, but nevertheless provided profound insight into why charisma is a popular—and dangerous—leadership trait.

My new boss was competent, caring, understanding. He had the abilities and skill to lead the organization, yet that was not good enough for me. I was sulking because my new boss was not charismatic like the old boss.

In looking back, I believe that I began to look at charismatic leadership in a different way because of the uncertain environmental conditions in Iraq in 2003. Although the Iraqi Army had been defeated and President George W. Bush had called an end to major combat operations, an insurgency was building, and the political-social-cultural-military situation was complex and ambiguous. In Iraq, I began to see the thirst for charisma all around me: in myself, my peers, my current organization, and organizations that I was no longer associated with.

I do not remember when I began to make the connections, but when my own lessons about the lure of charisma began to surface, I remember feeling embarrassed with myself. The embarrassment came from a shift in my own awareness, one of those rare moments where you see yourself and your own bias, stereotypes, and inadequacies as the problem instead of other people's problem. My experience, which I can still feel to this day, made this crystal clear.

I was in Iraq as a company commander of a three-hundred-soldier maintenance company. I was the leader and was supposed to set the example. I was supposed to be adult, selfless, level-headed, and positive. But I was not, and I had not been. I had been sulking privately to myself. Sulking does not fit into the category of "adult" or "selfless." Why? Let us look at some of the reasons, which illustrate the dangers of charismatic leadership.

I would have never classified charisma as a negative quality or shortcoming. But I began to see how charisma can be dangerous for an organization, even when it is used to bring change, inspiration, and vitality.

Charismatic Leaders Are a Tough Act to Follow

I was sulking because my new boss was not like my previous boss. He was not exciting or inspiring or cool. He did not make me think I could leap tall buildings in a single bound. Nor did he walk around as if nothing could stand in his way. I was dissatisfied with the new boss, and not for good reasons. My new boss was competent, caring, understanding. He had the abilities and skill to lead the organization, yet that was not good enough for me. I was sulking because my new boss was not charismatic like the old boss.

In those moments where I started to really see myself in my disappointment and disgruntlement with my new boss, I realized that I was caught in charisma's wake. My charismatic leader was gone, and my own deep psychological needs were no longer being fulfilled. I felt empty. The excitement was over, and now there was everything else: people to take care of, the responsibilities of my own leadership, and the demands of the uncertain mission itself. It was as if my favorite television show or a gut-wrenching and breath-taking playoff game was over, and I was surfing the channels looking for something that might entice me in the same way. Unfortunately, after your favorite show or a great sporting event, everything looks gray and slightly unappealing. So it is in the wake of charismatic leadership.

My old boss was unequivocally charismatic. He was also solidly competent and caring. He had the kind of charismatic leadership that I had looked for— he was like my first swim coach, Stu Greene. I would have never classified his charisma as a negative quality or shortcoming; in fact, I championed this aspect of his personality. But after he was gone, I began to see how charisma can be dangerous for an organization, even when it is used to bring change, inspiration, and vitality.

I began to ask myself why I was so attracted to these charismatic types. What had they done for me and for the organization that I now longed for?

Charisma is difficult to define, yet I almost always know it when I see it. Tom Cruise had it in *Top Gun*. Robin Williams had it in *Dead Poets Society*. Charismatic leaders appeal to the emotions, and they seem to exude personal confidence and belief in themselves. The people who have charisma inspire and create excitement with their presence. They have the uncanny ability to pay attention to others and make them feel good.

My desire for charisma biased my thinking and expectations. Expecting charisma was both selfish and inappropriate. Looking for charismatic leadership outside my organization prevented me from learning from my new boss.

Although my new battalion commander was competent, pleasant, and personally dedicated to the unit and the mission, he lacked charisma. He was not what I would call captivating and did not have magnetic energy. His personality did not draw me in. I sulked. In charisma's wake, I sought out other charismatic senior officers to be around when I should have been looking at myself, my new commander, and my own organization. I blamed my new commander for not being charismatic. I labeled this aspect of our leader-follower relationship as a negative quality—something that he lacked or failed to provide me as a follower. Charisma, unfairly, was my standard.

So I looked in other places for leadership instead of working on the relationship I had in front of me. I looked for guidance from my mentors and from trusted peers when I could have been building a relationship with a new mentor. I missed the excitement and the fearless self-confidence of the old commander. If I had not been so disappointed by my new boss's lack of charisma, I might have learned about new ways of doing things and new insights that he could have offered. I have since learned that my desire for charisma biased my thinking and expectations. Expecting charisma was both selfish and inappropriate. Looking for leadership outside my organization that satisfied my need to be affiliated with charismatic leaders prevented me from learning from my new boss.

What I learned from this experience is that charisma need not be a requisite quality for excellent leadership. I know that my own desires for a charismatic leadership are embedded in what I think a leader should be. Those who are led by a charismatic leader want the next leader to have the same kind of emotional effect. But charisma is an impossible expectation for some to fill—and it is just not the way some people move in the world. Some leaders are not charismatic but are competent and caring. Competence and caring are admirable leadership qualities, which should not be overlooked or diminished by a lack of charisma. Leading is not an act or an entertainment venue, and as followers, we cannot place entertainment or excitement over true competence and caring.

I imagine that charisma leaves a similar wake in a number of leadership and business contexts. Think of a time when you were around someone who was charismatic. Did it make the next person or leader to fulfill that role seem unexciting or lacking in some way? My fifth-grade history teacher, Mr. Matulewicz, was charismatic. He exuded personal confidence and inspired the same in his students. I remember him in front of class telling the story of Paul Revere's ride: he was magnetic, visionary, and passionate, even when teaching fifth-grade U.S. history in a tiny suburban elementary school in Massachusetts. He made the study of the American Revolution an emotional endeavor—a passionate pursuit of knowledge and a grand adventure—and he also made all of the other history teachers I had afterward pale in comparison.

Thereafter, I always looked for that Mr. Matulewicz–like charisma in the history classroom. In looking back, I am sure that expecting charisma in all history teachers was inappropriate as a standard, and it probably prevented me from giving other teachers a fair assessment of their own strengths as teachers and leaders. Charisma need not be a requisite quality for excellent leadership, but many of us (even the fifth-graders) expect it, and many organizations champion this aspect of a leader's personality.

I have come to see, however, that the lack of charisma is no reason to sulk or be disappointed in a leader. There are more important leadership qualities to look for: competence, caring, and commitment.

When charismatic leaders exit the organization, loyalty and commitment do not necessarily transfer to the new leader or back to the organization. The loyalty and commitment might walk out the door with the charismatic leader.

Charismatic Leaders Instill Devotion to Themselves, But Maybe Not to the Organization

Another potential problem of charismatic leaders is that they, perhaps unintentionally, inspire devotion to themselves but not to the organization. Charismatic leaders instill loyalty and commitment from their followers, which is almost always what we look for leaders to do in organizations. Unfortunately, when charismatic leaders exit the organization, loyalty and commitment do not necessarily transfer to the new leader or back to the organization. The loyalty and commitment might walk out the door with the charismatic leader. I believe that this is one of the real dangers of charismatic leadership. How do charismatic leaders ensure that the loyalty and commitment they engender become a lasting part of the organizational dynamic?

In Iraq, when my charismatic battalion commander left the organization, I was not the only person disappointed with the new boss because of his lack of charisma. My peers and I talked about the "good ole days" often. We commiserated. At watercoolers, coffeepots, and cafeterias all over the world, a similar dynamic happens when a charismatic boss leaves an office. As a group, we longed for the dogged self-confidence of the old charismatic leader because he made us feel self-confident too. But I began to see that our loyalty was not necessarily to the organization but to the leader. We were not as committed when he was gone, and we talked about leaving the organization often. I even looked for another job.

At the time, it was hard for me to see the effects that the wake of charisma had on the whole organization. Now I can see that my own frustration was multiplied many times over. Where I allowed my own loyalty and commitment to diminish when the charismatic leader left, I am sure that this was repeated throughout the organization, consciously and unconsciously. In government, private and public business, education, and sports, loyalty and commitment are often attached to a charismatic leader. So although it is often wonderful to have these people in our organizations, they present a danger when they leave.

The Power We Find in Charismatic Leaders Is the Type of Power They Personally Derive

Charismatic leaders have sheer power derived from their own personalities, which is very different from power derived from an organization. When I was a brigade-level staff officer, I had a charismatic brigade executive officer. A few months after he departed, I was in the office of the new brigade executive officer, briefing him on the plan for an upcoming training exercise. We had some significant obstacles to overcome in accomplishing our training mission, and I was proposing a change in the way we did business. Essentially I proposed that the executive officer make the changes happen by using his own power of persuasion. Thoughtfully, but also in a direct way, he said, "Dena, I am not Major Brown." He was dead on. He was not Major Brown, and he did not wield the same type of personal power in the organization. In the past, we were able to get a great deal done because of Major Brown's charisma. He was a master communicator, but he was also a master persuader, and people wanted to do what he asked.

The new brigade executive officer was more quietly competent. He was an outstanding leader and manager, but he was not charismatic. In all types of business, there are staff personnel who are quietly competent but not necessarily charismatic. Even in management positions, there are organizational dangers when a charismatic manager leaves and is replaced by someone who is not charismatic. In the headquarters where I worked, as a staff, we had relied on the charismatic power of the previous leader to produce needed change, not the power that came from his role or position. We were able to sidestep protocol and procedure because of the executive officer's charisma.

I know we used charisma to solve problems when we could have made new systems to solve problems. In the short term, this strategy might have been admissible, but in the long term, it was not necessarily better for the organization.

At the time, this type of power seemed like an asset to me: it made my job easier, and we got a lot done. I am sure private business abounds with similar stories about the power dynamics of charismatic managers. Charismatic managers have deep influence and engender personal devotion; their power is in their personality, not in their organizational job or role. In reflecting on the effects of charismatic leadership on organizational capabilities, I know that we used charisma to solve problems when we could have made new systems to solve problems. In the short term, this strategy of relying on charisma might have been admissible, but in the long term, it was not necessarily better for the organization. We look to charismatic leaders in times of crisis; instead, in a crisis, we must have the confidence to solve problems ourselves and trust our own abilities.

I believe that turbulence and ambiguity create a pull for charismatic leadership. Ambiguity can leave people feeling helpless. In emotionally charged situations, charismatic leaders point the way out of crisis. Usually they have clearly articulated goals and vision. In crisis, they can make obstacles seem smaller and surmountable, reducing anxiety and feelings of helplessness in the process.

I believe it was not a coincidence that I started to notice the pitfalls of charismatic leadership in Iraq. I needed, at a deep level, for a charismatic leader to reduce my own anxiety and stress. Upon reflection, I can see that on a personal level, I was under a lot of stress: I worried about my soldiers and their safety constantly. I also worried about the company's mission of supporting the five thousand soldiers in the brigade. I worried as well about the effects the Army was having on the people of Iraq. I worried whether we, as an army and as a foreign people, were doing the right thing by being in Iraq. The charisma of my leader alleviated some of my own stress and anxiety. In a way, charismatic leadership made me feel secure: my leader's unyielding confidence made me feel more confident.

The workplace is a home to crisis and fear as well. Layoffs, mergers, tough competition, win-lose sports games, and last-minute deadlines create moments where we feel helpless and full of anxiety. Even in these types of situations, we place our hope in a change leader, a coach, a religious leader, or a gifted manager to keep us from disaster.

I know that my preference for charisma speaks volumes about what I need as a follower in the leader-follower equation. I want my leaders to be undeniably self-confident and to inspire vision, dedication, and loyalty to the tasks at hand. At deeper levels, I take security and comfort in the dogged self-confidence of someone who is charismatic, especially when uncertainty is a characteristic of the business environment. These are all things that I thought I needed, or deserved, as a follower in Iraq. Often the things we need as followers get turned into our leader expectations. We look to our leaders for fulfillment of these needs when we could look inward and find these things in ourselves and be called to action. Finding in ourselves what we seek in our leaders is difficult but often necessary in times of crisis.

In the wake of Hurricane Katrina, the people of New Orleans, the people of the Gulf region, and the people of the rest of the United States looked for a charismatic hero to lead in the crisis that ensued. We expected someone to have undeniable confidence in his or her ability to restore our hope. We expected someone who would clear the path emotionally and physically to a sense of normalcy. At times when our own fears are strong and we feel personally unable to overcome the resistance forces to accomplish change, we look to charismatic leaders to do what we feel unable to do ourselves or what we are unable to see because of the conditions we are in.

Crisis, whether in combat, a natural disaster, or the workplace, cannot be solved by one person, even if that person is charismatic. It is a foolish wish. Often we as followers have the ability to navigate our way out of crisis. However, we may lack the confidence to see our abilities, and we lack the profound feeling of responsibility to do so. It is easier to look for a charismatic leader to lead the way out of crisis than to look to ourselves. As followers, we must learn how to deal with our own anxiety and tolerate ambiguity. Leaning on a leader to reduce our anxiety is not good followership. In a crisis, we must trust in our own abilities and take responsibility for what we can do. A charismatic leader, although perhaps comforting, cannot lead the way out of crisis alone. As followers, we must confront our own fears and take action. We must find those qualities in ourselves that we seek from our leaders.

*Charismatic leaders can create such a strong organizational
culture that people find it hard to criticize them or their ideas.
And when a subordinate does criticize a charismatic
leader, that subordinate can be seen as disloyal.*

Charismatic Leaders Can Create Organizational Cultures Where Dissenting Views Do Not Exist

Another potential danger in organizations led by a charismatic leader is that the leader's way might be dominant; therefore, other options or courses of action are not examined or suggested. During my time in Iraq, I watched this phenomenon occur in one of the sister units in my brigade. One of the infantry battalions had a commander whose charisma was legendary to both subordinates and superiors. After a short time under his command, even the Iraqi people knew of his infectious personality and unwavering confidence. He was one of those charismatic people who made you feel good to be around, and people were drawn to him like moths to a light at night. He engendered tremendous loyalty and commitment to himself personally from his subordinates. From an outsider's perspective, it appeared that he had magical powers over his people. Some of my peers who previously seemed to be fiercely independent and free thinking appeared to be under his charismatic spell.

Yet this was unfortunate for both the leader and the organization. This leader's charisma was so strong that his followers were blinded by his personality; as a result, they may have been unable to criticize his views or actions. Iraq was an ambiguous environment, and the costs of mistakes were often political and emotional. I believe these types of situations require leaders to have people around them who are their devil's advocates. These are the people who help their leader see the bigger picture or provide a different way of looking at things.

But charismatic leaders can create such a strong organizational culture that people find it hard to criticize them or their ideas. And when a subordinate does criticize a charismatic leader, that subordinate can be seen as disloyal by the other members of the organization who are captivated by the charismatic leader. Because of the strong pull for loyalty that charismatic leaders have, the people who challenge their organizational practices or specific leader actions are likely to be labeled and ostracized.

Charismatic Leaders Can Weaken Creativity

Charismatic leaders often emerge and make groups stronger. They create strong emotional bonds, and the groups that form around these strong bonds can be extremely cohesive, a quality that gets the group moving and thinking in the same direction.

However, although this trait is useful in accomplishing new or extremely difficult missions, the strong, cohesive qualities of the group may lead to like-minded and nonindependent thinking. It is hard for a cohesive group to see themselves, and the group can take on an arrogant quality, where their devotion to the charismatic leader's way becomes the only way and the best way. This like-minded thinking can work against creativity and new best practices. When the time comes for the group to move in different directions, it is unlikely that members will stray from the group or the charismatic leader.

It is hard for a cohesive group to see themselves, and the group can take on an arrogant quality where their devotion to the charismatic leader's way becomes the only way and the best way. This like-minded thinking can work against creativity and new best practices.

We Spend More Time Developing Charismatic Leaders While Neglecting Other Leaders

As a company commander, I looked to junior leaders who had the charisma to captivate their soldiers to accomplish missions in the company. When faced with a difficult, risky, or high-profile mission, I tended to turn first to the charismatic types. These were the junior leaders who exuded confidence and could communicate the importance of the mission to their people. Their confidence made me confident. Because of their charisma and my own attraction to this charisma, these junior leaders tended to be the ones that I spent more time developing.

In reality, these charismatic junior leaders needed me less than junior leaders who appeared to have other predominant qualities. I tended to place my emphasis where I felt comfortable: with the charismatic men and women who worked for me. Because the charismatic types get the focus of seniors, they tend to attract more work. I believe that many senior leaders rely on charismatic junior leaders in many organizations.

In fact, I have seen this pattern in all of the organizations I have been part of. Yet from a leader development standpoint, an organization does not benefit from a small group of people conducting the majority of the work for the organization, for several reasons: the charismatic people can get burned out, the uncharismatic people can feel neglected, and leadership experiences are not shared broadly across the organization, which can affect organizational learning.

Sergeant Elizabeth Bowles was a squad leader in my company. Midway through our deployment in Iraq, she interviewed to be the company's operations sergeant. In this capacity, she would coordinate training and organize the activities of a three-hundred-person maintenance company in a combat zone. She was intelligent and capable, but she lacked the charisma that many of her peers possessed, and I was reluctant to give her the job. She found me one morning after the interviews and told me in no uncertain terms that she not only wanted the job but that she knew she would perform well. This was one of those situations where I thought that a little charisma might get the job done easier or better.

Bowles proved me wrong. She had other strengths that I had neglected. Her quiet competence, attention to detail, and personal pride in her work took the company to a new level in operations administration. She was a masterful small team leader, and those who worked around her got things done, and done right the first time. Her leadership, although not charismatic at all, was a large part of why the company was successful in a number of areas.

We are able to see better the strengths and weaknesses of those leaders who are less charismatic. Our emotions get in the way of our judgment criteria when dealing with charisma.

It Is Hard to Evaluate a Charismatic Leader's Effectiveness

We do not judge charismatic leaders by the same standards as others. Charisma's alluring and captivating qualities can cause us to focus on certain aspects of a charismatic leader's skill set. Charismatic leaders often become larger than life, even heroic. We tend to dismiss their deficiencies in favor of their energy and the way they appeal to our emotions. For example, a star charismatic football player whose off-field antics are less than admirable does not often lose his hero-on-the-field status despite his questionable values. In the same circumstances, a less charismatic player might be kicked off the team, sidelined, or vilified. A similar dynamic exists in organizations. We are able to see better the strengths and weaknesses of leaders who are less charismatic. Our emotions get in the way of our judgment criteria when dealing with charisma.

In reality, a charismatic leader has leadership deficiencies that we do not want to see because this may conflict with our need for a heroic leader. We are able to ignore deficiencies in our charismatic leaders in order to play out our own deep psychological need to have everyday heroes in our midst.

How to Avoid the Pitfalls of Charisma

I still believe that charisma can be a positive leadership attribute, but there is a downside to charisma as well. Charisma can be mysterious, alluring, and seductive, and it is often the potent ingredient for bringing about organizational change. But I no longer associate exceptional leadership with charisma. Charisma is not part of my standard for excellence. Understanding the impacts of charismatic leadership can help us to avoid its hazards. Following are some guidelines, which I hope will help you be wary of charisma whatever your current role or position is.

What to Do If You Are a Charismatic Leader

If you know you are a charismatic leader, there are ways to avoid some of the pitfalls of charisma:

- Encourage dissent, and make sure you have people around you who can disagree with you without their feeling disloyal.
- Assess the environmental conditions that you lead in. Are they turbulent and anxiety provoking? Recognize that charisma creates safety in times of crisis but is less effective in times of stability. Rely less on charisma if appropriate.
- Use your charisma to overcome obstacles in the short term. In the long term, ensure that power in your organization in embedded in the organization, not in your own personal power.
- Plan your replacement or succession carefully. Know that your charisma has created a strong emotional bond to followers. Try to transfer those bonds back to the organization or to the new leader.
- Establish systems in your organization that will outlast your tenure.

What to Do If You Work for a Charismatic Leader

If you work for a charismatic leader, here are ways to minimize the effects of the wake of charismatic leadership:

- If charisma is one of the qualities you desire in a leader, do not expect that all leaders have the same amount or level of charisma.
- If a charismatic leader leaves your organization, be aware that you might look for charisma somewhere else.
- Be wary of trusting your leader more than your own immediate experiences. Do not let your loyalty to the leader overshadow your instincts about what is right.

How to Manage Charismatic Subordinates

If you have charismatic subordinates in your organization, here are some guidelines for managing the organizational dynamics:

- Know that the groups that form around charismatic leaders are often cohesive and can have rigid boundaries. Encourage intergroup interaction, and challenge these groups to come up with new, creative ways of doing things.
- Do not focus your attention on the charismatic types. Place leadership emphasis and development where it is needed, not where you feel comfortable.
- Evaluate whether responsibility in your organization rests predominantly with charismatic types. Distribute responsibility throughout your organization.
- Tell your subordinates that they are charismatic. Give them advice on how to manage their strong leadership qualities and how charisma affects organizational dynamics.

CHAPTER FOURTEEN

TRUST: THE KEY TO COMBAT LEADERSHIP

Patrick J. Sweeney

If your men trust you, they will follow you into any situation.

—PLATOON SERGEANT, 101ST AIRBORNE DIVISION,
TALL AFAR, IRAQ, MAY 2003

For military leaders, combat provides the ultimate test of their leadership abilities because it requires them to influence soldiers to *willingly* risk their lives to achieve the organization's goals. Based on my twenty-four years of leading Army organizations, I believe that trust is what gets soldiers to willingly follow their leaders into combat. The opening statement, from a platoon sergeant in combat, succinctly captures the notion that if soldiers trust their leaders, they will follow them in any situation. Therefore, leaders must earn their subordinates' trust before they can exercise a level of influence needed to lead effectively in combat. In fact, trust is the key to the exercise of leadership in any type of organization. Leaders must earn their followers' trust before they can truly lead. In this chapter, I define trust as one's willingness to be vulnerable to the actions of another person (leader, subordinate, or peer), based on a sense of confidence in the other person's competence to meet role requirements and character to behave cooperatively.[1]

Leadership is an influence process that takes place in the relationships between leaders and followers. Trust is the foundation that these relationships are built upon. Competent and caring leaders who work to establish positive cooperative relationships with their subordinates will earn their followers' trust. Competent and caring leadership reassures group members that the organization will accomplish the mission and that the leader will look after their welfare.

Once trust is earned, followers will allow leaders to influence not only their behavior but also their thoughts, attitudes, values, goals, and motivation. Thus, trusted leaders have the ability to impart positive developmental change in their subordinates. Followers may change their thought structures because they use trusted leaders as role models and adopt their attributes, traits, values, and beliefs. Or trusted leaders may persuade followers that the organization's values and goals are noble and worthy of being emulated. When followers start to view the leaders'/organization's values, beliefs, and goals as the correct way to think, feel, believe, and/or act, they will change their thought structures. This process of internalizing the leaders' and organization's values and goals greatly facilitates stable behavioral changes in followers. Group members are now internally motivated to act in accordance with the leaders'/organization's values and goals in order to maintain congruence with their own belief and value systems and not because of some external reward or threat of punishment. Thus, trust provides leaders with the ability to exercise a level of influence that literally transforms the followers and increases their willingness to work towards achieving the organization's objectives, even at high risk or sacrifice, which greatly enhances organizational effectiveness.

Compliance usually results from influence based on the leader's position power to reward and punish.[2] Leaders that exercise influence through the use of external motivators linked to their authority such as rewards or threats of punishment can be effective in low-risk environments. In compliance situations, group members will temporarily change their behavior to reap a reward or avoid a negative consequence; however, the behavior will only persist as long as the leader can monitor the behavior or has the means to provide rewards or deliver punishment. It is proposed that influence based solely on position power is not leadership but rather coercion or pushing.

On the other hand, in high-risk situations such as combat, firefighting, or law enforcement, leaders who rely on position power to influence will find it next to impossible to offer an external reward or punishment whose perceived value motivates followers to risk serious injury or death. In these situations, subordinates may reluctantly minimally comply while looking for ways to reduce their risk or they may outright disobey a directive.[3] In any case, followers will not have the motivation or will to face the dangers to achieve the organization objectives. This lack of commitment and motivation in group members will seriously hinder the organization's effectiveness.

To review, I believe that to effectively lead in demanding situations that require group members to assume risk or sacrifice to accomplish the organization's objectives, leaders must earn their followers' trust. Trust provides leaders with the ability to exercise influence beyond compliance, which is necessary to get individuals to put the concerns of the organization and fellow group members before their own. Group members will willingly follow a trusted leader into a high-risk situation because they are confident that he or she has the skills do the job, that the leader will look out for their welfare, and they believe that their actions are consistent with their own and the organization's values and beliefs.

Trusted Combat Leaders

By identifying the attributes comprising soldiers' ideal image (prototype) of a trusted combat leader and getting an assessment of each one's relative importance to establishing trust, leaders can gain insights into how to earn their subordinates' trust. A prototype is simply a commonly held set of attributes or characteristics typically associated with a member of a specific group or category.[4] Leaders can use the prototype of a trusted combat leader to assess and develop these important attributes in themselves and develop plans to communicate the possession of these attributes to group members.

The closer leaders match their subordinates' prototype of a trusted leader, the more likely it is that they will earn their subordinates' trust, which should lead to a greater ability to exercise influence and to greater organizational effectiveness. Furthermore, the exploration of soldiers' perceptions regarding the relationship between trust and influence provides insights into the role that trust plays in combat leadership. The lessons learned from this study of trust and leadership in combat are equally applicable and relevant to leaders of any type of organization.

I fought with the 101st Airborne Division during Operation Iraqi Freedom and took advantage of the rare opportunity to study trust and leadership in an actual combat environment in May 2003. The two main purposes of this study were to map the attributes contained in soldiers' prototype of a leader who can be trusted in combat and to explore the relationship between trust and influence in combat. Seventy-two members of the division completed an open-ended questionnaire designed to explore trust and leadership in combat. The soldiers were assigned to artillery and infantry units conducting combat and civil military operations in northern Iraq. I visited them at their respective base camps in Mosul, Tall Afar, and Qayyarah West Airbase. Mosul, the third largest city in Iraq, is located about 240 miles north of Baghdad. It is also the seat of the provincial government of Ninawa. The city of Tall Afar is located approximately 38 miles west of Mosul. Qayyarah West Airbase is an Iraqi military airbase located about 40 miles south of Mosul. These soldiers provided the information for this study in several ways:

- They voluntarily reported (in their own words) the attributes they look for in leaders who could be trusted in combat.
- They discussed why each attribute influenced trust.

- They rated the relative importance of each attribute to the establishment of trust.
- They shared their perceptions of how trust and leadership were related.

Ten Attributes of a Leader Who Can Be Trusted in Combat

After organizing the responses from the seventy-two soldiers into categories of attributes, importance ratings were summed to determine the top ten attributes soldiers look for in leaders who can be trusted in combat.

As shown in Exhibit 14.1, the results of this study suggest that a leader's competence and character in terms of loyalty and honesty/integrity are the core attributes that have the greatest influence on the development of trust in combat. In combat, subordinates depend on their leaders to develop and efficiently execute plans that accomplish the mission in a manner that minimizes the risk to their lives. Thus, subordinates looked for and placed greater importance on leader attributes that facilitate mission accomplishment and concern for their welfare, which serves to enhance their survival.

I sorted the attributes that were mentioned into categories based on the soldiers' labels and descriptions. If a soldier provided only a description of an attribute, the description was used to infer the underlying attribute and appropriate category. To facilitate interpretation of the data, I combined some attribute categories

EXHIBIT 14.1. ATTRIBUTES OF A LEADER WHO CAN BE TRUSTED IN COMBAT

1. Competent
2. Loyal
3. Honesty/good integrity
4. Leads by example
5. Self-control (stress management)
6. Confident
7. Courageous (physical and moral)
8. Shares information
9. Personal connection with subordinates
10. Strong sense of duty

Note: The attributes are listed in order of importance.

because they logically fit together and were also aligned with the Army's leadership framework—for example:[5]

- The attribute of leader competence was viewed as entailing a leader's job knowledge, intelligence, decision making, management, and interpersonal skills.
- The attribute of loyalty was viewed as encompassing concern for and support of subordinates, the chain of command, the unit, and the country. It also included the leader's willingness to place the needs of the unit and its members before his or her own (in other words, selfless service).
- The attribute of leadership by example was viewed as comprising leading from the front, modeling desired behavior, and sharing the dangers and hardships with subordinates.
- A majority of the soldiers in the study used "integrity" and "honesty" interchangeably; thus, these attributes were combined into the single category of "honesty/integrity."

The top ten attributes that soldiers identified as critical to the development of trust in combat are distinct attributes, but they are interrelated.

Soldiers cited leader competence as the most important attribute for influencing trust in combat. Soldiers depend on their leaders' technical and tactical expertise, judgment, and intelligence to plan and execute operations that successfully complete the mission with the least possible risk to soldiers' lives.

---

1. Leader Competence

Soldiers cited leader competence as the most important attribute for influencing trust in combat. Soldiers' responses indicated that a leader's competence plays a key role in ensuring the accomplishment of their missions and their survival in combat. They depend on leaders' technical and tactical expertise, judgment, and intelligence to plan and execute operations that successfully complete the mission with the least possible risk to soldiers' lives. Therefore, leader competence is essential to ensure the organization's success and the survival of its members.

Further analysis of their responses indicated that subordinates seemed to focus on leaders' job knowledge (technical) and decision-making (tactical) skills when assessing competence. They wanted leaders who possessed sound judgment and knew the technical aspects of their own and the subordinates' jobs and the techniques for employing personnel and equipment to achieve the mission efficiently. Leaders who mastered the technical and tactical aspects of their responsibilities seemed to bolster soldiers' confidence in the leader's and the unit's ability to complete the mission successfully.

Both technical and tactical competence provide leaders with the ability to make quick, accurate decisions to adjust to the dynamic nature of the battlefield. Combat is not the place for leaders to do on-the-job training; mistakes cost soldiers their lives. Therefore, leader competence, especially in combat, is critical to ensuring that an organization successfully accomplishes its missions while at the same time protecting and preserving the organization's most precious asset: its people. A competent leader increases the likelihood of soldiers' surviving combat; thus, it is adaptive for them to place the greatest importance on this attribute.

Leader competence also plays an important role in earning trust in a business setting. A longitudinal study investigating how company presidents develop working relationships with their subordinates found that the central factor in the development of these relationships was task accomplishment; therefore, leader competence played a significant role in the development of trust. In this study, employees judged leaders' competence in terms of functional or area expertise, general business sense, and interpersonal skills.[6] Similar to the military, a business leader's competence plays an instrumental role in the organization that is accomplishing its mission in an efficient manner. Employees are more likely to willingly assume the risks associated with change and growth such as bringing a new product to market, changing a business model, restructuring, or refining operations if they believe the leader has the competence to be successful.

The following situation illustrates the importance of leader competence in earning subordinates' trust, the accomplishment of the organization's objectives, and the survival of group members. Shortly after the start of Operation Iraqi Freedom, an infantry unit was tasked to enter the city of An Najaf, located about a hundred miles south of Baghdad, to complete a mission. Soldiers in the unit were apprehensive about the mission because they were not sure how the civilian populace would react to their presence and because of their lack of experience dealing with civilian crowds that spoke a different language, the potential that the Iraqi Army would set ambushes, and the restricted movement in the city. This was a highly dangerous mission, with the potential of entering a conflict with civilian supporters of Saddam Hussein. A sergeant who was an infantry company forward observer described the situation in this way: "The first time we had to go into a city and not knowing all the things we may encounter. My leader handled all situation changes with quick decisions to keep us from any wrongdoing, and the outcome was mission complete with everyone safe." This situation highlights how the leader's competence was instrumental to the safe and successful completion of a dangerous mission, which served to bolster the soldiers' trust in him.

The following statements from soldiers further illustrate the importance of leader competence to followers' safety and the development of trust:

> "A leader has to be technically and tactically proficient. If a leader displays that he is not or does not stay knowledgeable in his job, then he does not realize or care that the soldiers' lives in his hands depend on his ability to make correct decisions."—Private, Tall Afar, Iraq

> "Technical and tactical proficiency [of the leader]—Hard to trust someone who is not on top of their game."—Sergeant, infantry platoon forward observer, Qayyarah West Airbase, northern Iraq

> "[Leader] competence—Know your job. In combat, there is no 're-cock': you get one shot at it."—Second lieutenant, infantry company fire support officer, Qayyarah West Airbase, northern Iraq

---

Loyal leaders genuinely care about their soldiers, support them, place their soldiers' welfare before their own, and look out for their subordinates' well-being even if it incurs risk or cost for the leaders, allowing soldiers to depend on their leaders to protect their best interests at all times, especially when the risks are great.

---

2. Loyalty

Another critical leader attribute that significantly contributes to subordinates' survival is loyalty. The subordinates' view of loyalty was narrowly defined and focused on being concerned with and committed to looking out for their welfare. Responses from the soldiers indicated that loyal leaders look out for their subordinates' welfare by planning, executing, and accomplishing combat missions with the least possible risk to the lives of their soldiers. They genuinely care about their soldiers, support them, place their welfare before their own, and look out for their subordinates' well-being even if it incurs risk or cost for the leaders. Soldiers can depend on their leaders to protect their best interests at all times, especially when the risks are great. Therefore, it is adaptive for soldiers to trust leaders who are loyal to them because it helps ensure their survival in combat.

Leader loyalty is also important in business and political leadership. In fact, loyalty was so important to the development of trust and leadership that former New York City mayor Rudy Giuliani made it the cornerstone of his leadership philosophy and called it "the vital virtue." As he points out in his book on leadership, the willingness to take political heat to stand by employees facilitated the development of trust and devotion throughout his organization. Giuliani's loyalty facilitated the development of trust because city employees knew that in the toughest of situations, when most other politicians would run for cover, he would stand by them and protect their welfare.[7]

Leaders' demonstration of loyalty in the face of diversity communicates care and commitment and prompts followers to reciprocate in kind, which fosters the development of cooperation within the organization. Furthermore, a leader's loyalty encourages employees to exercise initiative and assume risk, which serves to bolster the organization's effectiveness. Loyalty provides followers with the sense of confidence that should their attempts at exercising initiative fail or draw negative reactions, the leader will stand by them and protect their welfare.

One story told by a lieutenant who was serving as an infantry company fire support officer illustrates how his commander's willingness to defy a directive during an attack in order to protect his soldiers' welfare demonstrated loyalty and served to bolster trust. The company was conducting an attack in An Najaf in full nuclear, biological, and chemical suits according to the battalion commander's guidance. The temperature during the attack was very high, and the unit suffered two heat casualties early in the attack. If the unit continued to attack with the protective suits on, the soldiers would suffer, and combat effectiveness would decrease. Here is how the lieutenant described the situation: "The company commander made the commonsense decision to wear just T-shirts and roll the pants to midshin. This may seem like an obvious decision, but it was going against command guidance, and the first sergeant wanted to remain in uniform. However, it greatly increased the trust in the commander across the company because it was a decision that put the soldiers and mission first, and not the all-important image depicted through the attached media."

This story clearly highlights that leaders who willingly incur personal risk or cost to protect their subordinates' welfare demonstrated loyalty, which serves to bolster trust. Furthermore, subordinates' responses indicated that leaders who demonstrated loyalty to their soldiers created the conditions for soldiers to reciprocate.

---

*A leader's integrity serves as a foundation for the moral and
ethical execution of missions, which protects his or her subordinates'
moral justification for fighting and sustains their will to win.*

---

3. Honesty/Integrity

Soldiers ranked leaders' honesty/integrity as the third most important attribute for influencing trust in combat. Honesty/integrity is a core character trait that entails a leader's truthfulness in word and deed. Soldiers must take action and risk their lives based on the information their leaders provide them; thus, they demand that leaders be honest and act according to their and the organization's values (integrity). Leaders' honesty and integrity allow followers to believe in them because subordinates know that in tough situations, leaders will walk their talk.

A leader's honesty/integrity is equally important for earning trust in a business or political organization. The longitudinal study investigating how company presidents develop relationships with key subordinates found that subordinates placed great importance on a leader's honesty/integrity. The employees wanted their leaders to behave morally and to be honest and open in discussing problems.[8] Honest communications also helps alleviate concerns regarding leaders' possessing hidden agendas or motives. Leaders with honesty/integrity provide employees with a sense of predictability of how the leaders will act in the future, especially in tough or morally challenging situations. This sense of confidence that leaders will be honest and behave morally regardless of the situation leads to the development of trust.

Leaders with integrity provide soldiers with reassurance that in the stress and chaos of combat, their welfare will be looked after and the mission will be accomplished in an ethical manner. A leader's integrity serves as a foundation for the moral and ethical execution of missions, which protects his or her subordinates' moral justification for fighting and sustains their will to win.

Regarding honesty, soldiers' responses focused on their strong desire to be given honest and candid information about the combat situation and future operations. Soldiers (like any other subordinates, even in a noncombat situation) wanted to know the truth about upcoming actions regardless of the situation. Honest and candid information seemed to help them control rumors and allowed them to form realistic expectations of the challenges ahead. Having an accurate sense of requirements needed to meet future combat situations can provide soldiers with a sense of predictability and control, which can help them manage stress. One sergeant's statement summed up the importance of honest communication in combat from a soldier's perspective: "Honesty, in my opinion, is what makes an effective leader. The executive officer of this unit kept us informed and never sugar-coated anything. If we were headed for some rough times, he flat out told us. He always kept us informed, and that is what soldiers need."

Leaders' honesty and integrity are essential character attributes necessary to exercise leadership in any type of organization. Followers expect their leaders to establish and live by high moral and ethical standards. Leaders' virtues and values shape the organizational culture through modeling, rewarding ethical behavior, and punishing unethical behavior. An organization's culture is a set of implicit beliefs and expectations of how employees should behave in conducting business outside the organization and how they should interact with each other within the organization.

Furthermore, leaders' honesty and integrity establish the ethnical boundaries for their employees to conduct business within. These boundaries established by the organization's culture promote the development of trust with clients and group members because people doing business with or working for the organization know they will be treated ethically. Thus, leaders' honesty and integrity provide employees a sense of moral direction, allow employees to believe in the leaders' word and deeds and the organization, promote cohesion and trust within the organization, and foster the establishment of cooperative and trusting business relationships with clients.

Conversely, unethical leaders can destroy their organizations and inflict severe financial hardships on their employees, shareholders, and retires, as was demonstrated in the Enron, Tyco, and Adelphi cases. Leaders' honesty and integrity are essential to leadership and greatly enhance organizational effectiveness.

Leaders who lead from the front communicate to their soldiers that they are confident in their own and the unit's abilities, have the courage to meet the dangers of combat, and would not ask soldiers to face a danger or do a task that they themselves would not be willing to do.

---

4. Leadership by Example

Leaders who live by their espoused values and lead from the front by willingly sharing the dangers and hardships with their soldiers enhance the development of trust, because leading by example bolsters subordinates' perceptions of their leaders' integrity and credibility. Leader credibility is based on perceptions of competence and character. Leadership by example, especially in combat, enhances soldiers' perceptions of leaders' integrity, because it is one thing to espouse certain values and beliefs and entirely another to act in accordance with those values and beliefs in an environment where one's life is at risk.

Thus, leaders who behave consistently with their values and beliefs during the stresses and dangers of combat reaffirm their integrity (that is, their character), which serves to bolster perceptions of their credibility. Soldiers know that leaders who can act according to their own and the organization's espoused values and beliefs in combat will develop and execute plans for combat operations, to efficiently accomplish the mission in an ethical manner, while minimizing the risk to soldiers' lives.

Leaders who lead from the front communicate to their soldiers that they are confident in their own and the unit's abilities, have the courage to meet the dangers of combat, and would not ask soldiers to face a danger or do a task that they themselves would not be willing to do. Also, leaders who lead by example and from the front link their survival outcomes with their subordinates' survival outcomes. This linkage serves to increase the interdependence between leaders and subordinates, which makes it more likely that the leaders will take advantage of opportunities on the fluid battlefield to minimize risk of life to accomplish the mission. Leaders who can demonstrate the character to lead by example by being out front in dangerous or crisis situations earn their subordinates' trust and bolster their subordinates' confidence to complete the mission and survive. The following observation, provided by an artillery platoon leader, captures the essence of how leadership by example influences the development of trust: "Leadership by example feeds on confidence and creates trust in subordinates because they know the leader will not expect his soldiers to do what he is not willing to do."

Leadership by example is important for developing trust with followers in any type of organization. Whether it is working long hours to meet a production deadline or sharing job security risks of a pending merger, leaders will enhance their credibility by standing side by side with their subordinates. Leaders who willingly share hardships and risks communicate to the group members the following positive traits:

- A sense of interdependence or community that leaders and group members are all in this together
- Selfless service
- A sense of concern for the organization and group members' welfare
- Confidence in their own and the group's abilities to handle the challenges

For instance, in 2006 in an effort to boost profits, General Motors (GM) laid off workers, reduced shareholder dividends, and reduced the salaries and benefits of its top managers. GM's CEO, Rick Wagoner, implied that senior management's pay and benefit cuts were symbolic to show that everyone would sacrifice to make the company profitable.[9] By leading by example and actively sharing in the pain of the cost-cutting measures, GM's top leaders linked their outcomes with those of their employees and shareholders, which made the cost-cutting measures more palatable and bonded them together to resolve the challenges the company was facing. In this case, top management's willingness to share in the hardships increased interdependence with employees and shareholders and bolstered their credibility, which should lead to cooperation and trust.

Leaders must be aware that subordinates are always assessing their reactions to stress to predict how they will react in extreme stressful situations where the consequences have the greatest importance.

---

5. Self-Control

Subordinates rated a leader's ability to maintain self-control in stressful situations as the fifth most important attribute for influencing trust in combat. The soldiers' responses indicated that they believed that leaders who can maintain their composure under the stress of combat are more likely to make better decisions. Leaders in any type of organization who can maintain their composure in stressful situations are able to fully apply their abilities and skills to make decisions to resolve the crisis in an efficient manner. In contrast, leaders who lose their composure tend to become overly aroused and emotional, which can greatly hinder sound decision making. Leaders' ability to handle pressure and remain calm in stressful situations serves to bolster perceptions of their credibility.

Soldiers perceive that a leader's stress management skills are necessary so that they can effectively use their competencies in combat. The following statements highlight subordinates' perceptions of the link between a leader's stress management skills and exercise of competencies under stress:

> "Cool and calm leadership style that does not get flustered under pressure [is] important to me, because if the leader stays calm, they usually make the best decisions."—Infantry company first sergeant, Tall Afar, Iraq

> "Tolerance of stress—how well they [leaders] handle stress [is important] because if they have a lot of stress, it could affect their judgment and leadership ability."—Sergeant, artillery gunner, Qayyarah West Airbase, northern Iraq

In addition, responses indicated that soldiers watched how their leaders reacted to stressful situations in peacetime to gauge how they would respond to the stress of combat. Subordinates in any type of organization use small, everyday stressful situations, such as receiving less-than-expected sales figures or a surprise inspection by the boss, as an indicator to project how their leaders will react in situations with great stress. Leaders must be aware that subordinates are always assessing their reactions to stress to predict how they will react when the consequences have the greatest importance. Consider the following comment, provided by a lieutenant who served as a battery fire direction officer: "A cool head [is important]—if he does not flip out over small stuff in garrison, then he will most likely be collected in combat."

Moreover, the following combat situation illustrates how a leader's lack of composure in a stressful situation can significantly reduce trust. An artillery unit was conducting a movement during the march to Baghdad and experienced three vehicle breakdowns simultaneously. Breakdowns during combat movements are significant because they place the vehicles, the supplies they are carrying, and personnel at risk. Stopping too long for repairs can disrupt time lines and cause a unit to fail a mission. It also places the unit at risk of becoming isolated and vulnerable to attack. Furthermore, abandoned vehicles are usually stripped by local residents in a matter of hours. Therefore, in the following combat situation, a commander was faced with three simultaneous vehicle breakdowns during a movement. A platoon leader, a subordinate officer, relates how the commander dealt with this stressful situation: "During a convoy movement we suffered three breakdowns almost simultaneously. My commander spent half hour yelling at people and placing blame. I lost trust in him because it made me doubt his ability to be decisive when it would have potentially mattered the most."

The commander's lack of composure during this stressful situation had a detrimental impact on the level of trust subordinates had in him. His lashing out at subordinates and placing blame on them for the vehicle breakdowns indicated his inability to remain composed and focus on what was important to resolve the crisis. As the platoon leader stated, the commander's lack of composure prevented him from acting decisively when it mattered the most.

A leader's self-control can also have an impact on subordinate-to-leader communication. Subordinates are less likely to provide candid information to leaders who cannot handle stressful situations, especially if the information is negative. In combat, leaders depend on their subordinates to provide them with information—good or bad news—about the unit and the enemy situation. This is true in any organization: leaders must rely on subordinates to keep them informed on the status of their units and on current conditions so they can adjust current and plan future operations. Leaders who cannot maintain their composure when given bad news and strike out at the messenger will shut down lines of communication with subordinates and isolate themselves. Subordinates may respond by hiding information, hesitating or delaying bringing information forward, or embellishing information to make it more acceptable to their leaders. In any of these cases, the leaders are isolated, which hampers their ability to make good and timely decisions.

Overall, followers in any type of organization are more likely to communicate with, trust, and follow leaders who can maintain their composure because they can depend on them to act responsibly in tough situations. Leaders who can manage stress and maintain composure have the means to apply their skills to make decisive decisions in tough situations. Also, their ability to maintain composure when and after receiving bad news facilitates the open flow of communication with subordinates, which greatly facilitates the leader's ability to make timely and informed decisions. Thus, a leader's ability to handle stress affects whether he or she can develop and maintain the trust of his or her subordinates.

6. Confidence

Leaders' confidence serves to bolster subordinates' confidence in the leader, their own abilities, and the unit's abilities, motivation, and willingness to follow. Leaders display confidence in their own abilities by making decisive decisions, especially during stressful situations such as combat.

Making a decisive decision during a crisis or stressful situation can be a challenge for leaders in any type of organization, because usually they do not have all the information they need to make an informed decision. They must rely on their professional judgment to make the best possible decision with the information and time available. They must be confident in their abilities to adjust the decision as the situation develops and more information becomes available. The key is to make a timely decision to get the organization moving and taking action to resolve the situation. Therefore, whether resolving an unforeseen problem in combat, fighting a hostile takeover in business, resolving a hostage situation in law enforcement, or fighting a complex multialarm fire, leaders must display confidence by making timely decisions and then adjusting them as needed.

Responses to the study indicated that subordinates used a leader's confidence as an additional indicator to reinforce their perceptions regarding the leader's competence to lead the unit successfully. This is a logical strategy because in most cases, leader confidence is built on a foundation of competence. This perception of the leaders' competence due to demonstrations of confidence appeared to increase subordinates' perceptions of their own and the unit's ability to accomplish the mission, which seemed to boost their will to fight. The following statement, provided by a soldier who served as an artillery computer operator, captured the link between leader confidence and subordinates' increased perceptions of the leader's competence: "I look to see how confident my leaders dealt with certain situations, so I could know and feel more comfortable that they know what they were doing."

Consider how the following statement from an artillery platoon leader highlights how a leader's confidence can serve to bolster subordinates' confidence and their will to fight: "[A leader's] confidence transposes to subordinates, prevents hesitation, and promotes the fighting spirit." In addition, a statement provided by a platoon sergeant in response to a question asking for a combat situation that changed his trust in the unit's leadership illustrates how a leader's demonstration of confidence can boost subordinates' confidence: "[The combat situation that changed the trust I had in my leadership occurred when] the platoon leader took total control and charge of a convoy in the war. He had a sense of brisk confidence that he infused in his subordinates." The following statement, provided by an artillery platoon sergeant, captures how a leader's confidence is directly linked to subordinates' confidence in the leader's decisions: "[Leader] confidence [is critical]—Someone [the leader] has to believe in what he is doing, or I will not believe in what he is doing."

The soldiers recognized that leaders will experience fear; however, they did not want their leaders to show signs of fear or be paralyzed by it.

---

7. Courage

Subordinate responses indicated that they view courage in a combat leader in two dimensions: physical and moral.

Importance of Physical Courage. A leader's physical courage seemed to entail the ability to overcome the fear of injury or death, hide or otherwise manage outward signs of fear, willingly share the risks of combat with their soldiers, and perform their duties in the face of danger.

The soldiers recognized that leaders will experience fear; however, they did not want their leaders to show signs of fear or be paralyzed by it. Leaders' physical courage seems to facilitate the development of trust with their subordinates because they could depend on courageous leaders to fulfill their responsibilities in combat, which seemed to increase subordinates' trust in the leaders and their willingness to follow them in combat, as shown in these observations:

> "[Leader] courage [is important because]—if you show your fear, no one will want to follow you into a situation where you are putting their lives

on the line."—Second lieutenant, infantry company fire support officer, Qayyarah West Airbase, northern Iraq

"There was a huge explosion at one of our positions. There were secondary explosions going off when we got there [at an abandoned Iraqi Army ammunition cache]. The fires were hot and causing a lot of explosions. I was there along with the commander, first sergeant, and ten other soldiers. We all went out to save the lives of five Iraqis knowing the risks. That definitely increased my trust in everyone there."—Specialist, cannon crew member, Qayyarah West Airbase, northern Iraq

"[Leader] courage [is critical]—I trust leaders who volunteer to share in any potential danger."—First lieutenant, artillery battery executive officer, Mosul, Iraq

Leaders' physical courage also sets the example and serves to enhance their soldiers' courage to face the dangers of combat. Conversely, leaders' lack of courage would increase their soldiers' fears. Soldiers are likely to make either a personal or situation attribution concerning a leader who is afraid to face combat. Subordinates who think that the leader lacks strength of character to overcome the fears of combat will make a personal attribution for the leader's demonstration of fear, which will decrease trust and the subordinates' willingness to face combat. Similarly, subordinates may believe that the situation is so grave that the leader's fear is justified and thus make a situational attribution. This attribution to explain the leader's fear would also decrease subordinates' willingness to face the dangers of upcoming operations. In either case, a leader's demonstration of fear will have a negative impact on subordinates' abilities and willingness to face the dangers to accomplish the organization's objectives.

A sergeant who served as an ammunition team chief provided the following response to why leader courage was important to the development of trust and subordinates' abilities to overcome the fear of combat: "[A leader's] personal courage to overcome fear [is important to the development of trust]. If the leader is afraid, it only makes the subordinates more afraid [to face combat]."

These insights regarding the importance of leaders' physical courage to the development of trust apply to all organizations that require its members to face physical danger to accomplish the organization's mission, such as law enforcement, firefighting, iron working, demolition, mining, commercial fishing, and oil drilling. Leaders' physical courage demonstrates to subordinates that they have the ability to manage stress, confidence in their ability to meet the challenges of the dangerous situation, a willingness to lead by example and share the hardships with subordinates, and strength of character to fulfill their role obligations in the most demanding situations. This is why a leader's physical courage increases subordinates' trust in the leader, their motivation to face danger, and their willingness to follow the leader into harm's way.

The Importance of Moral Courage. The second dimension of leader courage deals with leaders' moral strength to do the right thing in all situations. Moral courage entails a leader's strength of character to be willing to incur risk in order to act according to his or her values and beliefs and stand up to authority to protect his or her soldiers' welfare or defend his or her decisions. Thus, moral courage enables leaders to live with integrity, act to uphold the loyalty to their subordinates, and execute their duties with confidence. Subordinates can trust leaders who have the courage to act in accordance with their values because they know the directives they issue will be honest and based on values. Subordinates will not depend on or trust a leader who possesses good job knowledge, has a good set of values and beliefs, and has loyalty to subordinates but lacks the moral courage to put these skills, values, and beliefs into action. Therefore, a leader's moral courage provides the force of will to do what is right regardless of the situation and the costs the leader must incur. In combat, this is critical because leaders' moral courage and integrity define the moral and ethical boundaries that subordinates must operate within.

Furthermore, soldiers' responses indicated they would trust combat leaders who were not afraid to take a stand for what they believed in, the decisions they made, or what is the proper way to conduct business. Leaders must have the moral courage to handle the consequences of taking a stand with the chain of command to fight for what they believe is right. The following statements illustrate qualities of moral courage that lead to the development of trust:

> "[I place a high value on a leader's] strength when it comes to standing up to the company commander, so that fire-support team members were used properly and not as machine gunners."—Staff sergeant, infantry company fire support noncommissioned officer, Qayyarah West Airbase, northern Iraq

> "Courage [is important because] a leader must be able to take risks and not back down from confrontation."—Private first class, infantry company forward observer radio operator, Qayyarah West Airbase, northern Iraq

Moral courage is equally important to leadership in business, nonprofit, political, or any other type of organization. Group members always expect their leaders to have the moral courage to act in accordance with their own and the organization's values. Thus, leaders' moral courage provides group members with a sense of confidence that leaders will behave in a moral and ethical manner and take action to promote the best interests of the organization and its members. This confidence that leaders have the strength to act morally and ethically leads to the development of trust, which increases group members' willingness to follow.

Enron's, Tyco's, and Adelphi's senior business leaders lacked the moral courage to act in accordance with their own and their organization's values. The consequences of this leadership failure were devastating to the companies, the employees, retirees, and shareholders. Employees lost their jobs, retirees lost their pensions and sense of security, shareholders lost their equity, and the public lost trust in the companies. Whether these senior leaders actively participated in the fraud or tolerated it by not coming forward, they all lacked moral courage to do the right thing. Thus, the agency that comes with moral courage helps ensure group members that leaders do the right thing by the organization and all people associated with it.

Sharing information, especially in chaotic and dangerous situations, provides group members with a sense of predictability and control that they need and crave, which facilitates successful stress management.

---

8. Sharing Information

In combat, subordinates have a strong desire and need for their leaders to keep them informed about the current situation and upcoming operations. Continuous information flow enables subordinates to anticipate and prepare for future challenges physically and mentally. Regarding preparing for the physical challenges of combat, subordinates can gather and check their equipment, implement rest plans, and adjust duties as needed. In terms of preparing for the mental challenges, continuous information helps group members form realistic expectations about the demands of the current or upcoming mission; it also prevents rumors. Therefore, sharing information, especially in chaotic and dangerous situations, provides group members with a sense of predictability and control that they need and crave, which facilitates successful stress management. Consider these observations:

> "Keep soldiers informed—you do not need anyone lost or confused during combat. It is bad enough when bullets are flying and people are dying."
> —Specialist, forward observer, Qayyarah West Airbase, northern Iraq

"Keeping me and the soldiers well informed [is critical]. If there was no doubt on my mind what the mission was, with all the details, I know I would be good to go."—Specialist, artillery computer operator, Mosul, Iraq

"Giving out information [is so important], because if you know what is going on, the better you are able to prepare."—Sergeant, artillery gunner, Tall Afar, Iraq

"[A leader must be] informative—[this is] a must so soldiers are informed and not living in a 'rumor world.'"—Infantry company first sergeant, Tall Afar, Iraq

In any organization, leaders' willingness to share information, especially in a crisis, serves four important functions:

1. It allows subordinates to prepare for challenges and manage stress.
2. It demonstrates to subordinates that the leadership as an institution is not trying to hide anything.
3. It increases the interdependence in the leader-subordinate relationship.
4. It prompts subordinates to reciprocate in kind.

For instance, a company experiencing financial challenges may have to restructure to cut costs. By sharing this candid information with employees, the company leadership provides employees the time to prepare for possible cost-cutting courses of actions, employees may modify their behavior to cut costs to prevent the restructuring, and employees have the opportunity to provide senior leaders with ideas of how to cut costs without restructuring. This candid exchange of information on the organization's future increases the interdependence of leaders and subordinates and provides subordinates with a means to influence the organization's future.

Furthermore, the candid sharing of information prevents rumors, which allows all members of the organization to focus their energies on resolving the financial problems and not worrying about the validity of the last rumor. Therefore, candid sharing of information, especially in a crisis, meets employees' strong need to be kept informed in order to maintain a sense of predictability, prevents stress caused by rumors, and demonstrates the leadership's openness, which facilitates the development of trust.

This connection between the leader and subordinates is important because it increases the interdependence in the relationship and the likelihood that leaders will consider their soldiers as people and not simply as expendable resources.

---

9. Personal Connection with Subordinates

Leaders who took the time and made the effort to establish an interpersonal connection with their subordinates facilitated the development of trust in combat. The soldiers' responses indicated that they wanted leaders who made the effort to learn about them, listen to their concerns, and understand their basic needs. This connection or bond between the leader and subordinates is important because it increases the interdependence in the relationship and the likelihood that leaders will consider their soldiers as people who have families and aspirations, as well as fears, and not simply as expendable resources when the leaders are developing plans or issuing directives in combat. Also, this personal connection with the leader provides group members with a line of communication to potentially exercise influence over the organization's activities. Leaders are more likely to solicit from and listen to feedback provided by subordinates with whom they have a personal bond. Therefore, it is functional from the subordinates' perspective to desire a personal connection with the leader because it increases their chances of survival and also provides them with a means to exercise potential influence over their own and the organization's outcomes. Following are two statements from soldiers that accentuate the link between leaders' personal connection with their subordinates and the development of trust:

> "[I value] leaders who could relate to soldiers on personal and professional levels. It is important that the job gets done, but it is also important to know your soldiers. Soldiers will respect and trust these leaders more."
> —Specialist, radio repairman, Qayyarah West Airbase, northern Iraq

> "[I respect] a leader who is in tune with his men, knows them other than just another pack [racksack]—knows how they are feeling and can relate."—Sergeant, infantry company forward observer, Qayyarah West Airbase, northern Iraq

People join organizations to meet basic needs, such as earning money to provide food, shelter, and security, and to gain a sense of belonging and purpose. In most businesses, employees' basic needs are met through earning their salaries. This is a relationship where the employees exchange their work for pay from the company's leadership. Leaders who make the effort to form a personal bond with their followers learn about what truly motivates them and also provide group members with a sense of belonging. Leaders making the effort to get to know employees communicate to them that they are valued and respected members of the organization, worthy of the time needed to establish a relationship. This makes group members feel appreciated and strengthens their sense of belonging to the organization.

Furthermore, a personal connection with subordinates provides leaders with insights into each group member's sources of motivation, strengths, and weaknesses. This provides leaders the ability to tailor their influence strategies to reach all group members. Most important, this connection opens lines of communication with subordinates, which provides leaders with an invaluable source of information about the organization regarding all of the following and more:

- Perceptions about effectiveness of policies
- Feedback for improving organizational effectiveness
- Feedback on subordinate leaders
- Feedback on their own leadership effectiveness

This feedback from subordinates is critical for leaders' self-development and the organization's improvement. Leaders can also use these open lines of communication to communicate their vision and provide group members with feedback on how their work is making a contribution to the organization. This can help provide subordinates with a sense of purpose in their work. Thus, the establishment of a personal connection with subordinates benefits both group members and leaders.

10. Strong Sense of Duty

In combat, soldiers want their leaders to feel compelled and committed to meeting the responsibilities of their leadership positions. Leaders who have a strong sense of duty are more likely to fulfill their responsibilities, especially in the dangerous and stressful environment of combat. Thus, leaders with a strong sense of duty seemed to provide subordinates with a sense of confidence that their leaders would fulfill their responsibilities and accomplish the mission as well as take care of their soldiers, which served to facilitate the development of trust.

Below are several soldiers' responses to why duty was important to the development of trust. The three statements illustrate the connection joining duty, mission accomplishment, and taking care of subordinates' welfare:

"Duty—Mission first, soldiers always."—Sergeant, howitzer gunner, Mosul, Iraq

"Duty—Gets the job done, no matter what."—Specialist, infantry gunner, Tall Afar, Iraq

"Responsibility—it is good to know that you can look up to your leaders to do the right thing."—Private, infantryman, Tall Afar, Iraq

A leader's strong sense of duty is important to leadership in any type of organization. A sense of duty provides leaders with the motivation to meet their responsibilities in the toughest of situations. This increases group members' confidence that the leader will fulfill role obligations, which leads to the development of trust.

The Universality of the Leadership Attributes

The mapping of the prototype of a leader who can be trusted in combat provides all leaders with insights into the attributes that influence the development of trust with their subordinates. These insights regarding trust development in combat should be equally applicable to other organizational settings. Leaders can use this knowledge to do self-assessments, create plans to develop these critical attributes in themselves, and formulate strategies to communicate to their subordinates the possession of these attributes, especially when taking over a new organization. Leaders who diligently develop these important attributes should be able to earn their subordinates' trust and also provide them with a greater ability to exercise influence.

The Link Between Trust and Combat Leadership

When asked to describe in their own words how trust was related to leadership, the majority (78 percent) of the soldiers interviewed indicated that trust was necessary and essential for a leader to exercise influence in combat. This was a powerful finding because the results suggested that in extreme situations, where the subordinates assume the greatest risks, trust is the psychological mechanism that gets them to willingly accept leader influence, place their self-interests secondary to the organization's interests, and step into harm's way.

Leaders Can Be Effective Only If Their Subordinates Trust Them

To effectively lead subordinates in combat, leaders must first earn their subordinates' trust, as illustrated in the following statements:

> "I think trust is leadership. Leadership is the act of influencing soldiers to accomplish the mission by providing purpose, direction, and motivation. If soldiers don't know that they can trust you to feed them, let them rest, tell you what they are afraid of, then how in the hell are they going to follow you in any situation?"—Sergeant, artillery gunner, Mosul, Iraq

"If you trust your leader, you are willing to go to hell and back if need be."
—Sergeant, artillery gunner, Tall Afar, Iraq

"Soldiers first have to trust you to follow you. Following a leader and following orders are two different things. If they trust you and believe in you, there is nothing they won't do for you."—Second lieutenant, infantry company fire support officer, Qayyarah West Airbase, northern Iraq

"Trust to me deals a lot with leadership. The more I trust a leader, the more I allow him/her to influence me."—Specialist, artillery computer operator, Mosul, Iraq

"If you trust in your leaders, the soldiers will do more. On the other hand, if they do not trust their leaders, the soldiers will always second-guess their leaders before they do what they have to do."—Sergeant, mechanic, Mosul, Iraq

"It is like a field manual. The field manual is the leader. If I do not trust it, I would not read it. I would not take information from it or apply it or risk any lives. Trust in a leader allows you to listen and do what is expected of you. And because you trust the leader, you know that he will not foolishly risk your life and that of your peers/subordinates."—First lieutenant, platoon leader, Mosul, Iraq

---

Subordinates who did not trust their leaders would not willingly follow their directives, would question orders, and would not be willing to assume the risks of combat, which could put unit members' lives at risk and have a detrimental impact on the effectiveness of an organization.

As highlighted by these examples, subordinates viewed trust in leaders as necessary and essential to their willingness to accept leader influence and the risks of combat. Subordinates willingly followed the directives of leaders they trusted and seemed willing to put forth the extra effort and assume a greater degree of risk to accomplish the mission.

The finding that trust is necessary and essential to the exercise of effective leadership in combat can be applied to any type of organization. In general, people are more willing to be influenced by leaders who are competent to meet role responsibilities and have the character to behave in a cooperative and moral and ethical manner. The longitudinal study investigating how company presidents established relationships with key subordinates found that leaders' ability to exercise influence was a function of subordinates' trust in them. Thus, the findings from both studies strongly indicate that trust is the key to leadership.

The Lack of Trust Undermines Effective Leadership

The responses indicated that subordinates who did not trust their leaders would not willingly follow their directives, would question orders, and would not be willing to assume the risks of combat, which could put unit members' lives at risk and have a detrimental impact on the effectiveness of an organization. The lack of trust in the leaders would cause subordinates to focus on and worry about their personal safety and cause them to wonder about whether and question if the leaders' directives would result in accomplishment of the organization's objectives.

This questioning of leader directives and focus on personal safety could result in subordinates' adopting a protective or conservative attitude, which would decrease their motivation to face the dangers of combat. Subordinates will probably comply with nontrusted leaders' orders as a last resort; otherwise they will look for ways to change or get out of the leaders' directive in an effort to minimize risks to their own safety. In extreme cases, subordinates may even disobey the orders of leaders they do not trust. The following responses illustrate how the lack of trust in a leader decreases subordinates' willingness to accept leader influence:

> "If you do not trust your leaders, it can be difficult to follow orders, especially if death or dismemberment is an immediate result."—Sergeant, infantry company forward observer, Qayyarah West Airbase, northern Iraq

> "If you cannot trust your leader, you are going to have doubts about your safety as well as the safety of your fellow soldiers. You will not perform 100 percent for your leader if there is not trust."—Specialist, artillery gunner, Mosul, Iraq

> "If soldiers do not trust their leaders, it leads to second-guessing and possible disobedience of orders."—Staff sergeant, chief fire direction computer, Mosul, Iraq

> "You can tell a man to fight, as his leader; if he doesn't trust you, he will change the things you want. If he trusts you, he will do what you want." —Sergeant, supply noncommissioned officer, Qayyarah West Airbase, northern Iraq

> "Trust is the most important thing that can relate to leadership. Because if I don't trust my leader, I will question every order in my head, which can make me hesitate and may get me killed."—Specialist, infantry company armor, Qayyarah West Airbase, northern Iraq

> "The main foundation for leadership is trust. If you cannot trust the person or people who lead you, then basically you are lost. How can you be influenced to do something if you cannot trust the person telling you what to do?"—Sergeant, artillery gunner, Mosul, Iraq

EXHIBIT 14.2. COMBAT LEADERSHIP LESSONS FOR ALL LEADERS

Lesson 1: Trust is the key to the exercise of leadership.

Lesson 2: Competence is king in the development of trust in extreme situations such as combat.

Lesson 3: Lead by caring.

Lesson 4: Competence and character determine a leader's credibility.

Lesson 5: Leading by example enhances credibility and provides subordinates direction and motivation, especially in tough situations.

Lesson 6: Leadership is about creating relationships with people.

Lesson 7: Staying cool is a must to lead.

Lesson 8: Share information to lead, especially in tough situations.

Lesson 9: Never let them see you sweat—project confidence in all actions.

"A soldier who does not trust a leader will question decisions the leader makes and will not be willing to follow the leader into a dangerous situation."—Staff sergeant, platoon sergeant, Mosul, Iraq

"If a soldier does not trust his leader, he or she may hesitate in the time of need, costing lives or equipment."—Specialist, infantry antitank gunner, Tall Afar, Iraq

As highlighted by these examples, subordinates who did not trust their leaders did not willingly follow their leaders, questioned orders, and seemed to take measures to minimize the risk to their personal safety against orders. The results clearly indicate that in order to lead effectively, especially in the extreme situations such as combat, leaders must earn their subordinates' trust (Exhibit 14.2).

Notes

1. M. Deutsch, "Trust and Suspicion," *Journal of Conflict Resolution,* 1958, 2(4), 265–279.

2. J. French and B. H. Raven, "The Bases of Social Power," in D. Cartwright (ed.), *Studies of Social Power* (Ann Arbor, Mich.: Institute of Social Research, 1959).

3. G. Yukl, *Leadership in Organizations,* 4th ed. (Upper Saddle River, N.J.: Prentice Hall, 1998).

4. N. Cantor, "A Cognitive Social Approach to Personality," in N. Cantor and J. Kihlstrom (eds.), *Personality, Cognition, and Social Interaction* (Mahwah, N.J.: Erlbaum, 1981).

5. U.S. Department of the Army, *Army Leadership (Field Manual 22–100)* (Washington, D.C.: U.S. Department of the Army, 1999).

6. J. Gabarro, "The Development of Trust, Influence, and Expectations." In A. Athos and J. Gabarro (eds.), *Interpersonal Behavior: Communication and Understanding in Relationships* (Upper Saddle River, N.J.: Prentice Hall, 1978).

7. R. Giuliani and K. Kurson, *Leadership* (New York: Talk Miramax Books, 2002).

8. J. Gabarro, "The Development of Trust, Influence, and Expectations."

9. S. Carty, J. Healy, and C. Woodyard, "GM's Broad Cuts Aim to Share the Pain," *USA Today,* Feb. 6, 2006, sec. B, p. 1.

PART THREE

LEADING ORGANIZATIONS

CHAPTER FIFTEEN

SOCIALIZED LEADERSHIP

Todd Henshaw

I walked into the hallway of the fourth floor of MacArthur Barracks after taps one night. I was curious to see what happened when the officers were gone and cadets had their run of the place. When I entered the hallway, I heard someone crying. I approached the noise, turned the corner, and saw a huge shape in the dark hallway. The cadet's shoulders were shrugging as he wept, his body shaking uncontrollably. I caught the eye of the senior cadet in the hallway, who immediately approached to see who I was.

"Can I help you, Sir?" he asked.

"I'm LTC Henshaw, and I'm here doing research. Can you tell me what's going on?"

"Sir, I'm the squad leader, Cadet Jones. Well, Sir, this new cadet was being difficult, and we decided to take him through some physical exercises to get him to listen."

"What exercises did you have him do, Cadet Jones?" I asked.

"Sir, we had him do some flutter kicks and push-ups."

"Why is he crying?"

"Well, Sir, I guess we took him too far. He wasn't listening to us, so we were trying to break him down. We had him do a few push-ups, then a few flutter kicks. Then we had him do several repetitions of each. We got him to the point where he couldn't do any more. We wanted to get him to realize who is in charge. Once he got to the point where he couldn't do another flutter kick, he started losing it. He burst into tears and started sobbing. We haven't been able to get him to talk since."

This was one of many instances of cadet leaders trying to show new cadets "who's in charge." When I asked the cadet leaders where they learned these techniques, they usually responded, "Sir, this is the way it was done to me when I was a new cadet."

This story provides an example of the influence of culture on leadership development at West Point. Culture in the corps of cadets offers a prescription for cadet leadership, enforces understandings regarding who is in charge and what newcomers need to undergo before passage, and guides the leader-follower relationship.

Although most of us would agree that there are globally recognized measures or characteristics of effective leaders, the art and practice of leadership is inherently cultural and therefore local, informed and shaped by experience and social agreement. New leaders are required to learn the culture of the new organization quickly, albeit in conjunction with the skills and expertise associated with the new job. As they enter formal leadership positions or experience influence opportunities in the workplace, shared understandings regarding how to "be in charge" will frame their choice of leadership style and practice. Leveraging these common social understandings and confirming and reinforcing them in uncertain situations through symbolic behavior and language confirms and anoints leaders with cultural power.

The art and practice of leadership is inherently cultural and therefore local, informed and shaped by experience and social agreement.

The symbolic nature and forms of leadership have been discussed by management researchers in the past. Many suggest that leaders within organizations may influence and change the culture by manipulating a variety of levers to move social understanding or assumptions in the desired direction and motivate organization members to achieve goals and objectives. Indeed, if we agree to view organizations as cultures, and therefore systems of shared understandings, leaders must be aware of the culture within which influence is manifested and communicated.

The link less clearly established is between shared meanings learned by new organization members through early entry experiences and their future use in social interaction involving leadership. During entry experiences, new leaders learn not only how to interact with others in their new work setting; they actually learn how leadership is done in the organization. This is the case for novice and more experienced leaders entering new work settings.

During entry experiences, new leaders learn not only how to interact with others in their new work setting; they actually learn how leadership is done in the organization.

A great deal of management attention typically ensures that new workers are focused on learning the skills and knowledge associated with accomplishing tasks within the job description. If we were to consider that new employees are also learning the culture of their work group and the more general organization, we might further conclude that these newcomers are learning how veteran employees interpret their circumstances and ways to interact between members of the organization.

Just as socialization involves teaching new organization members appropriate organizational ways of thinking and behaving, leadership can be explained as the process of convincing potential followers that the interpretive capacities of the leader are worthy of their support.

Whether through formal authority or the confidence of followers, leaders are afforded the opportunity to read and define situations, influence others as to what is happening in a given situation and why, how to respond to the situation, and what to make of the response of the situation to the leader's action. The meanings derived from these interpretations, especially those connected to significant events, begin to form the culture that guides further interpretations and action. The experiences of followers are guided by these past interpretations of events. Leaders are subsequently accorded greater influence to determine how events are interpreted. The ways that leaders have responded to significant events become the ingredients of cultural forms such as organizational stories, myths, and legends and are often the foundation for ceremonies and rituals.

The power to communicate in symbolic ways is a necessary condition of leadership. Recent writings pointing to the link between leadership and storytelling emphasize the importance of enriched communication between leaders and followers and the necessary components of stories that tend to provide clarity of purpose and communicate greater transparency to followers. To be capable of inspiring subordinates to move in any particular direction, leaders must also be capable of leveraging a variety of meaningful communication practices and content that are culturally appropriate to ensure that the leader's message is properly understood and sufficiently symbolic to tap the emotions and motivations of followers.

When considering the social practice of leadership through this lens, the processes of newcomer socialization and leadership appear similar. Just as socialization involves teaching new organization members appropriate organizational ways of thinking and behaving, leadership can be explained as the process of convincing potential followers that the interpretive capacities of the leader are worthy of their support. Both processes result in increasing the level of social agreement regarding how we accomplish work, how we treat each other, and why we exist as an organization.

Cadet Basic Training and Socializing New Leaders

Several years ago, I was afforded the opportunity to observe cadet basic training (CBT, called "Beast Barracks" traditionally by alumni and cadets) at West Point. CBT not only socializes new cadets into military life, it also provides more experienced upperclass cadets (college juniors and seniors) an opportunity to practice leadership. During this eight-week summer training experience, socialization and leadership are intertwined, as cadre (the cadet leaders responsible for supervising and training new cadets) intend to show new cadets the ropes, or local cultural understandings, while they are teaching the more formally prescribed military tasks such as marching, rifle marksmanship, and how to wear the military uniform.

These new cadets will, in two years, be completing a learning cycle, informing their new cadets regarding local cultural definitions of leadership and using the same practices leveraged so effectively by their leaders to teach them the ropes.

The veteran cadre serve as role models as their experience approximates the relevant future experiences of new cadets. The new cadets are told that their initial year at the Academy involves learning to be a good follower, but they realize that at some point, they will be required to lead at West Point and eventually in the Army. The leadership practices modeled by the cadre and the cultural themes that they symbolize during these formative experiences offer new cadets lenses to interpret their experience and, more important to their future roles as leaders, recipes for their own future leadership situations. Although future leadership experiences as upperclass cadets will not mirror exactly those they observed as a new cadet, the context will be similar and will likely invoke the same situational definitions and actions demonstrated of their more experienced cadet leaders. These new cadets will, in two years, be completing a learning cycle, informing their new cadets regarding local cultural definitions of leadership and using the same practices leveraged so effectively by their leaders to teach them the ropes.

Cadet basic training at West Point offers an opportunity to witness the socialization of new leaders in progress. Senior cadets lead in ways that are informed by their cultural understandings as members and leaders in the corps of cadets. The cultural understandings that are taught new cadets through cadre behavior and language shape the ways that they will lead in the future. As they approach and consider the uncertainties inherent in early leadership situations in the future, new cadets draw on the same practices that are taught to them during this first formative summer.

New cadets are not merely passive receptors of the follower role; they are preparing for the future expectations accompanying the cadet leader role. They watch and learn, often assimilating understandings about leadership reflecting cadet cultural themes or understandings that conflict with formal Academy policies and leader intent. Much of the learning can be considered tacit cultural knowledge; it is neither prescribed in formal Academy policies or training programs nor openly discussed among cadre. It is often communicated through the practices leveraged by upperclassmen to maintain the social distinction between themselves and the new cadets.

This type of leadership maintains and reinforces current cultural themes and is maintained and reinforced by them. Leadership development within the corps of cadets at West Point, at least in its influence on new cadets, represents cyclical leadership learning and is reinforced each summer by the understandings of leadership that are shared among upperclass cadets.

Cadet Cultural Themes

In ten weeks of observing the cadets during CBT and through interviewing many of the upperclass cadre and new cadets, I learned much about cadet cultural understandings or themes that influence the way they socialize and lead new cadets. These themes, derived and content-analyzed from field notes and interviews, provide both content and process for what is taught by cadre to new cadets and inform the foundation for how they develop their roles and practices as new leaders during this CBT period (Table 15.1).

The cultural themes help explain what can be best summarized and described as upperclass leadership. This culturally informed style of leadership emphasizes status differences and associated privileges, is often punitive rather than supportive in nature, and uses traditions as justification to break down, weed out, and otherwise test the will and resilience of new cadets. This leader style is best appreciated by contrasting it to the explicit expectations of West Point and the Army, the organization that cadets are preparing to enter as leaders.

Table 15.2 points to the conflicting leader expectations of the explicit (formal, West Point and Army) and implicit (cultural) models. Academy expectations for leaders and leadership are consistent with those of the U.S. Army. Cultural expectations for cadet leaders within the corps of cadets emphasize defending corps traditions, ensuring separation between new cadets and upperclass students, regulating membership through breaking down and weeding out, and often manipulating subordinates as a means for entertaining and humoring upperclass students.

TABLE 15.1. CADET CULTURAL THEMES

Teamwork	"You must learn to count on others and contribute to the team."
Putting on the show	"We act one way when officers are around and another when it's just us cadets. We preserve our freedom of action by keeping officers in the dark."
Shared tribulation	"We went through this, and you should too. It made us who we are. We can't let you off easy. You'll appreciate this later."
Weeding out and gatekeeping	"The Academy lets you in, but the corps decides who stays. We'll test you, find your breaking points, and determine whether you should be here."
Developing mental toughness	"Combat requires leaders who won't fall apart under pressure."
We're still college kids; we like to have fun	"This is a serious place, but cadets must maintain a sense of humor to make it through."

TABLE 15.2. CONFLICTING LEADER EXPECTATIONS

Army or Academy Leader Expectations	Upperclass Leader Expectations
Inform followers	Withhold information to increase stress
Coach, teach, assist	Find and emphasize mistakes, failures
Manage stress; enable follower to achieve	Increase interpersonal stress and test resilience, find breaking points
Clarify task, standard, expectations	Confuse, disorient
Reinforce success; build confidence	Defeat, lay obstacles, break down
Respect followers	Belittle, demean, harass new cadets
Develop and learn	Use rites of passage, weed out
Remediate	Punish, coerce

West Point has articulated an elaborate leader development system configured to teach and promote effective leader behaviors and actions that reflect the explicit, espoused values of the institution. The shared cultural understandings and practices within the corps of cadets are quite different, however. These understandings regarding how leaders interact with followers are reflected in the leadership practices of the upperclass and in the culturally informed models of leading that they teach future generations of corps leaders.

While observing and interviewing upperclass cadets during cadet basic training, I witnessed the Army- and Academy-supported leadership practices, although the behaviors of most cadet leaders were more representative of the upperclass leadership practices reinforcing cadet cultural themes. This may point to individual differences in maturity or greater exposure to Army leadership expectations prior to entering West Point.

The differential requirements for a cadet to be a good upperclass student within the cultural expectations of the corps of cadets and a good leader (according to the Academy's own formal policy) are in conflict. The cycle of leadership development that prepares the new cadets for their future roles as cadet leaders supports and continues the cultural themes that are in conflict with the formal system of development, including the explicit guidance directed at cadet leaders by senior Academy officers. In fact, it defies the criteria used to evaluate cadet leadership performance.

This style of leadership does, however, meet the expectations of and fulfills their responsibilities to the corps of cadets, represented by the upperclassmen filling roles during the summer, and those who will inherit these new cadets when they return to their studies in the fall. The performance of the cadre in "whipping them into shape" will be evaluated by criteria that are different from those used more formally by the Academy. Summer cadre are responsible to the corps of cadets to produce followers who are prepared to assist them in maintaining a sense of humor and can persevere through demeaning treatment and hazing rituals integral to their passage into the realm of cadethood and acceptance. New cadets must be prepared mentally and physically to withstand the leader-induced interpersonal stress and learn the knowledge and skills associated with administering it when they become cadre. When new cadets enter their roles as cadre two years from now, they will have ready-made, culturally informed examples of leadership practices, with each reflecting the cultural meanings embedded in the upperclass leadership style.

Cadet leaders, in reacting to and trying to make sense of leadership situations, are likely to draw on practices that they have observed, are familiar to them, and have been used to discipline or train them in the past. Their cadet leaders inherited this system of leadership practices from their upperclassmen when they were new cadets and passed them to new cadets, never reflecting on the meanings symbolized in the behavior and language. When I would ask cadre what they had intended through enacting one of the various hazing rituals, they would either have no answer or would use what has become a shared rationale or justification for the practice.

Cadets build recipes for leadership and socializing subordinates based on their own socialization experience. It is a developmental cycle, and sometimes an abusive one, reflecting the nearly subconscious, automatic nature of cultural influence in leadership practices rather than reflective thought concerning what style of leadership would best serve the current situation or subordinates. In many cases, cadet leaders failed to consider the reasons that what they experienced during CBT would not necessarily be appropriate in this particular set of circumstances. It is imitation based on memories, partially reconstructed ones, where the harshness has been ameliorated and the successful outcome exaggerated.

It is a developmental cycle, and sometimes an abusive one, reflecting the nearly subconscious, automatic nature of cultural influence in leadership practices rather than reflective thought concerning what style of leadership would best serve the current situation or subordinates.

After lunch one afternoon, I was again walking through the barracks, this time in uniform. When I got to the top of the stairs, I heard yelling. Investigating further, I noticed that a new cadet had his back to the wall and was holding his arms straight out. This new cadet was having difficulty; he was obviously fatigued and could barely hold his arms out straight. When his arms fell, the upperclass cadet would yell, "Get your arms up!"

As I approached, the cadre member looked at me, then at the ground, and appeared guilty and ready to explain himself. I said, "You're not in trouble. I just want to know what is going on." As I spoke, the new cadet, back against the wall and arms out, began to belch involuntarily, as if he were going to vomit. The cadre member yelled down the hallway for someone to get a trash bag. Two other cadre members appeared carrying a black plastic bag and handed it to the cadet who had been administering the "discipline." Upon receiving the bag, the new cadet heaved, ridding himself of his lunch.

I pulled the cadre member aside and went through my usual line of questions. "Sir," he responded to my initial question, "the new cadet forgot to secure his lock box, and I was trying to teach him a lesson."

I asked, "How long has this been going on?"

"Sir, about thirty minutes. I had him doing Superman for the first fifteen minutes, then had him hold his arms out for the rest of the time."

"Superman?" I asked.

"Yes, Sir, we have them lay out on the floor with their arms stretched out in front like they're flying. The only thing touching the ground is their stomach. I had him hold his lock box like that until he couldn't hold it any more."

"What were you trying to accomplish with this?"

"Sir, when I was a new cadet, I forgot to secure my lock box. My cadre had me do Superman. I never forgot to lock my box again."

When I interviewed cadet leaders regarding what I had observed of their leadership in various situations, I asked them what they were trying to accomplish, where they had come across that particular practice, and what criteria they had used to evaluate the success of their method. Many cadet leaders spoke about ensuring that new cadets have a real experience, complete with the mental hardship and physical ritual, that they had survived during their cadet basic training summer. Cadet leaders share an understanding that tradition plays an important role in creating West Point leaders. Many leadership practices seem harsh and abusive to an outsider, yet many of the new cadets stated that this type of treatment was consistent with their expectations of the "Beast experience."

For CBT to be considered a meaningful experience, new cadets must persevere through extreme difficulty. If that mental or physical challenge was not produced by the Academy's formal training plan, upperclass cadet leaders would introduce it during lulls by adding physical punishment and mental stress, "increasing the volume" (yelling and verbal abuse), or entertainment episodes where they would have new cadets dance, sing, or, as in one case, form a band with dancers and complete a performance of a popular song to increase the stress. The officers who supervise cadets voiced concern that cadet leaders get carried away with this often harsh treatment of new cadets and told me that the cadets seem to enjoy it, not as a part of a formal program of events but as a form of entertainment.

When asked about the leadership practices, many of the cadre members could not articulate the exact function other than that the verbal abuse and often creative hazing techniques would test and develop the mental toughness of the new cadet and would allow them (at some point in the future) to say that they had survived a difficult CBT. This rites-of-passage perspective was not generally supported in the West Point formal program literature. Cadets were told by the Army officers that it was not their job to test, weed out, or otherwise determine the fate of new cadets.

Implications for Leaders

A primary responsibility of organizations is to develop new leaders. Integral to this process are the entry experiences or the socialization and early learning of those who will assume the mantle of leadership in the organization. As new leaders learn the culture, they are also learning appropriate ways to interact and influence others. Leadership is therefore culturally informed and shaped, and new leaders observe and replicate practices deemed appropriate through shared experience.

Organizations employ a variety of approaches and methods for managing the entry experiences of new leaders. Depending on the seniority and experience of the new leader, organizations may have no formal system in place, assuming that what the new leader sees and learns is appropriate and consistent with organizational direction, goals, and policies. Many organizations implement a detailed, formal process, ensuring that the new leader meets the right people and learns relevant job knowledge.

West Point, like many other typical organizations, assumes that formal programs and policies account for socialization and the entry experiences of new leaders. Yet this West Point example shows two competing systems in operation: the formal system, which is articulated and publicly acknowledged, and the informal, which is tacit though shared, maintained, and practiced by veteran insiders and exerts greater influence on new leader understandings regarding appropriate leadership in the organization. The expectations inherent in each system are different and, in the case of West Point, are near opposites.

Organizations cannot be assured that everything newcomers are learning is consistent with the formal program. In this case, informal social learning often contradicts and conflicts with the intent of formal leadership development programs. Cultural learning, especially the forms and practices of leadership that new leaders learn on entry, is related to the future practice of leadership in the organization and may be reinforcing vestiges of old culture. The socialization of new leaders therefore must not be taken for granted or assumed, but must be managed carefully to ensure that these first impressions are consistent with current organizational direction, goals, and philosophies.

Organizations cannot be assured that everything newcomers are learning is consistent with the formal program. In this case, informal social learning often contradicts and conflicts with the intent of formal leadership development programs.

John Dewey called this informal, veteran-administered social learning "miseducation" or "collateral learning," the idea being that what the organization intends may be only a portion of what is learned.[1] Organizational goals and objectives for learning represent only a small fraction of what newcomers actually learn. In the case of new cadets at West Point, military skills, cadet knowledge, and positive leadership represent the focus of Academy time and effort during this first summer. The formal training plan established by the Academy fails to address the powerful informal leadership training and development that occurs, mainly in interactions between upperclass leaders and new cadets. The institutional emphasis on explicit knowledge and skills and measurable outcomes leaves many of the traditional negative leadership practices in place.

This admonition to organizations speaks to the variety of cultural meanings in place within an organization that may or may not be consistent with formal policy or even functional for experienced members or novices. At West Point, these abusive practices are buttressed by traditions, defenses, and rationalizations in the name of future leadership challenges (combat, further hazing, maintaining a sense of humor). My West Point example highlights two systems of development operating simultaneously: one prescribed by the Academy to satisfy the institution's needs and the other culturally informed, intended to satisfy cultural demands and perceived developmental needs of new cadets.

There is indeed a conflict of intent here. Some unauthorized socialization practices are rationalized by veteran cadets as toughening and developmental, preparing the new cadets for hardships later in their cadet or military career. Cadet leaders defend their practices saying that they are the only actors who can identify the developmental requirements for the cadet role. They argue that officers supervising cadets cannot relate, do not remember what it is like, or did not graduate from West Point and therefore had not lived this experience.

Given two parallel systems at work, the result of socialization programs may be very different from what planners and supervisors of the program intend. What newcomers, especially future leaders, come away with is in a large part contingent on the leadership to which they have been exposed during these early interactions.

The informal or cultural systems are not necessarily changed by even radical shifts in policy. Cultural themes or understandings are resistant to the more formal systems and are often developed as a counter to them. In many cases during my observation at West Point, cadet leaders manipulated formal tasks to communicate their own cultural messages, confounding the Academy-stated purpose for the activity.

The cultural system recreates, reinforces, and defends itself as the task of socializing new leaders brings many of the tacit understandings to the surface. Many of the unstated assumptions go unchallenged throughout most of organizational life, as they are shared and accepted as appropriate by all socialized members. During new leader socialization in organizations, more experienced and senior leaders through their leadership (which includes cultural forms) shape the new leaders' understanding of what leaders are, what they do, how they define common situations and problems, and how they react to these situations. It forms a cycle of development passed on as generations of leaders and followers interact during these early socialization experiences. These meanings, which communicate to future leaders how to be a leader, are embedded in the practices and language used by more experienced leaders to socialize new leaders.

Support for this position comes from a wide range of studies indicating that early organizational learning is a major determinant of one's later organizationally relevant beliefs, attitudes, and behaviors. For new cadets at West Point, CBT represents the closest thing to "the Army" that they will see for at least their first year at the Academy. The lessons learned here are very powerful, more so than those learned during the academic year. Summer training represents the greatest military experience at West Point, the greatest immersion in an actual military lifestyle, rotating between garrison and field environment, and learning knowledge most relevant to future life as an officer in the Army.

So there is this issue of contiguity, or relevance and environment. Learning about leadership in a new organization that occurs during entry experiences is powerful and enduring for two reasons. First, the new leaders are more malleable and more impressionable than they will be at any other point in their organizational future. Everything is new, and each lesson prescribes how things are, what to make of things, how they should be reacted to and considered in interpretation and behavior. From that point on, situations and behavior either match what has been established or are anomalies. Second, the organization prioritizes the tasks to be accomplished and the knowledge learned during entry experiences as the most important or immediately relevant to the new leader. This establishes the relevance of the situations as those that will become critical later in their lives. They will be able to use this knowledge in the future, which makes learning it an imperative. Socialization plays a role in lasting images, understandings of how things are done, not merely new skills, roles, or an orientation to structure. Initial learning is learning that lasts and forms indelible impressions as to how to function as a member of a particular group. New leaders are more plastic, more impressionable than they will be at any point in the future. Even at this early stage in sense making, the new leader is discovering the requirements associated with the anticipated leader role.

West Point's view that new cadets are merely learning to be followers during these early experiences ignores their capacity to learn multiple roles simultaneously. New cadets are already piecing together their views of leadership and the practices and situations that will call out the various actions and reactions required in that role. They are leadership apprentices, observing and interpreting the behavior and language of relevant role models.

Socialization that is not managed can have unintended consequences. These unintended consequences are part of every socialization process and usually are not examined due to the lack of appropriate assessment, research, or evaluation approaches. West Point has been dealing with improper cadet leadership practices throughout its history. Many superintendents have tried, mostly through policy changes and personal influence, to change the patterns of upperclass leadership that remain. These patterns of leadership are informed by powerful cultural assumptions regarding the role of upperclassmen in the development of new cadets. The upperclass leadership style is promoted and informed by an underlying, tacit rationale that justifies unauthorized leadership practices. The cultural forms and practices communicate intended messages to new cadets early in their development—messages intended to convey upperclass status, dominance, and privilege. Although policy changes have influenced the practices themselves, the underlying themes remain. This has proven a very difficult problem for West Point. It has tried through formal mechanisms to extinguish these negative leadership behaviors and in their stead promote behaviors more consistent with those required of Army officers. The cyclical nature of leadership learning from generation to generation seems to be the most stubborn facet of the system to eradicate.

To change these traditional and culturally informed patterns of behavior, organizations must discover their sources.

What Are Organizations to Do?

It is critical for leaders to know what is being taught to new leaders entering the organization because what is taught might not always be consistent with organizational vision, strategy, or intent. Organizational leaders must ask themselves these questions:

- What is our current system or process for bringing in new leaders?
- What are the appropriate forms and practices of leadership in our organization?
- Are our higher and lower levels of leadership aligned in direction, goals, and message?
- How are cultural forms leveraged or appropriated in the organization?

The initial action for organizations to take in order to understand new leader socialization must be directed at understanding what is happening under the surface during these entry experiences. The only way to ascertain the underlying processes and forms of this behavior is by better understanding the culture. The organization must come to understand the common view of appropriate leadership practices within the organization, even at the lowest levels.

To change these traditional and culturally informed patterns of behavior, organizations must discover their sources. The cultural forms, the practices, language, and behavior themselves must be altered to promote enduring change.

Leaders within organizations should not think that they can merely write new policies to improve what is taught to new leaders. The underlying rationale must be changed to reflect a new set of responsibilities and role expectations for leaders in the organization.

For example, at West Point, the current rationale or ideology underlying upperclass forms of leadership implies that cadre must be enforcers—not of Academy standards but of the cultural themes that influence the early socialization of new cadets. The rationale also includes links between harsh interpersonal interaction and future challenges, such as requirements to deal with stress on the battlefield. Increasing mental toughness is used as an underlying justification for negative leadership. Breaking points are used as an indicator of future cadet performance and as a means to weed out those who may not meet the requirements for membership in the corps of cadets. Upperclass leaders are there to make the new cadet experience more difficult through interaction, not to enhance their probability of success through coaching and teaching. Their leadership roles and practices support themes of harsh treatment rather than promoting effective role modeling and mentoring behaviors as the Academy intends and prescribes.

The rationale must be changed by confronting cadets with the errors inherent in the traditional ideology. Connecting verbal abuse with combat in any way can be exposed as a justification for traditional practices. Cadets must be informed about the links between traditional practices, the accompanying cultural themes, and their nearly automatic adoption of these actions. Illuminating these links between themes and future behavior is critical to interrupting any socialization cycle. To interrupt this annual cycle of cultural reproduction, cadre must be convinced or their beliefs changed to reflect understandings about leadership more consistent with Academy themes. This requires exposing and dismantling the underlying rationale that currently justifies deviant leadership practices.

Meanings associated with normal entry activities in the organization must be changed to reflect the organization's intent for these activities. Leaders must determine if lower-level employees have turned these developmental activities into opportunities to communicate their own message. What is required is taking these leadership actions to a microlevel, to consider the motivations and intent of the leader actions prior to decision and action, and a thorough review of outcomes following these actions. Leaders must be more involved in coaching junior leaders and less involved in superficial actions, like making sure that the training events are on schedule. This will involve convincing higher-level leaders that their roles are primarily associated with leader development, not administrative tasks. Senior leaders play a critical role in the sense-making process for more junior leaders and must take the opportunity to shape and mold their interpretations to achieve the organization's expectations.

Meanings associated with normal entry activities in the organization must be changed to reflect the organization's intent for these activities.

Senior leadership could also be involved, prior to the entry of new leaders, in helping more junior leaders make sense of their new roles as leaders, especially those who have had little, if any, leadership experience. During this period, senior leaders in the organization and peers could provide feedback to junior leaders, reinforcing positive leadership and providing opportunities to change the more negative practices by isolating and questioning them. This early period would allow critical one-on-one time between senior leader and developing junior leader.

Organizational leaders should engage in the following activities:

- Provide senior leader involvement in the leader development process.
- Ensure a clear, consistent message.
- Get in touch with your culture, especially following change.
- Identify what you want in your leaders—what you want the leader development process to accomplish.
- Understand socialization as an opportunity for the culture to reinforce itself and resist change through new leaders or, conversely, an opportunity to accelerate change.

The only way to change socially reinforced systems of meaning is by employing methods of influence aimed at those very meanings. Leader interpretations of appropriate leadership in the organization are based on how they were led, complete with the shaping of their interpretations by other leaders before, during, and after these social interactions. To change interpretations, the very meanings themselves must change through changing the forms (practices, language, and behavior) or removing or changing those symbolic practices around which the meanings have been sustained. Cultural themes are reinforced and maintained each summer at West Point through the modeling behavior of upperclass cadets, supported by expectations and justified by rationale linking these behaviors with new cadet development. To change these cultural understandings, the rationale itself must be brought to the surface, questioned, and recast by leaders in an ideology more supportive of organizational goals and more consistent with their future roles as leaders in the organization.

Note

1. J. Dewey, *Experience and Education* (New York: Kappa Delta Pi, 1938).

CHAPTER SIXTEEN

LEADING AT THE
BUSINESS END OF POLICY

James Tuite

In most organizations, leaders are responsible for creating the policies, mission statements, and values that provide guidance to each member of the organization. These documents are essential for communicating the purpose of the organization and for laying out the framework for how work will be done, how customers will be treated, how the organization will operate, and so forth. Typically, though, the leaders who construct these policies are not the same people who must operationalize them on a daily basis. This responsibility is usually left to the people who work at lower levels of the organization. They are the ones whom the organization must rely on to execute its policies and behave in a way that embodies its values to accomplish its mission statement. They are, in a sense, at the business end of the organization's policies. Regardless of what is written, it is their individual actions that will collectively demonstrate the values and policies of the organization.

This idea is not a revelation. However, I suspect that many leaders do not understand how to lead in a manner that will inspire their people to behave in a way that embodies the values and the purpose of their organizations.

In your organization, your people are your company's agents. Each day, they are required to engage in activities that will collectively add up to accomplishing your company's goals. In doing so, they are either conducting their business within your company's espoused mission statement and policies—or not. And they are also acting as good stewards of your company's resources—or not. Rarely is there middle ground. In fact, with every action they take, they are either choosing to align with your company's espoused policies to add to the success of your company, or they are willfully choosing a lesser course of action.

---

*In most organizations, the leaders who construct the policies
are not normally the same people who must operationalize
them on a daily basis. People in your organization are executing
their duties as agents of your company, either within your
company's espoused mission statement and policies—or not.*

What Happens When Your People Ignore Your Policies

Recently I had the opportunity to observe this phenomenon from an outsider's perspective. Not too long ago, I awoke to the sound of screeching brakes as the garbage truck rounded the corner into my neighborhood. Realizing that I had not taken the trash out the night before, I jumped out of bed, threw on some clothes, grabbed the trash out of the kitchen, and then ran outside to beat the truck to the curb.

This particular morning happened to mark the second week of my community's new trash sorting and recycling program, so I wanted to make sure that my trash was in order. Under this new program, all cans, glass, and plastic containers were to be placed in a yellow trash can. All paper and cardboard products were to be placed in a blue trash can, and the remainder of the waste (everything that was not recyclable) was to be placed inside a clear trash bag and then placed inside a green trash can. Each type of waste was scheduled to be picked up on a different day of the week, and this morning was the day for the green can pickup.

When this new policy came out, we were told that the purpose of the clear trash bags was to allow the trash collectors to inspect each bag for compliance with the new policy. Any bag that was found to contain a recyclable item in it would not be picked up, and residents who repeatedly violated this new policy were threatened to lose their trash disposal privileges for an indefinite amount of time.

As the truck pulled up, I confidently handed my neatly sorted and freshly tied clear bag of trash to the collector and smugly waited for his inspection. I took pride in the fact that my trash was in compliance with the new policy, and I was eager to see the look of approval on his face as he inspected my well-organized refuse. To my surprise, he never even looked at the bag of trash that I had handed him; he simply grabbed it out of my hands and then quickly tossed it into the hopper on the back of the truck. He then went straight over to the other green trash cans that belonged to my neighbors and emptied them directly into the hopper without so much as a glance at their contents.

As I watched his actions, I thought, *Perhaps he didn't get the memo on the new policy; maybe nobody told him he was supposed to inspect the trash for misplaced recyclable items.* In just a few seconds, every trash can was emptied. Feeling slightly disappointed, I turned to walk back inside as the collector started to compact the trash. On my way in, I passed the back of the truck and could not help but notice all of the broken glass bottles and crushed soda cans that were in the bottom of the hopper. *Hey, aren't those recyclable items?* I thought. *Surely he had to notice this stuff inside the clear trash bags.*

Now I was curious. I had to find out why there was such a blatant discrepancy between what we had been told was going to happen under the new program and what I was actually seeing happen outside my front door. As the trash continued to compact and more broken glass bottles and crushed cans were exposed, I decided to ask a leading question of the trash collector: "Wow, it looks like there are a lot of people sneaking recyclables inside their regular trash, huh?"

Looking back on this exchange, I should have anticipated his answer. He turned to me, pointed at the green trash can and with a straight face said, "If you put it in that can, I'll take it." Well, there it was: the answer to my mystery. All of those aluminum cans and glass bottles were inside the truck's hopper because the trash collector—the last person in the chain of the company's new policy—decided, for whatever reason, that he was not going to inspect the trash bags.

You might ask, "What's the big deal?" After all, we are talking only about trash and one individual who decided not to follow and enforce a new policy. Although this might be the natural response, the details of what appears to be a minor incident reveal an important truth about leadership. It is not just about crafting sound policies and incentive programs; rather, it is much more about inspiring the people who implement the policies to care enough about the organization and each other so that they will act as good stewards of the organization even when no one is watching.

Furthermore, an individual's actions might reveal the true nature of an organization's culture. People tend to act within the norms of a company's culture. For instance, do you really think it is possible that I ran into the only trash collector who was not following the guidelines of the new policy? My guess is that there were probably others like him doing the same thing on their routes, and chances are, they all knew what each other was doing. Somehow this behavior became acceptable. What occurs at this point—the point where employees are free of supervision—reveals a company's true policy. It really does not matter what is written if the people at the business end of the policy do not follow it when the leader is not around. Your people are free to make decisions in your absence—and they will.

Now consider again the importance of each individual's actions within your organization. They *are* your organization. Their actions will not only define your company's policy but will also communicate the values of your organization to your customers and other employees. They are the business end of your policy, and you are fully reliant on them. So how can you ensure that they behave within the stated guidance of your organization and act as good stewards of your company's resources? How can you prevent your company from being overrun with "rogue" trash collectors? These are perplexing questions, and they are ones that I suggest you cannot effectively answer by simply adding more oversight or producing more incentive programs; rather, you must address them with people-focused leadership.

Identifying the Gap Between Espoused Policies and In-Use Policies

In the fall of 2000, I assumed command of an airborne infantry company at Fort Bragg, North Carolina. It was not long after I took command that I had the opportunity to observe how my company conducted business. After one week of being in charge, we were scheduled to execute a twenty-day field exercise that focused primarily on marksmanship and small unit battle drills. At the culmination of this field exercise, the platoons within my company were required to execute maneuvers on a live-fire range at night.

Short of actual combat, the night maneuver live-fire exercise is about as realistic as it gets for most infantry platoons. Try to picture thirty-five soldiers organized into three squad-size teams that are all moving around a four-kilometer range, engaging targets with live rounds, blowing things up, and using only radios and night-vision devices to communicate. This type of training is stressful and chaotic, but it is necessary to train soldiers so that they have the skills to meet the demands on the battlefield.

As an infantry company, one of our core competencies must be marksmanship. Being able to consistently hit a target is the first step in preparing for the night maneuver live-fire range. More important, being able to hit targets is one of the few skills that all soldiers must master to ensure their survival and the accomplishment of the unit's missions on the battlefield. Every person must be able to hit what they are aiming at the first time they fire because they might not get a second chance. To train soldiers to this level, the leaders in the company must be extremely competent and knowledgeable on marksmanship.

Thankfully, I had some highly experienced noncommissioned officers (NCOs) in my company. They had all conducted this type of training numerous times before, and they stated to me that they all knew what they were doing. As our field exercise approached, they assured me that our soldiers would be well trained and that they would be ready to execute the live-fire maneuver at the end of our two weeks in the field. When they showed me the training plan that they created for the individual marksmanship range, I was impressed with its level of detail and rigid standards. While they were briefing me on the plan, I could sense their ulterior message: they were telling me to back off. They wanted me to know that they could execute this training without my interference because they were more experienced and they fully understood the marksmanship standards.

Considering that I had been in command for only a week, I did back off. They had convinced me that they had it all under control, and it felt right to support them. I was glad to have them taking ownership of the marksmanship range and was confident, based on what they told me, that our soldiers would be well trained for the maneuver live fire. To my complete surprise, this was not the case.

After only two days into the training, I was dismayed at how mediocre my NCOs were at training marksmanship. The standards that they told me they were going to train to and what I was actually seeing did not match. Although I was new to the company, I had spent nearly two years in the 75th Ranger Regiment, where I learned a great deal about marksmanship from the NCOs in that organization, so I was confident that I knew what right looked like. In my mind, we had just wasted two days of training, but I decided not to say anything until I had given them more of a chance. Perhaps they were starting out slow on purpose.

I was dismayed at how mediocre my NCOs were at training marksmanship. The standards that they told me they were going to train to and what I was actually seeing did not match.

As the sun set on our second day of training, we broke for dinner before we prepared for our nighttime marksmanship training. Typically the first night of training consists of every soldier zeroing his weapon to his infrared laser at various ranges. Zeroing is the process in which an individual shooter adjusts his sights to match the point where the bullet hits the target. This can be a lengthy process, and it requires each shooter to have proper and consistent form. To zero an entire company (about 130 soldiers) is a methodical process. I have seen this training take nearly the entire night, so I prepared for a long night. At the end of our brief dinner break, I noticed that none of my NCOs or soldiers had the infrared lasers mounted on their weapons, and it did not appear that they were making any preparations other than putting on their night-vision goggles to conduct the training.

Confused, I went up to the NCO in charge of the range (the same one who had briefed me on the standards) and asked him what was going on. I asked where the lasers were and why they were not on the weapons. He replied, "Sir, we don't need those things. We usually just hang a chem light on the target and then use our day sights to hit it." *What?!* I thought. *Is he really serious? This doesn't match the standard that he briefed.* I then asked, "How do you intend to hit a target if it doesn't have a chem light on it, like an enemy soldier?" He answered, "Oh, if we deploy to combat, there'll be so many of us firing our weapons that odds are one of us will hit him." At these words, I was amazed and disappointed that they were coming from the same individual who had told me that our solders would be well trained. I started to wonder how he defined "well trained."

---

*I had leaders in my organization who were behaving in ways
that did not support the purpose of our organization. This was
the last straw: I knew it was time for me to get involved.*

A Beginner's Mistake: Attempting to Force Compliance with the Organization's Policies

Now I understood. Our training was poor not because we were starting out slow but because we were willfully choosing to train to a lower standard. As an infantry unit, our purpose and mission were clear: engage and destroy the enemy by means of firepower and maneuvers. Clearly we were not training to meet this mission, and after two days of observing and participating in poor training, I knew it was time for me to get involved.

I had to face my first leadership decision: How was I going to react to this situation? If I did nothing, I would be setting the precedent that this training was acceptable. If I decided to take charge, I might risk alienating my NCOs and soldiers because I was new and they might interpret my actions as a lack of trust. Truth be told, I honestly do not think anyone was even waiting for my reaction. Apparently this type of training had gone on for so long that I believe this substandard night marksmanship training had become the standard. As far as they were concerned, they were executing good training.

After considering my options, I decided on the latter course of action. After all, somebody had to speak up if the training was going to improve, and it was my job. So following the conversation with my NCO, I instructed the leadership of the company to send a party back to the rear to pick up all of the lasers and needed equipment and return to the range. When they returned, we distributed and mounted the lasers on every weapon. When this was completed, I instructed the leadership to return to the range shed for laser marksmanship instruction. For the second time that evening, I had the feeling that it was going to be a very long night.

When everyone had finally gathered at the shed, their resentment was palpable. I could see in their faces that they were upset and did not understand what all the fuss was about. To them, this training had worked fine for many years, and now the "new guy" wanted to change it. Because I could sense their frustration, I tried to encourage their participation by asking if anyone knew how the lasers worked so that they could teach the rest of us. No one spoke up, so now it was up to me. For the next two hours, I gave instruction on how to correctly mount, operate, and zero the lasers. I also described how being able to use the laser would allow us to accomplish our mission more effectively and probably bring more soldiers home alive. Not surprisingly, they were not too receptive to the insights I offered.

I could see in their faces that they were upset and did not understand what all the fuss was about. To them, this training had worked fine for many years, and now the new guy wanted to change it. Not surprisingly, they were not too receptive.

Following my instruction, we spent the next two hours making sure that every leader could mount, operate, and zero his laser and, more important, that each leader was prepared to teach his soldiers how to do it the next day. It was a long night when we finally left the range shed, and I was not surprised when everyone shuffled out quietly with their heads hung low after being released for the evening. I think they sensed that this was their first installment of many "good ideas" that the new commander was going to implement.

Throughout the rest of the field exercise, I noticed many things that people did that did not match what we had said we were about. It seemed as if everyone in the company enjoyed talking about how good we were, but when it came to actually executing, we were mediocre at best. All of our standards seemed to be at the lowest level of acceptability, and I did not see how that supported the effective accomplishment of our mission. I wondered why they did not care about being good and why they were content with the minimum standard. I was frustrated, and I had no intention of allowing the company to stay at this level. We were going to get better.

The more I observed my NCOs and soldiers doing the minimum, the more frustrated I became with them. And as a result, I gave them no quarter: I got involved in everything. Every time I witnessed poor performance, I made a correction; every time I saw a leader make a mistake, I made a correction. By my sheer will, we did improve—at least on paper. We improved not only in marksmanship but across the entire spectrum. We were better at physical training, better at maintenance, and better at battle drills. Although we did get better, I began to realize that my style of improvement came with a cost.

At the same time that everything was improving, I had quite a few individuals who were seeking a transfer out of my company. This surprised me a little, but I chalked up their leaving the company to their inability to be part of a great company. After all, it is not easy to be good, and it is harder to be great. It takes dedication and a lot of hard work. Maybe they just did not have what it takes.

Leadership is much more than simply getting the organization to improve performance. And although we improved in all of the objective measures, none of the improvements would have stood the test of time after I was replaced as the commander—not because they were bad standards but because no one other than me had truly internalized them.

One Person Enforcing a Policy Is Not a Policy—It Is Micromanagement

Now that I have had some time to reflect on what was actually happening in my company, I should not have been surprised when people were seeking to leave. I realize now that leadership is much more than simply getting the organization to improve performance. Consider my example. I was successful at getting people to improve their performance, but I had to be present. After a few months into my command, I do not think that there was a single person in the company who thought that he could get away with low performance. They all knew that if they let up, I would be there to make the correction, and if they did well, they might even earn some incentive. My leadership—or rather, my management of the company—was based mostly on exchange. I was all transactional: I used coercion and reward to gain compliance out of my solders. Unfortunately compliance is about the only thing that I gained. As a result of my actions, I had fostered an environment where I became the sole standard bearer in the company. I had become like Atlas holding up the world. This was my show.

I am quite certain now that when the leaders in my company raised their standards or made a correction on soldiers, it was probably to avoid my reprisals rather than because they truly believed in the higher standard. And although we improved in all of the objective measures, none of the improvements was lasting; none would have stood the test of time after I was replaced as the commander—not because they were bad standards but because no one other than me had truly internalized them. I am quite certain that during my command, my soldiers had numerous opportunities to make decisions that I would not find out about. I will never know how they behaved in these situations, but I can guess that they were probably very much like the trash collector that I encountered in my neighborhood.

I had micromanaged my company to success, but I did a poor job of building the team and developing the other leaders in my company. I believed that as a leader, if you lived the example and focused your efforts on the group's performance, you would build pride and cohesion and that would result in higher performance. I was wrong. True leadership must focus on the people in the organization; as a result, the organization comes together, and great performance follows. I learned this valuable lesson the hard way. During the first half of my command, the harder I tried to force my company to success, the more alone I felt in trying to reach our company's goals.

An Alternative Approach: Placing the Development of Your People Ahead of Results

After that first week and for the next ten months, I continued to drive my company to a higher level of performance. We continued to improve in every training event that we executed, but I began to notice that the improvements were only incremental. Although we were getting better, the amount that we improved did not seem to equal the significant amount of effort that I was putting in.

> *I had micromanaged my company to success, but as a result, I did a poor job of building the team and developing the other leaders in my company. True leadership must focus on the people in the organization. Then the organization comes together, and great performance follows.*

I was getting tired. It was exhausting to be involved with almost every decision and to inspect nearly everything we did for compliance. Many times, I thought: *Why don't these guys take pride in their own company? When will they start doing things because they care about this unit and being a professional as opposed to just avoiding my corrections? What's the matter with them?* My frustration was peaking, and something had to change; I could not last another year at this pace. Thankfully, I was presented with another opportunity to demonstrate what I cared about as a leader; only this time, I changed the focus of my leadership from our performance results to the development of my people.

At about the same time that my frustration was peaking, our battalion was scheduled to assume the highest state of deployable readiness on Fort Bragg, commonly called "assuming mission." This meant that for the next few months, if something were to occur in the world where an airborne unit with our capabilities was needed, we could potentially be the first to deploy. Therefore, all of our equipment needed to be maintained at its highest state of readiness, and all personnel assigned to the battalion had to be prepared to leave at a moment's notice.

To ensure that we were prepared to assume mission, the Fort Bragg inspector general (IG) team was scheduled to conduct an operational readiness survey inspection a few days prior to our assumption. This inspection consisted of multiple parts, and it took nearly an entire day to complete. Everything from medical records to training scores to vehicle and weapon maintenance was scrutinized to ensure that the assuming unit was at its highest state of readiness. If the sheer scope of the inspection did not raise eyebrows, then the threat of having to complete a reinspection and receiving a negative performance evaluation did.

Preparing for and passing this important inspection was a significant part of life on Fort Bragg: no one took this inspection lightly, especially not the IG team. Regardless, most of the soldiers in my company had already completed this inspection successfully multiple times. I too had passed one earlier in my command tenure, so it was nothing that really worried anyone in the company. Nevertheless, it did require a week of dedicated preparation.

As we started our preparation, I was confident that we could repeat our earlier successful performance. Every day began with a company formation in the motor pool, and then everyone was released to their platoon-level leadership for more detailed instructions as to what needed to get done that day. While the soldiers worked at the various locations around the motor pool and the company area, I would walk around to see what was happening, so that I could talk with them and to see if there were any issues that needed my assistance.

At the beginning of the week, I noticed that there was very little NCO leadership involved with our soldiers as they completed their tasks. It seemed as though we had a bunch of hardworking privates and specialists doing things the best way they knew how. This alarmed me for two reasons:

- Where was the lower-level NCO leadership?
- Who was making sure that our privates were maintaining our equipment to the published standard?

*In spite of all the deficiencies I saw, I purposefully did not
get involved. My leaders told me that they had a plan and
that if they were allowed to execute it, we would pass the
inspection. I needed to trust them, and I was tired of feeling
like the only person concerned with running the company.*

At our daily meeting later that afternoon, I mentioned my concerns about the lack of NCO leadership and supervision to my company chain of command. Their response was, "Sir, we've got it. We know the best way to prepare because we have been through this inspection many times. Let us run our platoons." As I listened, I thought, *I don't mind letting you run your platoons, but how can we effectively prepare for this inspection if no one is leading the effort?* My natural inclination was to take over, but going against what I had done during my initial ten months as the commander, I decided to back off. Instead of trying to control our performance on the inspection by telling them exactly how we were going to do business, I told them that I trusted them and that they had my confidence. By doing this, I figured one of two things would happen: either we would pass the inspection and my NCOs would start to take more ownership, or we would fail the inspection and possibly learn a valuable lesson as a company—if we survived the fallout.

For the rest of the week, things continued as I had seen them on the first day. Our soldiers would work on their own with little supervision and rarely did I see anyone using a technical manual while they conducted maintenance on our various pieces of equipment. But in spite of all the deficiencies, I did not get involved. I believed that to do so would have stripped my NCOs of the responsibility for the results of the inspection. My leaders told me that they had a plan and that if they were allowed to execute their plan, we would pass the inspection. I needed to trust them. After all, I was tired of feeling like the only person running the company.

When the day of the inspection came, everyone seemed to be in good spirits. There was a sense of confidence among all of our leaders and soldiers in the company because they felt that they had put in the appropriate amount of effort to pass the inspection. Unfortunately, their optimism was quickly dashed just three hours into the inspection when we earned the dubious honor of being the only company in the history of the 82nd Airborne Division ever to fail all twenty of our TOW (tubular-launched, optically wire guided) missile systems. This was a colossal failure. Not only did this failure earn us the right to a reinspection, but it also caught the eye of the division commander and his staff. Our seismic failure had the potential of delaying my entire battalion's assumption of mission, which would have ripple effects throughout the division.

This was a significant disaster and it did not bode well for my career. If having this humbling defeat dealt to me publicly in front of my entire brigade was not enough, I found out from my battalion commander that my job as the company commander was in jeopardy. He informed me that I could not weather a second failure on the reinspection and that I was given up to thirty days to schedule our reinspection with the IG's office. On this second inspection, 90 percent of our TOW missile systems had to pass in order to receive a passing grade.

That day, as the IG inspection wrapped up, everyone in the company was devastated and embarrassed. With our heads hung low, we slowly made our way out of the inspection area and headed back to our motor pool. On our way out, I informed all of my leaders that I wanted to see them after we put our equipment away.

Back in the company area, my leaders silently gathered in the motor pool and waited for me to speak. I was angry and frustrated, but as I looked around at all of them, I noticed something that I did not think was there before: they were all truly upset—not because they thought that I was going to scold them or berate them or because they thought the inspection was unfair; rather, they looked upset because they had been professionally embarrassed. This failure blindsided them, and they all knew that it was nobody's fault but their own. *Now*, I thought, *we're finally ready to commit to getting better.*

Development Produces Empowerment That Produces Lasting Results

After my leaders assembled, I began by asking what had happened and how we could have been so far off the mark. Both seemed to be rhetorical questions, and there was not a person standing there who did not fully realize that this failure was entirely his fault. They all knew that somehow they had allowed themselves to drift away from putting in the required effort needed to pass this inspection, and now we had paid the price. We had earned our failure, but it was time to move on.

As I spoke to them, I told them that I had scheduled our reinspection for the following week. Upon hearing this, every head raised and looked at me with disbelief. Seven days to prepare for the reinspection was unheard of. Nobody scheduled reinspection that soon, especially, as most of them knew, because a second failure might mean the end of my command. I think they were surprised that I would take such a gamble, but I also think that my decision demonstrated trust in them.

As I wrapped up our talk, I told them that I did not believe scheduling our reinspection after only one week was a gamble because I was certain of the outcome. I continued:

You told me last week that you all knew what you were doing and that you knew how to pass this inspection. Well, I believed you then, and if you tell me that we can do it now, then I'll believe you again. I don't know what happened here today. I don't know why we didn't see this coming, but I do know there isn't one person here who can honestly say that he gave his best effort during the preparation for this inspection. We all need to do better. We failed, it happened, and it's over. And we can either cry about this and point fingers at one another, or we can do the hard work that it takes to pass this thing and move on. I need your help, and we all need each other if we're going to prove that we are not failures. Without everyone's very best effort, we'll fail again. Of that I'm certain. So now, the only question is, What are we going to do?"

When I had finished speaking, the mood in the group was different. Their heads were no longer hanging low, and their look of embarrassment was gone. Many started offering suggestions as to how we could improve some aspects of our preparation, and some claimed the responsibility to make those suggestions happen. As they spoke, I carefully listened to each comment, and then a dialogue began. In no time, we had a plan. To me, this was no different from any other operation we had ever done; I often sought their input, but somehow this was different. By demonstrating trust and encouraging their input, this plan became more than just my plan: it was *our* plan.

In the days leading up to the reinspection, our company worked harder than I had ever seen them work before. Everyone was present and focused on the task at hand. By allowing my leaders the space to execute their plan and to see the results of their efforts (as ugly as they were), development occurred. They now had a better appreciation for the effort that it takes to be a good company. By not forcing my plan on them, I took away their safety net and gave them the accountability that comes with autonomy.

As I made my usual rounds in the company area, I saw only good things happening; my soldiers took pride in their work, and they were giving their very best effort. For the next week, this newly found motivation and dedication permeated the entire company, and seven days later, every missile system passed the reinspection. For the second time in one week, we set a new Fort Bragg record.

*My focus of improving the organization and
making it better never changed, but the way I went
about improving the company changed dramatically. In the
beginning, I was a transactional leader, but I did not care.
Clearly I was wrong. Although my intentions were good,
I was not leading my organization to success;
instead, I was trying to force it to success.*

The Lesson Learned: A Leader Cannot Force Success

In the three years since I relinquished my command, I have had the opportunity to reflect on my experiences. Although my command lasted a brief nineteen months, having the privilege to lead one hundred soldiers was truly one of the most personally demanding and rewarding experiences in my life.

I often think back on why leading my company in the beginning was so hard. My focus of improving the organization and making it better never changed over the entire tenure of my command, but the way I went about improving the company changed dramatically. In the beginning, my focus was on our performance as an organization and then putting systems in place that would improve our output. This meant that I had to create the systems and policies, and then I had to make sure that they were followed. This took a lot of effort and was incredibly draining. I was a transactional leader, but I did not care. My mind-set was that "I am going to hold you strictly accountable for everything you do and fail to do." I believed that setting the example and enforcing high standards was all that it took to inspire esprit de corps and high performance. Clearly I was wrong.

Although my intentions were good, I was not leading my organization to success; instead, I was trying to force it to success. This type of leadership was effective only at eliciting compliance (and, in some cases, covert resistance). How could I possibly inspire people to care about their profession and the company if they were concerned only about complying with what they considered to be my edicts? The answer is that I could not. When people do not see the need to change, then it is not likely that their behavior will change when you are not around. In fact, they are likely to act more like the trash collector in my neighborhood.

A Lesson in Leadership: Positional Power Does Not Facilitate Enduring Leadership

Some time later, I came across a reading in Gary Yukl's book, *Leadership in Organizations,* which discusses various perspectives on social power advanced by theorists such as John French and Bertram Raven, Bernard Bass, and Yukl himself.[1] In his passage, Yukl summarizes the different types of power that are commonly available to leaders and where this power comes from. The two most simple forms that power takes are positional and personal.

Positional power is the power granted to a leader by virtue of his or her role in an organization. For instance, a midlevel manager has a certain amount of power over subordinates to tell them what to do, grant rewards, and dispense punishment. In that same organization, the CEO normally has a much higher amount of those same powers over those same subordinates. This ability to influence stems from that person's position in the organization. It is only within the context of that specific organization that the leader has this power.

In my case, as the company commander, I could issue orders, give out awards, and punish in order to influence people, and I did. I used these powers to force improvement within the company, but this improvement came at the cost of alienating me from the company and relegating me to the position of the sole enforcer of our high standards. This should not have been a great surprise. When leaders tend to use their positional powers exclusively, they can at best expect only compliance and probably more often than not will incite resistance. *This was it,* I thought, as I read through the passage in Yukl's book. *This is why I felt that I had to be such a micromanager.* All I was gaining was compliance. Our mediocre performance was not all due to my leaders; my own behavior also influenced the situation.

The other form of power that Yukl describes in his book is *personal power.* It consists of two types: referent power and expert power. *Referent power* comes from the rapport and respect that the leader and followers have for each other. This rapport is forged over time, and it is based on a relationship built from trust. Interestingly, this power is not granted by any formal authority or from a position within an organization; rather, it is granted by the subordinate to the leader. The leader must earn this power. *Expert power* is also granted to the leader from the subordinate. It is only when the subordinate views the leader as an expert in his or her respective field that he or she can influence that subordinate with the leader's experience.

A leader who uses positional power will likely meet with compliance or resistance. This explains a lot of my frustration during the first half of my command. I viewed my subordinates as lazy and unprofessional, and I was unwilling to waste any time to let them slowly improve and develop. I wanted results, and in my mind, all I was asking them to do was to uphold the standards that they agreed to live by. To me, this was logical, so I used the appropriate positional power to get the results I wanted. Unfortunately, all I got was compliance (and some resistance). That was why I was exhausted and frustrated: by eliciting only compliance, I had to ensure that everything was getting done. As a result of my actions, I stripped away the responsibility of enforcing the standards from my other leaders in the company.

You cannot order esprit de corps or coerce high performance; instead, you have to inspire it. It was not until I started focusing on developing my people that things changed. To build the personal power needed to internalize high standards, I had to build a relationship with my subordinates. I had to demonstrate that I cared about and trusted them.

Later, I found out that this was not the best approach. I discovered that you cannot order esprit de corps or coerce high performance; instead, you have to inspire it. It was not until I started focusing on the development of my people that things changed. To build the personal power needed to inspire change and engender the internalization of high standards, I had to build a relationship with my subordinates. I had to demonstrate that I cared about and trusted them.

When I decided to allow them to prepare for the inspection the way they wanted to, I demonstrated trust. And when I put the security of my job in their hands, I strengthened this trust. To earn their respect, I had to give them respect first. By humbling myself and letting them know that I failed just as much as they did and that we all needed to work together, I demonstrated that I cared. I think that it was at that moment of our most public failure that they realized that I was not attempting to change the company simply to get a good performance report; rather, I wanted them to get better. If my intentions were self-serving, I do not think there was anything I could have done or said that would have changed their position toward me. By showing humility and sharing the risks with my subordinates, my actions demonstrated that I truly cared about them.

After ten months of command, I finally understood: leadership is about truly caring for your people and doing the things that demonstrate you care on a daily basis. Following our embarrassing failure and then our fantastic comeback, I viewed myself more as a servant to the company rather than the commander of the company. And it was through this shift in my perspective that my behavior toward my subordinates changed and I earned their respect and gained some personal power. No longer was I Atlas holding up the world; we were all holding it up together. From then on, two things happened during the remainder of my command: we all started to have a lot more fun and our performance as a company skyrocketed.

Leadership is not simply about getting performance out of an organization; it is about developing and inspiring the people within the organization to be their best. When you put your focus on your people and truly care about their development personally and professionally, you will earn their respect and loyalty. They will be willing to put in the extra effort even when you are not watching because they are confident that you will do the same for them. Development normally occurs with a dip in performance. If you are willing to underwrite this dip and invest in your people by doing what it takes to demonstrate that you care about them, then you will inspire excellent performance.

Note

1. G. Yukl, *Leadership in Organizations*, 6th ed. (Upper Saddle River, N.J.: Pearson Education, 2006). French and Raven authored the seminal paper on the subject in 1959, laying out five bases of social power: legitimate, coercive, reward, expert, and referent: J.R.P. French and B. H. Raven, "The Bases of Social Power," in D. Cartwright (ed.), *Studies of Social Power* (Ann Arbor, Mich.: Institute for Social Research, 1959).

CHAPTER SEVENTEEN

HARNESSING THE POWER OF CULTURE AND DIVERSITY FOR ORGANIZATIONAL PERFORMANCE

Remi Hajjar
Morten G. Ender

The U.S. Army provides valuable lessons on how to harness the power of culture and diversity to have a positive impact on mission performance, and these lessons are relevant to all types of organizations and their leaders. As the U.S. military and other professions, businesses, and groups aim to survive and flourish amid a sea of complex change, ideas on how best to leverage culture and diversity have become even more pronounced and important.

We learn culture through an ongoing process of socialization; we learn customs, mores, rules, values, laws, and other codes from the groups we enter in life.

What Culture Is, and Why It Matters to Organizations

The leaders of any organization require a thorough understanding of the multi-faceted concept of culture in order to truly harness its potential power. Culture consists of the collective values, beliefs, norms, underlying assumptions, languages, behavioral expectations, and artifacts that shape and define the social life of a group. Culture is to a group what personality is to an individual. It serves as an internal radar that enables us to discern others who are similar and dissimilar.

We learn culture through an ongoing process of socialization; we learn customs, mores, rules, values, laws, and other codes from the groups we enter in life. We join some of these collectivities by choice, and we become members of others by virtue of our particular life circumstances—such as our family, community, race, ethnic group, social class, sex and gender, nation and state, religious membership, and other associations greatly defined and molded by our family of origin and early life experiences. Within each of these groups, we learn to imitate socially appropriate behaviors and adopt accepted attitudes based on the normative expectations transmitted in each of these collectivities. We eventually internalize many of these well-entrenched social codes and thought processes in order to gain and maintain group acceptance.

Culture serves as a critical social boundary that divides accepted from unaccepted behaviors, beliefs, occupations, marital partners, lifestyles, and so forth. In sum, culture plays a monumental role in shaping how we act, feel, think, and live.

Understanding Core American Values

Knowing ourselves as an American culture is one step in the process in appreciating and harnessing diversity. Sociologists regularly ask Americans to identity their core values. There are fifteen that can be considered the core values of American society. Table 17.1 provides an alphabetical list of core values identified by adult Americans of all religions, genders, social classes, ages, races, ethnicities, sexual orientations, and abilities.

Some of the core values listed in Table 17.1 are fairly straightforward. For example, freedom is an important value for Americans that goes back to before the American Revolution. Americans are unlikely to support any rules, regulations, and initiatives that greatly restrict personal freedoms. Likewise, Americans greatly value progress—we love to build a better mousetrap, and this value spills over into our spirit of bold and enterprising initiatives in our capitalistic economy.

Other values are less straightforward. For example, individualism is a value that is very much taken for granted; we often do not articulate it among ourselves because it might be perceived as selfish. But historically, Americans have placed considerable value on individual achievement and success. We are a nation rich in lore of Americans who have come to this country with very little and pulled themselves up beyond their wildest expectations. Similarly, we generally hold individuals responsible for their actions.

The one value not often recognized by Americans entails racism and group superiority. But it is clear that American history includes 250 years of slavery and more

TABLE 17.1. CORE VALUES OF U.S. SOCIETY

Achievement and success

Activity and work

Democracy

Education

Efficiency and practicality

Equality

Freedom

Humanitarianism

Individuality

Material comfort

Progress

Racism and group superiority

Religiosity

Romantic love and monogamy

Science and technology

Source: From research in J. Henslin, *Sociology: A Down-to-Earth Approach,* 7th ed. (Needham Heights, Mass.: Allyn & Bacon, 2005).

than 100 years of fighting for racial desegregation, and our nation continues to struggle with race-based concerns. In addition, there is a great deal of self-segregation in America; visit any high school cafeteria, and you will see that students segregate themselves racially at lunch tables. Sunday is considered the most segregated day in the United States: races tend to attend churches with people of the same race.

It should be noted that values in American society are contradictory, and this is what makes us culturally unique. For example, although we are highly individualistic, we are also a highly humanitarian culture—with a great deal of concern for others, especially those perceived to be less fortunate.

In addition, some values cluster more or less with specific groups, which form unique value systems. These smaller-scale value systems (or subcultural value systems) are an organized set or pattern of values of a group or community where the unique values are interrelated with the larger societal values. In most cases, these value systems of specific groups show some similarity to and reinforce the greater national values. This system of supporting subcultures provides a framework for the various groups in U.S. society that influence people's social norms, ideas and ideals, beliefs, and most important, behavior.

Leaders must take into account that the people in their organizations exist in several cultures and subcultures simultaneously.

Understanding Core Army Values

In addition to the fifteen basic core values of all Americans in general, the U.S. Army has its own values system that connects everyone in the Army. It culturally creates a value orientation that is designed to influence behavior. The seven Army values, listed earlier in Exhibit 5.1, orient members of the U.S. Army into a collective and provide a culture of shared personal commitment to the greater organizational mission.

The Influence of Subcultures on a Larger Group

Subcultures are often erroneously viewed by the wider American society as deviant groups whose values greatly diverge from the mainstream, such as youth subcultures like hippies, punks, and hip-hop. However, research shows these groups generally transmit values that on the whole are consistent with the larger group, although some nuances exist that make them unique. And there are some subcultures with divergent value sets that clash with national values, such as the countercultures of militia or terrorist organizations.

Organizations need people who reinforce effective aspects of the preexisting culture, and they need members who innovate and challenge established procedures and beliefs to influence beneficial change.

Leaders must take into account that the people in their organizations exist in several cultures and subcultures simultaneously. For example, soldiers in the U.S. Army exist in an overarching professional culture with a noted values system, but they also work in distinct units that possess unique subcultures. For example, a Marine's personal demographics illustrate a set of cultural variations that distinguish her from peers, including sex or gender, race, ethnicity, religious affiliation, ability, social class background, and age. She might be stationed in a foreign culture as security for a U.S. embassy. In contrast, an Air Force captain might belong to civilian clubs, sports teams, or other nonmilitary organizations; each of these memberships transmits a distinctive subculture and value orientation that had an impact on the officer.

Thus, leaders must consider that multiple, dynamic cultures influence the diverse members of their organizations, which illustrates the leadership challenge to create a functional subculture based on organizational values that builds cohesion and also shows appreciation and respect for members' differences and varying identities. Building a solid subculture that integrates unique, diverse people and creates cohesion that contributes to optimal performance is a vital task for leaders in all walks of life.

Leaders must also perceive and leverage the different reaction values of organizational members to unit culture, which enhances the ability to leverage the power of culture. There are two types: organizational conformists and organizational mavericks. The first type of reaction is generally the conformist variety, where people abide by, apply, and expect fellow members to follow historically based cultural expectations, practices, mind-sets, and values. Conformists actively recreate organizational culture by reinforcing established values and traditions: this is the process of cultural reproduction. The second type of reaction to culture generally involves those who attempt to change culture and at times think and act differently from culturally prescribed expectations. One example entails organizational mavericks who act in new ways that are not in line with cultural norms: these members are also reacting to organizational culture. They are contributing to (or trying to spur) the process of culture change, and if their ideas or new behaviors prove relevant to the unit and subsequently become accepted and adopted, they help enhance the culture and ultimately the organization as a whole.

Both types of cultural reactions are essential for entities to survive and succeed. Organizations need people who reinforce effective aspects of the preexisting culture, and they need members who innovate and challenge established procedures and beliefs to influence beneficial change. Leaders cultivate and leverage both types of reactions to culture to help their organizations adapt and survive in a rapidly changing world. And an important subpart of an organization's culture entails its values and reactions to culturally diverse people.

Cultural Diversity?

We view diversity as differences among people that have an impact on a group or organization. There are several factors that differentiate people. We can categorize these as "the (un)lucky seven" as a framework for examining the most crucial elements of diversity in American society:[1] According to this framework, one is relatively lucky based on the value placed on the social characteristics. In American society, the "most lucky seven" are being male, young, white, Christian, hetero-sexual, able-bodied, and middle class. Further down the hierarchy, the most "un-lucky" are women, the aged, people of color, non-Christians, homosexuals, those who are disabled, and the underclass.

- Race and ethnicity
- Religion
- Social class
- Sex and gender
- Age
- Physical ability or disability
- Sexual orientation

In our sociology classes at West Point, we are rarely surprised by the signifi-cant variation in cadets' perceptions about the diversity of the United States, using the (un)lucky seven as a framework. In academic conferences, we have noted au-dience members giving similar, inaccurate answers to similar questions. For lead-ers in any organization, a necessary first step toward harnessing diversity begins by knowing how these groups are represented in the wider society, their commu-nity, their clients, and their organization. Here are some statistics on the (un)lucky seven characteristics, plus the U.S. population in general:

- *U.S. population:* Few Americans know the population of the United States. We have heard numbers from professionals ranging from 5 million to 3 billion. The actual number, as of the 2004 census, is 285,691,501.
- *Sex and gender breakdown:* Most might know that sex is distributed roughly evenly. Actually, in 2000 there were 96.3 males for every 100 females. There tend to be slightly more males for females between the ages of birth and thirty-four years of age, and the numbers reverse at age thirty-five through ninety and above because women tend to live longer than men.
- *Age:* The median age in the United States is 35.3. The largest percentage of people are between 35 and 44 years old (16.1 percent), with 6.8 percent under age 5 and 12.4 percent who are 65 and older.
- *Religion:* In terms of religious affiliation, data from the American Religious Iden-tification Survey in 2001 reported there were 159.5 million Christians in the United States.[2] Catholics, Baptists, Methodists, and nondenominational Chris-tians had the largest percentages of the thirty-five Christian groups recognized. There were also 7.7 million other religions, and 29.5 million listed no religious affiliation. Table 17.2 shows the distribution of the latter twenty-six different groups. All groups increased since 1990s, except for Jews and Rastafarians.

- *Disabilities:* There are 37.9 million Americans who are five years of age or older living in noninstitutionalized settings with a disability.
- *Sexual orientation:* The percentage of the homosexual population is estimated at 4 percent of the U.S. population. Some estimates have placed it as high as 10 percent and others at less than 1 percent. The percentages are likely to vary by region of the country, with higher percentages being more likely in urban, metropolitan areas.
- *Social class:* This is difficult to measure. One indicator of social class is income. The median income for a male, full-time, year-round worker, sixteen years of age or older was $41,194 in 2004. For a female, it was $31,374, with women earning roughly seventy-six cents for every dollar that a similar male earns. This income varies by education and other variables.
- *Race and ethnicity:* These are important elements of the (un)lucky seven. Racial and ethnic groups have been the most contentious in U.S. history. Table 17.3 shows the racial/ethnic groups in the United States as a percentage of the total population across years for four periods. The percentages are for 1980 and 2000 and are based on actual U.S. Census data. The second two are projected population distributions for 2025 and 2050. Whites are currently at about 71 percent. African Americans and Hispanic Americans are 12 percent each, and Asian, Native, Alaskan, and Aleutians make up the remaining ethnic groups.

The U.S. census has started to fully appreciate and recognize the complexity of ethnicity among Americans. Exhibit 17.1 is a reproduction of the questions on race and Hispanic origin from the census for 2000. Spanish/Hispanic/Latino is broken out into a range of groups, including Mexican, Puerto Rican, Cuban, and "other" groups, which might include Dominicans and Venezuelans, among others. Notably, there is now a category for people who identify themselves as biracial and multiethnic. Approximately 7 million Americans chose this category in 2000.

Leaders who ignore the diversity of the United States in general, their clients, their constituents, and their organizations are not fully leveraging the potentially rich, unique, and insightful range of ideas in the organization's members, and they also are potentially creating or reinforcing destructive obstacles to building solidarity and cohesion. In addition, leaders who fail to perceive, acknowledge, and leverage the diversity in their customers, peer competitors, and other people in their organizational environs miss tremendous opportunities to improve performance.

In contrast, leaders who embrace diversity and encourage their organizations to accept, understand, and ultimately value diversity build more cohesive and effective teams by leveraging differences among people. A salient question at this juncture, then, is why we emphasize these seven facets of diversity.

TABLE 17.2. SELF-DESCRIBED RELIGIOUS IDENTIFICATION OF THE ADULT U.S. POPULATION, 2001

Religion	Number of Followers
Jewish	7,740,000
Muslim/Islamic	2,831,000
Buddhist	1,104,000
Unitarian/Universalist	1,082,000
Hindu	766,000
Native American	103,000
Scientologist	55,000
Baha'i	84,000
Taoist	40,000
New Age	68,000
Eckankar	26,000
Rastafarian	11,000
Sikh	57,000
Wiccan	134,000
Deity	49,000
Druid	33,000
Santeria	22,000
Pagan	140,000
Spiritualist	116,000
Ethical culture	4,000
Other unclassified	386,000
Atheist	902,000
Agnostic	991,000
Humanist	49,000
Secular	53,000
No religion	27,486,000

Source: U.S. Bureau of the Census, *2000 Census* (Washington, D.C.: U.S. Department of Commerce, 2000).

TABLE 17.3. RACIAL/ETHNIC GROUPS IN THE UNITED STATES AS PERCENTAGE OF THE TOTAL POPULATION

Racial/Ethnic Groups	1980	2000	2025	2050
Non-Hispanic whites	81%	71%	62%	53%
African Americans	11	12	13	13
Native Americans, Eskimos, Aleuts	Less than 1	Less than 1	Less than 1	Less than 1
Asian and Pacific Islanders	2	4	6	9
Hispanic Americans	6	12	18	24
Total population	226,564,000	275,306,000	337,814,000	403,686,000

Note: 1980 and 2000: based on actual U.S. census data. 2025 and 2050: projected population distributions.
Source: U.S. Bureau of the Census. *2000 Census* (Washington, D.C.: U.S. Department of Commerce, 2000).

Why the (Un)Lucky Seven Receive Special Focus in Terms of Diversity

The (un)lucky seven categories exist because a critical mass of research has documented that these groups tend to suffer disproportionately from out-grouping and marginalization in American society (and in many cases, around the globe). In addition, the categories tend to create biased judgments and systematically unequal evaluations for both the historically dominant and the underprivileged groups in each domain; this phenomenon manifests itself across society and many organizations.

When cultural diversity reinforces these unequal categories, people end up with disproportionate access to valuable resources, including material goods, positions, opportunities, and experiences. In addition, they have uneven amounts of and potential to acquire wealth, power, and prestige. Groups at the top get more stuff: they are privileged in decision making and myriad other areas. Conversely, groups at the bottom have access to fewer resources: their voices receive less volume (or get muted altogether) regardless of the potential power inherent in their ideas and their special talents, abilities, and attributes that could contribute to organizational performance.

> *Leaders who fail to perceive, acknowledge, and leverage the diversity in their customers, peer competitors, and other people in their organizational environs miss tremendous opportunities to improve performance.*

EXHIBIT 17.1. HOW THE 2000
U.S. CENSUS HAS RECLASSIFIED RACE

**Reproduction of Questions on Race and
Hispanic Origin From Census 2000**

→ NOTE: Please answer BOTH Questions 5 and 6.

5. **Is this person Spanish/Hispanic/Latino?** *Mark* ☒ *the
   "No" box if **not** Spanish/Hispanic/Latino.*

   ☐ **No**, not Spanish/Hispanic/Latino   ☐ Yes, Puerto Rican

   ☐ Yes, Mexican, Mexican Am., Chicano   ☐ Yes, Cuban

   ☐ Yes, other Spanish/Hispanic/Latino — *Print group* ↗

6. **What is this person's race?** *Mark* ☒ **one or more races** *to
   indicate what this person considers himself/herself to be.*

   ☐ White

   ☐ Black, African Am., or Negro

   ☐ American Indian or Alaska Native — *Print name of enrolled or principal tribe.* ↗

   ☐ Asian Indian   ☐ Japanese   ☐ Native Hawaiian

   ☐ Chinese   ☐ Korean   ☐ Guamanian or Chamorro

   ☐ Filipino   ☐ Vietnamese   ☐ Samoan

   ☐ Other Asian — *Print race.* ↗   ☐ Other Pacific Islander — *Print race.* ↗

   ☐ Some other race — *Print race.* ↗

Source: U.S. Bureau of the Census, Census 2000 questionnaire.

The Danger of Stereotyping and Overgeneralizing

A grave danger that emerges from the (un)lucky seven categorization for the U.S. Army and all other organizations is stereotyping. Generally the dominant groups provide the standards by which unfavored groups are judged. Weaker groups are sometimes considered deviant or less worthy than the more powerful groups.

For example, the old standard on the U.S. Census shown in Exhibit 17.1 consisted of four racial categories plus the category "Other Race." People could pick only one category. Today the census contains six categories, including "Other Race"; more significant, respondents can choose more than one category. We see that the government finally "got it"—at least partially. Within the (un)lucky seven factors of race and ethnicity, people experienced enough difference and gained sufficient voice to influence the change to multiple categories. In essence, multiracials are now no longer "others."

The dangerous aspect of categorization, which is a mentally constructed process, occurs when people viewed as "others" fall into a stereotype of overgeneralizations, which are often negative, about a specific type or group of people. Although the generalization may capture some relevant characteristics and may have some usefulness, the assumption that all members of a group share the same characteristics contains pitfalls for organizations, especially in cases where stereotypes unjustly contribute to biases against certain people and subsequently perpetuates their muted voices and marginal or nonexistent influences in organizations.

The (un)lucky seven social categories also perform another important purpose for people. Categories provide the basis for some of our most important identities—the ways we see ourselves in relationship to the social world. These categories not only provide other people with clues about how to interact with us and how to expect us to act; they also provide us with a sense of what kind of people we might want to become and how we should act. Leaders need to recognize the identities of their people and create a unit subculture where these unique identities possess legitimacy, acceptance, and positive value.

But individuals do not always possess a strong sense of identity based on these categories, and the salience of their identities often varies across situations. For example, because she is surrounded by men and plays in an event historically and culturally defined as a male activity, teenage golf pro Michelle Wie is probably much more aware of herself as a woman than as a person of a particular social class when she is playing in the Professional Golf Association tournament. Similarly, a Jewish person might be much more aware of his religion when he attends a Christian wedding ceremony than when he is at work, unless a certain spirituality is (even subtly) culturally transmitted as the "right" faith at the office.

Similarly, if you have ever traveled outside the United States, then you probably have a better appreciation and feel for what it means to be American, although you might normally have trouble defining the specific aspects of an American identity. Experiences in other national cultures often provide a rich and valuable window through which we may gaze at our collective, culturally defined selves. The key summary point about the (un)lucky seven is that although these characteristics do not incorporate every form of cultural diversity, contemporary leaders in all organizations can view them as an important starting point in the vital project of harnessing diversity to enhance their units' performance.

*As a leader in your organization, do you try to downplay
or inadvertently ignore cultural diversity? Or do you realize,
acknowledge, and explicitly act with diversity in mind as
you work to influence people in your company?*

Diversity as a Force Multiplier in Organizations

As a leader in your organization, do you try to downplay or inadvertently ignore cultural diversity? Or do you realize, acknowledge, and explicitly act with diversity in mind as you work to influence people in your company? Organizations that leverage diversity view differences among people as an important resource to enhance performance, and they thereby foster a healthy approach toward making diversity a force multiplier. We argue that accepting, understanding, and valuing diversity enhances mission accomplishment. The first key step toward valuing diversity is to understand the fundamentals of processing cultural diversity.

Effectively Processing Cultural Diversity

The fundamentals of processing cultural diversity effectively are:

- Knowledge of the meaning and complexity of the concept of culture
- A refined sense of objectivity and genuine self-awareness, including how one's deeply held values, beliefs, and biases bear on thinking and can cause harmful ethnocentrism
- Awareness, understanding, acceptance, appreciation for, and, ideally, a thirst to learn about diverse cultures and people—practicing open-mindedness and cultural relativism

We will look at each of these three factors in more detail.

Understand the Concept of Culture. The first basic piece of effectively processing diversity entails an understanding of the complex and multifaceted concept of culture and how culture deeply influences human thought processes and behavior.

Be Objective and Self-Aware. The second fundamental requisite to processing cultural diversity effectively stems from a sufficient level of self-awareness of how your own cultural memberships contribute to your deeply held life values, philosophies, morals, and beliefs. Successful military professionals possess this essential knowledge of self as a first step to bringing adequate open-mindedness to their military missions. Accurately identifying and mentally managing potential biases and preconceived notions presents an enormous challenge. Because everybody possesses and applies thousands of mental categories or labels for different types of people, this cognitive structuring often causes faulty perceptions, where people see some things and fail to see or perceive others. To the extent that people's minds possess powerful labels for people of differing cultural backgrounds, these labels—such as the stereotypes generated from the (un)lucky seven categories—can create confusing emotions that impede logic and cause inaccurate perceptions about particular groups of people.

The U.S. military works to bring open-mindedness to the workplace where a diverse population constitutes its own ranks and contemporary missions will place the military in more frequent and intimate contact with diverse people. An accurate knowledge of self and effective management of one's potential mental impediments to open-minded thinking are essential to work effectively with those who are culturally diverse.

Embrace Cultural Relativism. To maximize effectiveness, U.S. military leaders employ cultural relativism and avoid ethnocentrism to effectively process cultural diversity. *Ethnocentrism* means judging another culture using one's own culture and related beliefs as a standard, with strong biases often damaging the perceptions of a different culture. In contrast, *cultural relativism* means viewing a different culture based on its own unique belief system, values, truths, traits, history, norms, artifacts, customs, and so on.

Cultural relativism does not mean completely shedding one's own personal beliefs or succumbing to an anything-goes frame of thinking and acting; instead, it means that military professionals must avoid rushing to judgment about diverse people and cultures. The most successful military professionals possess genuinely open minds and a sense of cultural relativism toward diverse people. Military leaders in particular must set the example by seeking understanding and appreciation for diverse others' cultural practices and beliefs so as to bolster a similar, collective attitude across their units to improve the accomplishment of their missions.

For example, when U.S. and coalition armed forces assign women military members to interact with indigenous Muslim women in Operation Iraqi Freedom (OIF) and Operation Enduring Freedom (OEF), this effective norm or technique shows appropriate awareness and sensitivity for important cultural customs associated with proper interaction between the sexes as practiced by many Muslims.

It seems reasonable to argue that success in OIF, OEF, and future nation-building campaigns will require hundreds, if not thousands, of similar culturally intelligent actions to effectively influence people to accomplish the mission.

Leveraging Culture and Diversity and Leading in the U.S. Army

Army culture, as in all other organizations, simultaneously embodies long-standing traditions, values, beliefs, norms, assumptions, and artifacts while it continuously changes to remain relevant and effective in a changing society. Its culture illustrates this dual nature.

On the one hand, Army culture is marked by adherence to a well-entrenched set of rules, standard operating procedures, a hierarchical organization with an array of positions of authority, and an expectation that its members will follow orders that enable their units to accomplish the mission. This is the part of Army culture that reinforces the established bureaucracy that manages the huge number of organizational soldiers and civilian members across the globe.

To remain relevant, the Army must be insulated and progressive. It must aggressively incorporate new technologies, innovate methods to wage war and military operations other than war (such as peacekeeping), rigorously self-assess to improve unit performance, and maintain a deep focus on its institutional values to unite its increasingly diverse membership.

The Army also uses internal and external specialists to examine Army culture, ensuring that the culture contributes to the profession's effectiveness. In this way, the Army constantly assesses and, when necessary, changes its culture. Thus, Army leaders at all levels lead in a culture that simultaneously possesses both bureaucratic and professional aspects.

It is important to understand the cultural diversity of the members of the Army. Consider the demographic statistics shown in Table 17.4.

Effective Army Leaders Leverage Culture to Maximize the Performance of Their Missions

From personal experiences in the U.S. Army since 1989, one of us (Remi Hajjar) has come to believe that effective Army leaders recognize the importance of culture and seek to leverage it to maximize the morale and ultimately the performance of their units. Leaders who fail to perceive the significance of culture often miss out on opportunities to improve their units.

When analyzing an organization's existing culture, a leader needs to pay attention to the distinction between stated values (what is said to be important) and the actual values (what is actually important).

TABLE 17.4. STATISTICS ON THE DEMOGRAPHICS OF THE U.S. ARMY

Race: African Americans make up 12 percent of the U.S. population but account for 22 percent of the military's enlisted ranks and 9 percent of its officer ranks.

Gender: Women comprise approximately 15 percent of the U.S. armed forces.

Age: The military is a young organization, with few members over age fifty-five.

Social class: The military draws primarily from the working and middle classes, and the enlisted ranks account for 85 percent of the organization.

Religion: Membership mirrors the U.S. population with a diverse array of affiliations.

Disabilities: There are few service members with significant disabilities, though the military is increasingly tolerating minor disabilities, particularly from veterans from recent wars who wish to remain on active duty.

Sexual orientation: Although we do not formally ask, estimates are that about 5 percent of the military are lesbian and 2 percent are gay—approximately thirty-six thousand active members.

Source: See D. R. Segal and M. W. Segal, "America's Military Population." *Population Bulletin,* 2004, 59(4). http://www.prb.org/pdf04/59.4AmericanMilitary.pdf.

But what specifically do Army leaders do to influence culture to enhance their organization's performance? The answer is twofold: (1) they assess and analyze the unit's existing culture, and (2) they reinforce elements of that culture that promote mission accomplishment and change parts of the culture to further enhance their units. Although this notion of assessing culture and then changing parts of it may seem straightforward, often it is quite difficult to do well. Based on my (Remi Hajjar) experiences, I have come to the conclusion that this is one thing that separates the best Army leaders from their contemporaries: using everything possible, including a culture game plan, to build the best winning teams.

Assessing the Culture of an Army Unit

The first aspect of leveraging culture is to conduct a solid assessment. Edgar Schein, in *Organizational Culture and Leadership,*[3] suggests we should examine three levels to assess an organization's culture.

Gain Understanding of the Organization's Culture. The first level is to gain an understanding of what is visible, heard, perceived, or sensed. It entails cultural artifacts such as signs, office equipment, unit organization, systems and procedures, and people (their words, appearances, demographic representations, dress, behaviors, and so forth). These are just a few of an infinite possible number of artifacts, all of which provide a veiled glimpse of the organization's values, the second level in which culture is revealed.

Recognize the Organization's Stated Values versus Its Actual Values. When analyzing the second level of culture, a leader needs to pay attention to the distinction between stated values (what is said to be important) and actual values (what is actually important). For example, a medical clinic that has a sign prominently displayed that discusses the importance of customer care has publicly stated the value it places on customer treatment. But if this clinic provides inadequate treatment to patients, its collective behavior clearly does not align with this stated value. Thus, the clinic's actual value would not be quality customer care but something else—perhaps tight control of patients and servicing a great volume of people.

As another example of actual values, the best Army units create a culture that reinforces the value of selfless service to such an extent that in times of combat, soldiers functionally perceive the importance of the collective group and its mission and survival as something worthy of potentially dying for. This becomes an operational value that the unit acts on—putting the unit's needs before an individual soldier's own needs. The automatic action of jumping on a grenade to protect one's unit is a manifestation of this actual value. An organization's actual values shed light into its most deeply held assumptions, the third level of cultural assessment.

Understand the Group's Collective Assumptions. Assumptions are the subconscious beliefs that lead to nearly automatic attitudes and behaviors among group members. These assumptions are to a group what a personality is to an individual. They help the group perceive and interpret stimuli, and then they help the group to act appropriately under different situations. (The next section of this chapter provides recommendations for changing the culture of a unit, which offers a specific example of artifacts, values, and especially underlying assumptions from the experiences of a company commander.)

To understand a unit's underlying assumptions, a leader needs to collect solid information about artifacts, stated values, and actual values. And it is crucial to understand these three levels of culture (artifacts, values, and assumptions) in order to assess culture to see whether it aligns with the mission. Army leaders perform cultural assessments through several techniques. For example, many officers request a unit climate survey, which gives them a snapshot of their soldiers' attitudes and feelings about a litany of topics. Army posts have a dedicated agency that conducts voluntary unit climate surveys for commanders who request them. Surveys provide important insights, such as on the following topics:

- The overall morale of the unit
- The existence of significant differences in opinions among different ethnic groups, sexes, or ranks within the unit
- The feelings of members about their ability to accomplish the mission

Army leaders also informally query many people to gain key insights into a unit's culture. They usually converse and gain the perspectives of three key echelons:

- Subordinate leaders and baseline soldiers
- Superiors and those in positions of authority over a given unit
- Peers from sister units

Leaders also gain valuable insights into a unit's culture by being with the unit during training, enabling them to see firsthand how the unit's culture affects how it operates.

Equal opportunity creates healthier competition and professionalism,
and diversity brings more skills and backgrounds.

Diversity Repercussions: When Army Leaders Fail to Lead

To better illustrate the positive aspects of leveraging culture, let us explore the opposite case. How does the failure of leaders to consider and act on the element of culture hinder organizations? As a company executive officer, one of us (Remi Hajjar) felt that his company failed to recognize and mold its culture to help the unit. The company commander rarely asked for input in decisions, and when he did ask for input, he never genuinely listened to subordinates. This contributed to an overly centralized unit culture.

This command team's failure to build a culture that solicited group input, ideas, and collective thinking not only decreased morale and motivation but failed to gain potentially creative, innovative, and useful insights. As a result, the unit performance was mediocre. The company's command team failed to leverage the process of cultural production to incorporate norms, values, and beliefs of a more collective and creative nature, which directly hurt the performance of its mission.

Changing the Culture of a Unit: A Case Study

Effective Army leaders leverage the process of cultural production to help set the stage for mission accomplishment. In the example of Remi Hajjar's experiences as a company executive officer, the command team failed to alter the culture (with norms, beliefs, and values that dysfunctionally reinforced rigid, centralized decision making and leadership), and it hurt the unit.

This experience during his lieutenant years helped him tremendously when assigned to command a company as a captain four years later. He had been informed by his new battalion commander and battalion command sergeant major of the numerous problems in his new company, and in the first few weeks of his new command, his preliminary observations reinforced some of these senior leaders' concerning insights. Many of them pointed to a problematic culture.

The new company had significant racial and gender diversity, but the culture of the unit caused people in the company to dangerously polarize around these differences. For example, many of the people said that certain company leaders favored women, whereas others favored a particular racial group. His observations shed some light on a troubling artifact: in most work settings, sergeants socialized together almost exclusively along racial and gender lines. This seemed to be the norm of the noncommissioned officers: they valued the company of demographically similar others and avoided dissimilar others whenever possible.

So although the Army's hallmark values of acceptance of diverse others and teamwork to accomplish the mission usually help to bond soldiers regardless of racial and gender differences, the actual values in this company reinforced cohesion along racial and gender lines—a dangerous situation that reduced the overall solidarity and effectiveness of the unit. Some of the underlying assumptions in the company included beliefs about in- and out-groups, based on cultural diversity.

Hajjar also noted an interesting cultural practice in the company as a new commander: some of the unit's subordinate leaders, many of them drill sergeants, were accustomed to almost demanding, rather than recommending, certain actions to the company's command team. He had been forewarned by the battalion's leadership that at times they were not sure who was really running the company: the company leadership or the drill sergeants. From observations and the way some drill sergeants treated him (or tried to treat him) in his first few weeks in command (these occurrences revealed artifacts, values, and assumptions in this unit), Hajjar concluded that previously established company norms reinforced audacious and presumptuous behavior from some of the drill sergeants.

In other words, two important cultural dysfunctions existed in the company he had just taken command of:

1. The culture transmitted messages that perpetuated polarization along racial and gender lines.
2. The culture included a norm whereby several drill sergeants lost sight of their chain of command and expected the company leadership to follow their every wish and demand.

We will look at how each of these problems was addressed.

Changing the Chain of Command. As a new commander, Hajjar immediately attempted to alter the unit's culture to build a winning team. He found that many of the unit's problems stemmed from the unit's senior sergeant (first sergeant); an investigation revealed many inappropriate behaviors on his part that helped create some of the cultural dysfunctions. Higher-level commanders decided to have this first sergeant transferred to another Army post to serve in a staff position for the final years of his Army career; he would never serve in an Army leadership position again.

A new company first sergeant was assigned to the command team. After agreeing on how the command team would resocialize some of the drill sergeants, the team met with the drill sergeants and discussed its views of professional dialogues between drill sergeants and the command team. But the norm change in the interaction between the company command team and the drill sergeants did not fully take hold until a few drill sergeants continued to attempt to make bold demands from the command team. When these attempts were promptly corrected—and clearly perceived as inappropriate—the cultural norm change began to take hold.

Eliminating Polarization Along Racial and Gender Lines. As for the racial- and sex-based divisions in the unit, the cultural changes began with the company's command team's influence. When the company needed to make important decisions about its vision, objectives, and short-, medium-, and long-term training strategies, collective thinking and brainstorming sessions that included every company leader (all demographics included) occurred. This practice countered what had happened in the past, where the unit norm for making big decisions involved bickering and infighting between a split command team, with each member of the team generally siding with subordinates from his or her demographic group. Clearly this former practice created a unit culture of distrust and dysfunctional alliances, and, ultimately, this was a fragmented unit that performed poorly.

We built a new culture that recognized, appreciated, and valued people's diversity, and this process of developing a new culture began by listening and giving equal credence to everyone's ideas for the company's future direction. Some company social events also helped to build solid cohesion in nonwork settings, which helped to transform the company's culture to one that did not perpetuate the idea that soldiers' demographics influenced how much power (or lack of power) they possessed in our unit. The new culture led to company solidarity and enhanced performance. Ultimately our unit's diversity became an asset, which illuminates the power of leveraging culture and differences in people.

Recap on Harnessing the Power of Organizational Culture

Leaders most effectively employ knowledge of culture to maximize their organizations' performance. To do this, effective leaders appraise their unit's culture from a variety of sources, using a variety of methods. After gaining a solid understanding of their organization's culture, they seek to change aspects of culture that are hindering performance, and simultaneously they reinforce the positive aspects of existing culture. They build leadership teams that can produce cultures to best support the mission. Just as the best Army units constantly assess their missions' performance in an attempt to ensure they are doing everything possible to perform at the top level, Army leaders continuously seek to ensure that their unit's culture best supports their mission performance. And the military's cultural value of respect and appreciation for diversity strengthens cohesion and has a positive impact on unit effectiveness.

Examples of Diversity Success in the U.S. Army

Racial integration in the U.S. armed forces, although not perfect, represents a monumental diversity success story that continues to set the example for American society at large. For example, we already noted the overrepresentation of African Americans in the U.S. military in terms of demographics.

To ameliorate the problem of racial strife in the ranks, the military established the Defense Equal Opportunity Management Institute (DEOMI) in 1971. In the 1960s and 1970s, the military had significant troubles with racial unrest and dysfunctions, and the turmoil plagued military installations and ships and had a negative impact on mission performance (an example is the grenade fragging of white officers and sergeants by racially diverse soldiers during the Vietnam War). DEOMI helped the Department of Defense address these issues and has become a hallmark division of the department. A success in its own right, today DEOMI (https://www.patrick.af.mil/DEOMI/DEOMI.HTM) trains military and civilian members of the Department of Defense and conducts research on equal opportunity and diversity issues to foster equal opportunity and understand and celebrate diversity.

Today race relations in the military represent an impressive, stark contrast to those in the Vietnam-era armed forces. As one small example, it is common to see soldiers of different races sitting and eating together in military mess halls and going out together on weekend passes, among other voluntary behaviors that provide evidence of genuine friendship and social bonds that transcend racial and ethnic differences. In contrast, one of us recently spent a few years at a large private university with a well-known reputation for academic excellence, and such sights such as mixed racial groups mingling and eating together in the cafeteria were not nearly as evident.

Another example of the success story of racial integration in the armed forces is a ubiquitous feature of military life whereby African and Hispanic Americans routinely order around Caucasian Americans, something that is far less prevalent in mainstream U.S. society. In the end, the military effectively influenced a major change in its own value system toward respect for diverse others (particularly on the basis of race and ethnicity) through a command emphasis and a solid educational program (with organizations such as DEOMI) for the force at large.

This monumental accomplishment took much time and command emphasis, and the project of fully incorporating and leveraging racial and ethnic diversity in the armed forces continues now and will remain an important focus for the future. Leaders in all organizations can learn much from the lessons of the U.S. Army and military in the realm of leveraging race and ethnicity to promote effectiveness.

The Leading Diversity Initiative: An Emerging Next Step in the Project

About a decade ago, the Leading Diversity Working Group (LDWG) emerged at the U.S. Military Academy (USMA) at West Point. The group's thought, findings, and vision seem quite germane to the project of diversity, and in this vein it represents another developing, potential success story.

The LDWG represents a microlevel example of the armed forces' emphasis to keep the profession on target regarding cultural diversity. Interestingly and necessarily, the LDWG created a point of tension with some of the philosophy of one of the military's founding fathers on diversity (DEOMI); specifically, the LDWG questions the validity of a philosophy that permeates the culture of the U.S. military. The LDWG suggests that major faults emerge from the general philosophy that because all military members wear the same green uniform and work under the same set of professional values that cultural variations matter little—that the force should more or less ignore these differences.

In contrast, the LDWG poses the opposite case: because military members are not the same underneath the uniform, despite their shared military attire and professional values, cultural differences matter tremendously. And it states that if the military wishes to evolve to the next level of cultural intelligence with regard to diversity, then collectively the armed forces must enhance their ability to accept, understand, and value differences in people.

The USMA aims to inculcate graduates with a solid cultural perspective. Culture awareness is one of eight major academic goals the Academy aspires to in its rigorous core curriculum. The cultural awareness goal has several supporting objectives, including educating cadets on the culturally diverse Army and that they will lead soldiers from diverse backgrounds, and the knowledge of different global cultures where these soon-to-be young officers should expect to work effectively with unique, diverse people.

As an illustration of the Army's diversity, the photograph shows the 4th Platoon Bravo Company, 27th Main Support Battalion, 1st Cavalry Division—a transportation platoon in January 2005 in the eleventh month of a twelve-month tour of duty in Iraq. It is commanded by a West Point lieutenant—the only officer in the photograph. The remainder of the photograph is made up of a diverse array of active-duty enlisted soldiers of the platoon. We challenge the reader to identify the West Point platoon leader. The answer is found at the end of the chapter.[4]

The LDWG's new vision and thoughts on cultural diversity symbolize an emerging new wave of progress in the project of thinking of how to better leverage diversity in the new millennium, and its impact is felt at USMA. Certainly other organizations have developed similar working groups, and ideally these entities take a similar approach, whereby cultural differences matter significantly and leaders set the example toward understanding, valuing, appreciating, and leveraging diversity.

An Example of a Cultural Diversity Challenge Confronting the U.S. Army

The U.S. military profession—similar to the society it serves but generally to a greater collective extent—possesses a dominant Christian spiritual emphasis, which presents certain benefits and costs to the armed forces. The religious diversity found in the larger society is somewhat reflected in the armed forces.

Having a Christian umbrella as the dominant faith of choice in the military facilitates cohesion among military members and military families of similar spir-

A PICTURE OF DIVERSITY

ituality, particularly when Christian-based activities and services bring these families together. This spiritually generated camaraderie forges strong in-group bonding, which fosters a degree of healthy, functional cohesion in the U.S. military.

Nevertheless, this prominent spiritual emphasis carries certain costs. One is potential out-grouping of spiritually diverse others, which relates to the possibility for faulty processing of spiritual diversity in the U.S. military. In extreme cases, a failure to process this type of cultural diversity can create unprofessional conduct, harassment, and even abuse of spiritually dissimilar others in the force.

The profession has identified this potential issue, and it has communicated and reinforced the idea that spiritual tolerance is a military value. And when a few cases emerged that illustrated ignorance of this value of respecting spiritually diverse military members (recently, some U.S. Air Force Academy cadets showed disrespect to spiritually diverse peers), leaders stepped in and educated particular units to build greater appreciation for this organizational value. On the whole, the military undertakes the project of diversity in order to maintain and improve its cohesive, diverse team to effectively serve the nation.

Benefits to Society of Leveraging Cultural Diversity Effectively

One of this chapter's themes is that a connection exists between effectively processing cultural diversity within the ranks of the armed forces to applying the same skills with diverse persons who do not wear the U.S. military uniform. Should a force with some members harboring and practicing closed-mindedness toward diverse military peers expect open-minded thinking and associated behaviors when these people work with culturally different people outside its ranks?

The fundamentals of processing cultural diversity apply similarly regardless of the particular circumstances of their use. By building a stronger base of basic culture processing skills, including an understanding of the complexity of culture, heightened self-awareness, a knowledge of the dangers of ethnocentrism, and sufficient open-mindedness that leads to cultural relativism, the military will better accomplish its multiple charters. By continuing to apply the fundamentals of processing cultural diversity, the armed forces bolster service cohesion and forges solid working relations with diverse others outside the military. As the U.S. military needs to bond more effectively with diverse people through culturally intelligent behavior, its ability to process cultural diversity takes on even greater importance.

Conclusion

Leaders should consider the benefits of leveraging cultural diversity, which include both internal organizational and external environmental factors:

1. Potential internal organizational benefits of leveraging diversity:
   - Equal opportunity creates healthier competition and professionalism.
   - Diversity brings more skills and backgrounds.
   - Less human energy is wasted on the (un)lucky seven discrimination; healthier orientations are developed toward diversity; and accepting, understanding, and valuing diversity builds solidarity and bolsters effectiveness.
   - New ways of organizing, thinking, and innovating are fostered.
2. Potential benefits in the external environment by leveraging diversity:
   - Diverse organizations are more legitimate in the eyes of Americans, our allies, and our detractors.

- Success can be achieved in new and diverse markets, and among unique customers.
- Working with external organizations—with multilateral organizations, allies, the media, nongovernmental organizations, and host nations—is more effective than not.

Knowledge of culture, diversity, and how to process cultural diversity effectively takes on ever increasing importance. Lessons from the U.S. Army underscore the power that results for leaders and organizations that wisely and effectively leverage culture and diversity. For leaders who aspire to the next level of organizational success, the expectedly unsurpassed, exponential rise of interconnectedness in this era of globalization demands an even greater ability to harness the power of culture and diversity.

Notes

1. "The (Un)Lucky Seven" is the title of the introductory chapter of an undergraduate textbook that is relevant to understanding cultural diversity: M. Ender and B. Lucal, *Inequalities: Readings in Diversity and Social Life* (Boston: Pearson Custom Publishing, 2004).
2. B. A. Kosmin, E. Mayer, and A. Keysar, *American Religious Identification Survey 2001* (New York: Graduate Center, City University of New York, 2001). http://www.gc.cuny.edu/faculty/research_studies/aris.pdf.
3. E. Schein, *Organizational Culture and Leadership* (Hoboken, N.J.: Wiley, 2004, rev.).
4. The lieutenant is the female on the far right standing, now CPT Halaevalu Ball, formally Helu. She is the first female Tongan American graduate from the U.S. Military Academy. A former captain of West Point's women's basketball team and a sociology major, CPT Ball is a transportation officer who successfully led her platoon on regular transports across Iraq with no casualties. She attributes her success to her platoon sergeant, SFC Michael Pitz, second row, third in from the right.

CHAPTER EIGHTEEN

DEVELOPING ORGANIZATIONAL COMMITMENT BY PUTTING PEOPLE FIRST

Todd Woodruff

Commitment and sacrifice are commonplace for U.S. soldiers and their families. More than twenty-five hundred troops have died in Iraq and Afghanistan, and most soldiers can measure the time spent away from their families, friends, and home life in years rather than months or weeks. Compounding these wartime demands are the routine demands of Army life that include unpredictable short- and long-term schedules, physical hardships, frequent moves, housing concerns, detriments to spousal employment, increased need for child care, decreased support from and access to extended families and friends, the absence of the soldier from critical family events, and disruptions in friendships and education for children and the spouse.

Despite these sacrifices, the military continues to retain highly committed, skilled professionals without the benefit of large salaries. The importance of developing and retaining highly committed soldiers cannot be overstated. Unlike civilian counterparts, virtually all soldiers enter at the lowest enlisted or officer rank and are trained, developed, and promoted into positions of increasing responsibility. There is no lateral entry from the civilian sector, making the retention of junior and midlevel leaders enormously important.

The deep commitment of soldiers and their families is evident in the example of my long-time friend Sergeant First Class Arthur. Arthur, his wife, and the Army have been a team for almost two decades. In a four-year period, Arthur was separated from his wife and two boys for a one-year assignment to South Korea, a six-month wartime deployment to Afghanistan, and a thirteen-month wartime deployment to Iraq. Despite the repeated separation, the enormous physical risk, and the fear and anxiety it created for his family, they remain committed to each other and the Army. This is not an isolated case: for the past four years, the Army has exceeded its retention goals by progressively larger margins each year. In 2005, the Army raised its retention goal by eight thousand soldiers and still managed to exceed its objective significantly.

How has the Army developed committed soldiers and families, given the increasing level of demands that are placed on soldiers and their families? Among the many reasons soldiers cite are these:

- Having a sense of purpose
- Developing a bond with fellow soldiers
- Leadership climate
- Having the support of and serving the interests of their families
- Being able to use the skills they have developed

Academic research identifies numerous factors that contribute to organizational commitment,[1] including:

- Autonomy
- Responsibility
- Empowerment
- Task variety and meaningfulness
- Leader support
- Development and investment in members
- Professional opportunities
- Work-family balance
- Pay and benefits

Soldiers want to know they are risking their lives for a higher purpose, for a mission that has meaning to them, and that they contribute to the greater good.

Soldier commitment to the Army is no exception, and though Army missions may differ from the private and nonprofit sectors, the leadership processes that have produced millions of highly professional and committed soldiers are often applicable to organizations outside the military. This chapter examines how these leader actions and principles influence soldier commitment through the soldier's belief in the mission, the development of cohesion, positive perceptions of the unit, Army values, the soldier's satisfaction and welfare, work-family balance, and aspects of how the soldier perceives his or her job.

Developing Multiple Supportive Commitments

One explanation for why soldiers develop powerful commitment to the Army is the ability to create multiple related commitments that support commitment to the Army. One soldier's example of a network of related commitment may help illustrate this point:

> I'm a soldier, and my friends are soldiers. That's my best friend, Mike, and those three soldiers are my good friends also. The rest of these guys are my platoon, kind of like my second family. My sergeant there is like my big brother; he kicks my butt, but [he] takes care of me no matter what. He doesn't let anyone else mess with us. The other soldiers in this building all belong to my company (100–150 soldiers). They're my "Band of Brothers," I'm friends with a bunch of them, and I spend most of my free time with people from this unit.
>
> This complex of buildings is the Rakkasans' area (Rakkasan is the name the regiment earned while fighting the Japanese during World War II). It's the home of the best unit in the division. I could tell you all about our history, but it would take a while because they have done so much. Of course, the Rakkasans are part of the 101st Airborne Division, Screaming Eagles. I asked to serve here because it's the most prestigious and capable division in the Army, plus they are headed to Iraq this year, and if you're going to be a soldier, you might as well do it where the rubber meets the road and you can make a difference. Plus, I need to help take care of these guys.

As this example suggests, soldiers develop commitment to:

- The mission (in this case, Iraq)
- Their buddies, leaders, and team (personal relationships and cohesion)
- Their units (in this case, the Rakkasan Regiment and 101st Airborne Division)
- The Army ("I'm a soldier")
- The Army's values system (soldier care, service, and family)
- Serving the nation

Figure 18.1 illustrates this well. These multiple points of personal identification and commitment are powerful enough to influence a soldier to volunteer for missions that include exposure to great physical risk and hardship; to forgo greater financial rewards (although soldiers' salaries have improved and reenlistment bonuses are averaging $6,000 to $12,000); accept tearful good-byes with their children, spouse, other family, and friends; and dedicate himself or herself to lifelong service. The first section of this chapter discusses how leaders develop commitment through ideals, people, and nested commitments to subordinate and higher organizations.

Purpose: "I Will Always Place the Mission First"

Army wife Diane Campbell, in an interview with *Washington Times* writer Thomas Ricks, spoke of her daughter's turning to her during a movie and saying, "My daddy's saving the world."[2] That is the power of purpose. Soldiers want to know

FIGURE 18.1. A SOLDIER'S COMMITMENT TO IDEALS, PEOPLE, AND ORGANIZATIONS

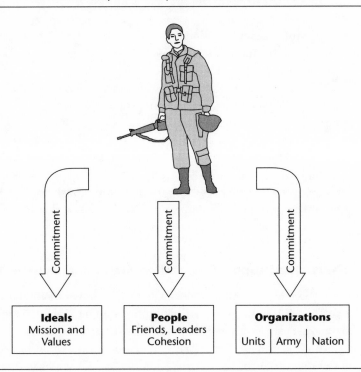

they are risking their lives for a higher purpose for a mission that has meaning to them and that they contribute to the greater good.

Research indicates that the personal meaningfulness of serving and wanting to contribute to something larger than themselves is a powerful enlistment motivation for many soldiers. The same is true outside the Army. Tom Henry is an example of why even successful members may lack commitment if meaningfulness is absent. Tom left a successful career in the restaurant industry when he began feeling his work was not significant: he then cofounded Feed America First of Tennessee, a nonprofit organization dedicated to providing food to those who feed the hungry by collecting food donations and distributing them to local charities within the middle Tennessee communities.[3] Whether in the Army, private business, or the nonprofit sector, intrinsic caring about a task, the task having personal meaning for the individual, and the individual believing that his or her efforts have a positive and substantial impact on the lives of others and importance beyond the immediate situation all contribute to empowerment and organizational commitment.

The Army has an advantage over most private sector organizations because of the nature of its role, but even in the military, fully leveraging the effects of a meaningful mission does not happen by accident. Soldiers are reminded at every opportunity that what they do has great meaning. Through deliberate exposure to the Army's institutional ethos, vision statement, comments of institutional leaders, and professionally produced media products, soldiers are reminded almost constantly of the importance of their service and the Army's contributions to the United States and its ideals.

Although these methods are important, they are insufficient. Unit leaders must also articulate to soldiers the importance of their efforts and how each task and mission contributes to the success of the larger operation. As part of this culture, Army leaders demonstrate the importance of a task by sharing in hardships and risk and by demonstrating a willingness to do any task asked of soldiers. A leader appearing in the middle of the night in freezing rain to tell a soldier he or she is doing a great job protecting the unit from attack does far more to communicate the importance of standing guard than telling that soldier the next morning after climbing out of a warm, dry sleeping bag.

Values: "I Serve the People of the United States and Live the Army Values"

Army values are common across all levels of the Army's nested commitment and serve as an additional source of commitment. The Army advertises its values, deliberately socializes its soldiers into the values system, uses them as a measure of performance, and reinforces Army values in everything it does. (Chapter Five addresses the topic of values further.) There is ample evidence that soldiers commit to the Army partly because of its values. Most soldiers who join the Army do so for primarily intrinsic reasons, such as a desire to serve or to find merit-based, racially unbiased opportunities, and they may be committed to the Army because they identify with an ideal that is inextricably linked to the Army. In other words, the positive association a soldier has for the values system carries over to commitment to the institution itself. This is consistent with business sector findings that the congruence of member values with the overall organization's values contributes to commitment to the organization.

Conversely, soldiers who do not identify with the Army's values may be less likely to commit. For example, a soldier who is in the Army only for college money or his or her own personal development may be less committed to the service than people who join because they want to serve their nation or a cause larger than themselves. But even in these situations, because the Army values are inculcated over time, its values of loyalty, duty, and selfless service may create the conditions that promote commitment. It is not difficult to imagine a soldier who joined for selfish reasons yet over a period of socialization begins to identify with the Army's values of loyalty and duty, and then develops commitment to the Army itself.

People: "I Will Never Leave a Fallen Comrade"

The Army is people. The soldiers placing their boots on the ground, making decisions, and personally influencing the situation define this organization. By its nature of shared hardship and risk, long periods of time spent in close living conditions, a shared values system, self-selection into the Army, and a host of other factors, soldiers form a special bond at the small unit level. These types of friendly and supportive relationships with coworkers and supervisors have been found to have a positive effect on organizational commitment, and I would argue that this effect is magnified in the Army.

Although most people might not consider the Army a warm organization, in some ways it is. We practice tough love and ask soldiers to exercise violence on behalf of their nation and to endure the most difficult situations, but at the same time, soldiers often speak of their bonds with their buddies and the depth of their personal commitment to them. These personal ties to other soldiers are predicated on membership in the Army and help form the bedrock of commitment to the Army.

Soldiers often share a family-like bond. They call each other "brother" and use the word *love* in describing their relationships. For some, their loyalty to their comrades is so powerful that it becomes their primary motivation for taking risk in combat. The thought of failing their buddies is a powerful motivator. This relationship is typical between peer soldiers, but it can also exist between the leader and the led.

For example, at a memorial ceremony in Iraq, which was documented by the PBS program *Frontline*, Sergeant Gabriel Garcia recounted the words of his fallen soldier, Specialist Travis Babbitt. Garcia, repeating Babbitt's words through his tears, said, "Sergeant . . . Sergeant Garcia, I'll never let anything happen to you. I always got your back." Babbitt was shot through the chest and died doing just that: protecting his brothers in arms. Even after receiving the mortal wound, Babbitt returned to his weapon and killed the enemy threatening his comrades. Garcia said in his remarks, "If it wasn't for him, I wouldn't be here talking to you." No leader or friend could ask for anything more.[4]

Babbitt's company commander, Captain Whitely, when informing his soldiers of Babbitt's death, said, "We all loved him like a brother. . . . I love each of you like my brother. . . . I love each and every one of you and I'm proud of what we do here." This closeness horizontally between peers and vertically between leaders and their subordinates can result in job satisfaction and powerful commitment to your organization. Garcia was asked if he needed a break following Babbitt's death, to which he replied, "That's not even a question for me, there's no way I'd leave the team. No way." This commitment is repeated throughout the Army.[5]

Although the conditions of Army life lend themselves to developing social cohesion, cohesive groups can be dysfunctional if they are opposed to the vision of the organization and operate outside its values system. Therefore, Army leaders go to great measures to build cohesive teams and ensure these teams support the Army's mission and values. Although some of the methods for developing these bonds and unit cohesion may differ from the private sector (for example, collective physical training, exposure to situations that requires complete and mutual trust, or shared risk), many of the methods (for example, frequent social events for members and families, caring leaders, common goals, stable and supportive work relationships, exposure to challenging situations, and creating wins for the team) are just as applicable to any business or nonprofit organization and are consistent with much of the research on cohesion and team building.

---

*Soldiers desire to be a part of a unit with a history of
achievement and excellence, to contribute to its storied
history, and to live up to the standards of its past heroes.*

Esprit de Corps: "I Will Never Accept Defeat, Never Quit"

Research indicates that members of an organization tend to have the strongest commitment to their most immediate units and that as units become more distant, these effects are weakened. Despite this added challenge, the Army is successful at developing commitment to mid-echelon units above company level, and the Army provides an excellent example for overcoming the effects of distance that result in reduced commitment. The Army has managed to develop strong commitments to both the more proximate units (squad, platoon, and company) and to units that are four to six echelons removed from the soldier (battalions, regiments, brigades, and divisions), because they have reduced the conceptual range to these echelons. In other words, despite being four to six echelons removed, soldiers develop strong social and psychological identification with their units.

The effects of social cohesion and direct leadership that are significant at the team through company level begin to lose influence at the battalion level and higher, but these higher units have other powerful mechanisms to develop commitment. In the Army, we refer to them collectively as "esprit de corps," which includes spirit and pride in the unit's history, heroes, and achievements. As part of the Army's culture, soldiers learn the history of their unit, and leaders perpetuate the perception that their unit is special. Soldiers desire to be part of a unit with a history of achievement and excellence, to contribute to its storied history, and to live up to the standards of its past heroes.

It is not uncommon for soldiers to identify themselves as a member of a midlevel unit such as a regiment or division and maintain powerful commitment to these units. Recall the example of the soldier in the 101st Airborne, quoted at the beginning of this chapter. He could tell you about its impressive history, parachuting into Normandy during World War II, its contributions in Vietnam and the Gulf War, and its two deployments to Operation Iraqi Freedom. Similar stories could be recounted for the soldier's battalion or regiment.

When I was a sergeant with the 187th Regiment, I would have told you, "My unit is called the Rakkasans, and we're the only airborne regiment in the history of the U.S. Army to fight in every war since the inception of airborne tactics: we parachuted in to fight the Japanese and North Koreans, and we kicked ass at Hamburger Hill in Vietnam." Soldiers in that regiment today would add that they conducted the largest and deepest air assault helicopter operation in history during the Gulf War, fought al Qaeda in the mountains of Afghanistan, and have been back to fight insurgents and terrorists in Iraq twice. Those soldiers could also tell you about the unit's Medal of Honor recipients and how they are currently contributing to the unit's history and proud traditions. The commitment to these units can last long after a soldier has left the unit, with the soldier seeking to return to the unit and former members attending battalion, regiment, and division reunions for decades after leaving the Army. I have served in numerous battalions, regiments, and divisions, and this level of identification and commitment is almost always present.

Commanders and key leaders in these midlevel units are similarly affected by the dynamics of esprit de corps, but cohesion and strong social networks among this group of leaders can play an important role in creating commitment between horizontal and vertical units. Their personal relationships and ties with other leaders within the parent unit help bring this unit identification back down to the soldier level. Soldiers see their leaders are fully committed to the unit (the battalion through the division) and other leaders within that unit, and this knowledge helps reinforce the influences of their own identification with the unit.

For example, in Hawaii as part of the 25th Infantry Division and the Wolfhound Regiment, my battalion commanders would frequently hold social gatherings for the unit's officers and senior noncommissioned officers (NCOs). Our unit leaders and their families would meet for weekend barbecues at a leader's home on the beach, meet frequently to welcome new leaders and say farewell to those leaving, conduct leader sports events and competitions, and complete professional development exercises followed by an "officer call" (code for having a few beers). Over time, we developed close ties that reinforced our membership with the Wolfhounds.

In another battalion (an all-male unit), we had the Bayonet Brotherhood. When they first arrived at the unit, officers and senior NCOs were inducted into the Brotherhood, issued a numbered regimental coin, and officially became part of the team. The formal affiliation was reinforced with frequent social events at the old officers' club and more formal events that celebrated the unit's history. The relationship that existed between these thirty to forty key leaders was the glue that tied together the unit of almost seven hundred soldiers.

It is also important to mention that our commitment to the regiment or division was not mutually exclusive with commitment to the Army. In addition to commitment to the unit, we continuously reaffirm our commitment to the Army, our loyalty and relationships to other soldiers, and our core values and missions. The way the Army perpetuates the pride in unit and Army history and heroes can be used similarly in the private sector. Continental Airlines is an example of how storytelling can be used to develop an emotional commitment to the organization. Just as Army leaders share stories of its units' and soldiers' accomplishments to leverage an emotional commitment to the unit and to articulate desirable behavior, Continental Airlines trains and uses deliberate storytelling of past events to build an emotional commitment from the member to the leader and organization.[6]

Higher Commitments: "I am a Guardian of the American Way of Life"

Just as leaders are able to develop commitments to units that are subordinate to the overall organization, they can and should leverage how commitment to the organization serves other social identities the member may have. In the case of the Army, there are natural relationships between serving the Army and service to America, society, and the ideals of freedom and the American way of life. For some soldiers, serving the Army allows them to support their commitments to their family or religion. Although leveraging this relationship may be more obvious for the Army, leaders in the private sector may also be able to develop relationships between their organization and higher-order societal structures or ideals. For example, leaders at Microsoft could leverage the linkage between their company and its support to education, national security, or the American quality of life.

Leader Lessons for Developing Multiple Supportive Commitments

Soldiers can maintain strong commitment to people, purpose, principles, and units, all nested within their commitment to the Army and the nation. The story of Specialist Casey Carroll illustrates the power of this nested commitment. Carroll was sent home in March 2005 after he lost a finger and took shrapnel in his hip and foot from an improvised explosive device that killed one soldier and wounded three others. "They sent me home for good, but I went home to build myself back up so I could get back to my unit," said the young father of two. One month later, Carroll was on his way back to Iraq, saying he had a duty to his country, a responsibility to this unit, and owed it to his children.[7] For Carroll, his service in the Army and returning to Iraq was a product of related and nested commitments to his unit and his fellow soldiers, his country, and his values (duty), and it enabled his family relationship. By creating numerous points of commitment to the organization's ideals, people, and multiple levels of work units that most members are part of, leaders can generate potent organizational commitment in their people:

- Ask, "How can I get my members to commit to each other, their leaders, their immediate team, other higher-level units in the organization, and the organization's missions and values system?" Alignment of these commitments takes deliberate analysis and leader actions, but consider the following lessons for developing commitment in business, nonprofit, and governmental organizations. Explain to your members why their job and tasks are important, how they add value to the organization, and perhaps how they serve society.
- Encourage and facilitate friendly, professional relationships between members and between leaders. Take measures to build and maintain small unit cohesion.
- To generate commitment to midlevel units, build relationships among midlevel leaders to function as the social glue between units. Insist that midlevel leaders be highly visible role models to all members, from entry level to direct-subordinate level.

- Ensure your organization promotes values people can be proud of and encourages them to serve the organization and other members.
- Live the values that you espouse.

A Climate of Caring

I enjoy watching movies portraying military leadership styles. My favorite is the Marine drill instructor in *Full-Metal Jacket* who is enormously impressive in his ability to enforce discipline, create fear, curse, and transform young men into marines. My own Army drill sergeants were cast from this same mold, and they were some of the toughest men I have ever known, but their approach to leadership was situationally based. That is, it was appropriate for basic training and transforming a civilian into a soldier, but it is seldom used in leading soldiers in operational units. After all, who would voluntarily subject themselves to this form of leadership over a prolonged period—particularly soldiers with their own families?

The climate that leaders set in a unit has great influence on a soldier's commitment to that unit and desire to remain a soldier. The degree to which leaders seek to improve satisfaction with the soldier's work, general quality of life, personal development, work-family balance, and family care has enormous influence on the level of organizational commitment that exists. This is reflected in the Army's reenlistment missions. Commanders at all levels are tasked with a reenlistment goal and held accountable for their ability to meet this goal. The ability to retain soldiers in their command is seen as a reflection on leadership and command climate. I believe most Army leaders would agree. Other things being equal, supportive and caring leaders tend to do very well, and those who are perceived as uncaring, self-serving, or hard on families often fail to retain soldiers.

It is because we ask so much that leaders must also care so much.

Caring for Soldiers

Leaders demonstrate caring by knowing their soldiers, understanding their needs, and placing the needs and interests of the subordinate, the unit, and the Army before their own.

Good leaders are supportive and develop personal caring relationships without compromising their leader-led relationship. Recall Captain Whitely saying to his soldiers, "I love each of you like my brother. . . . I love each and every one of you, and I'm proud of what we do here." The genuine emotion in his voice and in the hug he gave a grieving soldier were clear. Immediately following this statement, he had them reset their vehicles, weapons, and gear and then sent them back into harm's way the next morning.

This leadership approach may surprise some people who are unfamiliar with the Army and its culture. Barry Posner, coauthor of *The Leadership Challenge*, visited the U.S. Military Academy at West Point to discuss his research on the qualities subordinates desired in their leaders.[8] In an informal poll of the military audience, caring was selected at a higher frequency than he found during his research. As we talked afterward, he mentioned that he had expected the opposite, that he had not expected caring to be as important in a hypermasculine, warrior culture. I explained that in the Army, we must care deeply for our subordinates, because we ask them to risk their lives and subordinate their own well-being to the unit's, trusting to their leaders and peers for their safety and welfare. It is because we ask so much that leaders must care so much.

The previous discussion on people and cohesion and a forthcoming discussion on soldier development both address some ways that supportive and caring leadership can generate organizational commitment. Although these actions may be adequate for single soldiers without children, caring for soldiers with families requires additional discussion.[9] The discussion of care and support of Army families is highly applicable to business and nonprofit organizations where work-self balance and work-family balance are equally critical. Studies have found that more than 75 percent of personnel consider the balance between work and personal life their top priority and that more than two out of three male workers would give up pay, power, and status for more family time.

Leader Support of Army Families

For a majority of the Army, a caring and supportive leadership climate is equally critical to the development of both the family's and the soldier's commitment to the Army. Not many years ago, the Army had the saying, "If the Army wanted you to have a family, it would have issued you one." Today the saying is, "We reenlist families," acknowledging that spousal and family satisfaction with Army life is highly influential in the decision to stay with the Army.

In today's Army, Sergeant Arthur's family situation (mentioned at the very beginning of this chapter) is not uncommon. Family members outnumber soldiers by a ratio of three to two, and 60 percent of soldiers are either married or have children. Like other organizations, the Army faces many of the same social and family trends, such as increasing numbers of dual-income households, single parents, and women in the organization and a decreasing willingness of families to tolerate the demands of work at the expense of the family.

This final trend is particularly important because the influence of the family is incredibly powerful. Married soldiers and soldiers with children are nine times more likely to consider their family role and identity more important and self-defining than their soldier role and identity. This is surprising because soldiers experience significant socialization to their units and the Army and tend to develop close, caring relationships with other soldiers. For leaders, this means that soldiers with families are more likely to behave in a way that is consistent with expectations, values, and norms of their family rather than the Army. It is crucial that leaders develop a situation where families and soldiers believe that Army and family life are compatible. Without this approach, soldiers and their families are unlikely to remain committed to the Army.

Leaders who believe that families are not their concern fail to mobilize the support and influence of the family, generate resistance from spouses, and reduce performance in the organization.

The profound impact that leadership plays in soldier commitment and family satisfaction is clear in the story of Adam and Autumn Martinez. Adam Martinez is a soldier and a husband who was looking forward to being a great father. The Martinezes were expecting their first child while Adam would be in Afghanistan, about midway through a ten-month deployment. Adam's leaders knew the unit would be gone, and they recognized how important it was for Adam to be an active partner in the pregnancy and to be there for his wife, Autumn. They made it a point to have Adam make the doctor's appointments, hear his unborn son's heartbeat, and care for Autumn during her worst periods of morning sickness. Adam had not asked for this time off, but his leaders made it a point to know when Autumn's appointments were and when she was not feeling well.

This level of leader support and individualized consideration continued throughout Adam's deployment to Afghanistan. He was able to call and e-mail home daily, and when his wife went into labor, he was immediately sent to the unit headquarters. While Autumn delivered their child, Adam Martinez was on the phone coaching her, and the wife of the company commander, Susan Moore, held the phone to Autumn's ear in a delivery room a half-world away. Autumn and Adam Martinez were only one of six families in this organization of 120 soldiers to have babies while the unit was deployed. Each time the company commander, Captain Tobby Moore, ensured the soldier was sent to the headquarters and participated in the delivery by telephone.

When I met Autumn, she repeatedly spoke about how supportive her husband's leaders and other spouses in the unit had been and about the importance of the new relationships she has developed with these spouses. It is no coincidence that Adam Martinez reenlisted or that the company to which Adam Martinez belongs had the highest retention rate of almost thirty companies in the brigade.

This example illustrates the two-pronged approach that the Army uses to care for families. First, the Army has family-friendly programs and policies. Like many other organizations, it has invested heavily in family-friendly policies and programs, such as family support groups, affordable child care, medical care, and systems so spouses can communicate during periods of separation. Over the past fifteen years, the focus on families has produced a much-improved system of support, resulting in almost two-thirds of spouses rating the family support as excellent or good.

Second, the Army has family-friendly leadership. Although family-friendly policies and programs are important in reducing work-family conflict and developing commitment, they are only part of the solution, and they are much more effective when combined with supportive leadership. By themselves, these policies and programs offer an incomplete solution that would achieve only partial success at best, particularly as the level of demands made by the organization increases. Imagine how ineffective higher-level policies and programs would have been if Adam Martinez's leaders had limited his involvement with caring for Autumn before he deployed, not let him communicate with her during their separation, and prevented him from being involved in the birth of his son.

Despite the risk and the family separation, Army leaders have had success in creating an environment where most soldiers and the families believe a person can be a great father or mother, husband or wife, and a great soldier. In this approach, the leader's focus is on enhancing the compatibility between the two roles rather than winning a competition for the soldier's limited time and energy. Although family policy and programs play a role, it is front-line leaders who have the greatest impact on the satisfaction of soldiers and their families.

Leaders must understand how their actions impinge on the lives of soldiers and families and how families influence the effectiveness of the unit.

Army leaders are expected to be caring, compassionate, and accommodating of soldiers and their families. It is these leaders whose decisions, behaviors, knowledge, skills, and abilities make the greatest difference in the lives of families, and it is the junior-level leaders who, because of their frequent and intimate contact with soldiers and their families, are the most influential in their day-to-day lives.

Human issues can never be outsourced to family support programs and policies; instead, the focus must be on caring, individualized leadership. Leaders who believe that families are not their concern fail to mobilize the support and influence of the family, generate resistance from spouses, and reduce performance in the organization.

The Martinez case demonstrates the effect of caring leadership on the day-to-day lives of soldiers and families. Leaders understood the needs of the unit's families and provided the individualized support that each required. They sent the message that families are part of the team, resulting in the development of a trusting relationship between the unit leadership, their soldiers, and the soldiers' families. Ultimately this results in increased retention, satisfaction, and organizational commitment.

The experiences of Army leaders, supported by substantial research, have shown that families have a significant impact on organizations. Leaders influence this impact by affecting the quality of the families' lives and the families' perception that the unit leaders are supportive and accommodating of their needs. When families believe that the leaders are supportive and take measures to increase families' satisfaction with the organization, the unit is likely to experience reduced work-family conflict and increased commitment, retention, satisfaction, and performance; and families are likely to experience increased marital and family satisfaction, cohesion, and stability; lessened child developmental problems and family conflict; and improved individual well-being. Cumulatively, the evidence strongly suggests the relationship shown in Figure 18.2.

When leaders fail to create the perception that they care about families, soldiers are more likely to experience work-family conflict, and in the long term, they

FIGURE 18.2. THE INFLUENCE OF A LEADER'S ACTIONS

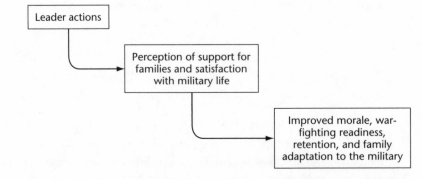

are more likely to resolve that conflict in the interest of the family, and thus at the expense of the Army. There are plenty of leaders who still view families as a distraction that they need to buffer their organization from and who fail to see how their decisions touch the lives of their soldiers' families.

Caring is not enough. Just as leaders must be technically and operationally competent, so must they be competent in ensuring the well-being of their soldiers and their families. Leaders must understand how their actions impinge on the lives of soldiers and families and how families influence the effectiveness of the unit. They must also develop the necessary skills and knowledge to care for families and be accommodating of their needs.

Leaders who care but are ineffective in developing the perception that they are caring or have little positive impact on families' satisfaction with the organization are only marginally better than leaders who do not care at all. This requires leaders to know their soldiers and their families and routinely demonstrate individualized concern for each. Leaders must have an understanding of the specific leader behaviors likely to be perceived as supportive and result in improved family satisfaction with the Army or unit.[10]

I have already discussed the importance of camaraderie and cohesion among soldiers. The Martinez story highlights the important role informal social networks play in the satisfaction of families with Army life. In addition to their help during the pregnancy and birth of Autumn's baby, the spouses in the organization helped by bringing food and visiting frequently after Autumn returned from the hospital. The development of these types of relationships between the spouses of soldiers is critical.

Research has shown that friendships between spouses tend to parallel the organizational structure. Soldiers' friendships at work are likely to carry over into their free time and home life, resulting in friendships between couples. Friendships between spouses also occur because leaders routinely include families in our unit activities. Leaders use parties, picnics, formal ceremonies, dances, unit sports events, information meetings, and less structured events that include socializing with small groups of subordinates and their families outside work. This makes a huge difference when a family needs help, and it increases family commitment to the Army.

When leaders develop relationships through repeated interaction between their unit's families, they are developing a network of family support. Army families take care of each other, and they do so because the leader has developed an organization that includes families as part of the team. This is particularly important when soldiers are deployed away from home. Families that cope the best in a wartime environment cite the solidarity and friendships they have developed with other spouses as critical. "We have become a sorority of separation," said one Army spouse, playing on the "band of brothers" slogan.[11] It is not uncommon to hear from people who left the service that they miss the quality of friendships they experienced in the Army. The spouses are no different. Their happiness and satisfaction is tied to the unit through the many friendships and bonds they share with other spouses in the organization. My wife is a perfect example: of her three best friends, two of them have spouses whom I work with every day, and the third is a spouse of my fellow commander from my previous assignment.

Although each family may differ, there are critical core family care skills and knowledge that should be developed in all leaders. Exhibit 18.1 includes lessons for Army leaders that also have application for most civilian organizations.

Soldier Training, Education, and Development

Training, education, and developmental programs go beyond increasing performance: they also increase members' organizational commitment by creating the perception that the organization values the member and by acting as a symbol of the organization's commitment to the member. In fact, single soldiers without children tend to consider their personal development one of the most important factors in their continued commitment. The Army engages in these practices to a level seldom matched by other organizations. This is partially a product of the Army's lack of lateral entry, requiring it to develop leaders and skilled soldiers from their point of initial entry, but it is also a means to operational excellence. Lifelong learning and leadership development are highly valued and necessary components of our culture. As leaders, one of our core responsibilities is to train soldiers and units to be prepared for a full spectrum of tasks and operations.

My own enlisted and officer experiences may provide an idea of the magnitude of the Army's investment in training, education, and development. During my first four years of enlisted experience, I spent the equivalent of one year in schools and training outside operational units, attending three months of basic and initial entry training, three leader development courses, and numerous skill-producing schools and programs. When on-the-job and operational training with my unit are added, the preponderance of my time was spent in activities geared toward my leadership and skill development. I attended college and earned an M.B.A. using the GI Bill and Army College Fund and continued to attend Army schools and training during Reserve Officer Training Corps. As an officer, the Army's investment has been even more pronounced. I have spent four of eleven years in full-time educational experiences away from operational units, completing many skill-producing schools; a full-time, Army-funded master's degree in sociology; and three professional development schools, each lasting six to ten months.

EXHIBIT 18.1. LESSONS FOR
BUILDING MEMBER AND FAMILY COMMITMENT

All leaders should:

Consider families to be part of your organization and not a distraction.

Know your unit's families and their issues and concerns.

Seek to identify new ways to increase spousal satisfaction with your organization.

Train leaders in family support and model these practices in your own leadership.

Allow families as much control over their family situation as possible, provide the most predictable schedules possible, and do not waste members' time.

Listen to families' problems, show real interest in the well-being of families, and treat members and families with respect.

Include families in unit activities.

Communicate with spouses and provide avenues for spouses to communicate with unit leaders.

Provide quality sponsorship to new members and families.

Understand how and why leader decisions affect families. Recognize that even routine decisions can have consequences for families (for example, keeping members later than scheduled and beyond the family's day care hours).

Understand how families perceive your decisions and behavior and how to create the perception (and fact) of caring, accommodating leadership.

Know how to identify and help high-risk families (for example, very young families, new parents, families new to the Army, single parents, and families with special needs).

Know the various support agencies and other forms of assistance that are available to families, and know how to encourage their use.

Understand the demands of child rearing and the limitations of child care facilities.

Know how to develop informal spousal-support networks in the unit.

Senior leaders must also:

Hold subordinate leaders accountable for the support they provide to families.

Ensure that the plan and support for families is nested at all levels of the organization so that each unit is working together and augmenting the support provided by higher and subordinate commands.

Institutionalize leadership practices that promote care for members and families.

Source: M. W. Segal and J. Harris, *What We Know About Army Families* (Alexandria, Va.: Army Research Institute for Behavioral and Social Sciences, 1993).

A point worth reinforcing is that the Army does more than invest in directly applicable skills. It uses a program of developmental schools that prepares NCOs and officers for their next level of responsibility and leadership and also invests heavily in soldiers' general education. Soldiers are eligible for substantial tuition assistance for college; they may have their previous educational loans repaid; those found deficient in academic skills may be sent to school to address this deficiency; and many officers attend full-time, fully funded graduate schools.

There is more than anecdotal evidence that this investment enhances commitment to the Army. For example, consider the following facts pertaining to soldiers who participate in Army continuing-education programs such as college tuition assistance:

- They were 7 percent more likely to reenlist.
- They were 5 percent more likely to complete their term of service.
- They had higher performance ratings.
- They were promoted earlier.

In addition, officers attending Army-funded graduate schooling are also more likely to remain in the Army until retirement.

Perhaps most important, training and development are not limited to schools and classes outside operational units. Although soldiers have substantial opportunities for focused training and education away from other day-to-day responsibilities, I would argue that it is within the unit that the most important training and development occurs. Training occurs almost every day, and leaders and peers dedicate substantial energy to training other soldiers within the unit. Unit leaders routinely counsel, coach, mentor, and provide soldiers and subordinate leaders opportunities to try new jobs and train in positions of greater responsibility. Even when a unit is deployed to war, training and development do not end.

This significant and continuing investment in soldiers serves to develop a sense of competence in the soldier and serves as a symbol of the leader's and the Army's commitment to the soldier, both of which result in the soldier's greater commitment to the Army, unit, and leader. Leaders can also degrade a soldier's commitment by failing to balance the short-term performance of the unit against the long-term needs of the soldier and the Army. Countless times I have seen leaders faced with the decision of either sending the soldier to a school or postponing or denying the educational opportunity so the soldier could participate in an exercise or a deployment. Although the soldier may help the unit with the exercise, denying the schooling opportunity typically results in a loss of commitment and trust unless the reasons for the decision are carefully communicated and the soldier agrees with the logic of the decision. This is just as important in the public, nonprofit, and business sectors as it is in the Army. Numerous researchers have found that investment in training and employee development has impacts on both the rational and emotional commitment of the member to the organization and overwhelmingly positive effects in improved productivity.

Do not undermine commitment by placing the leader's
short-term performance needs before the developmental needs
of the member or the long-term needs of the organization.

Opportunities for Excellence and "Being All You Can Be"

Work redesign or job enhancement is one of the core areas of focus for the development of organizational commitment. It is also one of the areas where I believe the Army has made the most progress, and it helps to explain its success in soldier retention during this period of war. One key factor I have discussed previously is meaningfulness of the work and having a powerful sense of purpose. Meaningful work and military service seem a natural fit, but empowering members and generating job satisfaction with increased responsibility, discretion, feedback, and job variety may not fit the stereotypes of Army leadership or the public's perception of what it is like to be a soldier. Some people might pull up the image of the sergeant yelling at a soldier saying, "We don't pay you to think, we pay you to follow orders," and the soldier standing at attention, eyes forward, yelling, "Yes, Sergeant!" This behavior is unlikely to generate commitment and is the exception rather than the rule in the Army.

Soldiers develop powerful commitment for many of the same reasons identified in job enhancement and redesign research, including empowerment, increased responsibility, discretion, task variety, and opportunities to demonstrate competence. Although the Army has its share of micromanagers and risk-averse leaders, most leaders in today's Army speak of the necessity of empowering our soldiers and junior leaders. The term *strategic corporal* is often used in discussing this issue, referring to the fact that the Army's most junior leaders are making decisions and taking actions that have strategic implications and possibly influence global opinions.

For example, the nature of combat and information availability in Iraq and Afghanistan has created a situation where squad and platoon leaders are making decisions that would have been reserved for company and battalion commanders only a decade ago. Because combat operations in Iraq and Afghanistan are highly complex and decentralized in their execution, junior leaders are required to make immediate decisions, often under media scrutiny and without time to consult higher authorities. These tactical decisions have strategic impacts, so junior leaders and soldiers must understand the purpose of their mission, what the commander intends to accomplish, and how it fits into the big picture. This awareness combined with the Army values helps junior leaders take initiative, anticipate situations, use creativity, adapt to the adversary and environment, execute complex problem solving, and make decisions under stress.

Soldiers spend a considerable amount of time and energy to develop these skills and abilities, so it is not surprising that many soldiers deployed to combat often cite the opportunity to use their training as a reason for their continued service in the Army. When not deployed, soldiers exist in a perpetual state of training and preparing to deploy. Just as an athlete prepares for and anticipates a big game or season, many soldiers seem to gain commitment when they have the opportunity to put their skills, leadership, and decision making to good use.

An example can be seen in a platoon in Iraq that was tasked with ensuring that a local mosque was not being used to store weapons for a Shiite militia. As it approached within sight of the mosque, the platoon was surrounded by a hostile mob intent on denying the platoon's advance. The leader had to consider what to do and the consequences of each action. Media were present, and the use of force would have likely undermined the strategic effort to gain the Arab population's support. Leaving could encourage similar actions in the future and fail to complete the current mission. There was no textbook solution, and the decision could not be delayed. Situations like this are not uncommon, and they provide ample opportunities for soldiers to demonstrate their competency.

The variety and complexity of the missions and tasks also contribute to organizational commitment. In the past, task variety came in the form of different combat missions, whereas today's tasks and missions are just as likely to be tied to local economic development, promoting governance, establishing essential services and infrastructure development, or training the host nation's police and military. For example, in the first year of operations in Iraq, young lieutenants, just two years removed from college, found themselves serving as interim mayors of Iraqi villages, providing medical services, restoring electrical power and water, appointing local Iraqi leaders, fighting insurgents, and solving numerous problems. On any given day, a soldier in Iraq or Afghanistan may be assisting in the opening of a school in the morning, responding to an insurgent attack at midday, and negotiating for local labor in the afternoon.

Discretion and great responsibility are equally commonplace in today's Army and also serve to enhance commitment. The Army is constantly faced with doing more with less and increasing soldier-to-task ratios. Although it might be nice to have all the resources and soldiers needed, it has forced the Army to provide greater discretion and responsibility to soldiers and leaders.

Staff Sergeant Horn was a radar operator who supported a field artillery unit. Horn was tasked with reducing rocket and mortar attacks against the American base. Under less restrictive combat conditions, he would have identified the point of origin of enemy fire and directed artillery to destroy it. But because this would risk innocent lives and damage the town the unit was trying to protect and rebuild, Horn had to identify and pursue alternate methods that largely focused on influencing the local population to provide information about the insurgents who were conducting the attacks, many of whom were likely from their own clan or tribe.

Horn knew little about the local society, but he quickly educated himself about the Iraqi people and villages, developed personal relationships with the local leaders, and identified the concerns and problems of the local population. Using information gained from these relationships, Horn was able to loosen the local population's support of the insurgents by helping to direct financial aid to solve some of their problems, such as providing clean water to thirty villages.

Given the complexity and rapidly changing nature of the environment, it is difficult to know what tasks to train for and even more difficult to find the time to do so. As a result, the focus has shifted from perfecting a few core tasks to instead focusing on the development of initiative, flexibility, and decision making. In the past, a platoon might have executed a training exercise and after each iteration conducted a critical review to determine what was done well and what needed to be corrected. The platoon would then repeat the action until it was considered fully trained.

In contrast, today, rather than seeking mastery of a task through repetition, it is more likely that the platoon would execute a series of tasks under situations and threats that changed significantly at each iteration. Developing flexibility, initiative, and rapid decision making under stress has become more important than task mastery. This has created a situation where soldiers and leaders experience increased responsibility, discretion, task variety, and opportunities to demonstrate competence in training and during operational deployments.

In the Army, training for a wide array of missions is a core activity, driven by the realities of a complex and changing global environment. These same global changes create increased complexity and rapidity of change in the business environment, making the need to develop flexibility and adaptability equally critical to many businesses. By providing leadership training and deliberate developmental experiences that force leaders to cope with ambiguity, apply initiative, and make difficult decisions, organizations not only increase their agility and flexibility but also increase member satisfaction and sense of competence.

Soldiers develop powerful commitment for many reasons,
including empowerment, increased responsibility, discretion,
task variety, and opportunities to demonstrate competence.

Lessons for Leaders

People want to be developed, to feel that they have importance to the organization. Although most organizations provide training for their members, they may not be fully leveraging this as an opportunity to development commitment. How could you use the investment in your people that is already occurring to build the perception that they are valued?

People also have a need to demonstrate their competence, exercise greater autonomy, and be entrusted with increased responsibility. How can you help your people realize these interests while still managing the initial risk? When people are given these opportunities, how will you use the experience to generate commitment?

These are some of the ways Army leaders have answered these questions:

- Invest in your members' training, education, and development.
- Ensure this investment is viewed by the member as a sign of his or her value and the leadership's commitment to the member.
- Do not undermine commitment by placing the leader's short-term performance needs before the developmental needs of the member or the long-term needs of the organization.
- Communicate the task and mission, your intent, how it fits into the big picture, and your desired end state. This sets the conditions for the member's greater use of discretion and creativity. It also empowers the member to generate task variety.
- Provide opportunities for the member to use new skills, assume greater responsibilities, and exercise initiative within the leader's intent.

Conclusion

The Army is a unique institution, and although the demands it faces, the methods it uses, and its environment may differ greatly from other organizations, the principles for developing organizational commitment remain the same. Army leaders develop commitment by putting people first and developing personal relationships that are tied to the organization.

Army leaders help soldiers build and maintain strong commitments to people, purpose, principles, and units, reinforcing their commitment to the Army and the nation. They build cohesion within small units and create social networks of leaders that tie together subordinate organizations. They also form the perception that the soldier's efforts make a difference to the mission, their buddies, the unit, the Army, and the nation and that by serving the Army, they are serving the best interest of their brothers and sisters in arms, their families, and themselves. Leaders role-model and mentor their soldiers in the importance of the Army's values, and they continuously remind soldiers of how they are continuing the proud traditions of their units and the Army.

Army leaders must develop a culture of caring and individualized consideration for their members and their families, where a person can honestly say, "I can be a great member of this team and a great parent and spouse." Army leaders are supportive and accommodating, and they demonstrate care for their subordinates and their families, taking observable, tangible actions to increase families' satisfaction with the organization. They recognize that the care of subordinates and their families is not adequately addressed simply through family-friendly policies or programs and that developing deeply rooted, long-term commitment from soldiers and families is their responsibility.

Finally, leaders communicate to their soldiers that:

- The Army has and will continue to invest in their training, education, and development.
- They have a future in the Army.
- Their service is appreciated.

Effective leaders provide soldiers the opportunity to exercise their skills and exercise responsibility and initiative.

Maintaining a highly committed force during a period of great risk and difficulty is not easy, and without highly effective leadership, it would be impossible. Army leaders make this happen by doing all of the following:

- Building the soldier's belief in the mission
- Developing cohesion and positive perceptions of the unit
- Living the Army values
- Improving soldier and family satisfaction and welfare
- Maintaining work-family balance
- Investing considerably in personal and professional development, and positively influencing how the soldier perceives his or her job

The approach of developing multiple supportive commitments that reinforce attachment and engagement with the parent organization; creating a caring and supportive climate; investing in member training, education, and development; and providing ample opportunities for excellence is valid across the full spectrum of organization types. Although it is not intended to be a cookie-cutter solution, leaders who know their organizations and people should find this framework useful in aligning the elements that contribute to organizational commitment.

Notes

1. Organizational commitment is commonly defined as strong belief and acceptance of the organization's values and goals, motivation to exercise considerable effort for the organization, and a powerful desire to maintain membership in the organization: R. T. Mowday, R. M. Steers, and L. W. Porter, "The Measurement of Organizational Commitment," *Journal of Vocational Behavior*, 1979, *14*, 227–247. In the Army's case, I would add willingness to accept risk and personal sacrifice.

2. T. Ricks, "Army Spouses Expect Reenlistment Problems," *Washington Post*, Mar. 28, 2004, p. 9. These findings were based on a poll conducted by the *Washington Post*, Henry J. Kaiser Family Foundation, and Harvard University, plus dozens of supplemental interviews. The poll was the first nongovernmental survey of military spouses since the terrorist attacks of September 11, 2001. The survey included more than a thousand spouses living on or near the ten most-deployed-from Army posts.

3. "Engineers Who Make a Difference," *Industrial Engineer*, May 2005, pp. 26–33.

4. *Frontline*, "A Company of Soldiers," Feb. 22, 2005, PBS.

5. *Frontline*, "A Company of Soldiers."

6. Corporate Leadership Council research, http://www.corporateleadershipcouncil.com/CLC/1,1283,0–0-Public_Display-115952,00.html.

7. Carroll's story is in "Soldiers Stories" at the Army's home page, www.Army.mil.

8. J. Kouzes and B. Posner, *The Leadership Challenge*, 3rd ed. (San Francisco: Jossey-Bass, 2003).

9. Many of the general principles for creating a supportive and caring climate for families can also be applied to single soldiers' quality of life.

10. T. D. Woodruff and T. A. Kolditz, "The Need to Develop Expert Knowledge of the Military Family," in B. M. Snider and L. J. Matthews (eds.), *The Future of the Army Profession*, 2nd ed. (New York: McGraw-Hill, 2005).

11. Ricks, "Army Spouses Expect Reenlistment Problems," p. 9.

CHAPTER NINETEEN

MANAGING EXPECTATIONS WHEN LEADING CHANGE

Everett S. P. Spain

Expectations need to be managed from the beginning, and throughout the process—which requires a major effort of public information and education. . . . Otherwise expectations are unrealistic, and [people] are inevitably disappointed. When disillusion sets in, . . . people can easily turn against the . . . agreement they had at first welcomed.

—KOFI ANNAN, SECRETARY GENERAL, UNITED NATIONS, OCTOBER 14, 2004[1]

Understanding the importance of managing expectations is tough, and doing it well is even tougher. In managing expectations, a change leader seeks out and builds effective communication bridges between the leader and his or her stakeholders, while thoughtfully using those bridges to understand and help those stakeholders understand the realisms of the change process, while maintaining an overall positive perspective. Although managing expectations can significantly influence the success of one's efforts to lead change, managing expectations is a complex process that takes a conscientious leader's focus to succeed.

Teachers, parents, managers, and educators all need to learn how to manage expectations. Perhaps there is nowhere else that managing expectations is more significant right now than in Iraq, as the U.S. government, led by the U.S. Army, works to lead a massive transformational change in a sovereign nation-state. If the United States is going to be successful in leading an effective transformation of Iraq, many organizational leaders must make the conscious choice to manage the expectations of their key stakeholders. This holds true for all levels of leadership during the change process.

For example, in providing oversight and legitimacy for Operation Iraqi Freedom, President George W. Bush is attempting to manage the expectations of the U.S. Congress, the global media, and international leaders. Down lower but also of strategic importance is U.S. Army Lieutenant Jeremy Holman, who is in charge of the security of the al-Kinde neighborhood in Baghdad: he is simultaneously working to manage the expectations of the local tribal councils, his military bosses, and the disenfranchised yet influential former members of the Baath regime living in the area. The president and the second lieutenant have a similar challenge, in that the support of their stakeholders through managing expectations is the keystone of their successes.

In 2004, Major Christina Schweiss, a friend of mine who was then serving as a professor at West Point, had a great idea to build an academic course to teach seniors about how to lead successful stability operations as young officers; she named the course "Winning the Peace." To determine the curriculum of the forty lessons with thoughtful due diligence, Schweiss surveyed returning commanders from U.S. combat units deployed in the Middle East and asked them what topics should be included to prepare future second lieutenants to hit the ground running with the skills and thought processes needed to make immediate positive impacts in Iraq and Afghanistan. The colonels listed "expectation management" as one of their major themes.

Knowing I was serving as the West Point course director for a course called Leading Organizations Through Change, Schweiss asked if I would develop and teach the lesson on managing expectations for the new course. I knew I would be forced to learn about leading change in the process. My assumption was quite correct.

Soon after our conversation, I went to the USMA library and used its comprehensive in-house and online worldwide sources to gather all existing published information on the subject that I could. Surprisingly, I noted a distinct lack of coherent information about how a leader actively manages the expectations of various stakeholders. The only significant resource I found was a book written by Naomi Karten in 1994, *Managing Expectations,* which generally focused on influencing customers' expectations in the sales and service industries.[2]

The absence of an existing community of knowledge about managing expectations was both a curse and a blessing: it was a curse because I had to spend a lot of time reflecting on my life experiences in managing expectations while using the frameworks I taught in my course Leading Organizations Through Change to understand the full potential of managing expectations. The absence was a blessing for that same reason.

This chapter defines in detail what is required when managing expectations, and it offers nine lessons that leaders should keep in mind when trying to effect change in their organizations. It draws not only on experiences in Iraq, but also offers a nonmilitary case study of how one determined school principal was able to change the culture of a troubled, dangerous high school in the Bronx, New York, by implementing these principles and lessons in leading change by managing expectations.

*Does the success of this leading change effort depend significantly
on this person's active support, participation, or approval either now
or in the future? If the answer to that question is yes, then that
person most likely is one of your key stakeholders.*

As a Change Agent, You Must First Identify Your Stakeholders

As an organizational leader and change agent, you should know that the perceptions of your key stakeholders almost always determine the actual success; therefore, identifying who those key stakeholders are becomes the first crucial step toward success in leading change. Here are some examples of the infinite range of who your key stakeholders could be:

- If you are a U.S. Army company commander in Iraq, your key stakeholders could include your soldiers, your soldiers' families, your battalion and brigade commanders, the local Iraqi leaders, and the global media.
- If you are a consulting firm vice president, your key stakeholders could include your team, your managing director inside the firm, the leaders of the firm you are consulting for (your client), and often the key influencers of the employees of your client.
- If you are a professor and head of a college academic department, your key stakeholders could include the dean, your students, the other department heads, the professors in your department, and even the school newspaper staff.
- The key stakeholders of the president of the United States include the Congress, the citizenry (via political action committees, media, legislature, and U.S. corporations), political parties, leaders of multinational and state organizations, and other nation-state leaders.

The major categories of the stakeholders are surprisingly similar. In fact, most organizational leaders have the following categories of stakeholders they should actively manage the expectations of:

- Employees
- Boss
- Key influencers (and potential spoilers) in the customer base (those external to the organization)

- Key influencer (and potential spoiler) peers inside the organization (those internal to the organization)
- The media

In addition to going through this list to identify key stakeholders, an organizational leader should ask the following question to determine if a person or a group of people is actually a key stakeholder: "Does the success of this leading change effort depend significantly on this person's active support, participation, or approval either now or in the future?" If the answer to that question is yes, then that person most likely is one of your key stakeholders.

The U.S. government has somewhat recognized the need to manage the expectations of key stakeholders for Iraq and has taken some efforts in this direction. For example, in summer 2005, the White House created the Office of Strategic Communications and Planning (OSC), which is currently headed by former presidential adviser Karen Hughes and commissioned with the following mission statement: to "ensure consistency in messages that will promote the interests of the United States abroad, prevent misunderstanding, build support for and among coalition partners of the United States, and inform international audiences."[3]

Managing expectations effectively calls for the establishment of two-way communication, not just unidirectional influence.

Similarly, as the war in Iraq entered the stability phase following the end of major combat operations in the spring of 2003, the U.S. Army began an initiative to double the size of its inventory of active-duty psychological operational (PSYOPS) soldiers because one of the PSYOPS primary missions is to convince the local population to support the democratically elected government of Iraq and legitimate Iraqi security forces.[4] Also, the U.S. Army had just formed information operations (IO), a separate branch for select officers to enter as full-time jobs; the goal is to head the Army's information coordination effort, including communicating a consistent and effective message with multiple stakeholders, including the American public back home (through public affairs officers) and the Iraqi citizens (through organizations such as civil affairs).

Although these steps by the U.S. government and Army are building systems that enable mechanisms to more effectively manage expectations, these efforts in themselves may not be enough because these efforts primarily concern one-way communication. The OSC, PSYOPS, and IO branches are designed to send messages, but not as much emphasis is put on receiving messages from stakeholders.

Managing expectations effectively calls for the establishment of two-way communication, not just unidirectional influence.

Managing Expectations Defined

"Managing expectations" can be defined as consistently communicating with your key stakeholders to understand their spoken and unspoken expectations, while realistically shaping their perceptions of:

1. Your true character and intentions
2. The benefits of the long-term change process
3. What constitutes short-term success
4. Stakeholders' specific responsibilities required to achieve the short- and long-term outcomes

Managing expectations thoughtfully is a decision that is made; it is not left to chance. Believing that stakeholders will have a realistic and positive view of the managing expectations perceptions without your deliberately helping them get there is preposterous and overly idealistic. A change leader has too many key stakeholders who may have too many diverging goals and internal influences to leave managing their expectations to chance. The next sections of this chapter explore each of these perceptions in more detail.

If you are leading change to serve rather than to manipulate, you had better prove it fast. The first aspect of effectively managing expectations is to realistically communicate your organization's actual character intentions.

Realistically Shaping Perceptions of Your Character and Intentions

I know everyone from my civilian life, so I have extra incentive to get them all home alive. When we get home, I've got to look at all of their mamas.

—STAFF SERGEANT STEELE, SQUAD LEADER, 1-153TH INFANTRY,
ARKANSAS NATIONAL GUARD, SERVING IN IRAQ

If you are leading change to serve rather than to manipulate, you had better prove it fast. The first aspect of effectively managing expectations is to realistically communicate your organization's actual character intentions.

When the U.S. Army's 3rd Infantry Division attacked in Iraq in 2003, it expected to be treated by most of the population as liberators. Although this was the case in some instances, many Iraqi people turned out to be distrustful of the American soldiers, because the Americans' true intentions and character were unknown. Similarly, some members of the global media and the U.S. population believed the United States was attacking Iraq for the primary purpose of securing U.S. access and profits to the oil resources in the region. Although the U.S. government expressed that it was attacking to enforce United Nations resolutions, suppress terrorism, free the Iraqi people from Saddam Hussein's oppressive regime, and promote true democracy in the Middle East, many of the Iraqis did not accept this message because they did not trust the U.S. government.

Trust is the key to succeeding in this managing expectations perception, and it can be built only over time and with effort. For example, to establish trust with the global media, the U.S. military now facilitates embedding reporters with deployed military units on a massive scale. Brigadier General Vincent Brooks, the director of public affairs for the U.S. Army, says a key for effective communication and building trust in people's perception of your intentions is to give people both access and context.[5] Let them know and see for themselves what is going on (provide access), while making a deliberate effort to explain why the U.S. actions are what they are (include context) whenever possible. For example, when local Iraqis and the world saw U.S. soldiers passing out food and providing medical treatment to local residents, their perception of the soldiers' true intentions and character changed dramatically.

Another essential factor when building trust is to study and respect the culture of stakeholders in order to be able to better listen to and understand them. By working to understand why stakeholders think what they do and practicing reflective listening with them, a change leader communicates that his or her stakeholders have important values and needs themselves. Although stakeholders will not always agree with a change agent's course of action, if you take active steps to influence their positive trust for you by giving them access, context, and reflective listening, they will begin to understand and trust you and have a positive perception of your value and intentions.

Building Their Faith in the Long-Term Process

A leader's job is to give their people hope.

—RUDY RUETTIGER, NOTRE DAME FOOTBALL PLAYER AND SUBJECT OF THE 1993 FILM *RUDY*[6]

A change leader must help stakeholders visualize the end state. Challenge and hardships are often associated with change, and rightly so; therefore, it is important that the leader help the stakeholders understand the value of reaching the goals of the long-term change process and having faith in the plan to get there.

Danny Hassig, a U.S. Army reserve civil affairs officer, arranged a meeting with Sheik Saad, an influential Iraqi who lived in the Karada Peninsula (which is the Baghdad equivalent of Manhattan). Because Saad was a major informal leader, Hassig deliberately introduced himself to Saad and made an effort to meet with him every few weeks in order to manage the expectations of the Iraqi people regarding the U.S. forces operating in Karada.

For his part, Sheik Saad was risking his life to periodically meet with Hassig; the sheik had been wounded from an assassination attempt a month prior and now walks with a cane, even though he is only in his late thirties. After exchanging pleasantries for some time, Hassig asked Saad what the local residents were currently thinking about the Americans. Saad explained that his people were pleased that the United States had followed through on its promise to transfer sovereignty from the coalition provincial authority (CPA) to Iraqi Interim Prime Minister Allawi and his temporary government. Saad also commented that his people had recently seen new soccer fields and new gardens installed in their communities, courtesy of Hassig and his U.S. forces funding local Iraqi contractors. The Iraqis were thankful they had seen the American soldiers patrolling as partners with the Iraqi police and were seen mentoring the embryonic Iraqi democratic government.

Hassig believed that Saad now had trust in Hassig's character and intentions, so Hassig used that trust as a foundation when he asked Saad to apply for a coalition-funded economic development loan, a move that would potentially energize the economy of the sheik's neighborhood. Saad would do it only if he felt the United States was viable, pro-Iraqi, and trustworthy, because a large loan would tie Saad to a long-term business relationship with the coalition. Saad acted on this faith and applied for the $3.5 million loan. Hassig smiled as he took the completed loan application and U.S.-style income statement from the sheik, promising to deliver it to the right people. Sheik Saad returned the smile and summarized his people's new faith in the long-term process by concluding, "When we see the U.S. Army in Iraq, we feel safe."

A wise expectation manager understands this and feeds this hope without promising time lines and things that they cannot guarantee. Author and psychotherapist Viktor Frankl wrote about his experiences as a prisoner in the Auschwitz concentration camp during World War II: his reflections on his experience conclude that someone's attitude in a time of difficulty can overpower negative actual circumstances and give that person hope. Frankl shared the example where, in the fall of 1944, his fellow prisoners spread rumors that they would be liberated by Christmas. When they were not liberated by Christmas, an unusually high percentage of them passed away in the month after Christmas: their expectations had been too high, and their hopes were crushed.[7]

Managing expectations is a long-term process, but a
change leader can influence those expectations only
within the context of consistent short-term actions.

Realistically Shaping Perceptions of What Constitutes Short-Term Success

The Iraqi people know the U.S. has put men on the moon, so they don't understand
why they still don't have electrical power 24 hours a day, even though they didn't have
100% power under Saddam Hussein.

—MAJOR GENERAL RON JOHNSON, FORMER COMMANDER, U.S. ARMY
CORPS OF ENGINEERS, GULF REGION DIVISION[8]

Managing expectations is a long-term process, but a change leader can influence
those expectations only within the context of consistent short-term actions. U.S.
Army Captain Darin Thomson did exactly this when leading his company in Iraq
in 2003.

Two weeks after coalition forces liberated Iraq from the Baath Party, Thomson and his infantry troopers (known as the Bravo Bushmasters) received the mission of securing and stabilizing the town of Taliyah, about fifty kilometers south
of Baghdad. Although he and his troopers did not experience any hostilities from
the fifteen thousand local residents during their first seventy-two hours in town,
Thomson was concerned that he needed to connect quickly with the local leaders, especially because he had no idea of how long his company would be assigned
to stay in Taliyah.

Because his boss, a lieutenant colonel, had stopped briefly in the town and
had a short meeting with some local leaders before moving north, Thomson had
to manage the expectations of the local residents that it was he, a captain, who
was actually in charge before he could even start to manage their expectations for
the more complex short- and long-term issues involved.

At the sessions, Thomson quickly discovered that most of the established local
government officials were Baath Party and had left town in front of the arriving
Americans. Although the formal government was defunct, four local residents
came forward and claimed major leadership roles: a representative from the town's
dominant tribe, the town electrician and water engineer, the town food distribution supervisor, and a seemingly shady gentleman who claimed security expertise.
The priorities of each of these emerging leaders were different. After a few hours
of an active and volatile conversation, Thomson heard a message loud and clear:

that they desperately needed and expected U.S. aid with medical care, fresh water, food distribution, and local security.

Regarding medical care, the Taliyahians had an out-patient medical clinic that was out of almost all supplies, including medicine, but continued to treat many sick people, including several wounded (likely from combat). The tribal chief supported medical care as the main need of the town.

Drinking water was also a major problem in Taliyah. The city historically received its fresh water from a pipeline that originated in a larger city to the north, but because the power generation facility outside town was not working, the pumps that ran the pipeline were not operational either. Most of the large pumps had blown gaskets, and only 25 percent of the homes in town were connected to the fresh water network through underground piping. The town was surviving on imported bottled water, and those supplies were getting low. The town electrician said this was the most pressing need.

Decent food was scarce. The Baath Party had distributed food to the city monthly from supply trucks, and the residents would use their government-issued ration cards to request their family's share, but the most recent food delivery had come more than a month ago. The food delivery Iraqi leader argued that this was most pressing for his people.

Finally, security was an issue. The prewar police force in Taliyah was led by Baath Party members who had left town soon after the invasion, with all of the police's small arms with them. The Iraqi who claimed security expertise said they needed 150 weapons and help from the U.S. soldiers patrolling the city because their citizens were experiencing an increase in crime, especially in violent carjackings.

Clearly the overall challenge for Captain Thomson was remarkably similar to the same one that affects many city managers today, especially during times of catastrophe, in that there were too many needs and not enough resources. In assessing his capability to assist the Taliyahians, Thomson counted his 125 combat infantry soldiers, fourteen Bradley Fighting Vehicles, and six Hummers. His unit had no engineer capability, but it did have small maintenance, medical, and food sections and several soldiers who had various civilian skills they learned prior to joining the service that might be capitalized on.

Being a skilled expectations manager, Thomson knew that he was indeed the de facto government in that town, and he realized he needed to frame what short-term success was in the eyes of the residents, or he would risk losing his credibility quickly. Therefore, he called a second meeting for the town, where he showed the tribal leaders that he had no resources available to have a positive effect on most of the issues facing the town except for security. After much conversation, Thomson got the tribal leaders to agree in concept that security was the top concern and that restoring a functioning and legitimate security force in the town was the most realistic short-term goal to work toward achieving. Thomson also let the Iraqis know that he was not able to provide them large-scale assistance with their immediate food and water issues.

As for medical care, Thomson told them what his unit was capable of and did what he promised, which was to give them a couple of boxes of surplus supplies, including water purification tablets, and when possible and on a case-by-case basis, Thomson's unit would do its best to treat wounded Iraqis that the Iraqi clinic could not handle.

In that planning session, Thomson and the emerging Iraqi leaders worked out a security plan where U.S. forces would immediately begin patrols in order to reestablish security and safety in the community. Thomson coordinated to get the local leaders a few firearms to enable them to start a small, reconstructed police force. His security plan of patrolling and empowering the new police force was successful. He had gotten the emerging Iraqi leaders together to agree that security was the primary short-term goal for Taliyah. The Iraqi leaders and local residents viewed it as a great success instead of becoming frustrated that the U.S. forces were unable to help significantly with the Iraqis' other areas of need. Because the security provided by the Bravo Bushmasters met the Iraqis' expectations of success in the short term, the Iraqis were pleased with Thomson and the American presence.

The leader of the change effort must clearly communicate his or her expectations of what the people must do (both individually and collectively) to make the transformation a success.

Realistically Shaping Perceptions of Your Stakeholders' Own Responsibilities

Captain Larry, when am I going to be able to go to the United States and see your universities and set up exchange programs?

—DR. ATABEE, DEAN OF THE COLLEGE OF SCIENCE, BAGHDAD UNIVERSITY

Managing expectations is also about getting stakeholders to do their part. Captain Larry Geddings was the commander of a mechanized infantry unit and was assigned oversight of the sector of Baghdad that included Baghdad University.

When he and I met with Dr. Atabee, Dean of the College of Sciences, I listened to the dean as he pressured Geddings into somehow buying him plane tickets and granting him authorization to travel to U.S. universities to collaborate and create teacher and student exchanges. Geddings just smiled and responded that he would look into it, knowing that he did not have authorization to grant Atabee's wishes and knowing that perhaps Atabee and Baghdad University had their own work to do before this would become a reality.

Geddings was concerned that several problems at the university remained that needed to be resolved before he could do anything to promote an exchange program with an American institution. For example, security at Baghdad University was a major issue: an unarmed American soldier had been killed near a dozen students while walking in the center of campus a few months earlier, but no potential witness would admit to seeing anything.

University concern for basic sanitation was also a problem, as evidenced by the poor condition of the visitor rest room across the hallway from the college president's office.

Finally, Baghdad University's degree legitimacy was in question: the university had conferred advanced degrees to Saddam's sons—a doctorate in political science to Uday Hussein and a juris doctorate to Qusay Hussein—even though Atabee admitted they had not spent much time in class.

Nevertheless, Atabee was ready to go to the United States and begin exchanges, and he told Geddings that was the way it needed to be. Even so, Geddings knew that before starting an exchange program, Atabee realistically needed to ensure his campus was safe, the degrees granted were earned prior to enacting exchanges, and fundamental things like sanitation at his university was reasonably acceptable.

People within an organization that is changing typically must take deliberate action to effect some of the change themselves and not just wait to be changed by the system. As part of a transformation, the leader of the change effort must clearly communicate his or her expectations of what the people must do (both individually and collectively) to make the transformation a success.

Table 19.1 is a rough snapshot of the broad changes the coalition forces are working on to transform Iraq. Each of these characteristics requires the individual people to take some action themselves.

Although the transformation of all of the areas of change shown in Table 19.1 involve significant understanding, perhaps managing the expectations of the role of the common people in a change is the most crucial to the macrochanges being successful. The Iraqi people during Saddam Hussein's time were not allowed to vote, were not required to pay income taxes, and had their power, water, and often

TABLE 19.1. CHANGES SOUGHT IN IRAQ

Area of Change	Before the War	Goal for Change	Fundamental Action Needed by Iraqi Individuals
Government	Totalitarian	Democratic	Run for office, vote, support elected officials
Economy	Socialist	Capitalist	Risk money and time via entrepreneurship, compete
Role of common people	Subjects, paid no income taxes	Citizens	Pay income, sales, and property taxes
Equality and suffrage	Male only	Equal rights for women	Males accept gender equality
Political process	Only Baath Party, only Arab, discrimination and distrust	Multiparty, multiethnic	Campaign openly, support all popularly elected officials, respect all

their food given to them by the Iraqi government, which used oil revenues to fund this socialist and dependency-fostering environment. The Iraqi people were accustomed to paying for gas, at, in the summer of 2004, eighteen cents a gallon. This subsidized rate resulted in huge lines at the few gas stations that existed because very few entrepreneurs would build a gas station with no profit potential involved because they would have to compete against the few government-run and subsidized stations.

Clearly, American commanders like Captain Geddings must communicate the expectation that Iraqis do their part and vote, adopt an entrepreneurial culture, pay taxes, accept gender equality, and support popularly elected officials if this transition was going to work. If done well, this step will take stakeholders from customers and make them into partners. Stakeholders are much more likely to accept their own responsibilities in facilitating this change if they first trust the change agent's character and the organization's intentions, have faith in the benefits of the overall long-term process, and understand what constitutes short-term success.

Wise change leaders will always ensure they have a robust enough system to accomplish their promised goals, even if Murphy's law hits them in the nose several times along the way.

Lessons Learned in How to Manage Expectations

Following are eleven lessons I have learned while attempting to manage expectations in my career or when observing others trying to do the same. Using them as a guide can put a change leader on a path toward creating positive and consistent communication channels with their stakeholders.

Lesson 1: Underpromise and Overdeliver

*We believe the [U.S./NATO] mission [in Bosnia] is
limited and achievable within approximately a year.*

—VICE PRESIDENT AL GORE[9]

Vice President Gore's effort on expectation management may have held some traction at the time, but it quickly backslid into a ditch when the United States stayed in Bosnia past the one-year mark and is still there more than ten years later. Gore was likely advised by his experts that his claim was reasonable at the time, but the fact remains that it did not strengthen his stakeholders' beliefs in the organization (the U.S. government) or the process itself (peacekeeping in the Balkans) by claiming something that did not actually come true. The fact of the matter is that the United States cannot totally control when it will successfully complete a peacekeeping operation. Every situation will be different, and claiming an end date before beginning is like adding a mathematical sum before discovering the actual amounts to be added together.

Wise change leaders will always ensure they have a robust enough system to accomplish their promised goals, even if Murphy's law hits them in the nose several times along the way. In service professions such as engineering, customers (who are stakeholders) depend on you to do a job for them, on time, on budget, and meeting all quality standards. A customer, boss, or peer probably will not have a clear understanding of the particulars of the job (including the technical and logistical requirements) and the impact of environmental factors (weather, politics, other requirements) that will significantly influence when you can finish. Therefore, it is up to you, the organizational leader, to define the measures of success yourself by setting and communicating the time line and standards that you are trying to meet.

Suppose you are the platoon leader with the 1st Cavalry Division's 8th Engineer Battalion, with responsibility to oversee the infrastructure rejuvenation of the town of Zapharania, a poor suburb of Baghdad located about ten kilometers southeast of the city center. After driving around the town, you noted that liquid sewage was collecting on the sidewalks in many of the neighborhoods. Further research showed that the main cause of the pooling wastewater was due to dilapidated and overwhelmed underground wastewater pipes. The city leaders asked for your help with this problem.

An expectation manager is fundamentally a communicator, and repetition and simplicity are crucial for effectiveness.

You decide to work with the city hall officials and local contractors, and you conclude that you can contract for a complete renovation to the cities' wastewater lines that will be finished within two to three months, depending on a variety of factors. Your and your soldiers' level of motivation is not a variable; you will work just as hard regardless of what you cite as a finish date. Further assume that you want to announce your intentions at tomorrow's district adviser council (DAC) meeting with the Iraq authorities. You know that the completion date you cite in that meeting will affect the Iraqis' perceptions of you and the U.S. Army. If you say two months, the residents will like that better than if you say three months, but that sets you up for failure.

A wise expectation manager will cite a three-month (a long-finish) date. Your unit may be able to finish early and exceed expectations, but if the external factors turn against you during the project, your stakeholders (the Iraqi citizens) will still see you holding up your end of the deal. Remember to promise only things that are within your power to deliver.

Lesson 2: Set Short-Term Goals with Key Stakeholders

In addition to setting realistic end dates for a project, you can (and should) manage expectations by setting interim short-term goals with key stakeholders, especially those who have to take specific actions to ensure those goals are realized. This will assist you with building trust with them and in getting their commitment toward their own responsibilities.

Wise change leaders must be cautioned that they must change the message appropriately whenever the truth or situation changes. Otherwise they risk alienating stakeholders.

Lesson 3: Have Stakeholders Commit in a Public Setting

Always choose the locations strategically with regard to who else will be present when formally asking stakeholders to commit to action in order to help reach the change effort's short-term goals. Public meetings are typically effective settings for verbal commitments of stakeholders due to the potential peer accountability involved. The perceptions of their peers and neighbors often will hold much more influence on their following through with their promises than their agreement with you alone. Your stakeholders will realize that others are expecting them to hold up their end of the deal as well, resulting in the stakeholders' often being more willing to follow through with their commitments and becoming more partners in the change process than customers of it.

Lesson 4: Use Message Repetition to Communicate Clarity

An expectation manager is fundamentally a communicator, and repetition and simplicity are crucial for effectiveness. Patrick Lencioni, in his book *The Four Obsessions of an Extraordinary Executive,* presents three of his four "obsessions" as having to do with creating and communicating clarity on what the organization is doing and why.[10] Furthermore, presidential adviser Karen Hughes stated, "As a communicator, I like to boil things down and make them easy to remember. I also realized that about the time the rest of us get sick of hearing about them, is about the time when . . . they'll begin to stick and people will actually remember them."[11]

Lesson 5: Changing the Message Is a Strength, Not a Weakness

Wise change leaders must be cautioned that they must change the message appropriately whenever the truth or situation changes. Otherwise they risk alienating their stakeholders, who will perceive them as a propaganda machine rather than an authentic communicator. Stakeholders' needs will change, and they will actively seek to discover whether you are listening to them by watching to see if your actions change as a result of their new needs and requests.

If you do not listen and keep the same message and same actions, you are likely to lose their support because you lose their trust. You cannot make all stakeholder groups happy all of the time, and you must publicly accept and address this fact so it does not torpedo your change efforts. If you change in response to stakeholder needs when possible, you will build strength to your overall change efforts.

> *Stakeholders just want to be informed and can handle bad*
> *news: they just want to hear it from the change leader, and*
> *they lose trust when they hear it from someone else.*

Lesson 6: Set Up Regular Meetings and a Communication Center

Wise change leaders should establish a primary, easily accessible central information clearinghouse for updated status and information about the short- and long-term goals. The central information clearinghouse could be a public Web site that is updated frequently, a bulletin board in an area accessible by all, or a daily newspaper with write-in features.

The consistency of the communication events is much more important than the consistency of the message itself. Stakeholders want to be informed and can handle bad news: they just want to hear it from the change leader, and they lose trust when they hear it from someone else. Similar to a civil engineer's charts that track the status of engineer projects against the plan, these central information clearinghouses enable communication with stakeholders, especially when the clearinghouse presents both positive and negative factual stories, while providing a simple mechanism for the stakeholders to send their thoughts back to the change leader.

Lesson 7: Managing Expectations Calls for Establishing Two-Way Communication

Two-way communication with stakeholders is critical. It is not enough to simply communicate one way by lecturing or making formal statements to stakeholders. Research stakeholders' culture, unspoken expectations, and body language. Ask them to speak their minds clearly and frankly.

Listen reflectively. Bracket yourself mentally into their positions, and think about what your expectations would be. This two-way communication will help you understand the values their culture holds dear so you can work to build their perception of your intentions by understanding and integrating their values when possible.

Lesson 8: Always Communicate What Is Not Possible and Why

Do not be afraid to say no, and stick to your guns if that is realistic. You stand the risk of stakeholders' losing faith in you if you promise and cannot deliver (recall lesson 1). This will not happen by status quo, and a change leader must always be clear about limits.

Captain Doug Copeland was the commander of Bravo Company, 2–7 Cavalry, and was responsible for providing security in the central Baghdad neighborhood of Salhiya, just north of the International (Green) Zone. His company raided the house of an insurgent and took him into custody in June 2004. A few days later, Copeland took a U.S. patrol to the home of the insurgent to inform the wife about the status of her husband and to return his wallet and some identification papers that she might need in his absence.

As Copeland knocked on the door with an Iraqi translator on one side and a large soldier as his bodyguard on the other, the wife came to the door and requested her husband be returned. Copeland quickly gave the wallet and identification back to the wife and told her, "Your husband is going to jail for attacking coalition soldiers, and he will not be back for a long time." He also told her everything he knew about the situation, including where her husband was most likely going to be incarcerated. Copeland did not have to return the wallet and identification or speak to the wife, but he wanted to ensure he managed the expectations of one of the Iraqi citizens in his security area.

Lesson 9: The Organizational Leader Should Lead the Managing Expectations Efforts

Especially in regard to building stakeholders' faith in the overall long-term process, there is no substitute for stakeholders' hearing the most recent managing expectations message from the organizational leader and being able to communicate openly with him or her. If managing expectations responsibilities are assigned to a staff officer or assistant, the organizational leader sends the message that managing expectations is an auxiliary task and that the value of that stakeholder is not as important as if the organizational leader communicated directly. That is not the message to send to your stakeholders.

Lesson 10: Being Positive Is a Catalyst in Managing Expectations

Even when you are unable to meet expectations, giving enthusiastic and cheerful communication about why not and what you are capable of will help people see the glass is half full, versus half empty.

Lesson 11: Don't Fear Inevitable Incidents; Just Respond Promptly to Them

In almost any long-term change effort, there will be negative press, rumors, or claims against your leadership efforts. Sometimes the claims will present true incidents that when taken alone, appear to hurt your cause, and your stakeholders lose trust in your situation. This train of thought influences leaders to centralize control of their messages and limit the communication and initiative of their subordinates in communicating (for example, some theaters of operation in the U.S. Army require general officer approval of any psychological operations product). We all know of individual incidents that have captured the world stage through the global media, but a wise expectation manager will not let the potential of a bad communication stifle the ability to conduct communication through decentralized multiple levels of their organization.

Most change leaders work hard to keep their organizations morally straight and honorable, but especially in large organizations, there will periodically be incidents where individuals who represent the organization will display a lack of values and bring discredit to their team. These unfortunate incidents can cause a temporary loss of trust with target stakeholders. What most expectation managers do not realize is that people expect organizations to make mistakes and typically have a much higher capacity to forgive them than the leader imagines—but only if the organization responds swiftly and publicly with appropriate corrective action. In doing so, the organization will almost always restore that trust.

If stakeholders sense a cover-up of any type, you will lose their long-term trust and your ability to manage their expectations. Cover-ups are what destroy trust, not the sporadic incidents that will inevitably rise during the efforts of any change leader, so do not limit communication in fear of such incidents. You cannot prevent them all, and sealing off communication prevents you from dealing with them productively when they do occur.

Know Your Context to Focus Your Efforts

Wise change leaders use multiple lenses when looking at their situations to help clarify and understand the managing expectations landscape in order to tailor their actions appropriately within the context of their idiosyncratic (and fluid) situation. Calibrating the strategy for managing expectations will differ depending on whether the change leader is trying to primarily influence people inside his or her organization (internal) or outside it (external), or both. Also, change agents must understand what context of managing expectations they are targeting: strategic (when they are attempting to manage the expectations of large organizations or societies) or tactical (when they are attempting to manage the expectations of a more limited group of people, where a leader is able to directly communicate with most of them personally if he or she chooses to do so).

The central themes of managing expectations and the four key perceptions pertaining to managing expectations listed at the beginning of this chapter remain the same no matter what the context of the situation is. Table 19.2, however, looks at four different situations involving managing expectations, and it

TABLE 19.2. HOW TO MANAGE EXPECTATIONS IN FOUR DIFFERENT SITUATIONS

Level	Strategic/External	Strategic/Internal	Tactical/External	Tactical/Internal
Context	External (group outside your organization)	Internal (employees inside your organization)	External	Internal
Example	You are commander of Coalition Forces, Baghdad, and are trying to influence the Iraqis in Baghdad to reduce violence and actively support the newly elected government.	You are the commander of Coalition Forces, Baghdad, and are trying to influence your soldiers to stay polite, professional, and prepared to kill the enemy.	You are an Army company commander in Baghdad and are trying to influence the Iraqis in one neighborhood to reduce violence and actively support the newly elected government.	You are an Army company commander in Baghdad, and you are trying to influence your soldiers to stay polite, professional, and prepared to kill the enemy.
Example stakeholders	Iraqi tribal leaders; Sunni, Shia, and Kurd Party leaders; local imams; city council members; leaders of insurgency	Your subordinate commanders (Brigadier Generals, Colonels, and others)	Tribe leader, neighborhood council leader, police district leader, and neighborhood electrician	Your lieutenants, senior noncommissioned officers, and soldiers
Global media influence over your stakeholders	High	Low	Medium	Low
Consistency of the same message required	High	Medium	Low	Low
Amount of two-way communication (listening required)	Medium	Low	High	Medium
Frequency of status updates you must provide your key stakeholders to be credible	High	Low	Medium	Medium
Most important of the four managing expectations perceptions	Their faith in the overall long-term process	Emphasis on stakeholders' responsibilities	What constitutes short-term success	Emphasis on stakeholders' responsibilities

suggests my perceptions on the ideal key variables in the leader's execution of managing expectations:

- The impact of global media
- The consistency of theme required
- A priority on listening
- The need to update your message
- Most important, the four key perceptions related to managing expectations

A Nonmilitary Case Study: Managing Expectations at a Troubled High School

The lessons learned in Iraq about managing expectations are the same ones that adept civilian change leaders are employing at home. JFK High School in New York City is no exception.

In February 2003, Anthony Rotunno took over one of the most violent and troubled high schools in the New York City system when he agreed to become the principal at JFK Public High School in the Bronx. Rotunno then presented a tour de force of successfully leading change, using managing expectations as a key enabler of his efforts.

Just before Rotunno was hired, a JFK student had been shot and killed in a scuffle outside the school, and widespread student horseplay in the hallways had resulted in an assistant principal's ankle being broken when she was not fast enough to get out of the way. Absenteeism and tardiness were rampant, the graduation rate was down, and the JFK academic and athletic programs were mired in mediocrity. At the time, it was not uncommon for students to launch chairs from the upper-story windows of the eight-floor building onto the sidewalks below.

The Challenge: To Change the Organization's Culture and Systems

Rotunno knew that he wanted to change the culture and systems within the school in order to make it an excellent place to learn and work. He felt that going to high school should be the best time of students' lives, and he set out to create that experience at JFK High School. He also knew he would have to manage expectations along the way if he were going to succeed. In leading change and managing his stakeholders' expectations along the way, Rotunno's foundational belief was, "I must prove to everyone that change started with me."

His first task was to identify his major stakeholders. He keyed in on the teachers' union and the students, even though he knew the school board, city administration, and various microschools within Kennedy also had influence. Of all of these, Rotunno realized the students and teachers' union were the two most important stakeholders initially, so he opened up a deliberate communication channel with them immediately, because the teachers and students were the ones most likely to make or break the change process.

To open the lines of communication with the teachers, Rotunno held a town hall meeting with them to hear their concerns. Their primary concerns were truancy, academic standards, and creating specialty academic programs, of which Rotunno listened to and took into account when making short-term goals. He also discovered that everyone knew that Rotunno had been promoted up through the school security field, so many of the teachers doubted his qualifications for handling the leadership of the administrative, educational, athletic, and related areas at JFK High.

Rotunno knew he had to make moves to improve the school's security before he could broach any administrative and educational challenges. But he also knew that adding additional security procedures at an already tense school would not be popular with the students, and a lack of focus on academics would not be popular with the teachers. Believing security had to come before students and teachers would feel safe enough to reach their potential, Rotunno spoke to the teachers and students and clearly communicated that security was the initial priority (based on his broad school discipline experiences), and he let them know that academic improvement was on the way, but only after security was in order.

Rotunno was persistent, and he received agreement from the teachers' union and students to establish security as the primary short-term goal. Almost immediately, he closed all entrances and exits to the school except one, where he installed airport-style metal detectors that everyone had to walk through when entering the building. Some of the teachers' union members and students were angry, but Rotunno knew this physical channeling of the high school community also provided an opportunity to build the students' and teachers' positive perceptions of Rotunno's true intentions and character.

Never daunted, Rotunno saw the single entrance as an opportunity to manage expectations daily, so he greeted the students and teachers there every morning. Daily at the single entrance, he spoke to as many students and teachers by first name as he could remember. Rotunno would engage any student or teacher about any subject that was on his or her mind, and he gave them a heartfelt smile as they departed.

---

*Managing expectations is an essential part of the fuel
required to make the impossible into a reality.*

Rotunno's continuous mode of information sharing was his omnipresence: he attended all major sporting events personally, and by being there every morning and during extracurricular activities, he reinforced the students' and teachers' perception of his intentions and character. Rotunno's deliberately positive attitude, welcoming smile, and choice to maintain eye contact with everyone who spoke to him demonstrated to his stakeholders that he truly felt that all should be treated with dignity and respect. The students and teachers began to think that Rotunno cared about them and valued their opinions.

As a foundation for all he was doing, Rotunno worked to build his teachers' and students' faith in the potential of the long-term process of change. By coining the motto "The Pride Is Back!" (which referred to the JFK High School of twenty years ago, then among the finest high schools in the city academically and athletically), Rotunno made that motto ubiquitous throughout the school, printing it on T-shirts, posters, and correspondence, and telling anyone and everyone who would listen. He knew that the four-thousand-student inner-city school had the potential to again be one of the safest schools in the city, one where students and teachers worked together to achieve academic and athletic excellence.

The Result: "The Pride Is Back!"

When I visited the school in early 2005, while Rotunno was walking me out, we passed a seemingly insignificant hallway corridor that led from the school building to the athletic fields. That hallway was not insignificant to Rotunno. We stopped, and he shared the story of the pep rally before JFK's recent district championship football game, where the JFK students and faculty used their motto "The Pride Is Back!" to motivate their team the entire week of the big game. Rotunno spoke in detail of the final pep rally that the school had held in that corridor, and he could tell from the spirit that day that the school was turning the corner and was on its way back toward a great place for young people to learn and grow. Rotunno did not tell me in his story if the team won; that was not what was important to him. (I discovered later they did win that game.) What was important was that his key stakeholders—the students and teachers—were starting to believe in the positive benefits of the long-term change process—and it showed.

As he built the students' and teachers' trust in his intentions and their faith in the long-term change process, Rotunno continued to manage expectations by gaining consensus on what everyone should consider were short-term successes and the corresponding student and teacher responsibilities required to get there. For short-term goals, the teachers would be responsible for moving consistently disruptive students to more appropriate alternative-education programs outside

JFK High School and performing sweeps of all the hallways after the start of each period for security. And the students would be responsible for getting to their assigned classes on time and respecting the facilities, the other students, and the administrators.

The real test of managing expectations is not whether the communication has taken place, but whether the lines of communication are successfully opened and if the perceptions of the key stakeholders have been shaped as intended. The teachers and staff successfully placed most of the disruptive students in alternative-education programs; they also formed security teams that swept the hallways between periods by starting on the eighth floor and sweeping all the way to the ground floor and sent kids who were avoiding class to a supervised holding room outside the school.

Not surprisingly, the students had done their part by minimizing fighting, reducing absenteeism and tardiness, and increasing their respect for the teachers and facilities (which Rotunno catalyzed by reopening all of the student bathrooms that his predecessor had locked due to vandalism and vagrancy). In all these things, Rotunno's consistent communication of "The Pride Is Back" motivated all of his stakeholders to believe in the long-term process, even when initially Rotunno may have been the only one who held an honest belief that JFK could be turned around.

As JFK started to turn the corner toward becoming a safe place again, at the one-year mark in the job, Rotunno got his teacher and staff cabinet together, listened to their desires, and concluded that security was under control and no longer the top priority; instead, instruction and education were now the school's focus. As a result, Rotunno and his staff established numerous short-term academic goals with the support of his faculty and staff, including a math excellence program, an environmental/science excellence program, a bilingual honors program, and a plan to improve the JFK athletic program. JFK's results seem to be working, as the scores on state Regents Examinations and the related graduation rate have increased from approximately two hundred just a few years ago to four hundred graduates in 2004, and a goal of five hundred graduates on JFK High's near-term radar screen.

As we reflected on that recent victorious evening and what it meant to him, a JFK senior named James walked by with his book bag, and when Rotunno smiled at James and asked him how he was doing, James stopped on his own accord to speak to us. When we asked his experiences at JFK High School, James volunteered that as an underclassman, he had been making bad decisions and was going nowhere; "Now, thanks to Mr. Rotunno and what he has done with JFK High School, I am out of trouble, back on track, and planning on going to college."

Conclusion

Managing expectations is fundamental when leading change. Wise organizational change leaders will work to identify their key stakeholders, build a bridge of two-way communication with them, and work to understand their spoken and unspoken expectations while realistically shaping the four key perceptions of managing expectations:

1. The leader's character and intentions
2. The benefits of the long-term change process
3. What constitutes short-term success
4. The stakeholders' specific responsibilities required to achieve the short- and long-term outcomes

Doing so will empower an organizational leader to understand the complexities of the change situation, enable alignment of goals with stakeholders, and provide mechanisms to promote understanding and teamwork towards achieving those goals. Whether it is a U.S. Army company in Iraq or a public high school in the Bronx or any other organization, managing expectations is an essential part of the fuel required to make the impossible into a reality.

Notes

1. K. Annan, *Learning the Lessons of Peace Building*, Oct. 2004. http://www.un.org/Depts/dpko/dpko/articles/sg_article181004.htm.
2. N. Karten, *Managing Expectations* (New York: Dorset House, 1994).
3. K. Hughes, undersecretary of state for public diplomacy and public affairs, http://www.state.gov/r/us/2005/55165.htm.
4. S. Stern, "Military 'Transformation' May Not Mean Smaller Forces," *Christian Science Monitor*, May 7, 2003.
5. V. Brooks, address to class of 2006, Command and General Staff College, Fort Leavenworth, Kans., Oct. 2005.
6. *Rudy*, 1993. The comments are from Rudy Ruettiger at the conclusion of the Special Edition DVD.
7. V. Frankl, *Man's Search for Meaning* (New York: Washington Square Press, 1984).
8. R. Johnson, keynote address, Kansas City District, U.S. Army Corps of Engineers Conference, Nov. 2005.
9. A. Gore, quoted in *USA Today*, Feb. 14, 1996.
10. P. Lencioni, *The Four Obsessions of an Extraordinary Executive* (San Francisco: Jossey-Bass, 2000).
11. Hughes, Department of State Web site, http://www.state.gov/r/us/2005/55165.htm.

INDEX

H

Hajjar, R., 313, 327, 330–332
Hall, P., 142
Handbook of Leadership Development (Center for Creative Leadership), 16
Handshakes, 227
Hannah, S. T., 88
Harris, B. M. "Mac," 171
Harris, J., 355
Harvard Business Review, 16, 25
Harvard Business School lessons: Beech-Nut case study, 55; being preyed upon, 45–46; Johnson & Johnson case study, 55–56
Hassig, D., 369
Hastings, G., 32
Helu Ball, H., 337
Henshaw, T., 281
Hesselbein, F., 171
High-impact leadership: components of authentic and, 90–94; leader's authenticity as core of, 89
High-potential talent: of Lotus Release 5 team, 146–149; the problem with, 133–134; of U.S. Skydiving Team (1991), 133, 143–144; of U.S. Skydiving Team (1994), 135–141, 153–158; of West Point's Sprint football team, 135, 142–145
High-risk situations. *See* Extremis leadership
Hilmes, A., 65, 66
Hilmes, J., 65–66
Hollander, E., 96
Holman, J., 363–364
Honesty: as combat leader attribute, 259–261; West Point Honor Code on, 59–61, 85. *See also* Ethics; Integrity
Honor Code (West Point), 34
Horn, Staff Sergeant, 359
Hoyvald, N., 55
Hughes, K., 366
Human shield tactic, 50
Humility, 150–153
Hunter, Private First Class, 52
Hurricane Katrina, 246
Hussein, S., 373

I

Idiosyncrasy credits, 96
Illustrator gestures, 227
Inauthenticity, 89–90
Integrity: assessing junior leader's character and, 121; assessing NCOs (noncommissioned officers), 127; assessing senior leader's, 118; as foundation for ethical execution of combat missions, 259–261. *See also* Character; Ethics; Honesty
Intention: communicating, 207–210; fostering initiative and growth through clear, 210
Iraq War: changes sought in Iraq, 374t; charismatic leadership examples during, 240–241, 245–246, 247, 249; example of soldier commitment to, 347; examples of quiet leadership during, 209; female military interactions with indigenous Muslim women during, 326; importance of core values in, 63–65, 70; learning about extremis leadership during, 162, 166, 167, 168, 178–179, 181, 186–187; managing expectations during, 363–364, 366, 369, 370–376, 379; relationship and bonds between soldiers of, 343–344; strategic corporal leadership in, 357–359. *See also* Combat leadership; Extremis leadership; Global War on Terrorism

J

James, W., 88
Jargon language, 235
Jason's story, 59–61
Jefferies, H., 136
Jefferies, J., 133
JetBlue Airways, 47, 48
JFK High School case study (New York City), 382–385
Johnson & Johnson Credo, 82
Johnson & Johnson (J&J), 55–56, 82, 83

Johnson, R., 370
Jones, E., 97
JRTC (Joint Readiness Training Center) [Fort Polk], 20, 214
Junior leaders assessment (Bench Project): behaviors setting apart exceptional, 120e; communication skills, 122; competence, 120–121; development of subordinates, 122; focus of, 119–120. *See also* Subordinate leaders
"Just make it happen" attitude, 53–54

K

Kail, E. G., 3
Karten, N., 364
Keen, K., 12–13
Kegan, R., 104
Kinesics: interpretation of nonverbal movements and, 229t; overview of, 224, 227, 230–232
Kirkby, M., 136, 137–138, 140
KIS (Keep It Simple), 208
Kohlberg, L., 104
Kolditz, T. A., 107, 120, 160
Kosovo air campaign: example of environmental proxemics, 227; story illustrating nonverbal gestures and movement during, 229t
Kotter, J., 179
KSAs (knowledge, skills, and abilities), 177, 184

L

Language: jargon, 235; paralanguage, 224, 232–233; sharing common understanding of, 175. *See also* Communication
Lavery, J., 55
LDRSHIP values internalization: step 1: self-identification and selection, 69–71; step 2: early socialization process, 71–75; step 3: use of role models, 75–79; step 4: sharing of stories and examples, 79–83; step 5: feedback and performance evaluations, 83–86; steps listed, 69e